WORLD WAR
HULK

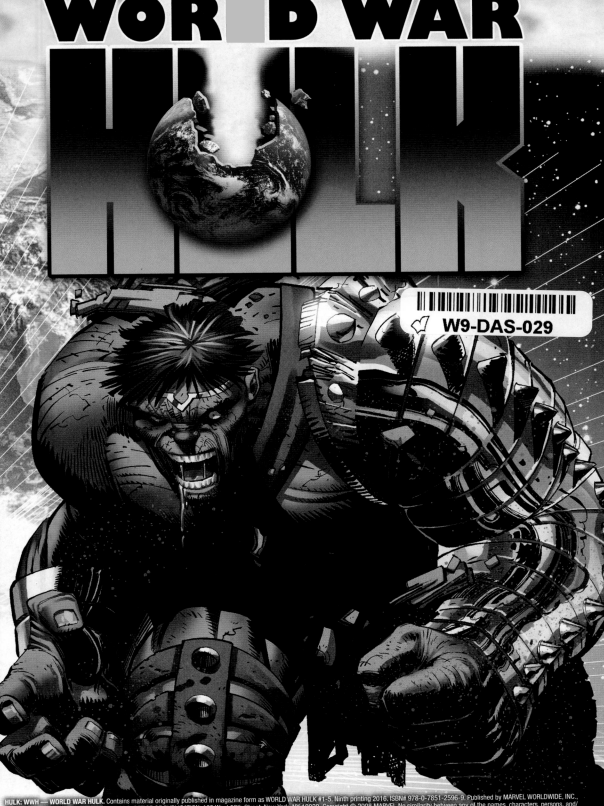

W9-DAS-029

HULK: WWH — WORLD WAR HULK. Contains material originally published in magazine form as WORLD WAR HULK #1-5. Ninth printing 2016. ISBN# 978-0-7851-2596-9. Published by MARVEL WORLDWIDE, INC., a subsidiary of MARVEL ENTERTAINMENT, LLC. OFFICE OF PUBLICATION: 135 West 50th Street, New York, NY 10020. Copyright © 2008 MARVEL No similarity between any of the names, characters, persons, and/ or institutions in this magazine with those of any living or dead person or institution is intended, and any such similarity which may exist is purely coincidental. **Printed in the U.S.A.** ALAN FINE, President, Marvel Entertainment; DAN BUCKLEY, President, TV, Publishing & Brand Management; JOE QUESADA, Chief Creative Officer; TOM BREVOORT, SVP of Publishing; DAVID BOGART, SVP of Business Affairs & Operations, Publishing & Partnership; C.B. CEBULSKI, VP of Brand Management & Development, Asia; DAVID GABRIEL, SVP of Sales & Marketing, Publishing; JEFF YOUNGQUIST, VP of Production & Special Projects; DAN CARR, Executive Director of Publishing Technology; ALEX MORALES, Director of Publishing Operations; SUSAN CRESPI, Production Manager; STAN LEE, Chairman Emeritus. For information regarding advertising in Marvel Comics or on Marvel.com, please contact Vit DeBellis, Integrated Sales Manager, at vdebellis@marvel.com. For Marvel subscription inquiries, please call 888-511-5480. **Manufactured between 8/17/2016 and** 9/19/2016 by QUAD/GRAPHICS WASECA, WASECA, MN, USA.

WORLD WAR HULK

Writer: **GREG PAK**
Penciler: **JOHN ROMITA JR.**
Inker: **KLAUS JANSON**
Colorist: **CHRISTINA STRAIN**
Letterer: **CHRIS ELIOPOULOS**
Cover Art: **DAVID FINCH, DANNY MIKI,
CHRISTINA STRAIN** & **FRANK D'ARMATA**
Variant Cover Art: **JOHN ROMITA JR.,
KLAUS JANSON** & **CHRISTINA STRAIN**
Production: **BRADFORD JOHANSEN**
Assistant Editor: **NATHAN COSBY**
Editor: **MARK PANICCIA**
Special thanks to **IRENE LEE**

Hulk created by Stan Lee & Jack Kirby

Collection Editor: **MARK D. BEAZLEY**
Associate Managing Editor: **KATERI WOODY**
Associate Editor: **SARAH BRUNSTAD**
Senior Editor, Special Projects: **JENNIFER GRÜNWALD**
VP Production & Special Projects: **JEFF YOUNGQUIST**
SVP Print, Sales & Marketing: **DAVID GABRIEL**
Book Designer: **RODOLFO MURAGUCHI**

Editor in Chief: **AXEL ALONSO**
Chief Creative Officer: **JOE QUESADA**
Publisher: **DAN BUCKLEY**
Executive Producer: **ALAN FINE**

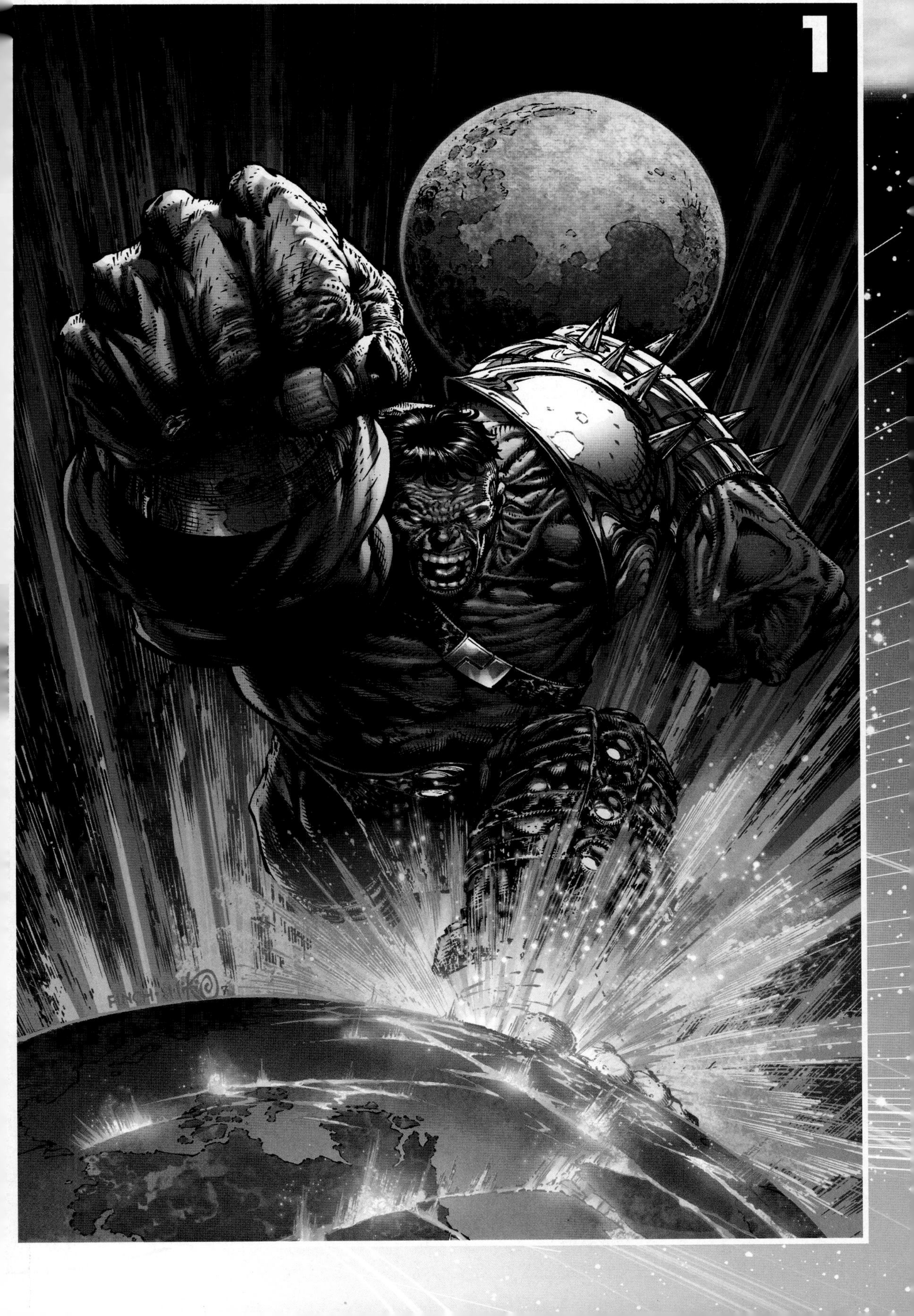
1

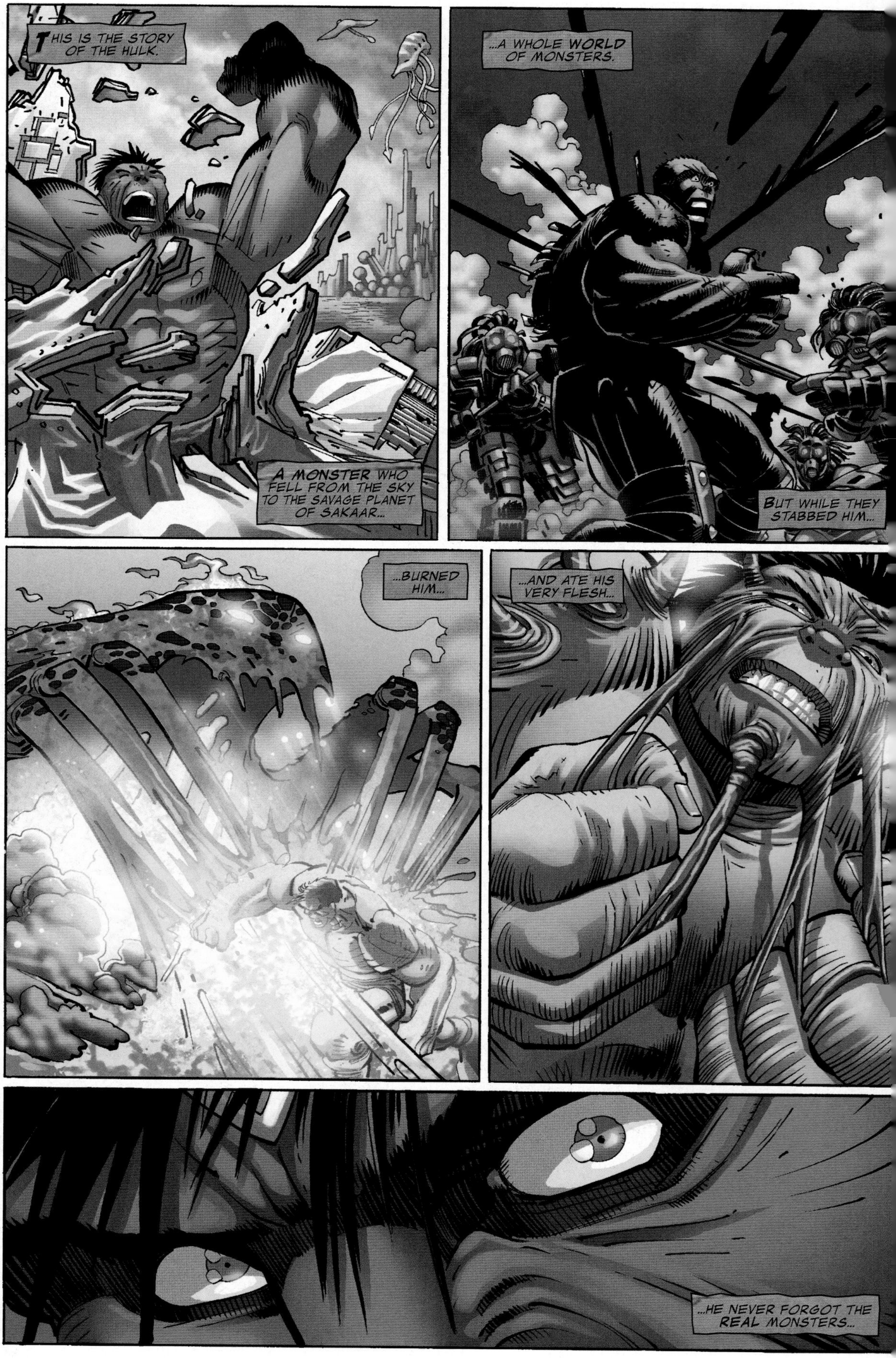
THIS IS THE STORY OF THE HULK.
A MONSTER WHO FELL FROM THE SKY TO THE SAVAGE PLANET OF SAKAAR...
...A WHOLE WORLD OF MONSTERS.
BUT WHILE THEY STABBED HIM...
...BURNED HIM...
...AND ATE HIS VERY FLESH...
...HE NEVER FORGOT THE REAL MONSTERS...

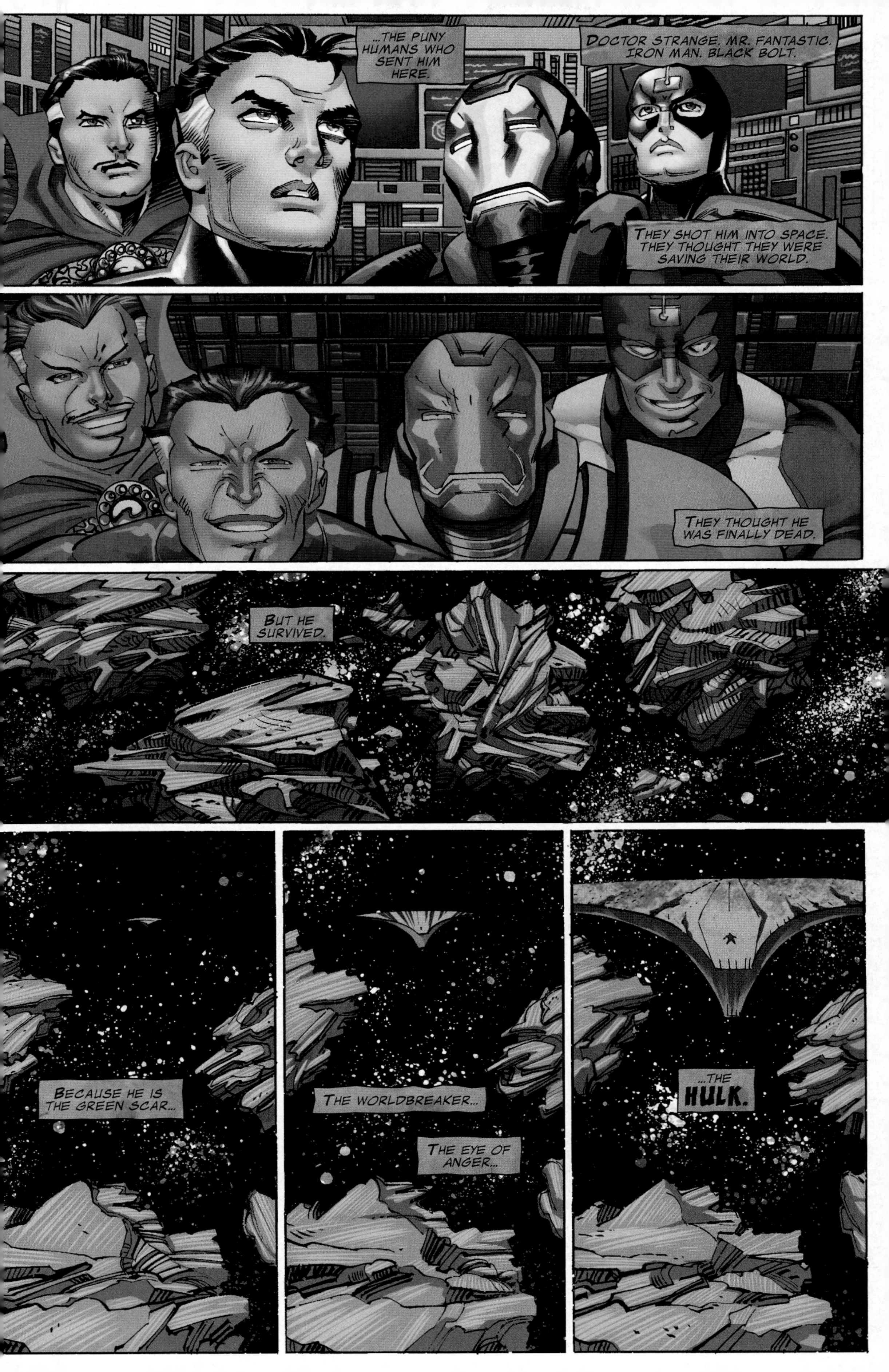
...THE PUNY HÜMANS WHO SENT HIM HERE.
DOCTOR STRANGE. MR. FANTASTIC. IRON MAN. BLACK BOLT.
THEY SHOT HIM INTO SPACE. THEY THOUGHT THEY WERE SAVING THEIR WORLD.
THEY THOUGHT HE WAS FINALLY DEAD.
BUT HE SURVIVED.
BECAUSE HE IS THE GREEN SCAR...
THE WORLDBREAKER...
THE EYE OF ANGER...
...THE HULK.

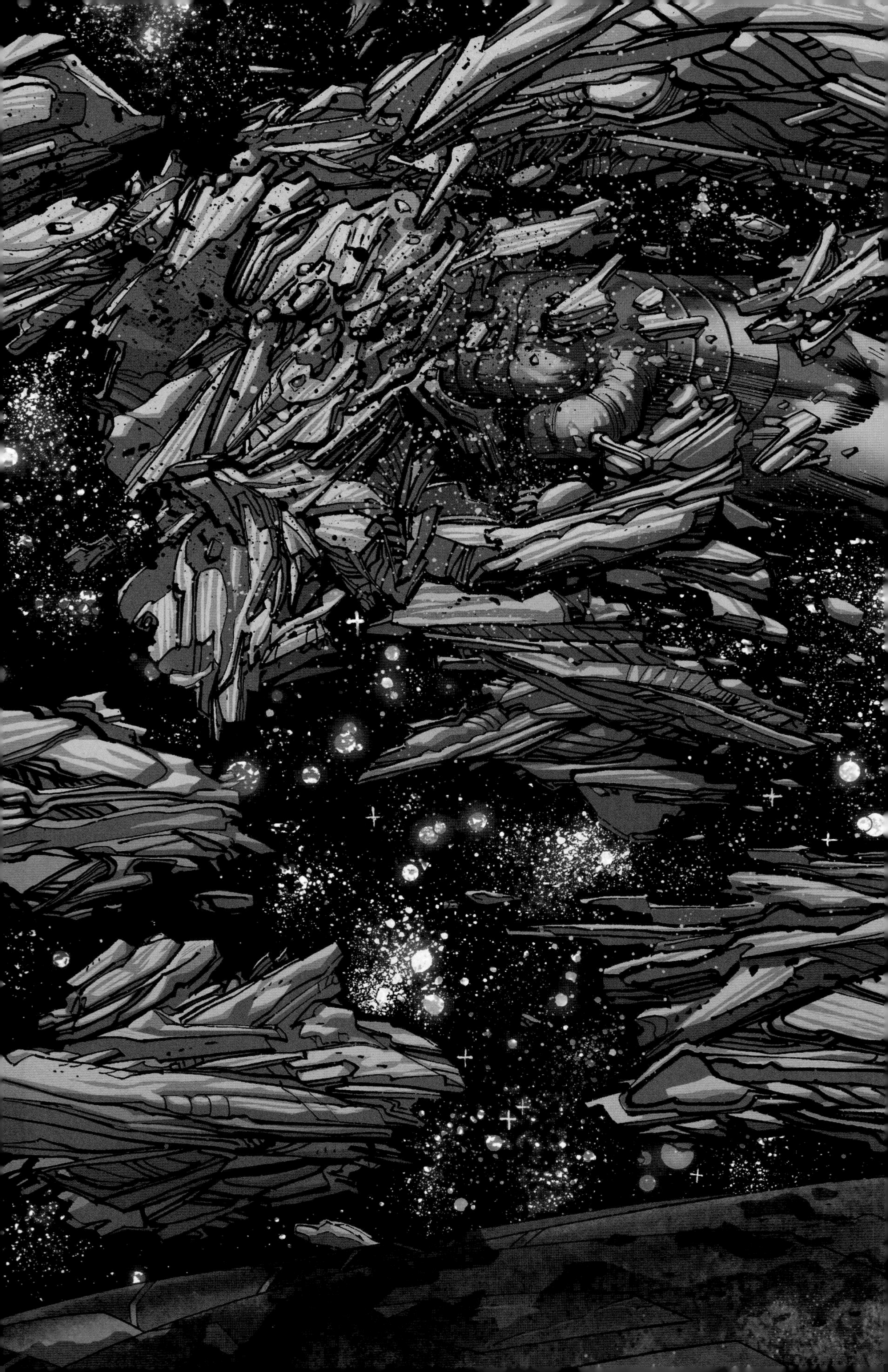

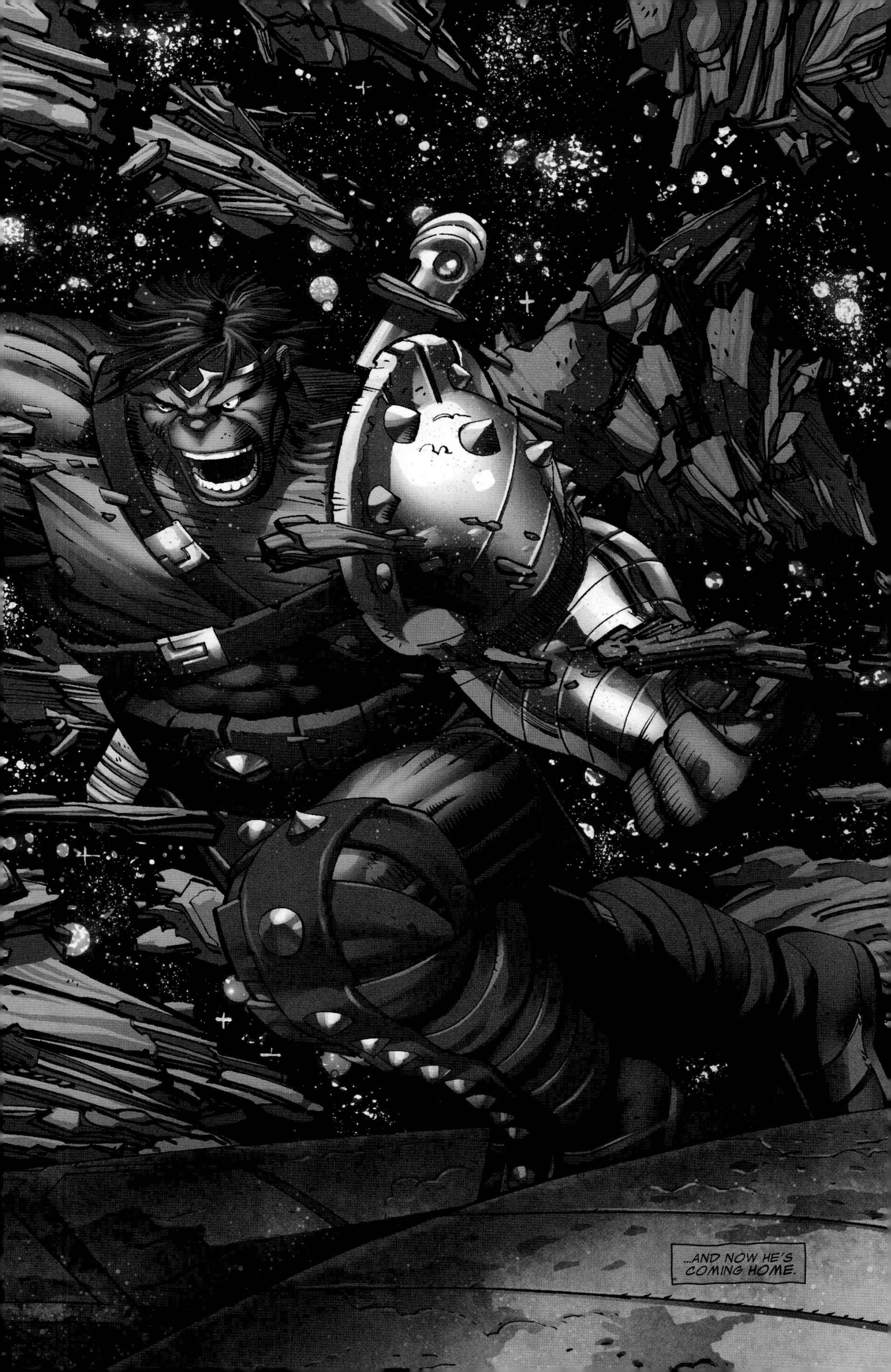
...AND NOW HE'S
COMING HOME.

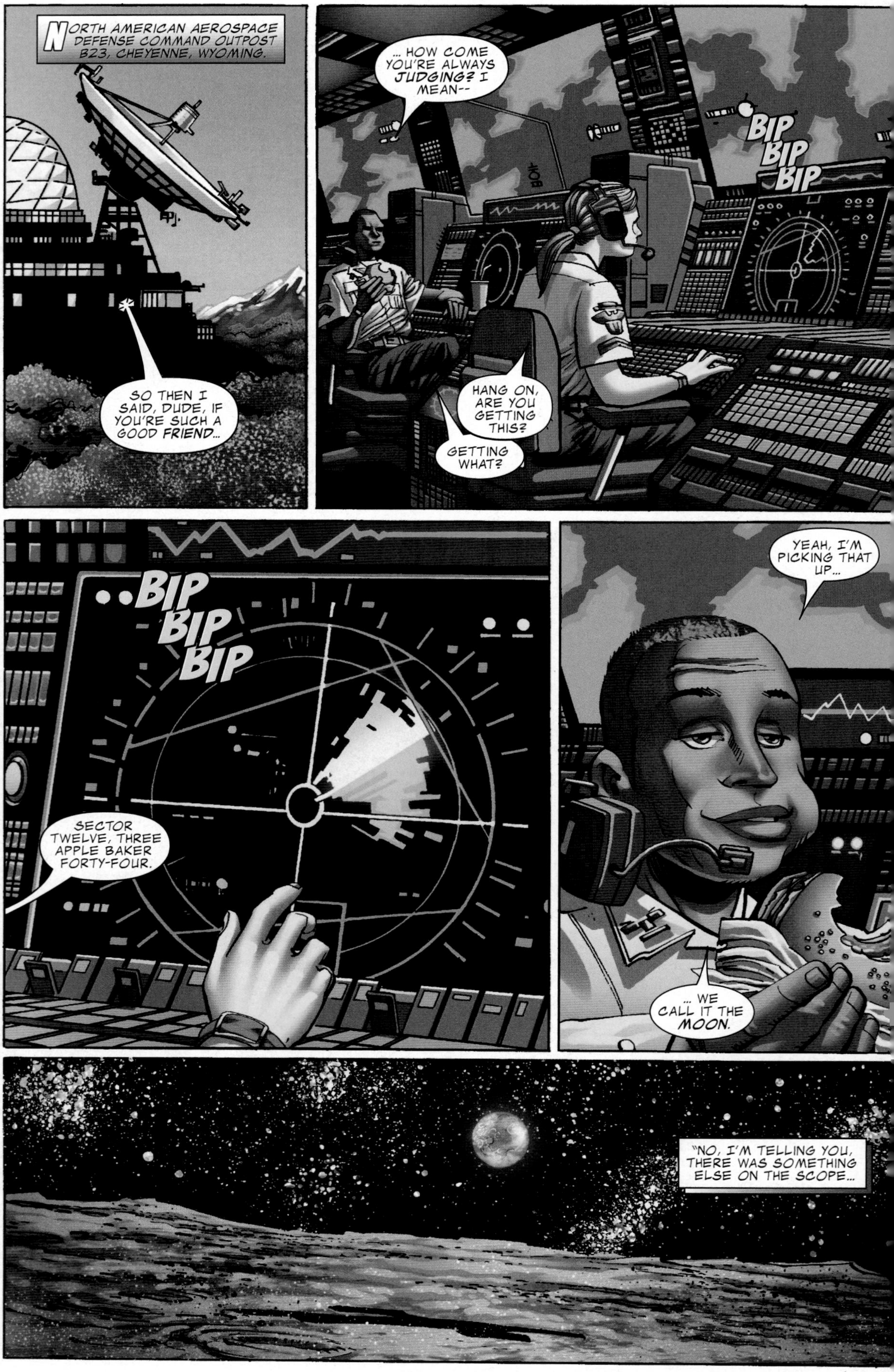
NORTH AMERICAN AEROSPACE DEFENSE COMMAND OUTPOST B23, CHEYENNE, WYOMING.
SO THEN I SAID, DUDE, IF YOU'RE SUCH A GOOD FRIEND...
... HOW COME YOU'RE ALWAYS JUDGING? I MEAN--
BIP BIP BIP
HANG ON, ARE YOU GETTING THIS?
GETTING WHAT?
BIP BIP BIP
SECTOR TWELVE, THREE APPLE BAKER FORTY-FOUR.
YEAH, I'M PICKING THAT UP...
... WE CALL IT THE MOON.
"NO, I'M TELLING YOU, THERE WAS SOMETHING ELSE ON THE SCOPE...

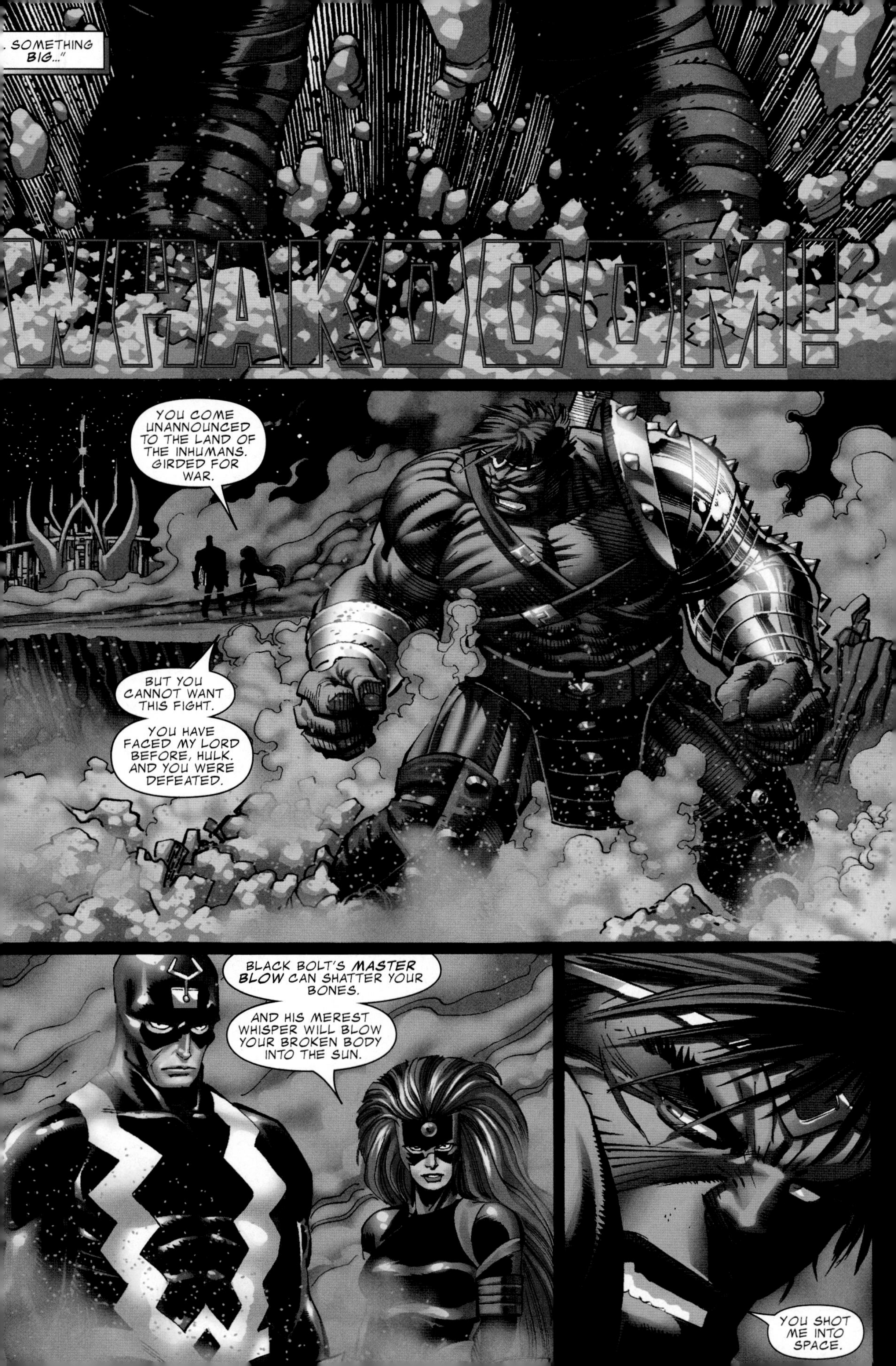

...SOMETHING BIG..."
WHAKOOOM!
YOU COME UNANNOUNCED TO THE LAND OF THE INHUMANS. GIRDED FOR WAR.
BUT YOU CANNOT WANT THIS FIGHT.
YOU HAVE FACED MY LORD BEFORE, HULK. AND YOU WERE DEFEATED.
BLACK BOLT'S MASTER BLOW CAN SHATTER YOUR BONES.
AND HIS MEREST WHISPER WILL BLOW YOUR BROKEN BODY INTO THE SUN.
YOU SHOT ME INTO SPACE.

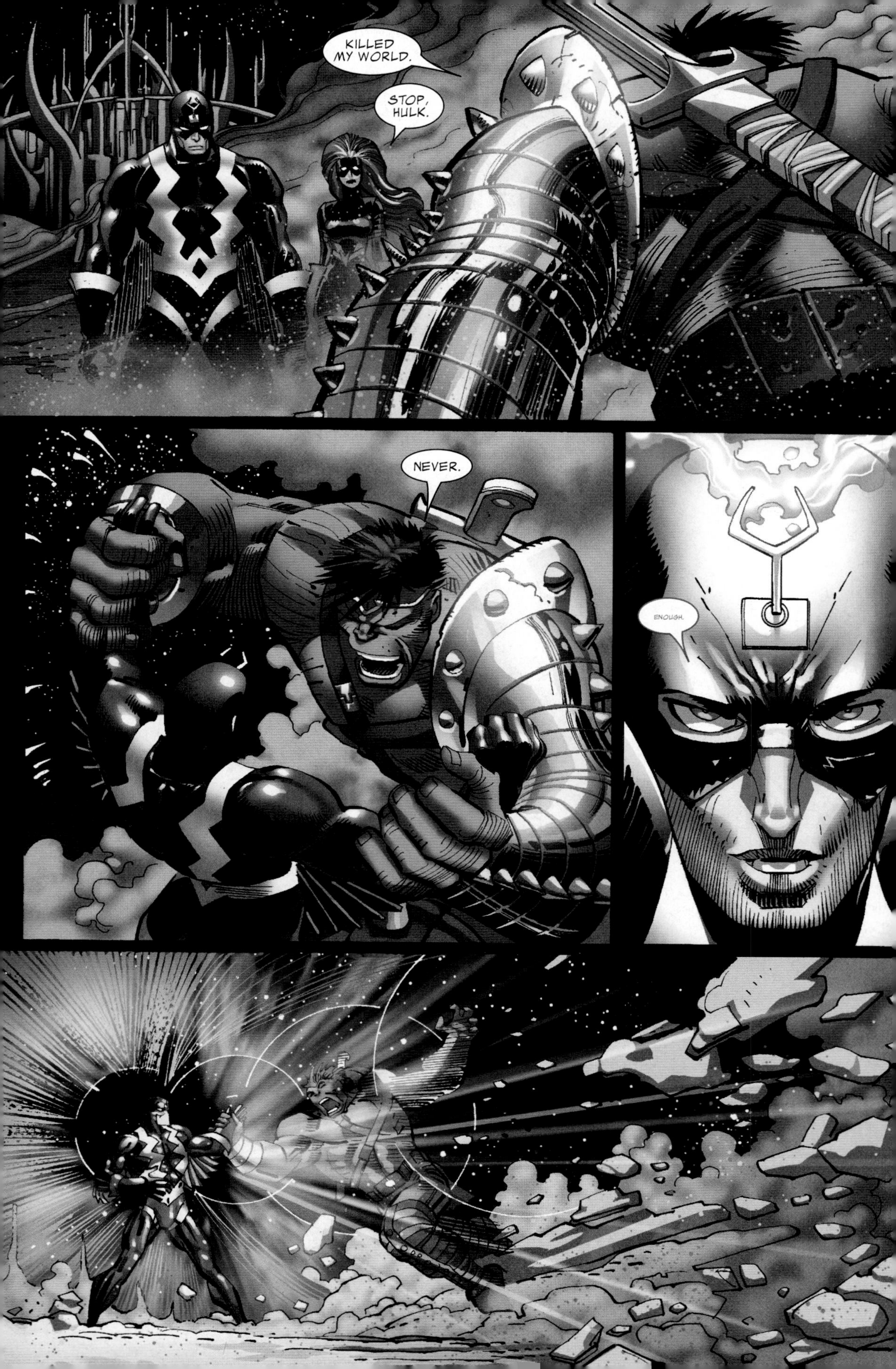
KILLED MY WORLD.
STOP, HULK.
NEVER.
ENOUGH.

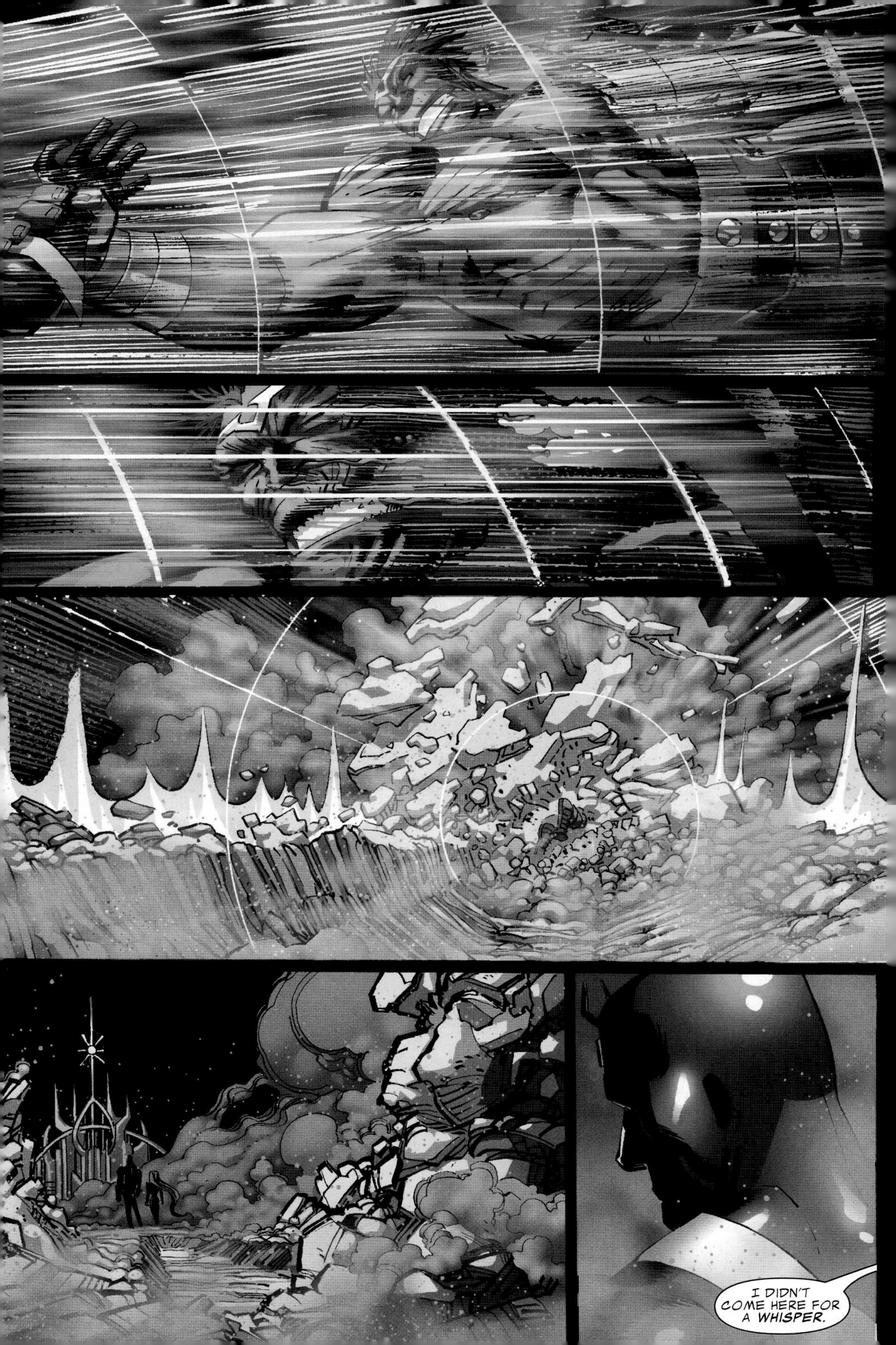
I DIDN'T COME HERE FOR A WHISPER.

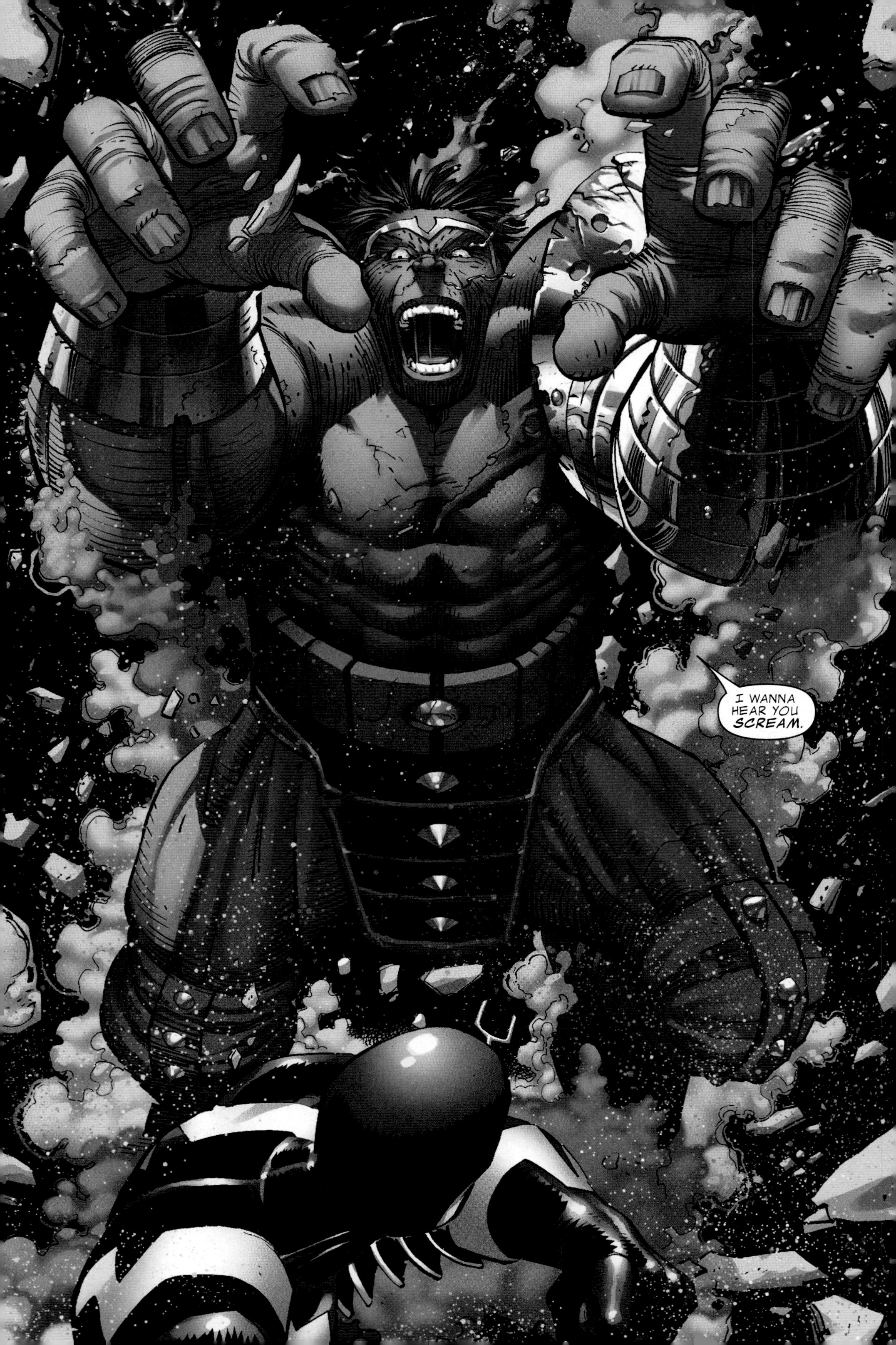
I WANNA HEAR YOU SCREAM.

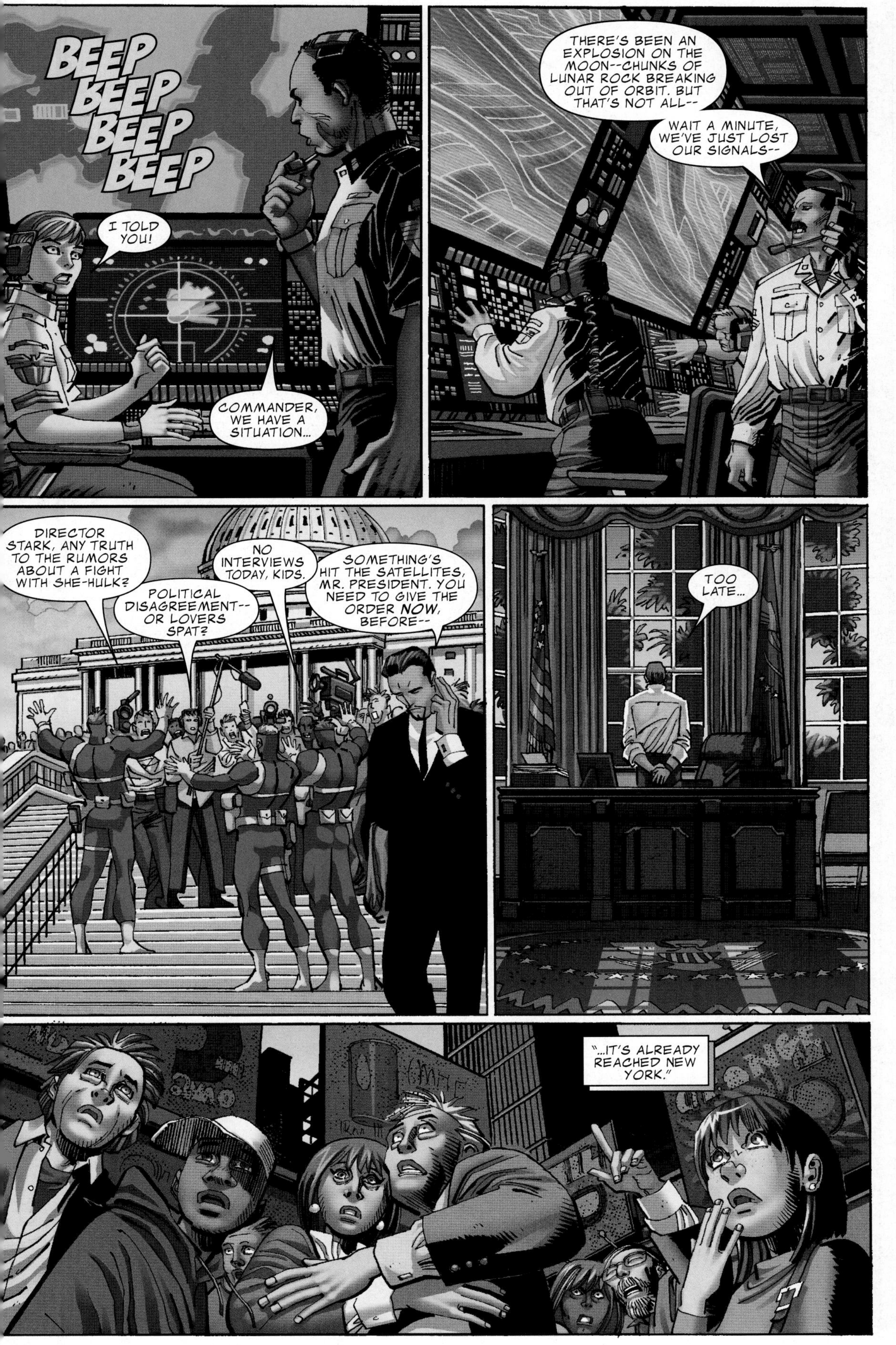
BEEP BEEP BEEP BEEP
I TOLD YOU!
COMMANDER, WE HAVE A SITUATION...
THERE'S BEEN AN EXPLOSION ON THE MOON--CHUNKS OF LUNAR ROCK BREAKING OUT OF ORBIT. BUT THAT'S NOT ALL--
WAIT A MINUTE, WE'VE JUST LOST OUR SIGNALS--
DIRECTOR STARK, ANY TRUTH TO THE RUMORS ABOUT A FIGHT WITH SHE-HULK?
POLITICAL DISAGREEMENT--OR LOVERS SPAT?
NO INTERVIEWS TODAY, KIDS.
SOMETHING'S HIT THE SATELLITES, MR. PRESIDENT. YOU NEED TO GIVE THE ORDER NOW, BEFORE--
TOO LATE...
"...IT'S ALREADY REACHED NEW YORK."

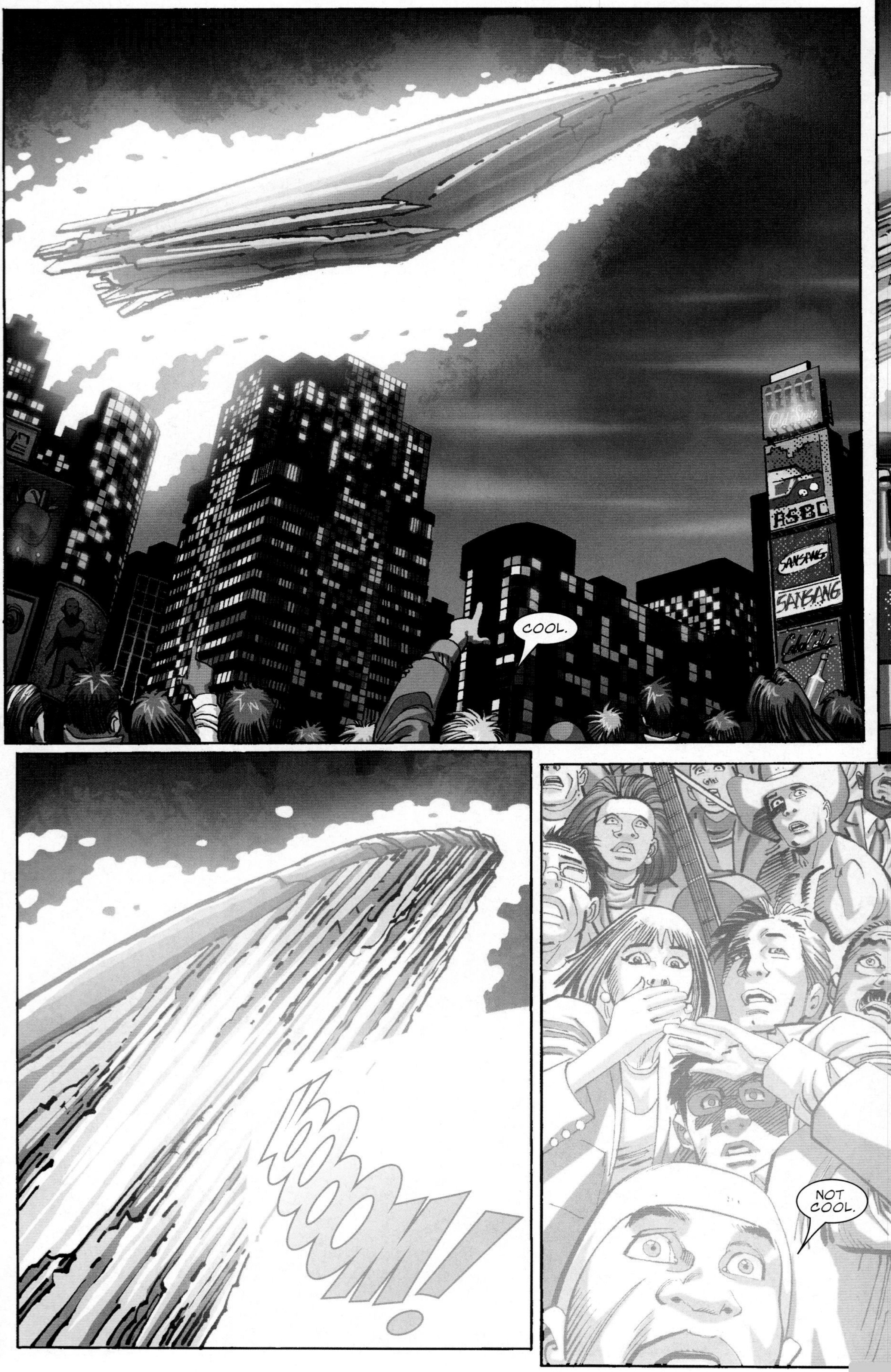
COOL.
VOOOOM!
NOT COOL.

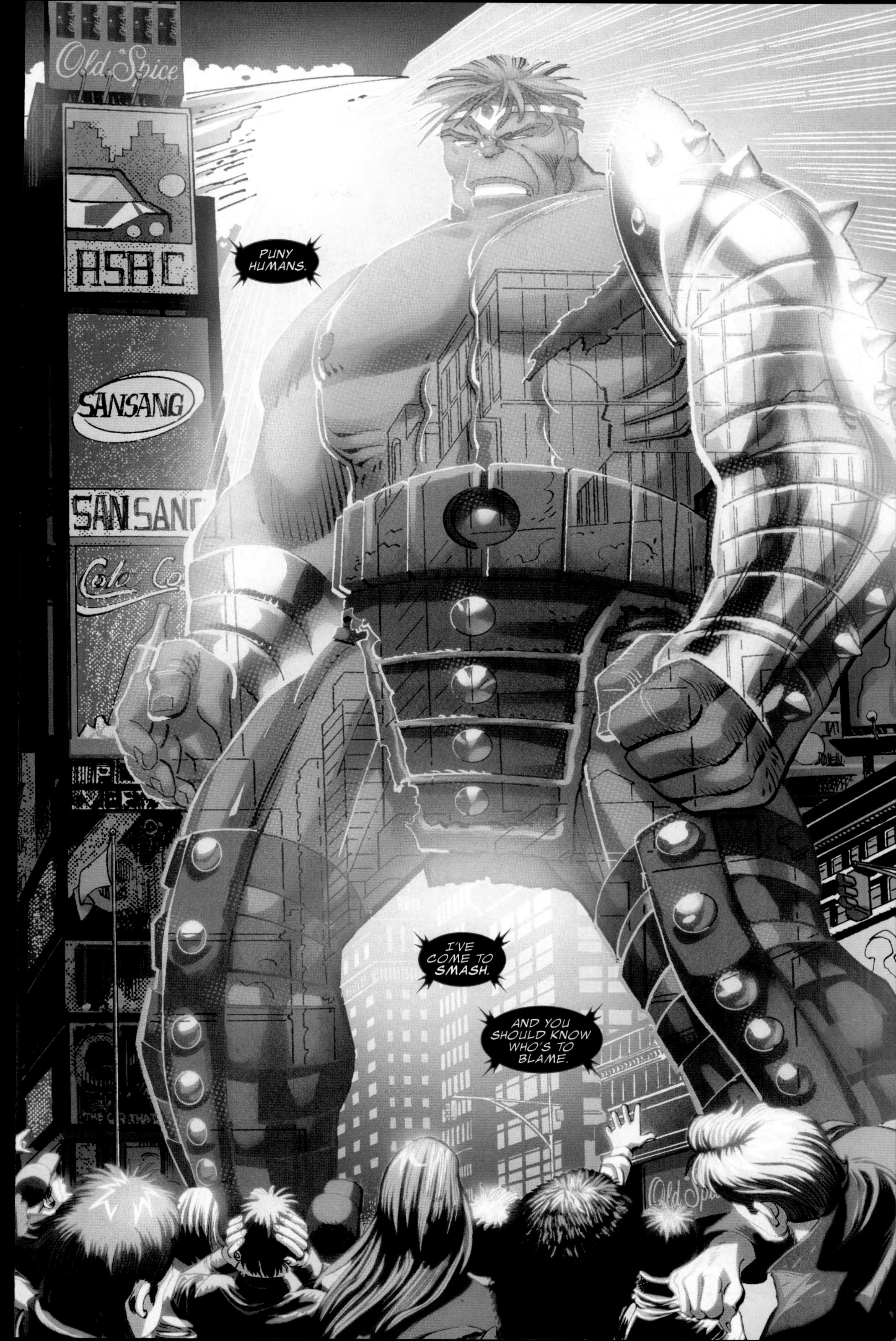
Old Spice
ASBC
SANSANG
SANSANG
Cola Co
PUNY HUMANS.
I'VE COME TO SMASH.
AND YOU SHOULD KNOW WHO'S TO BLAME.

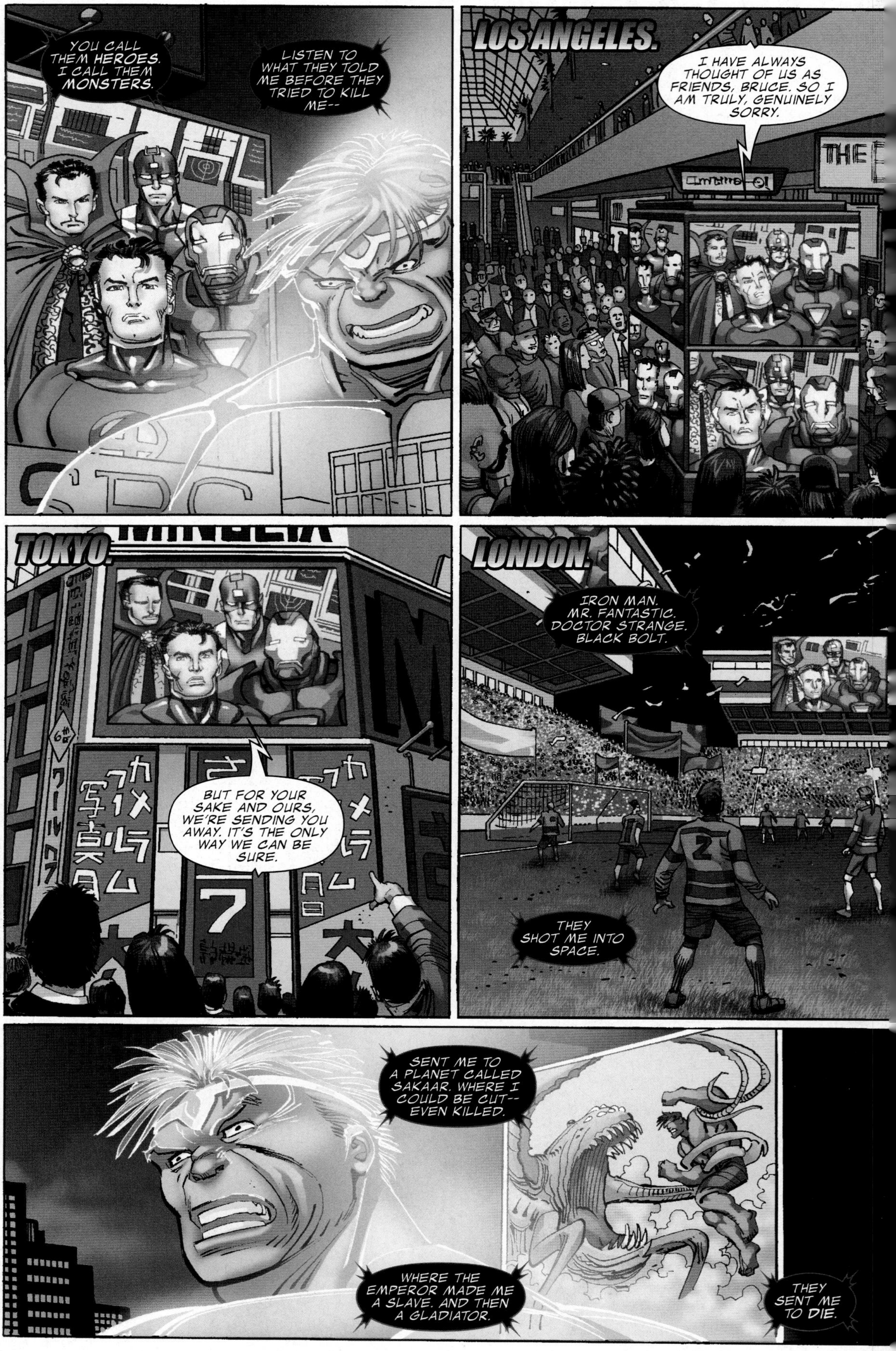
YOU CALL THEM HEROES. I CALL THEM MONSTERS.
LISTEN TO WHAT THEY TOLD ME BEFORE THEY TRIED TO KILL ME--
LOS ANGELES.
I HAVE ALWAYS THOUGHT OF US AS FRIENDS, BRUCE. SO I AM TRULY, GENUINELY SORRY.
TOKYO.
BUT FOR YOUR SAKE AND OURS, WE'RE SENDING YOU AWAY. IT'S THE ONLY WAY WE CAN BE SURE.
LONDON.
IRON MAN. MR. FANTASTIC. DOCTOR STRANGE. BLACK BOLT.
THEY SHOT ME INTO SPACE.
SENT ME TO A PLANET CALLED SAKAAR. WHERE I COULD BE CUT-- EVEN KILLED.
WHERE THE EMPEROR MADE ME A SLAVE. AND THEN A GLADIATOR.
THEY SENT ME TO DIE.

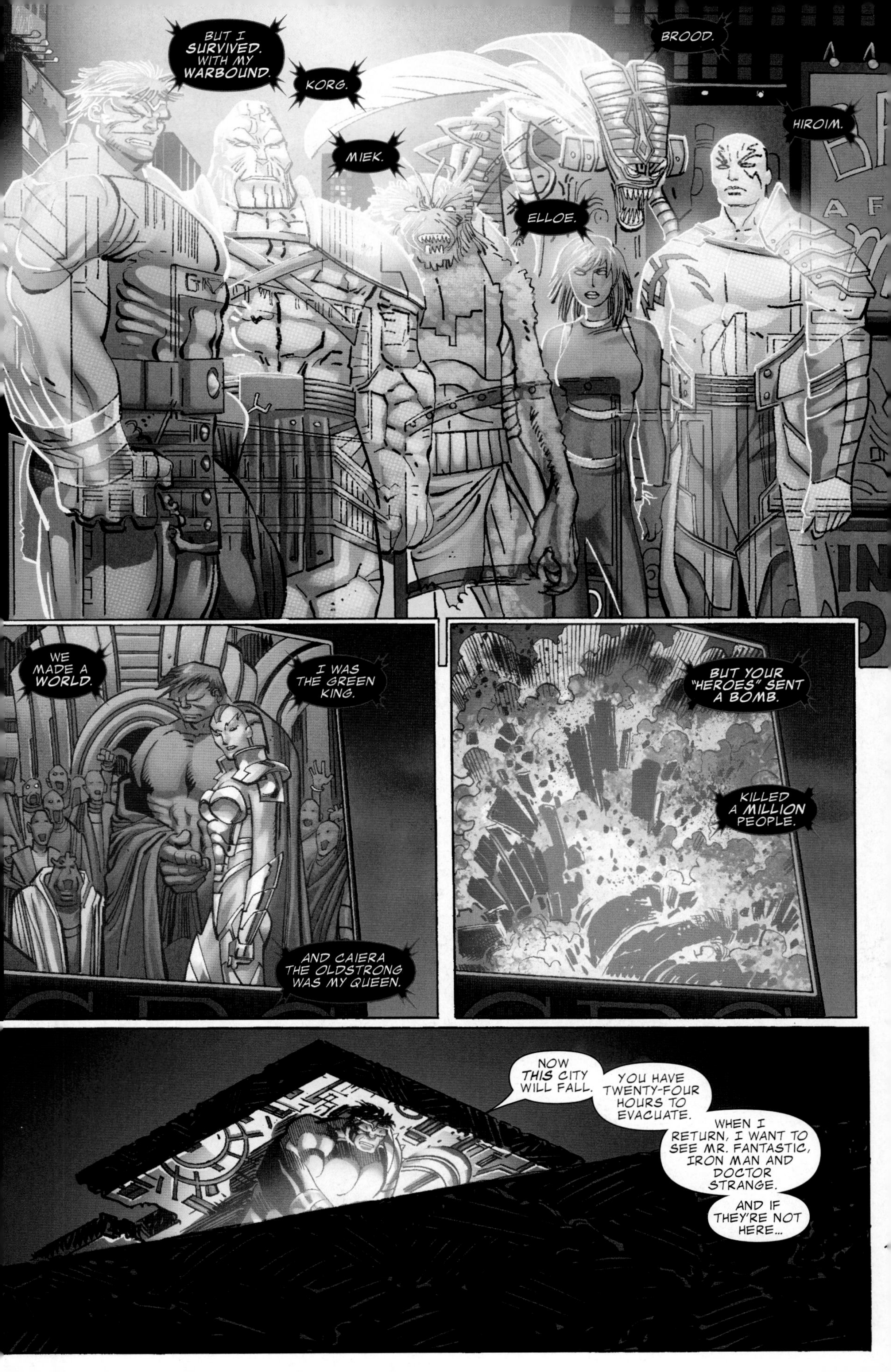
BUT I SURVIVED. WITH MY WARBOUND.
KORG.
MIEK.
BROOD.
ELLOE.
HIROIM.
WE MADE A WORLD.
I WAS THE GREEN KING.
AND CAIERA THE OLDSTRONG WAS MY QUEEN.
BUT YOUR "HEROES" SENT A BOMB.
KILLED A MILLION PEOPLE.
NOW THIS CITY WILL FALL.
YOU HAVE TWENTY-FOUR HOURS TO EVACUATE.
WHEN I RETURN, I WANT TO SEE MR. FANTASTIC, IRON MAN AND DOCTOR STRANGE.
AND IF THEY'RE NOT HERE...

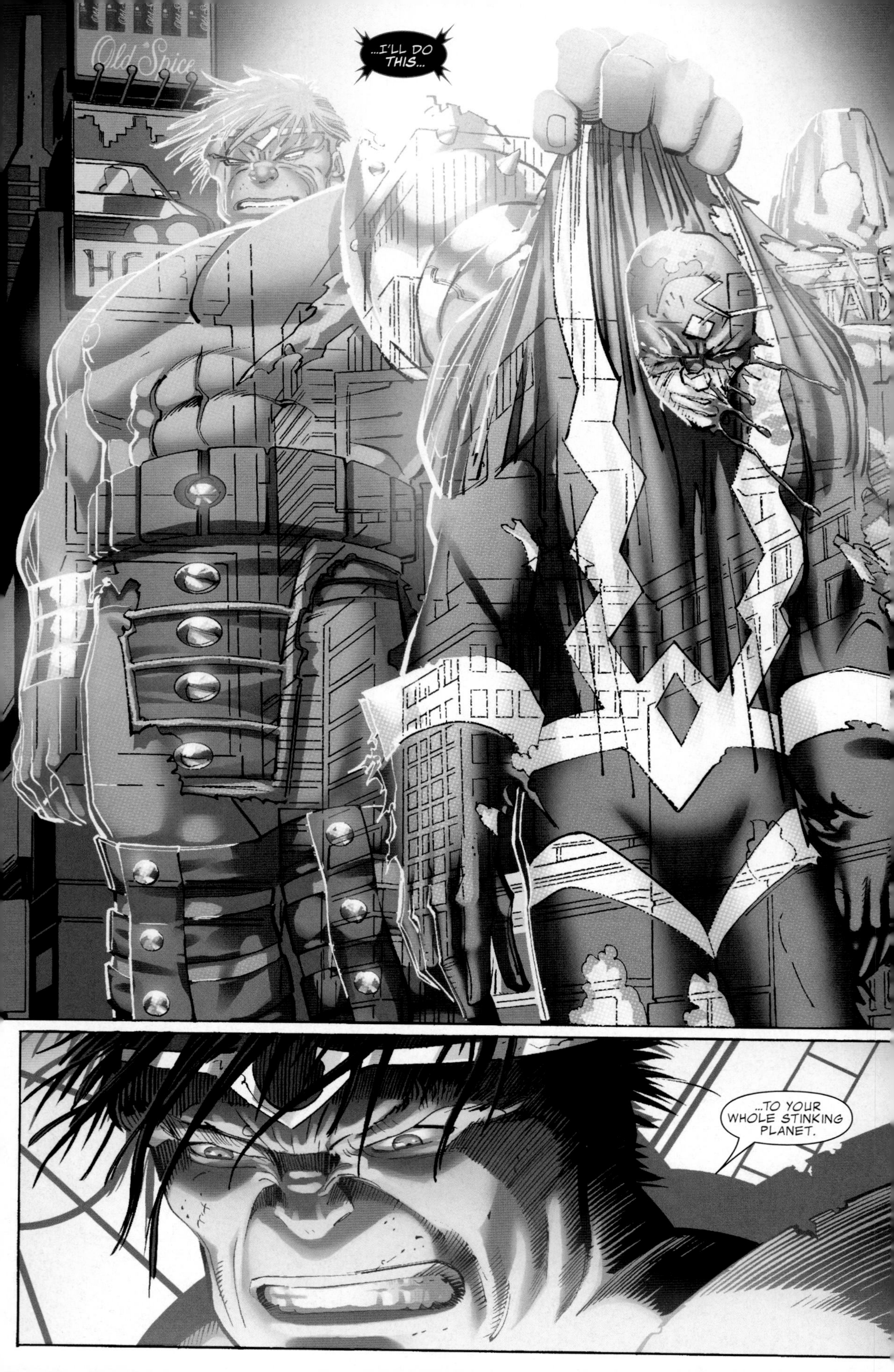
Old Spice
...I'LL DO THIS...
...TO YOUR WHOLE STINKING PLANET.

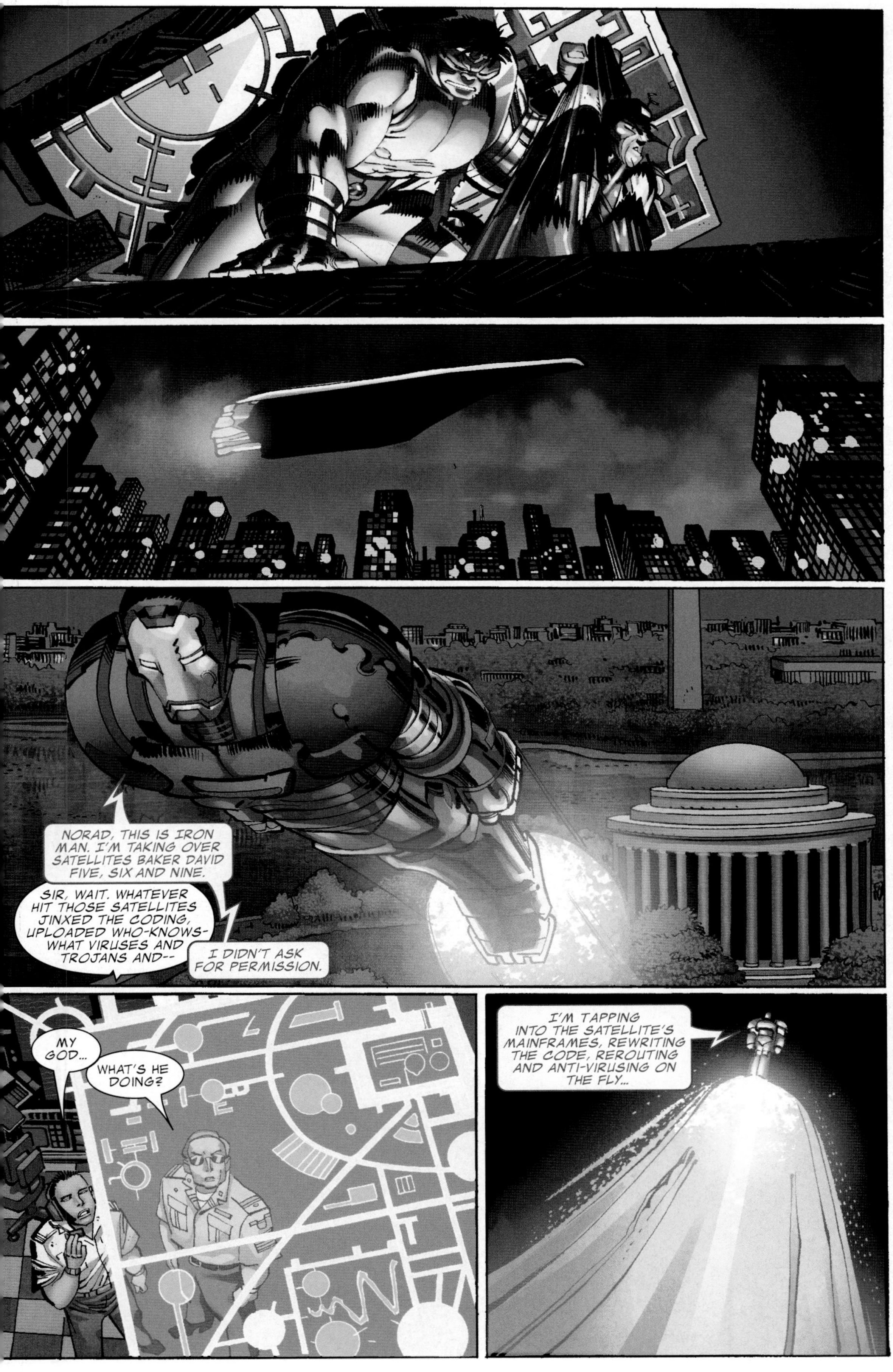
NORAD, THIS IS IRON MAN. I'M TAKING OVER SATELLITES BAKER DAVID FIVE, SIX AND NINE.
SIR, WAIT. WHATEVER HIT THOSE SATELLITES JINXED THE CODING, UPLOADED WHO-KNOWS-WHAT VIRUSES AND TROJANS AND--
I DIDN'T ASK FOR PERMISSION.
MY GOD...
WHAT'S HE DOING?
I'M TAPPING INTO THE SATELLITE'S MAINFRAMES, REWRITING THE CODE, REROUTING AND ANTI-VIRUSING ON THE FLY...

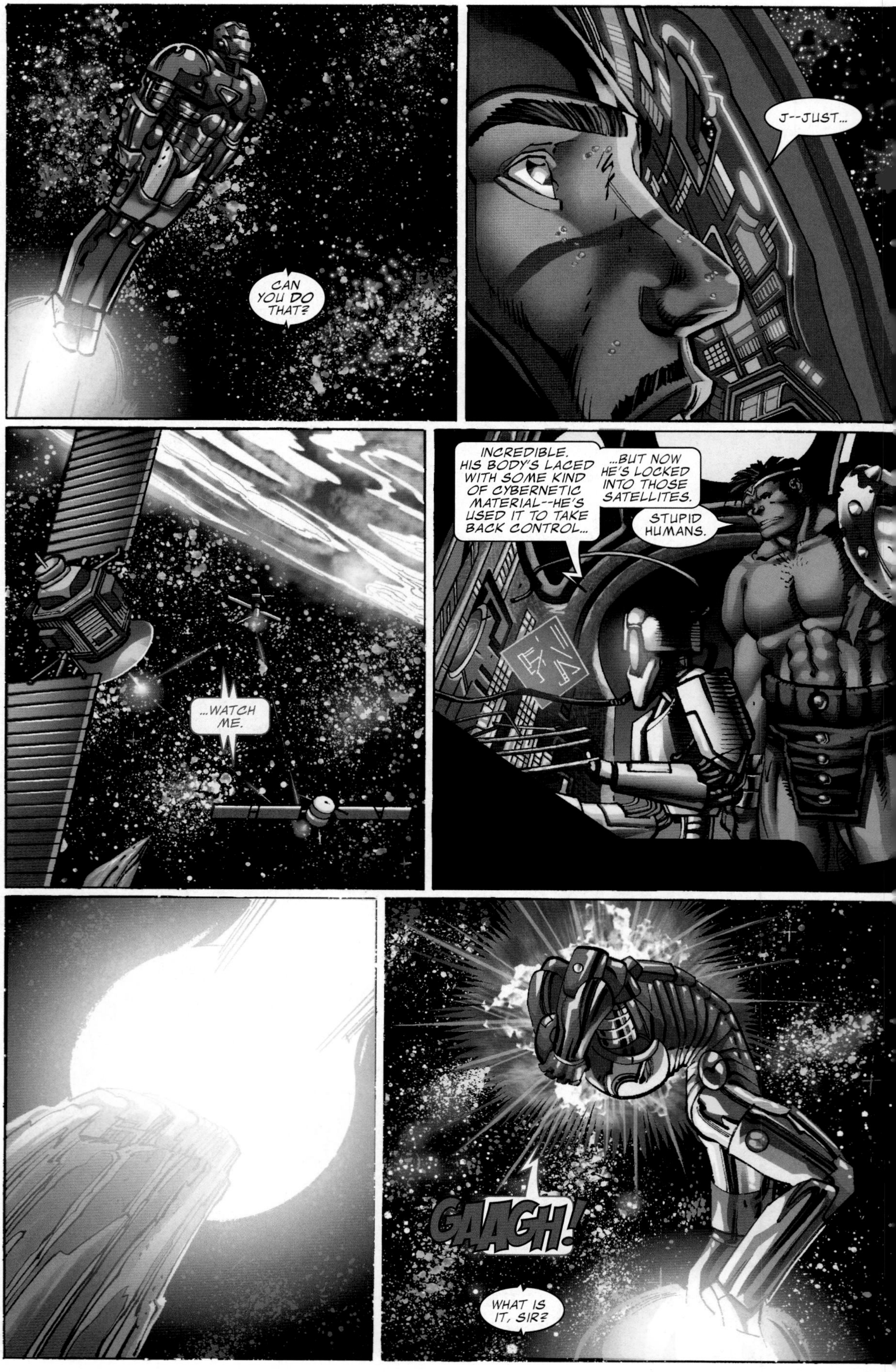
CAN YOU DO THAT?
J--JUST...
...WATCH ME.
INCREDIBLE. HIS BODY'S LACED WITH SOME KIND OF CYBERNETIC MATERIAL--HE'S USED IT TO TAKE BACK CONTROL...
...BUT NOW HE'S LOCKED INTO THOSE SATELLITES.
STUPID HUMANS.
GAAGH!
WHAT IS IT, SIR?

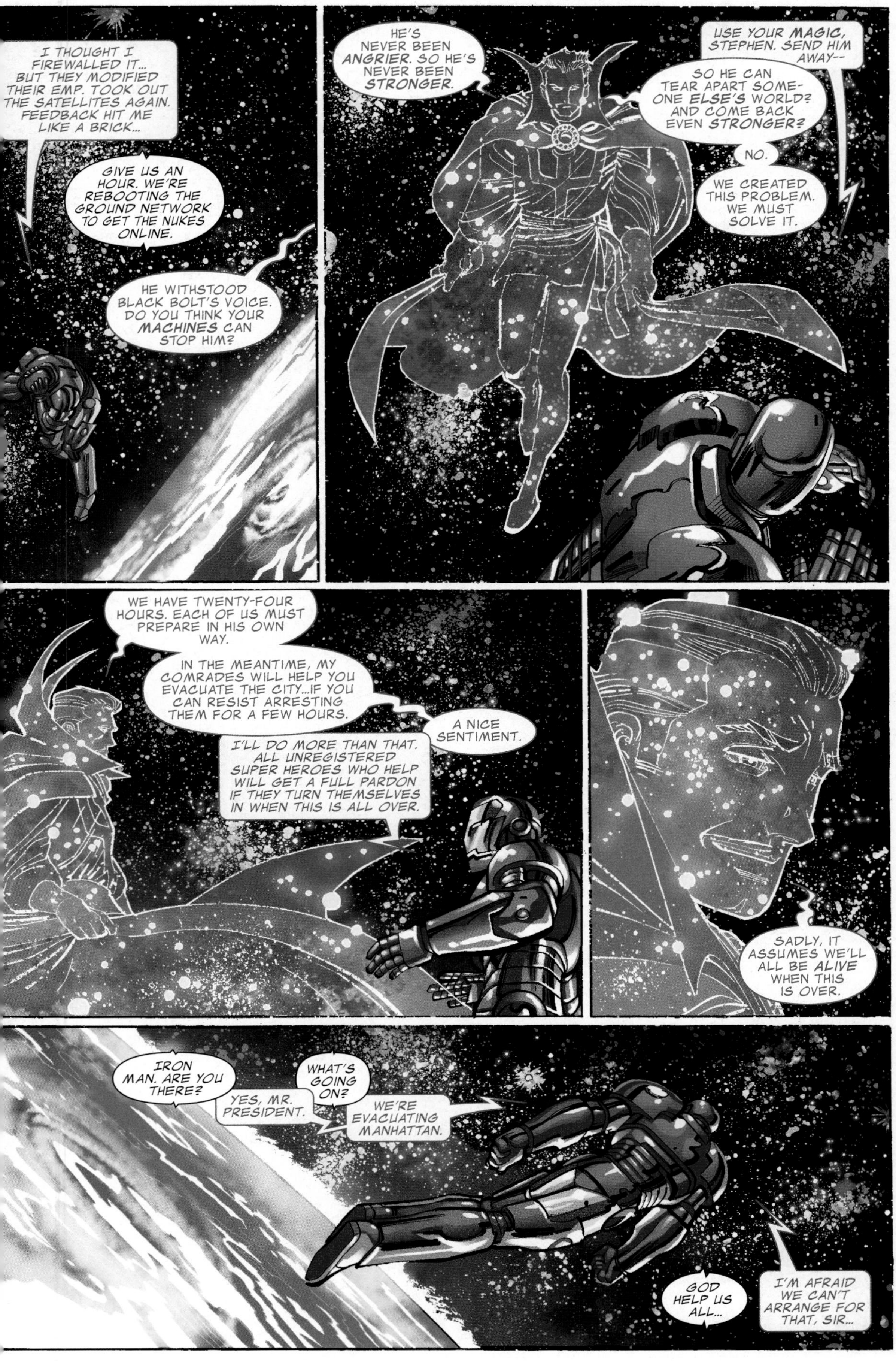
I THOUGHT I FIREWALLED IT... BUT THEY MODIFIED THEIR EMP. TOOK OUT THE SATELLITES AGAIN. FEEDBACK HIT ME LIKE A BRICK...
GIVE US AN HOUR. WE'RE REBOOTING THE GROUND NETWORK TO GET THE NUKES ONLINE.
HE WITHSTOOD BLACK BOLT'S VOICE. DO YOU THINK YOUR MACHINES CAN STOP HIM?
HE'S NEVER BEEN ANGRIER. SO HE'S NEVER BEEN STRONGER.
USE YOUR MAGIC, STEPHEN. SEND HIM AWAY--
SO HE CAN TEAR APART SOMEONE ELSE'S WORLD? AND COME BACK EVEN STRONGER?
NO.
WE CREATED THIS PROBLEM. WE MUST SOLVE IT.
WE HAVE TWENTY-FOUR HOURS. EACH OF US MUST PREPARE IN HIS OWN WAY.
IN THE MEANTIME, MY COMRADES WILL HELP YOU EVACUATE THE CITY...IF YOU CAN RESIST ARRESTING THEM FOR A FEW HOURS.
A NICE SENTIMENT.
I'LL DO MORE THAN THAT. ALL UNREGISTERED SUPER HEROES WHO HELP WILL GET A FULL PARDON IF THEY TURN THEMSELVES IN WHEN THIS IS ALL OVER.
SADLY, IT ASSUMES WE'LL ALL BE ALIVE WHEN THIS IS OVER.
IRON MAN. ARE YOU THERE?
YES, MR. PRESIDENT.
WHAT'S GOING ON?
WE'RE EVACUATING MANHATTAN.
GOD HELP US ALL...
I'M AFRAID WE CAN'T ARRANGE FOR THAT, SIR...

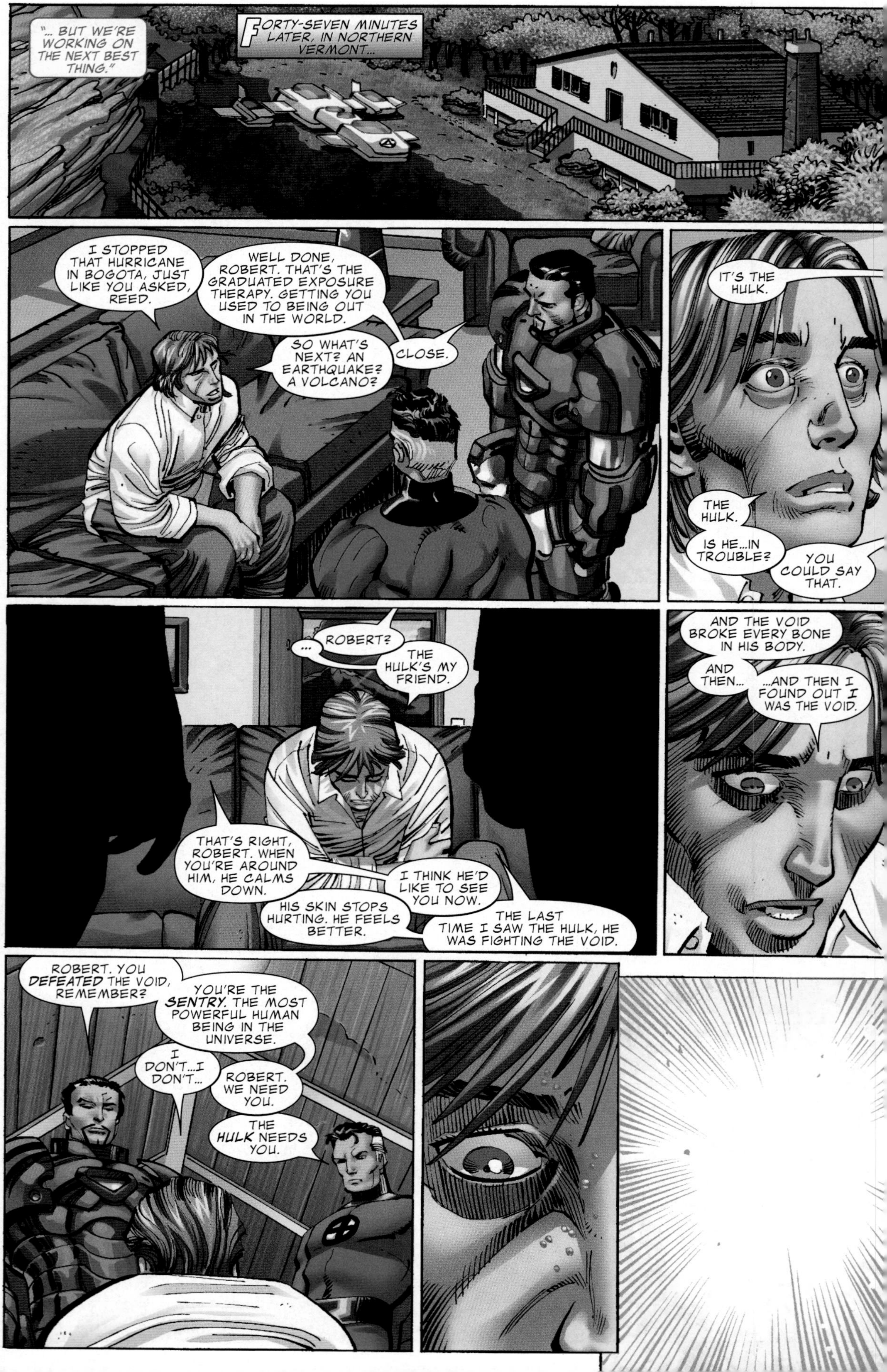
"... BUT WE'RE WORKING ON THE NEXT BEST THING."
FORTY-SEVEN MINUTES LATER, IN NORTHERN VERMONT...
I STOPPED THAT HURRICANE IN BOGOTA, JUST LIKE YOU ASKED, REED.
WELL DONE, ROBERT. THAT'S THE GRADUATED EXPOSURE THERAPY. GETTING YOU USED TO BEING OUT IN THE WORLD.
SO WHAT'S NEXT? AN EARTHQUAKE? A VOLCANO?
CLOSE.
IT'S THE HULK.
THE HULK.
IS HE...IN TROUBLE?
YOU COULD SAY THAT.
...
ROBERT?
THE HULK'S MY FRIEND.
THAT'S RIGHT, ROBERT. WHEN YOU'RE AROUND HIM, HE CALMS DOWN.
I THINK HE'D LIKE TO SEE YOU NOW.
HIS SKIN STOPS HURTING. HE FEELS BETTER.
THE LAST TIME I SAW THE HULK, HE WAS FIGHTING THE VOID.
AND THE VOID BROKE EVERY BONE IN HIS BODY.
AND THEN...
...AND THEN I FOUND OUT I WAS THE VOID.
ROBERT. YOU DEFEATED THE VOID, REMEMBER?
YOU'RE THE SENTRY. THE MOST POWERFUL HUMAN BEING IN THE UNIVERSE.
I DON'T...I DON'T...
ROBERT. WE NEED YOU.
THE HULK NEEDS YOU.

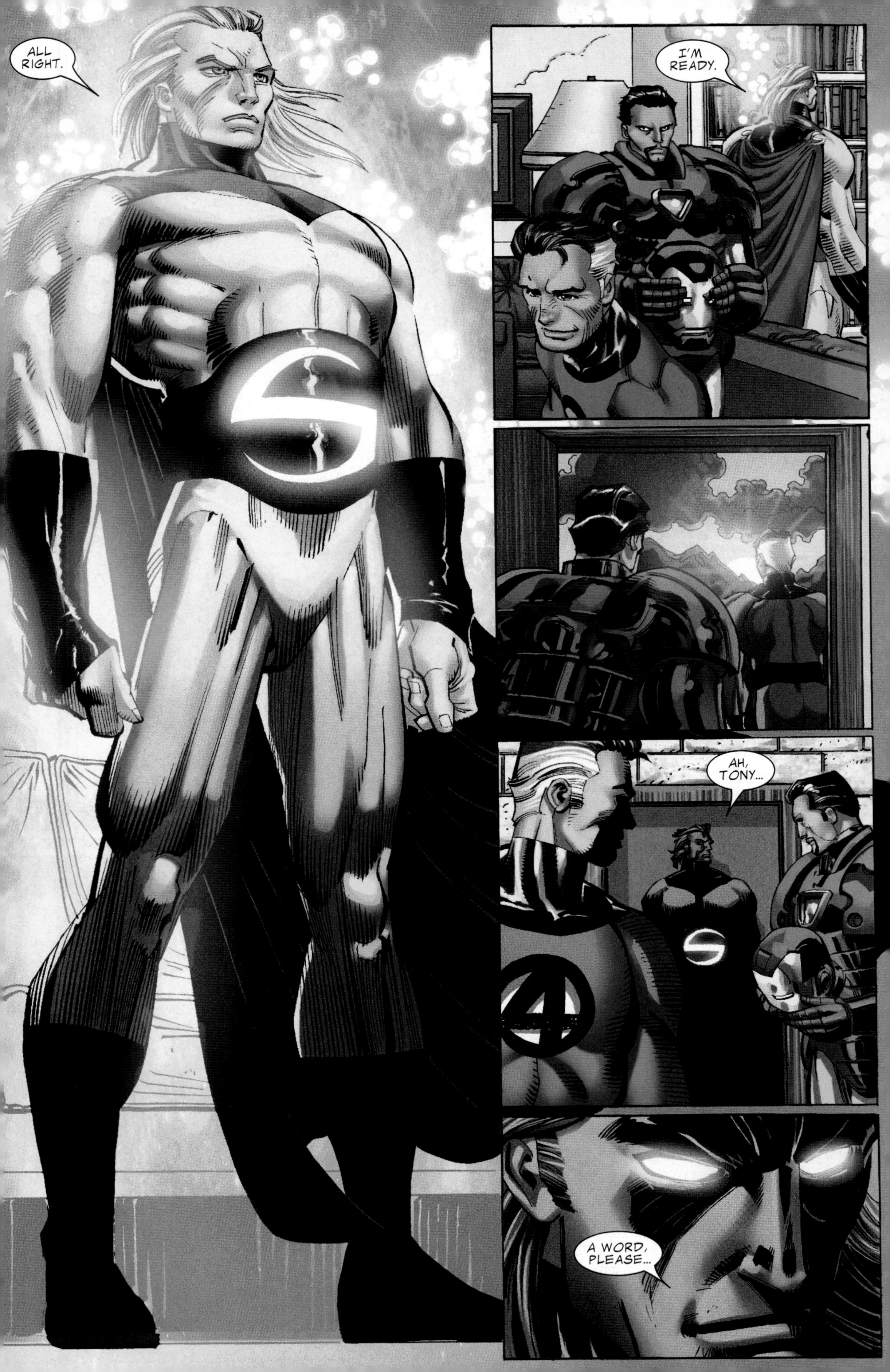
ALL RIGHT.
I'M READY.
AH, TONY...
A WORD, PLEASE...

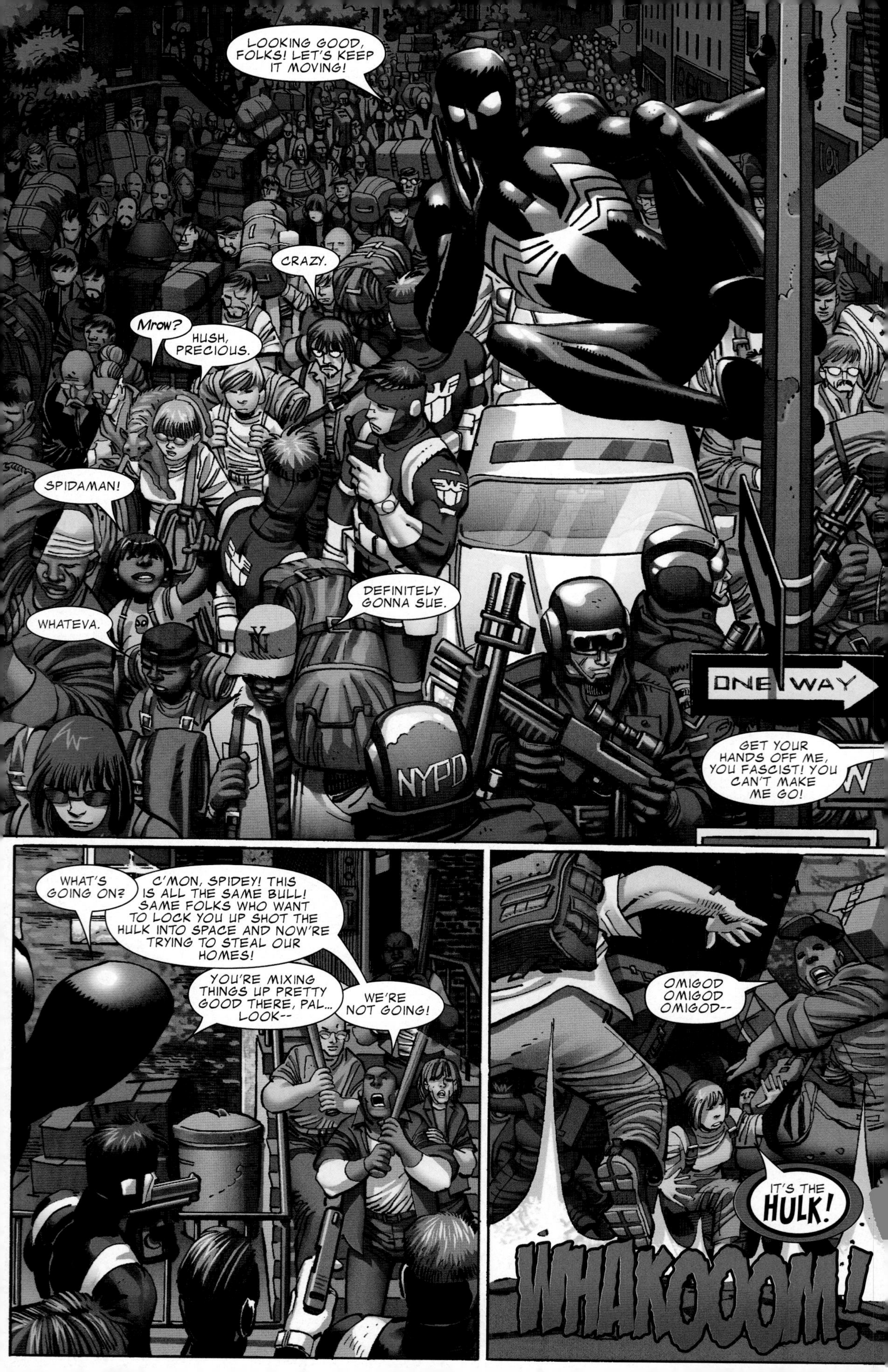
LOOKING GOOD, FOLKS! LET'S KEEP IT MOVING!
CRAZY.
Mrow?
HUSH, PRECIOUS.
SPIDAMAN!
DEFINITELY GONNA SUE.
WHATEVA.
ONE WAY
NYPD
GET YOUR HANDS OFF ME, YOU FASCIST! YOU CAN'T MAKE ME GO!
WHAT'S GOING ON?
C'MON, SPIDEY! THIS IS ALL THE SAME BULL! SAME FOLKS WHO WANT TO LOCK YOU UP SHOT THE HULK INTO SPACE AND NOW'RE TRYING TO STEAL OUR HOMES!
YOU'RE MIXING THINGS UP PRETTY GOOD THERE, PAL... LOOK--
WE'RE NOT GOING!
OMIGOD OMIGOD OMIGOD--
IT'S THE HULK!
WHAKOOOM!

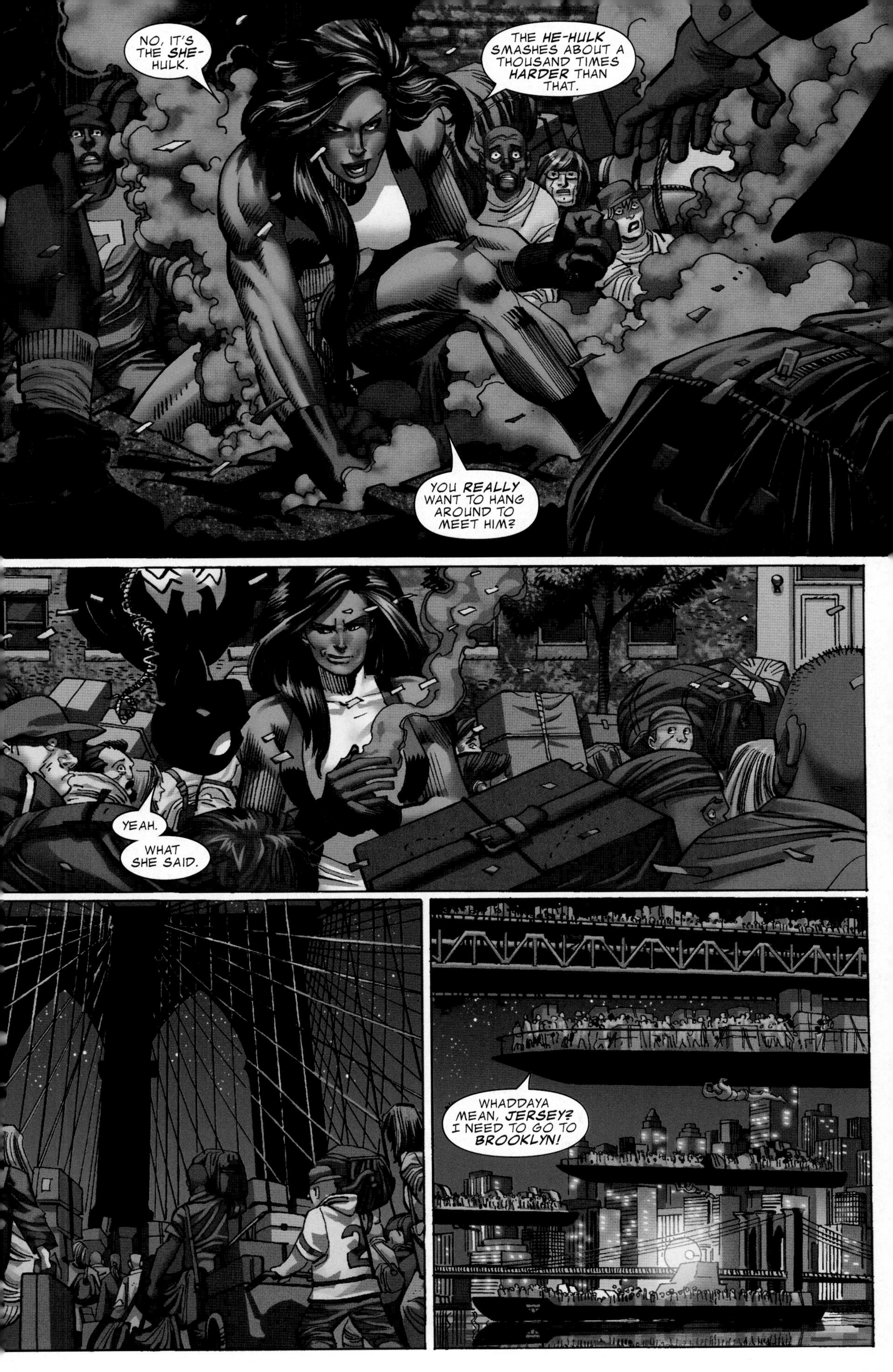
NO, IT'S THE SHE-HULK.
THE HE-HULK SMASHES ABOUT A THOUSAND TIMES HARDER THAN THAT.
YOU REALLY WANT TO HANG AROUND TO MEET HIM?
YEAH.
WHAT SHE SAID.
WHADDAYA MEAN, JERSEY? I NEED TO GO TO BROOKLYN!

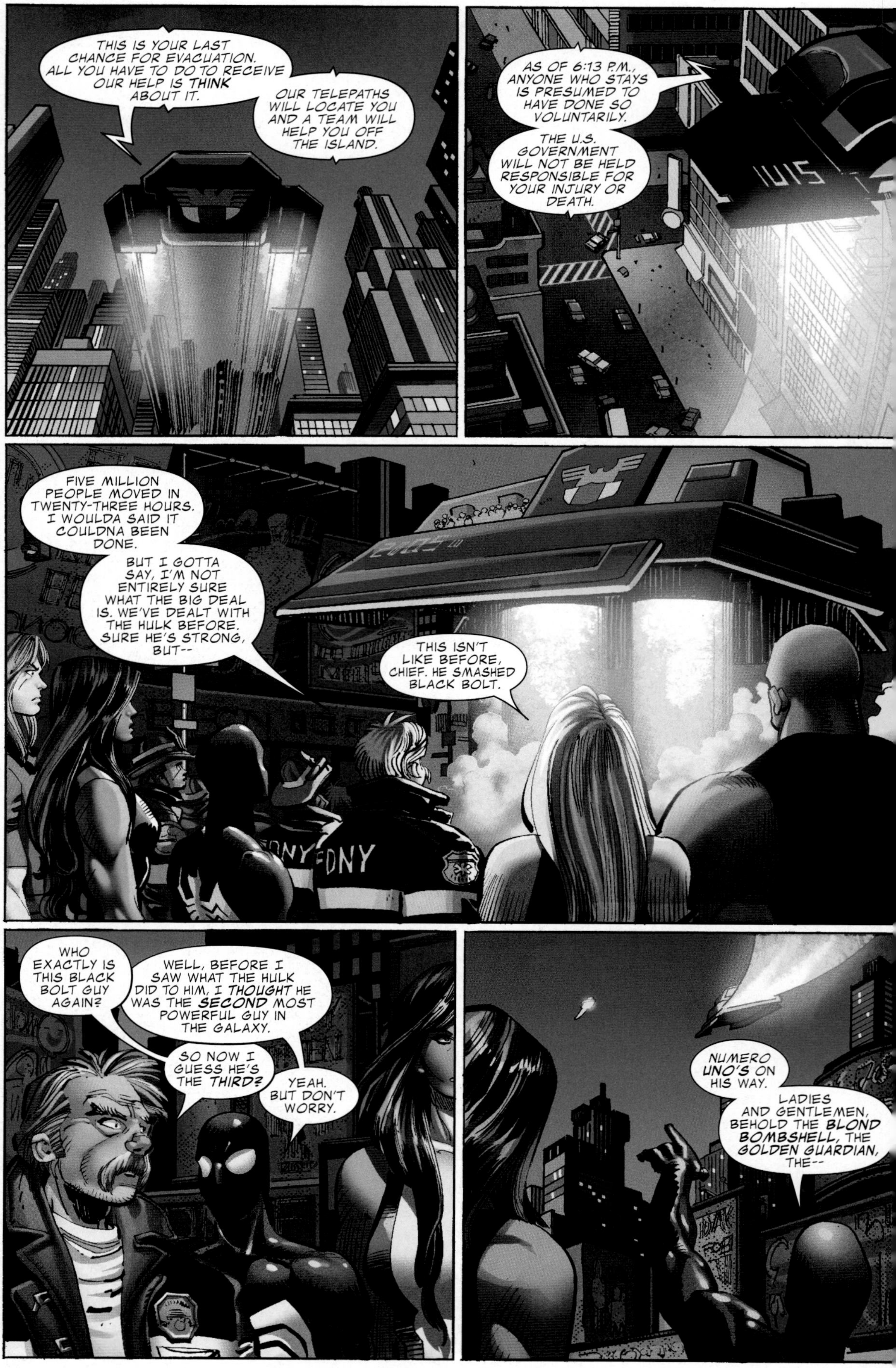
THIS IS YOUR LAST CHANCE FOR EVACUATION. ALL YOU HAVE TO DO TO RECEIVE OUR HELP IS **THINK** ABOUT IT.
OUR TELEPATHS WILL LOCATE YOU AND A TEAM WILL HELP YOU OFF THE ISLAND.
AS OF 6:13 P.M., ANYONE WHO STAYS IS PRESUMED TO HAVE DONE SO VOLUNTARILY.
THE U.S. GOVERNMENT WILL NOT BE HELD RESPONSIBLE FOR YOUR INJURY OR DEATH.
FIVE MILLION PEOPLE MOVED IN TWENTY-THREE HOURS. I WOULDA SAID IT COULDNA BEEN DONE.
BUT I GOTTA SAY, I'M NOT ENTIRELY SURE WHAT THE BIG DEAL IS. WE'VE DEALT WITH THE HULK BEFORE. SURE HE'S STRONG, BUT--
THIS ISN'T LIKE BEFORE, CHIEF. HE SMASHED BLACK BOLT.
FDNY
WHO EXACTLY IS THIS BLACK BOLT GUY AGAIN?
WELL, BEFORE I SAW WHAT THE HULK DID TO HIM, I *THOUGHT* HE WAS THE ***SECOND*** MOST POWERFUL GUY IN THE GALAXY.
SO NOW I GUESS HE'S THE *THIRD?*
YEAH. BUT DON'T WORRY.
NUMERO ***UNO'S*** ON HIS WAY.
LADIES AND GENTLEMEN, BEHOLD THE ***BLOND BOMBSHELL***, THE ***GOLDEN GUARDIAN***, THE--

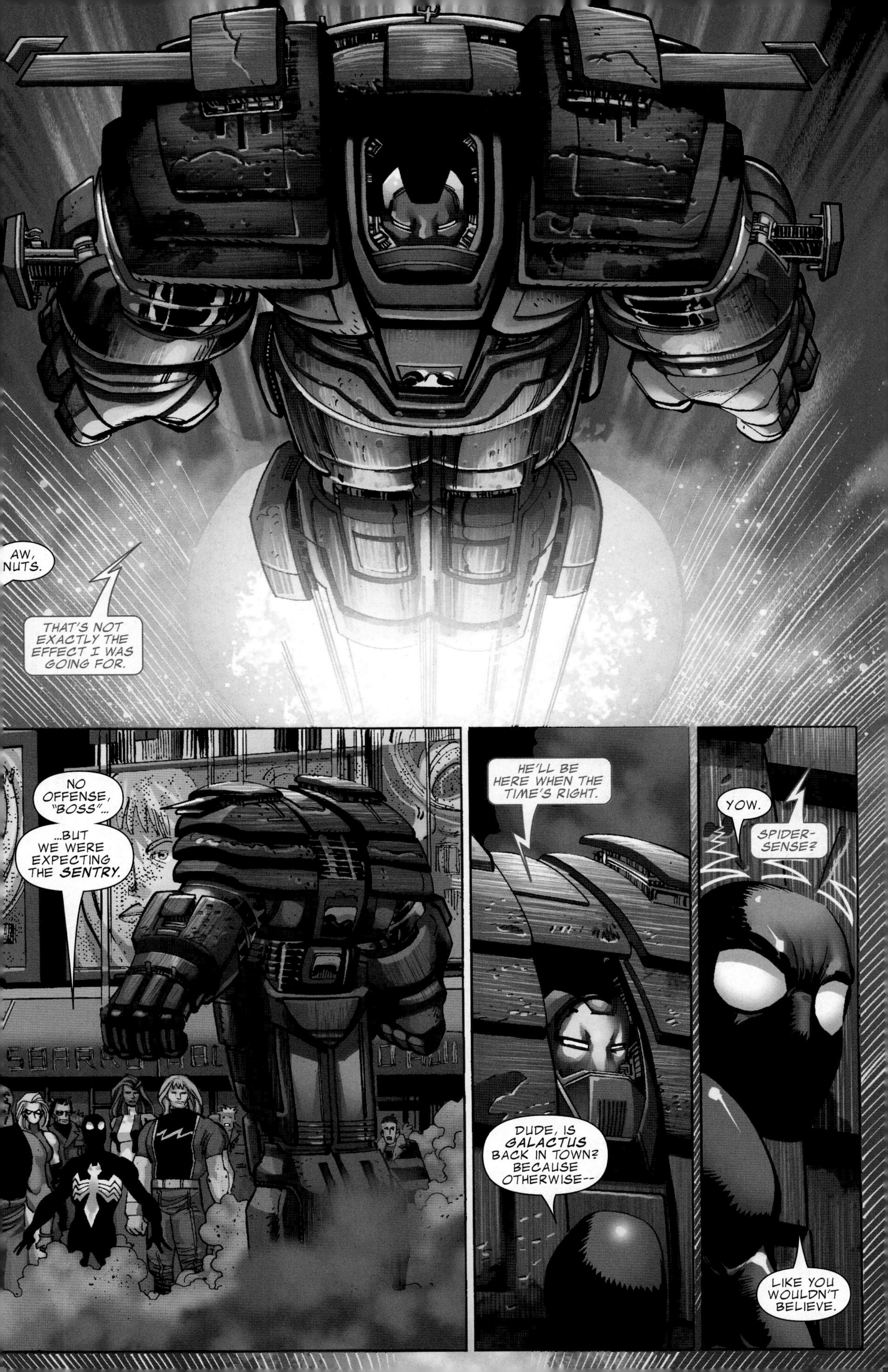
AW, NUTS.
THAT'S NOT EXACTLY THE EFFECT I WAS GOING FOR.
NO OFFENSE, "BOSS"...
...BUT WE WERE EXPECTING THE **SENTRY**.
HE'LL BE HERE WHEN THE TIME'S RIGHT.
DUDE, IS ***GALACTUS*** BACK IN TOWN? BECAUSE OTHERWISE--
YOW.
SPIDER-SENSE?
LIKE YOU WOULDN'T BELIEVE.

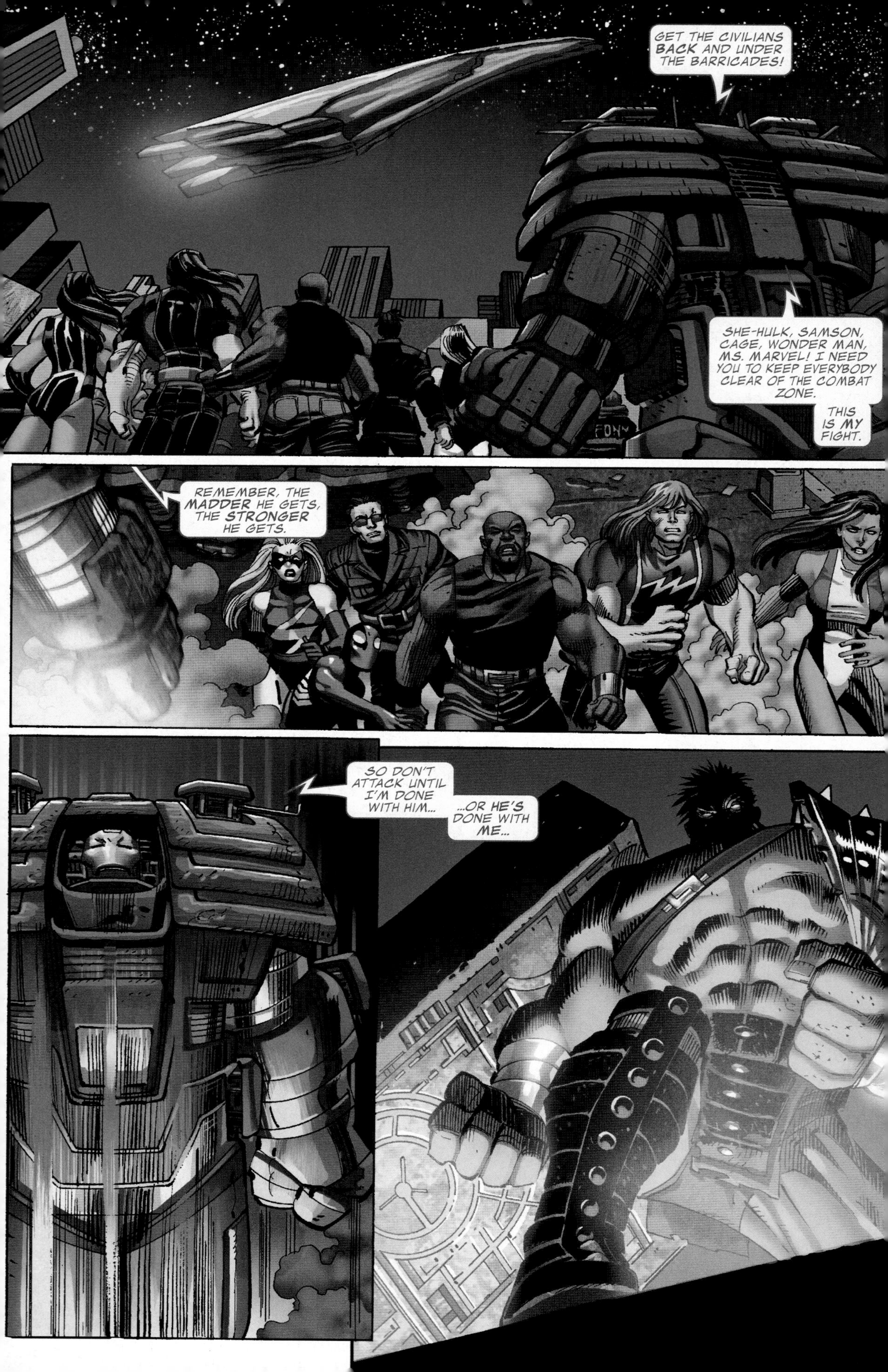
GET THE CIVILIANS BACK AND UNDER THE BARRICADES!
SHE-HULK, SAMSON, CAGE, WONDER MAN, MS. MARVEL! I NEED YOU TO KEEP EVERYBODY CLEAR OF THE COMBAT ZONE.
THIS IS MY FIGHT.
REMEMBER, THE MADDER HE GETS, THE STRONGER HE GETS.
SO DON'T ATTACK UNTIL I'M DONE WITH HIM...
...OR HE'S DONE WITH ME...

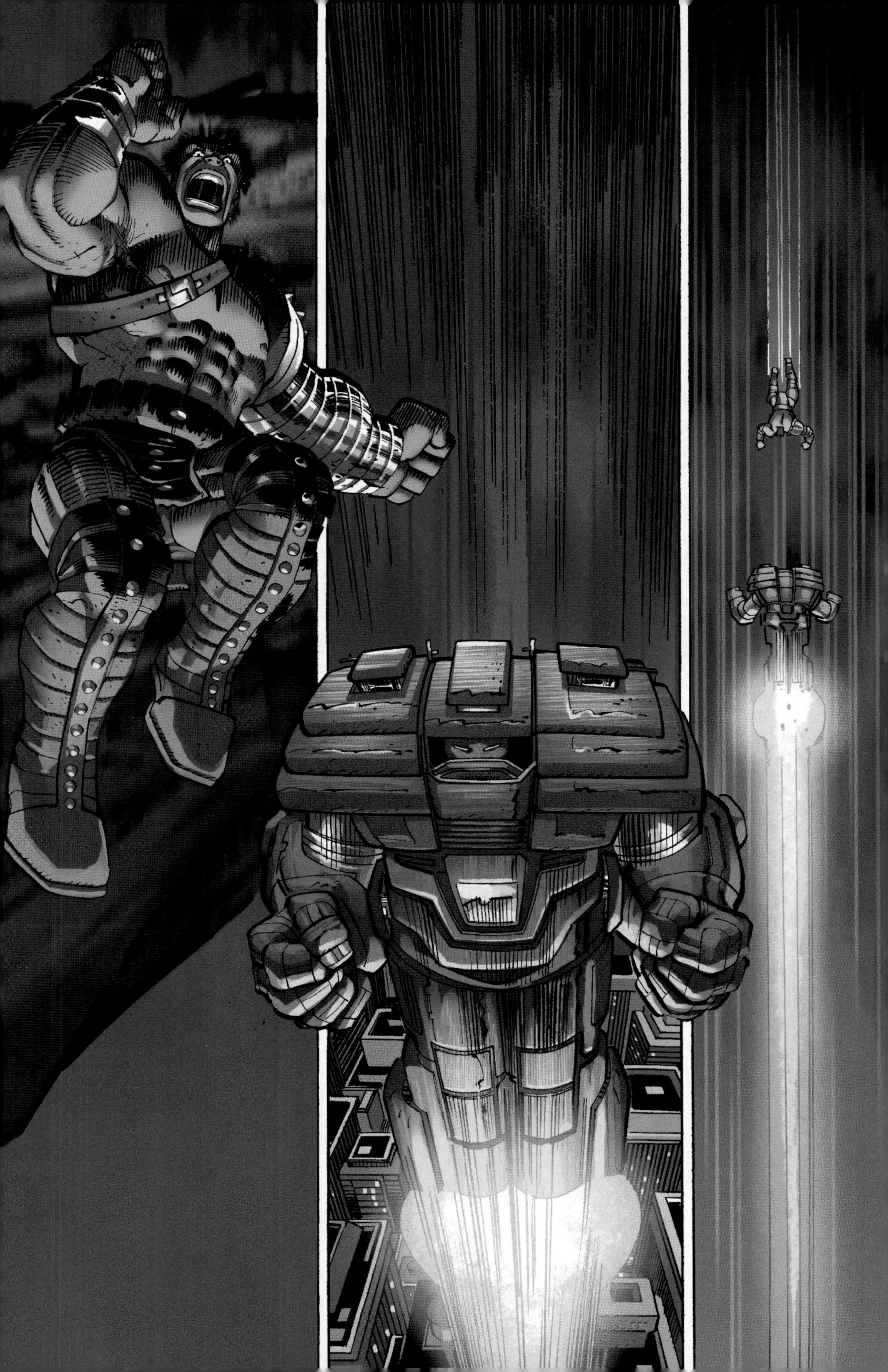

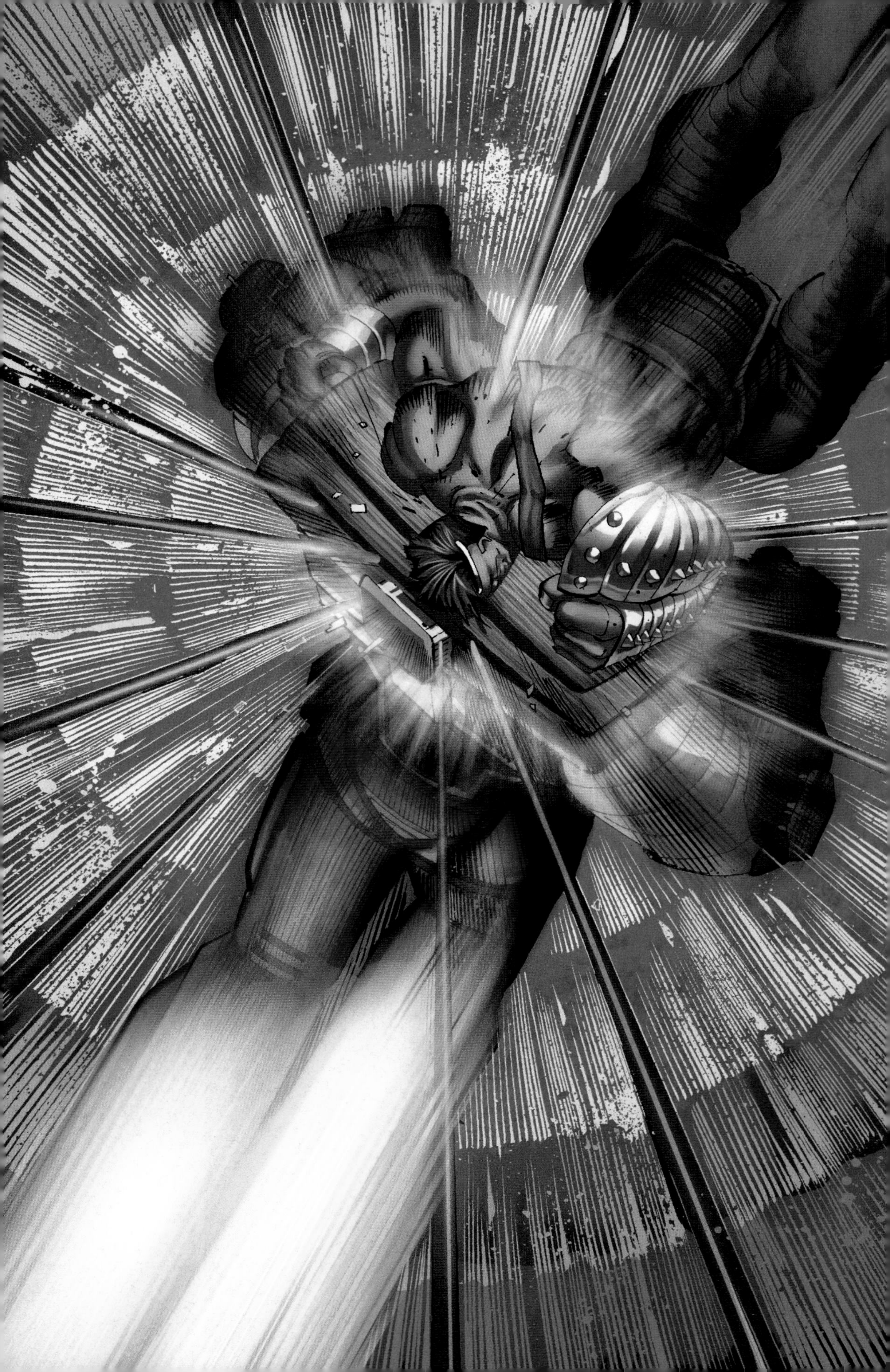

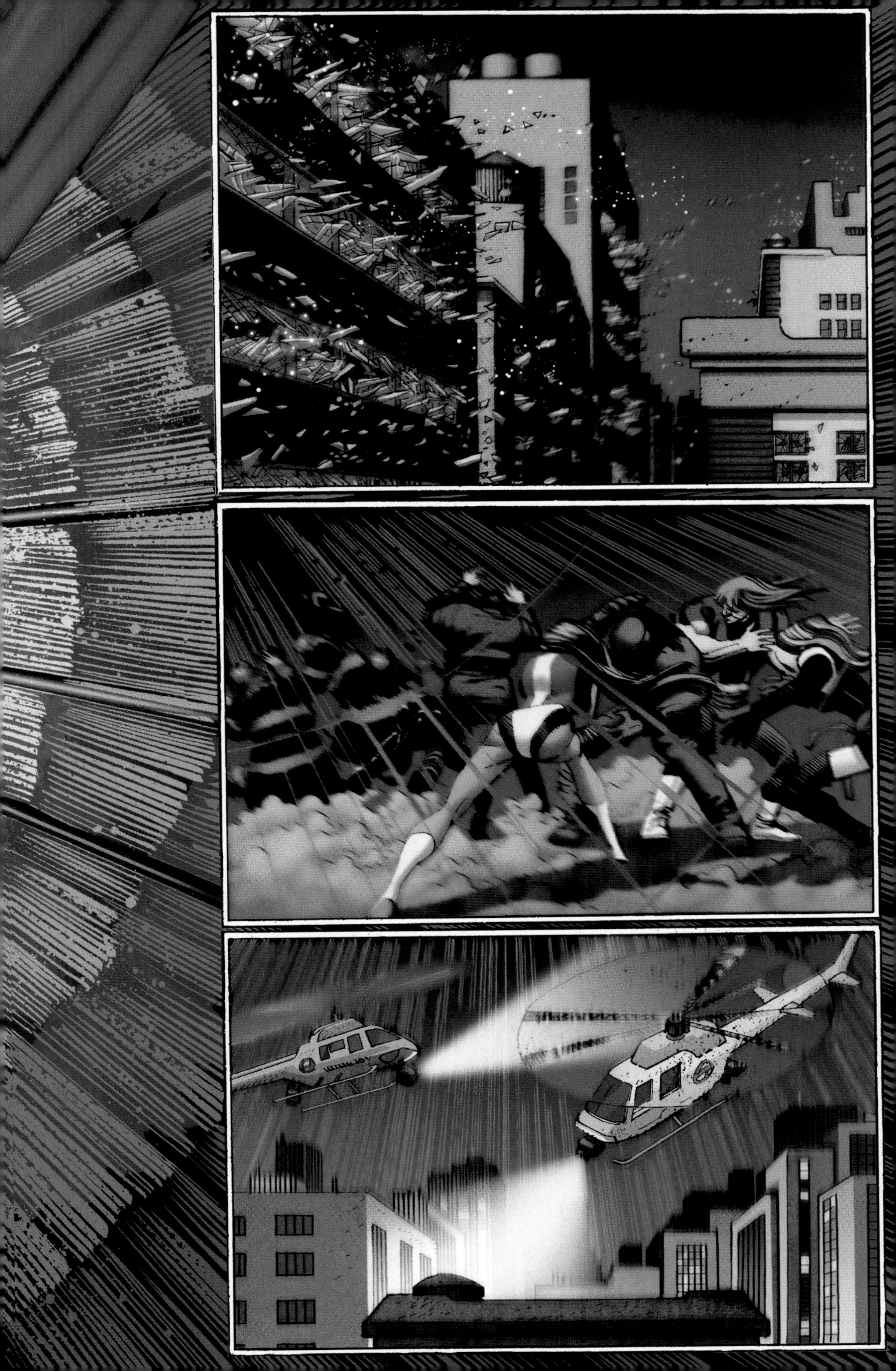

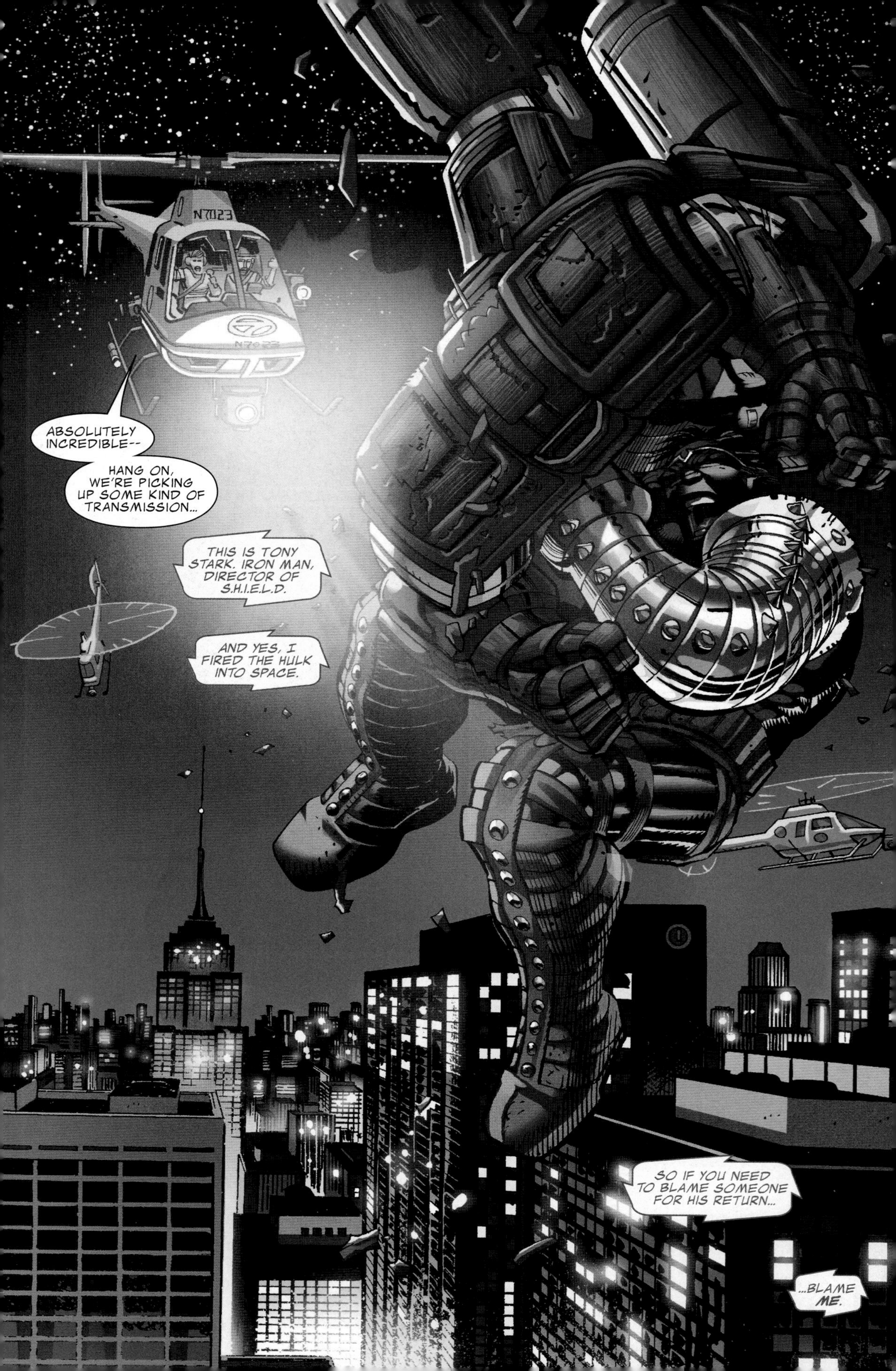
ABSOLUTELY INCREDIBLE--
HANG ON, WE'RE PICKING UP SOME KIND OF TRANSMISSION...
THIS IS TONY STARK. IRON MAN, DIRECTOR OF S.H.I.E.L.D.
AND YES, I FIRED THE HULK INTO SPACE.
SO IF YOU NEED TO BLAME SOMEONE FOR HIS RETURN...
...BLAME ME.

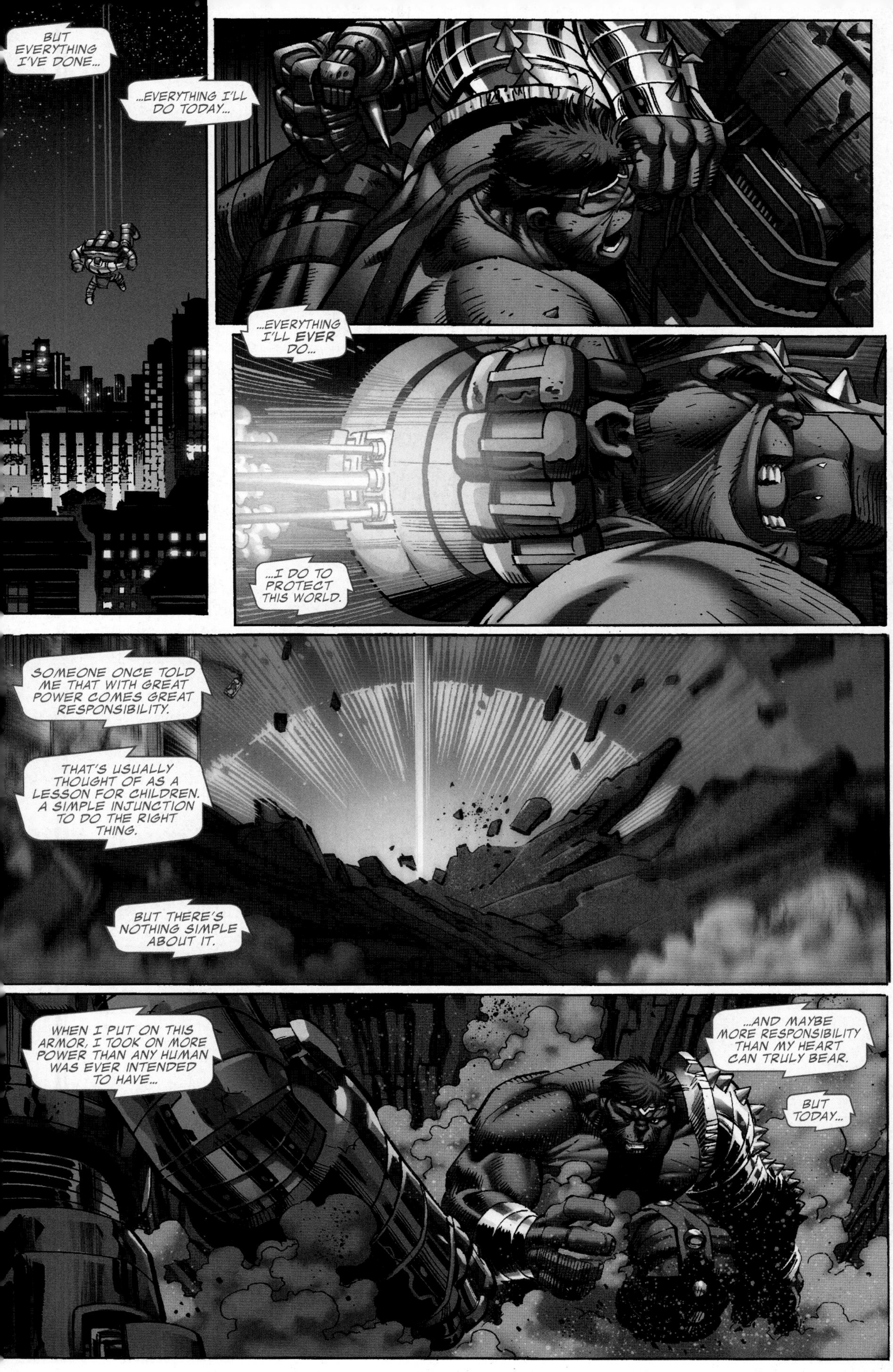
BUT EVERYTHING I'VE DONE...
...EVERYTHING I'LL DO TODAY...
...EVERYTHING I'LL EVER DO...
...I DO TO PROTECT THIS WORLD.
SOMEONE ONCE TOLD ME THAT WITH GREAT POWER COMES GREAT RESPONSIBILITY.
THAT'S USUALLY THOUGHT OF AS A LESSON FOR CHILDREN. A SIMPLE INJUNCTION TO DO THE RIGHT THING.
BUT THERE'S NOTHING SIMPLE ABOUT IT.
WHEN I PUT ON THIS ARMOR, I TOOK ON MORE POWER THAN ANY HUMAN WAS EVER INTENDED TO HAVE...
...AND MAYBE MORE RESPONSIBILITY THAN MY HEART CAN TRULY BEAR.
BUT TODAY...

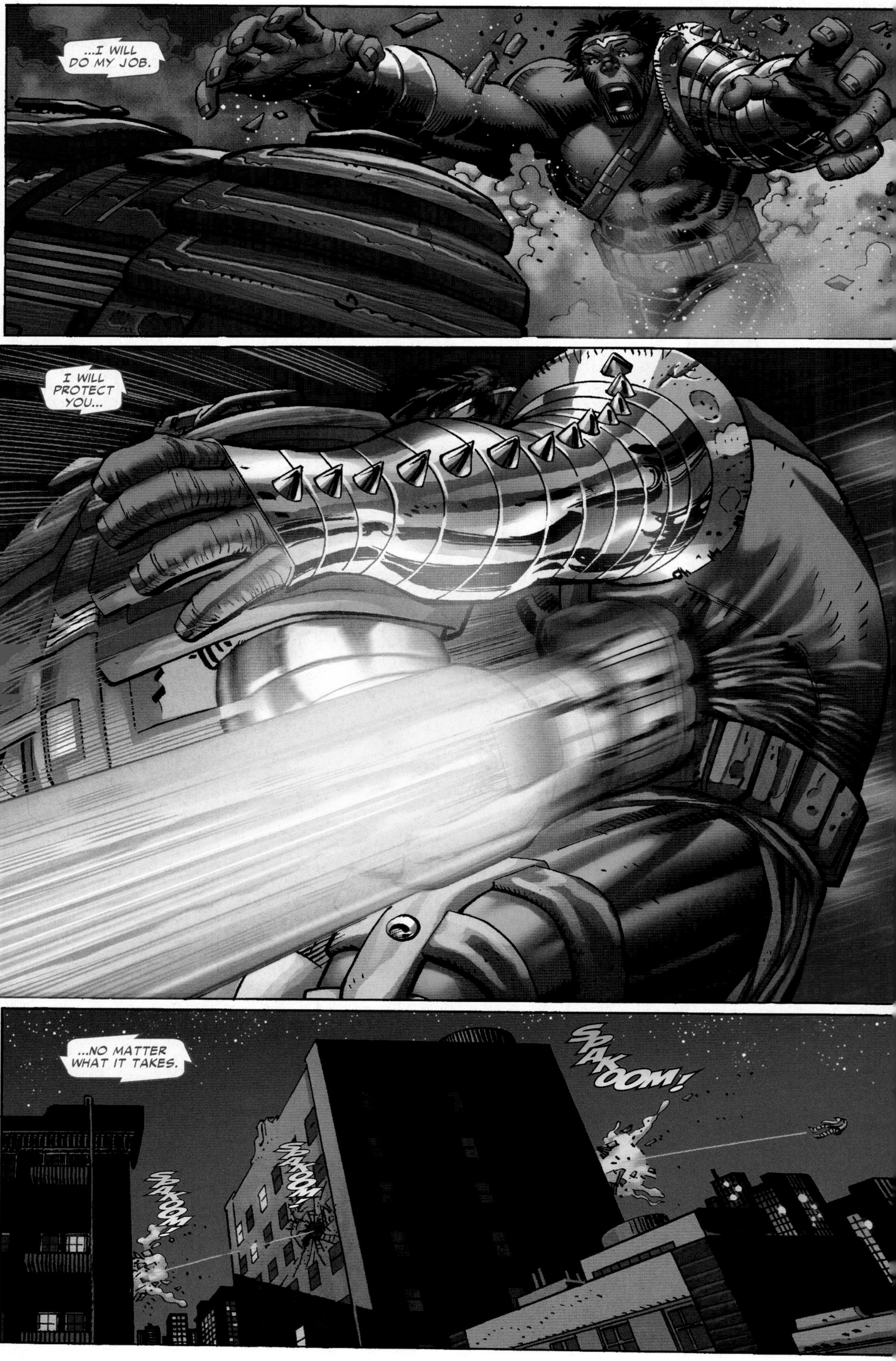
...I WILL DO MY JOB.
I WILL PROTECT YOU...
...NO MATTER WHAT IT TAKES.
SPAKOOM!
SPAKOOM!
SPAKOOM!

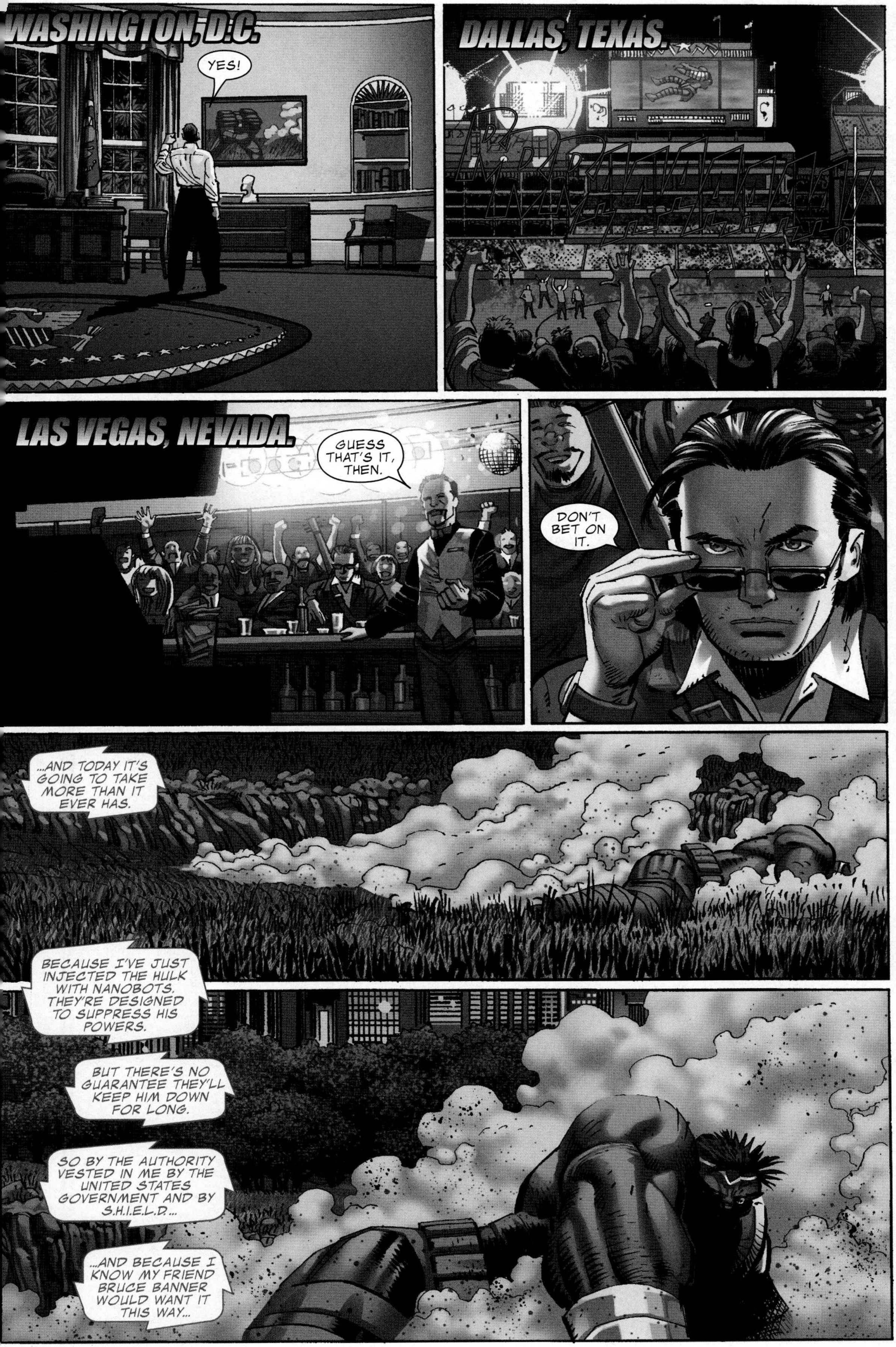
WASHINGTON, D.C.
YES!
DALLAS, TEXAS.
LAS VEGAS, NEVADA.
GUESS THAT'S IT, THEN.
DON'T BET ON IT.
...AND TODAY IT'S GOING TO TAKE MORE THAN IT EVER HAS.
BECAUSE I'VE JUST INJECTED THE HULK WITH NANOBOTS. THEY'RE DESIGNED TO SUPPRESS HIS POWERS.
BUT THERE'S NO GUARANTEE THEY'LL KEEP HIM DOWN FOR LONG.
SO BY THE AUTHORITY VESTED IN ME BY THE UNITED STATES GOVERNMENT AND BY S.H.I.E.L.D...
...AND BECAUSE I KNOW MY FRIEND BRUCE BANNER WOULD WANT IT THIS WAY...

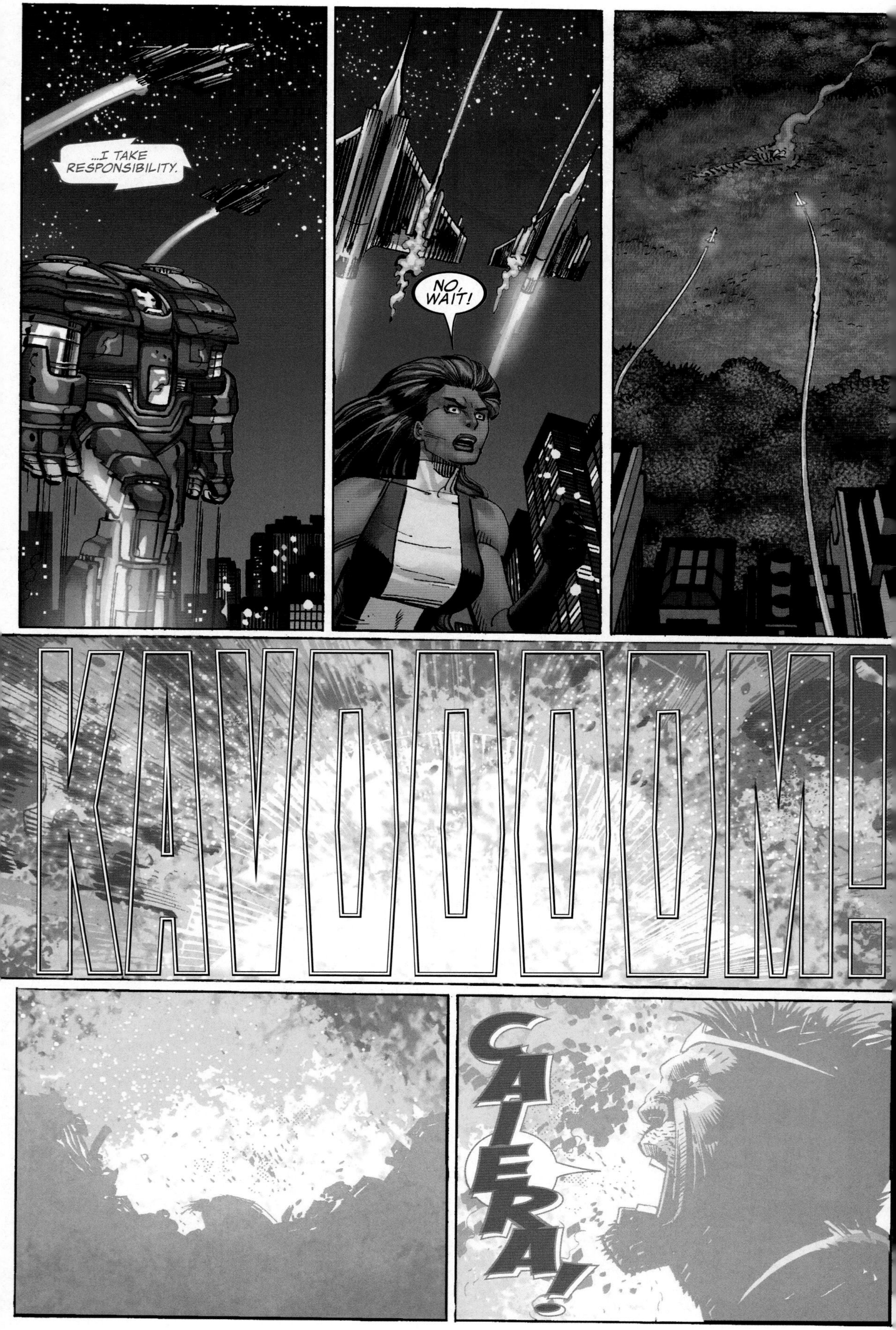
...I TAKE RESPONSIBILITY.
NO, WAIT!
KAVOOOOM!
GAIERA!

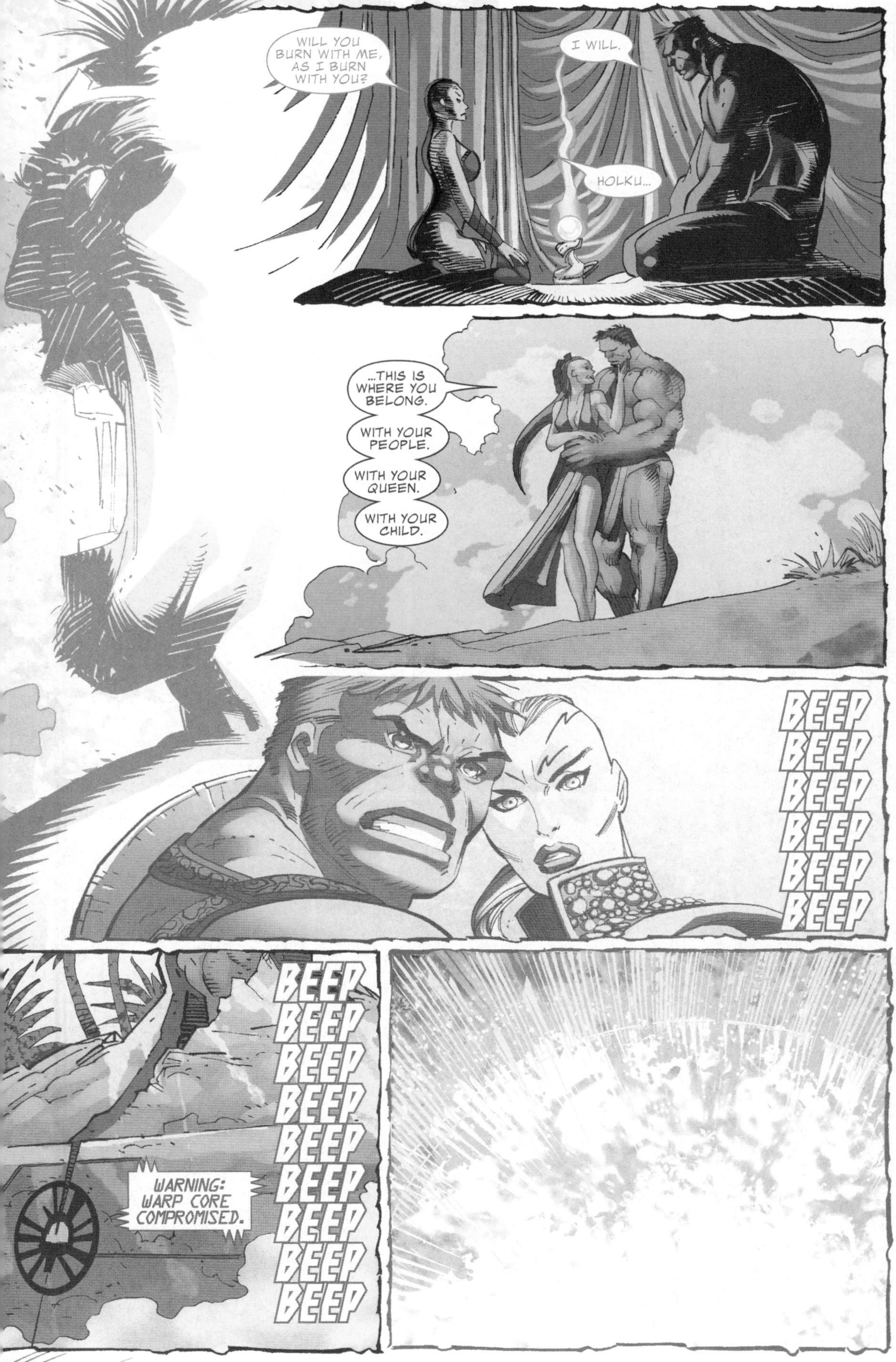
WILL YOU BURN WITH ME, AS I BURN WITH YOU?
I WILL.
HOLKU...
...THIS IS WHERE YOU BELONG.
WITH YOUR PEOPLE.
WITH YOUR QUEEN.
WITH YOUR CHILD.
BEEP BEEP BEEP BEEP BEEP BEEP
BEEP BEEP BEEP BEEP BEEP BEEP BEEP BEEP BEEP
WARNING: WARP CORE COMPROMISED.

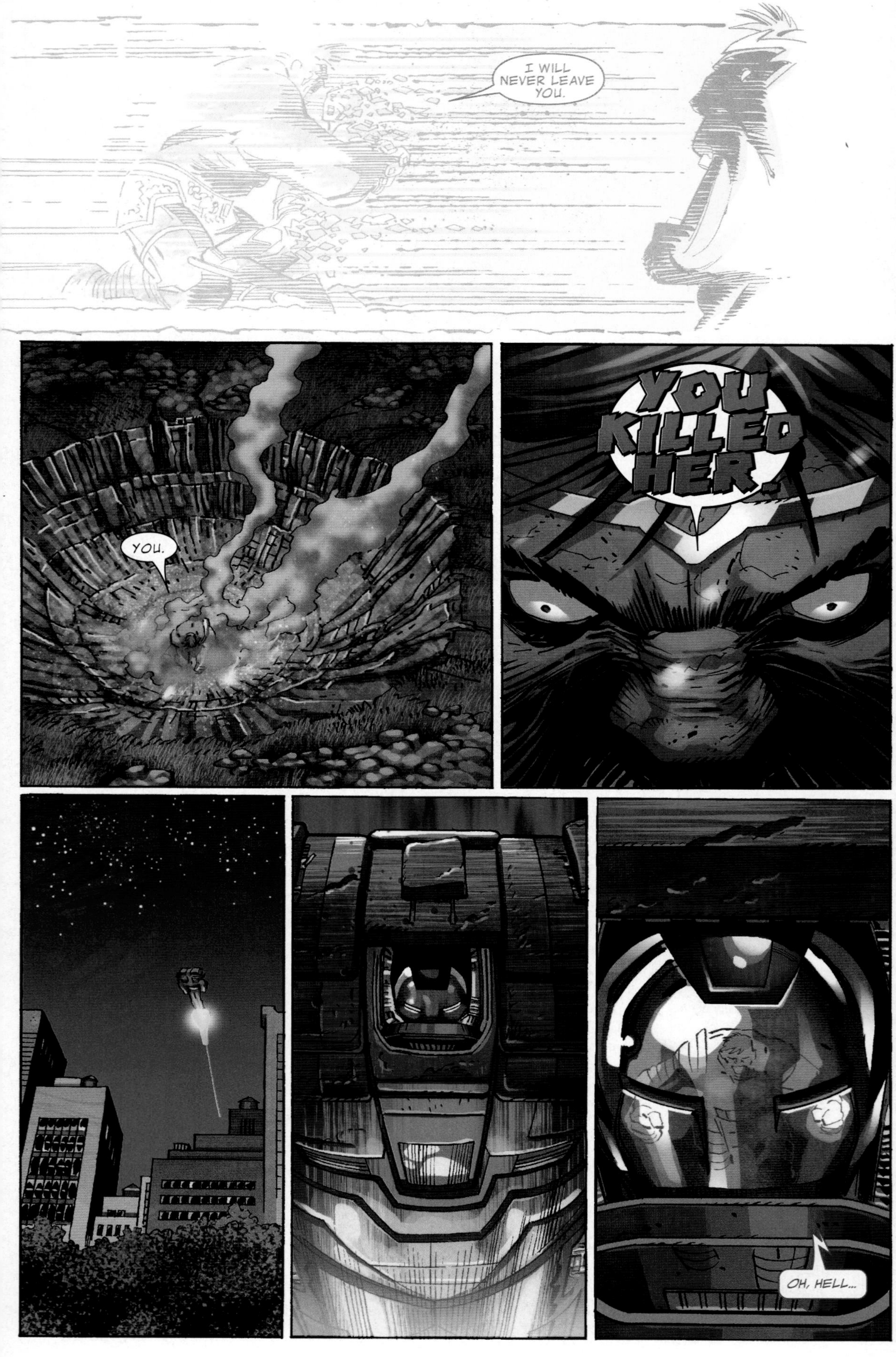
I WILL NEVER LEAVE YOU.
YOU.
YOU KILLED HER.
OH, HELL...

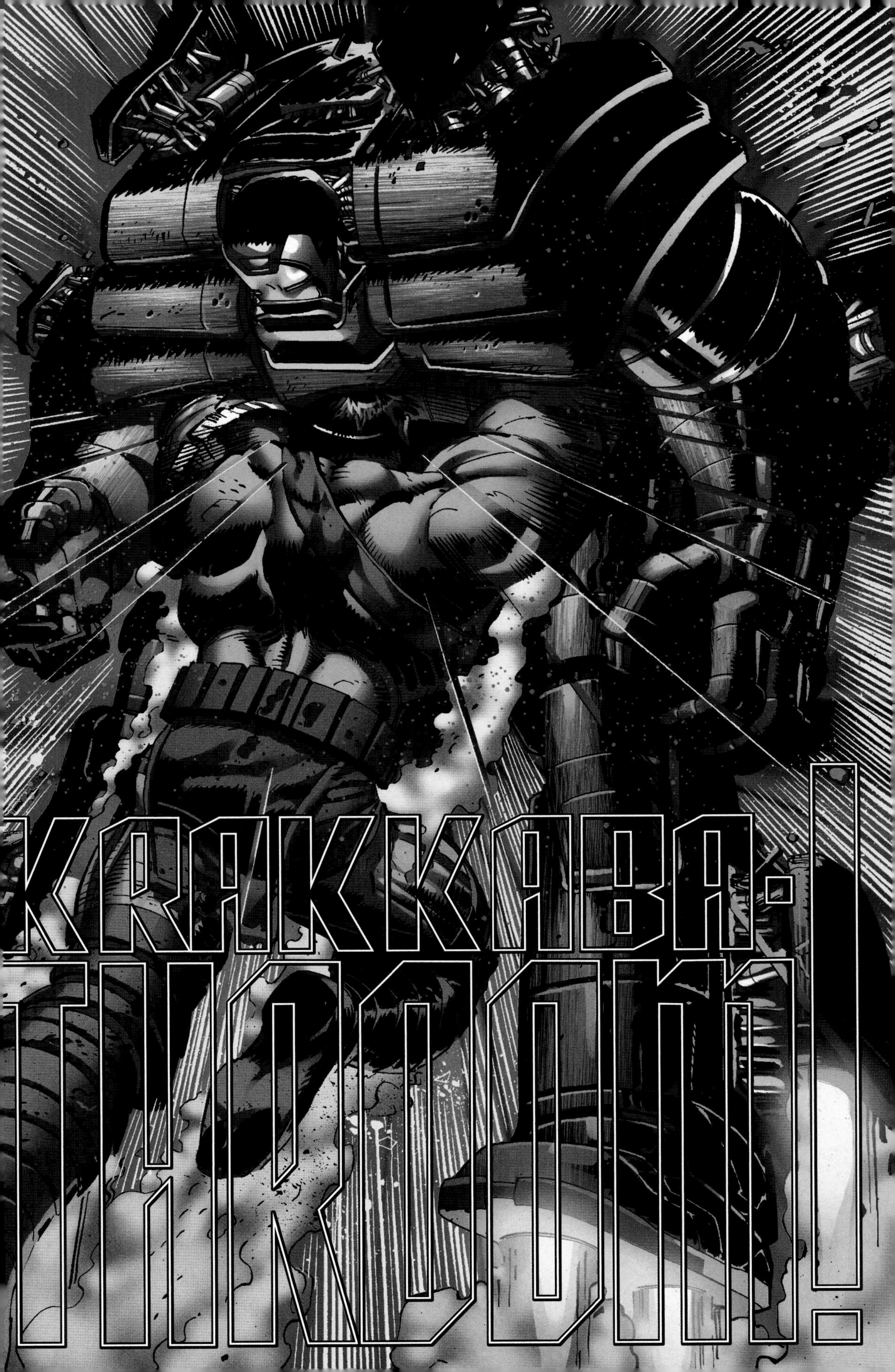
KRAKKABA-THOOM!

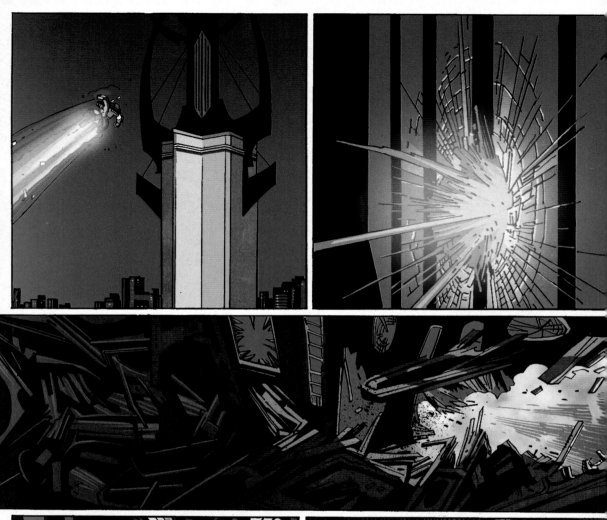

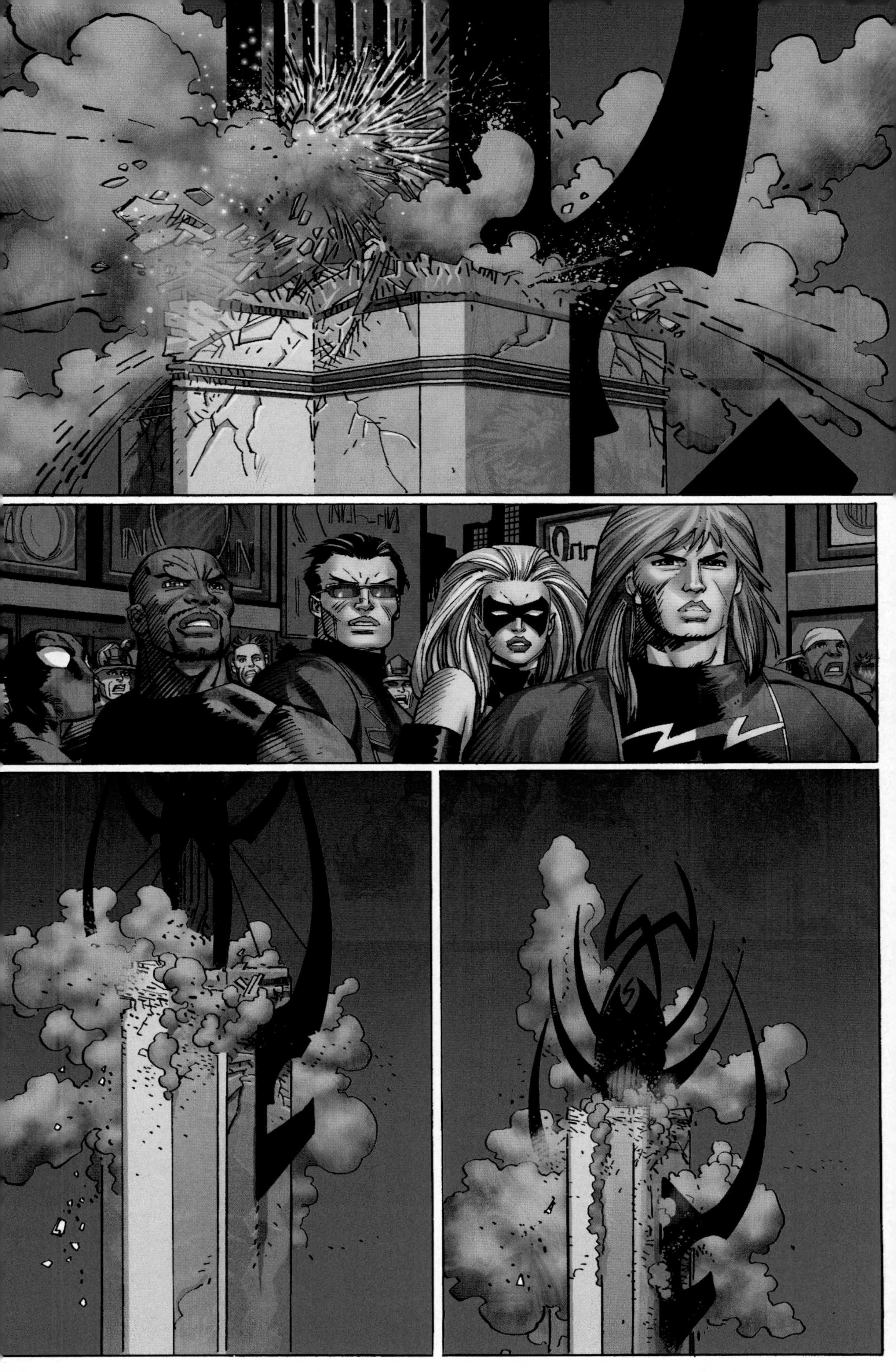

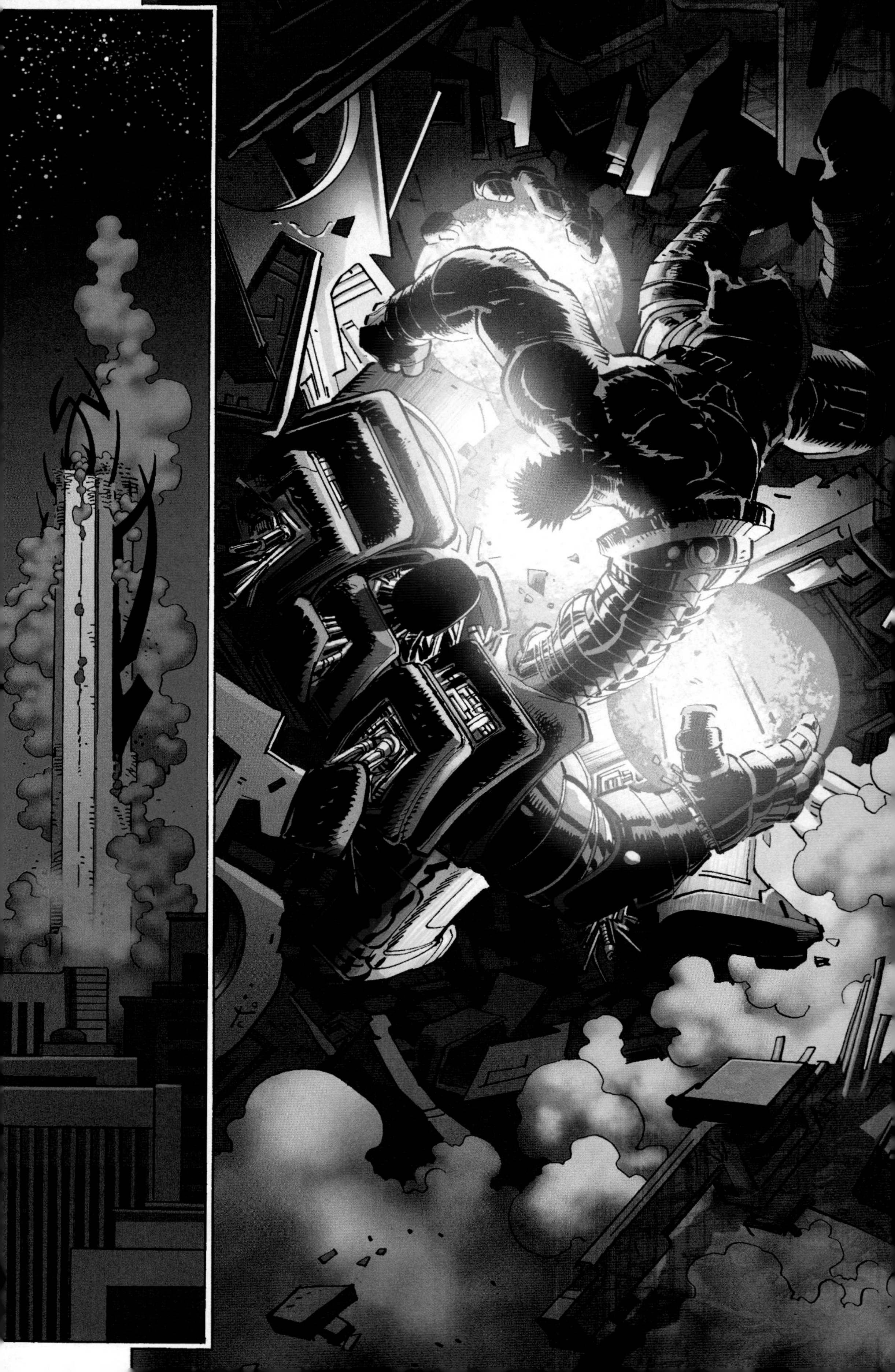

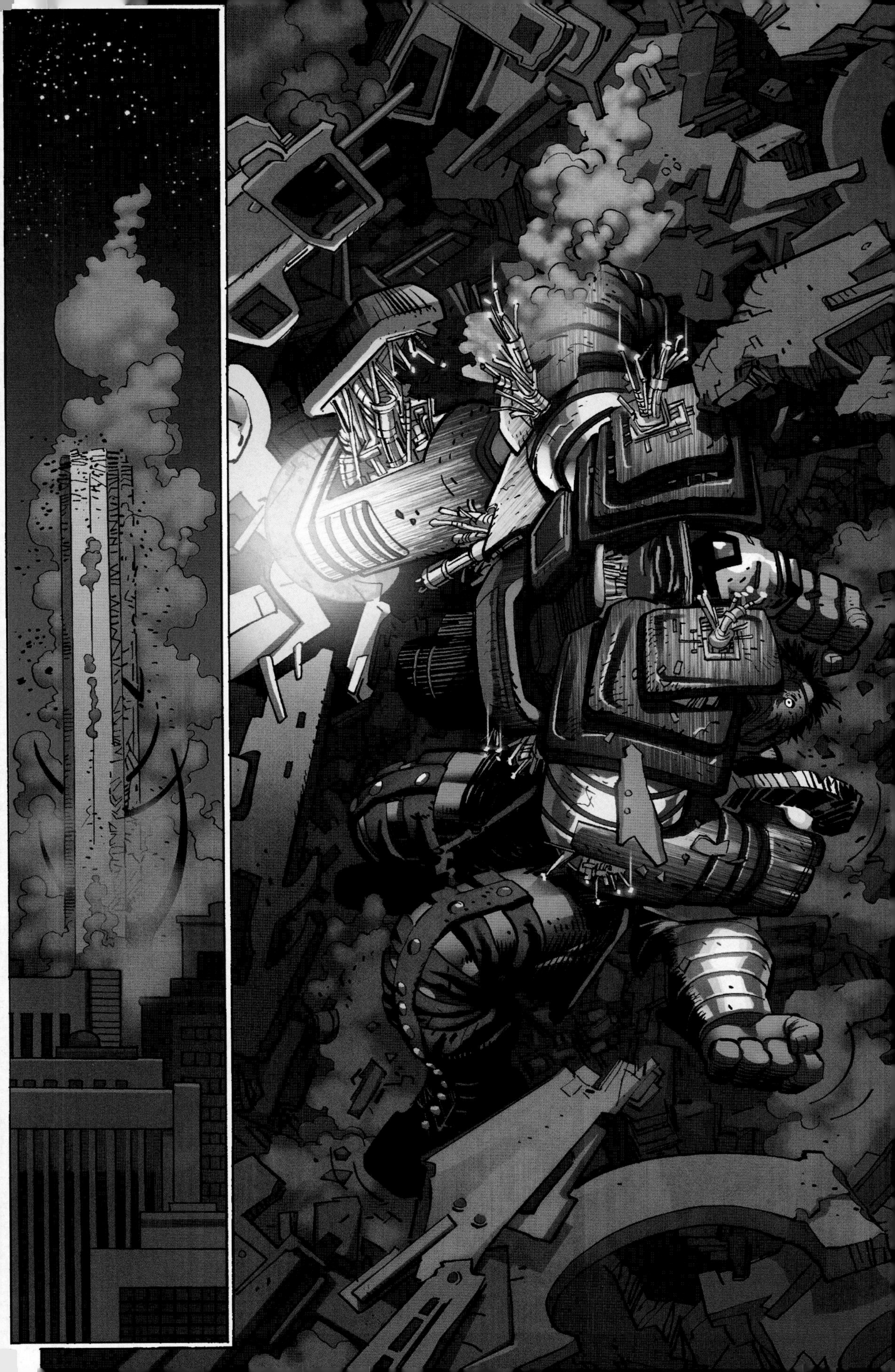

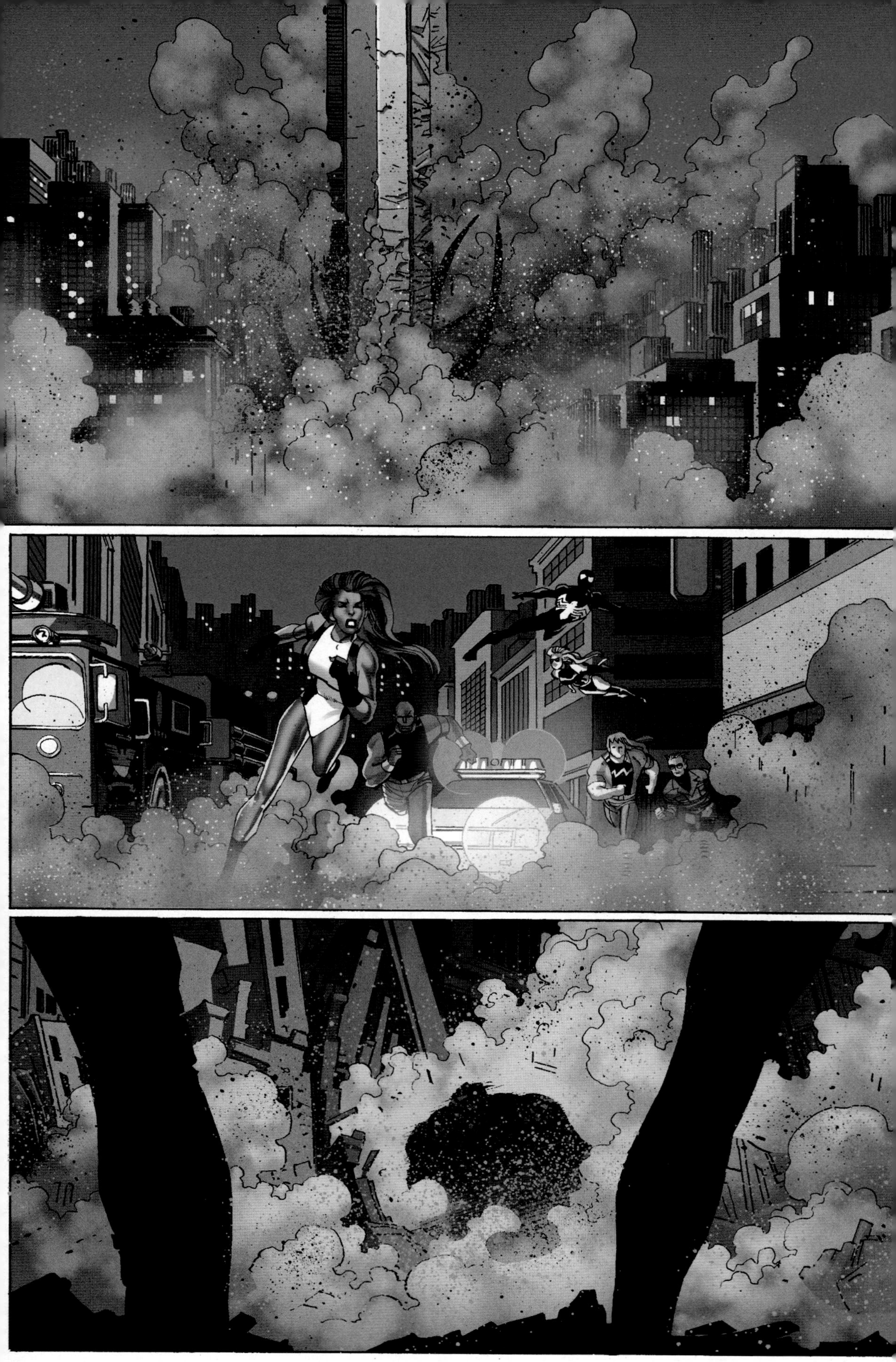

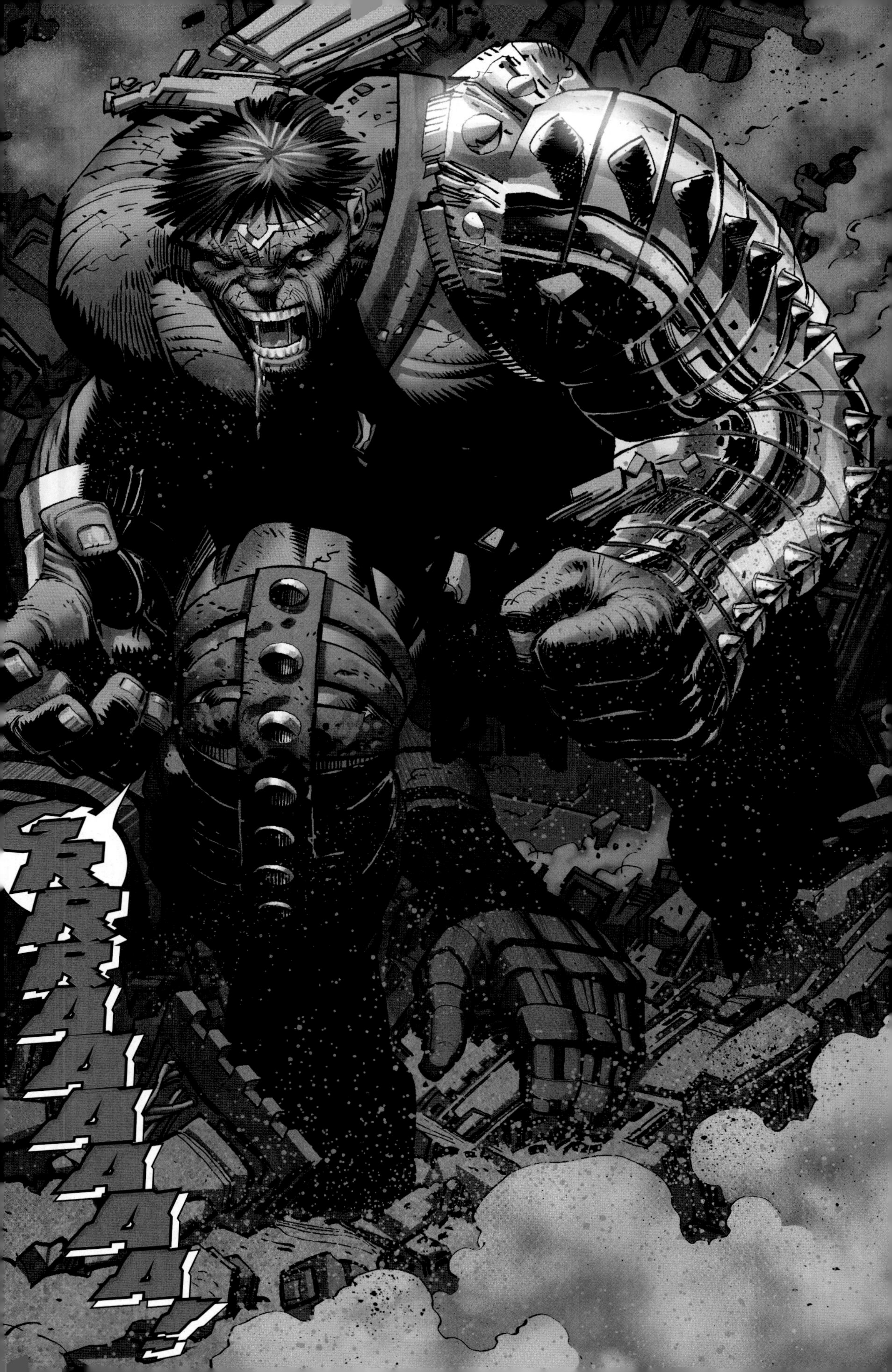
RRRAAAAAA

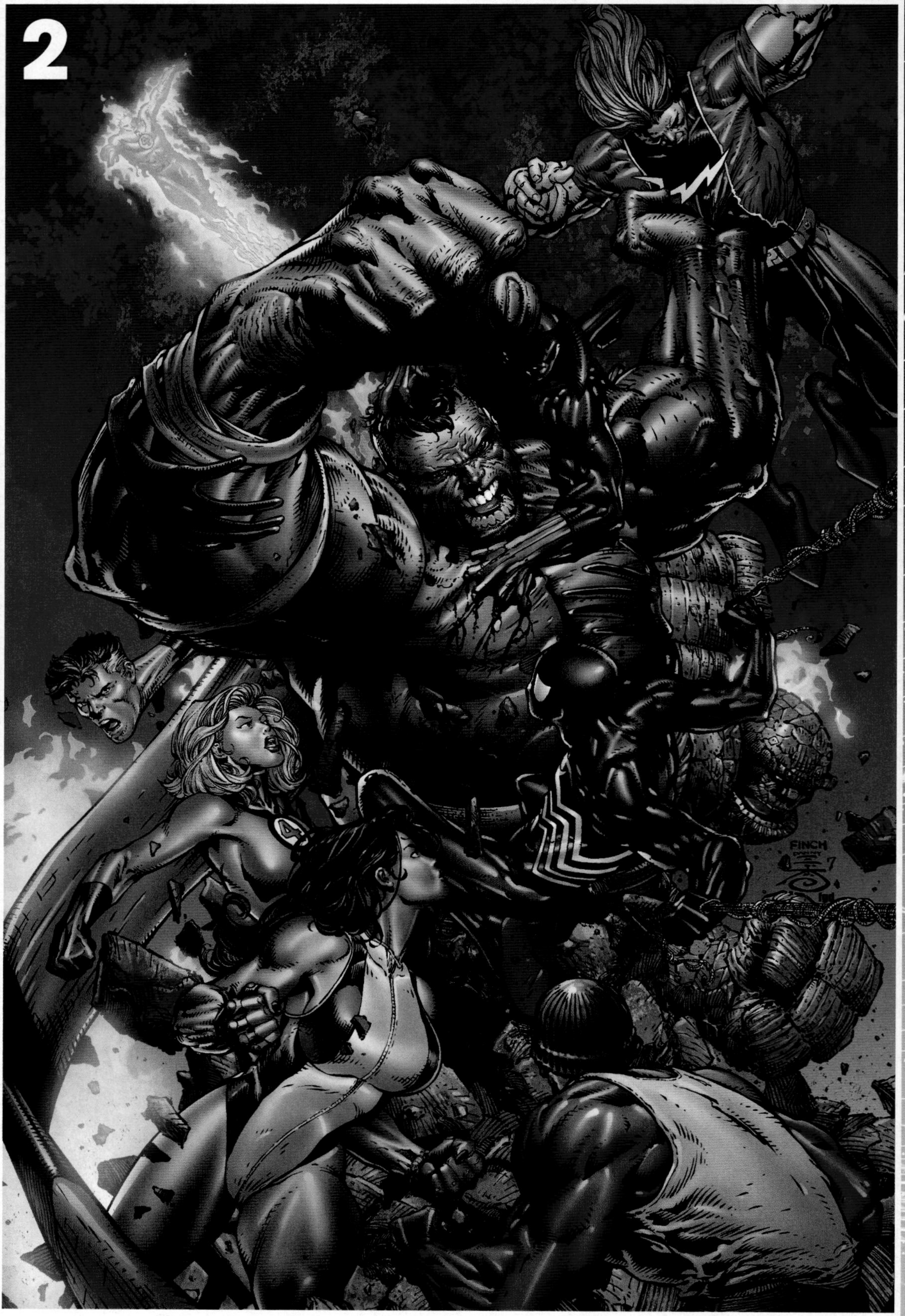
2
FINCH

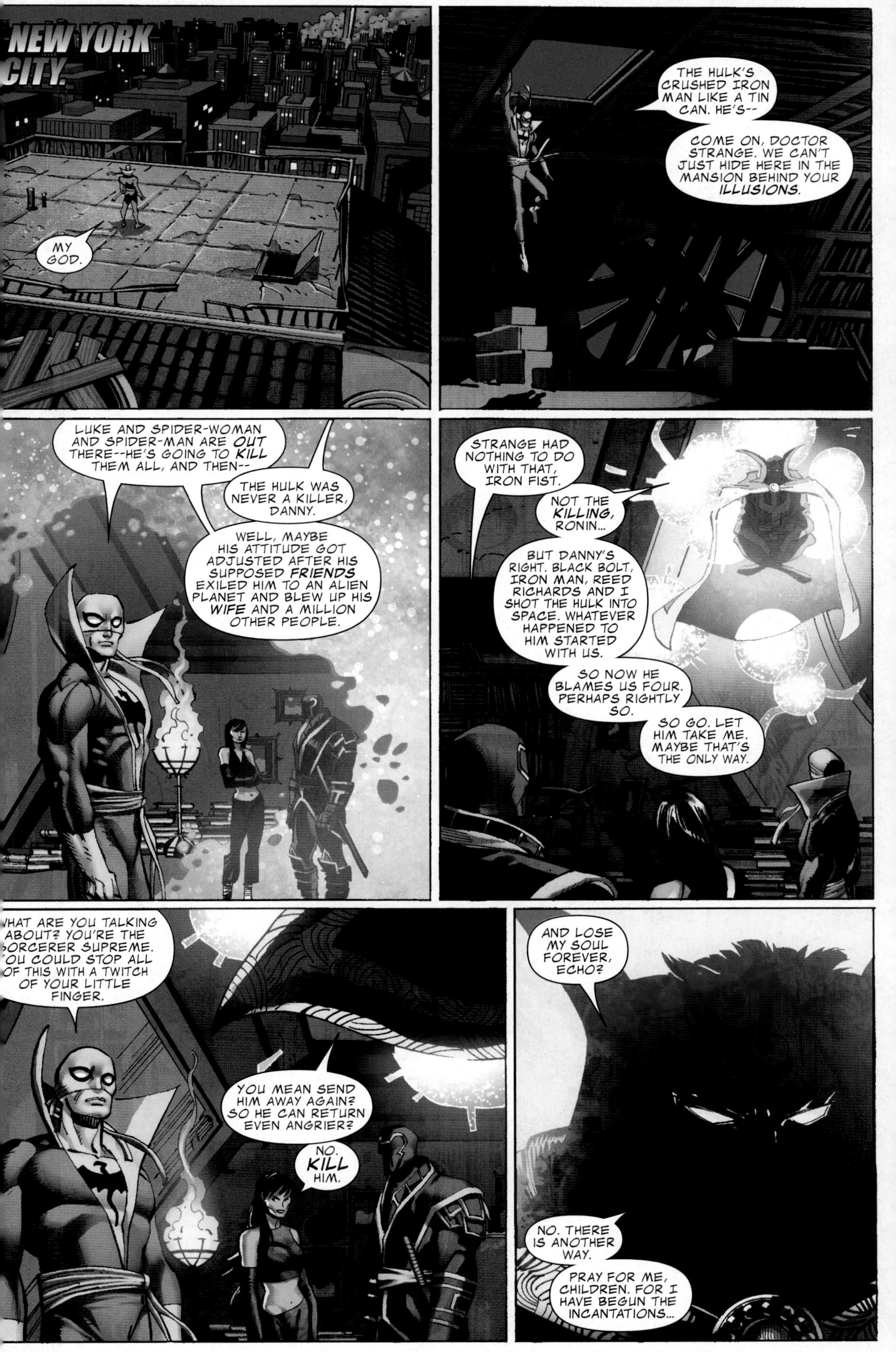

NEW YORK CITY.
MY GOD.
THE HULK'S CRUSHED IRON MAN LIKE A TIN CAN. HE'S--
COME ON, DOCTOR STRANGE. WE CAN'T JUST HIDE HERE IN THE MANSION BEHIND YOUR ILLUSIONS.
LUKE AND SPIDER-WOMAN AND SPIDER-MAN ARE OUT THERE--HE'S GOING TO KILL THEM ALL, AND THEN--
THE HULK WAS NEVER A KILLER, DANNY.
WELL, MAYBE HIS ATTITUDE GOT ADJUSTED AFTER HIS SUPPOSED FRIENDS EXILED HIM TO AN ALIEN PLANET AND BLEW UP HIS WIFE AND A MILLION OTHER PEOPLE.
STRANGE HAD NOTHING TO DO WITH THAT, IRON FIST.
NOT THE KILLING, RONIN...
BUT DANNY'S RIGHT. BLACK BOLT, IRON MAN, REED RICHARDS AND I SHOT THE HULK INTO SPACE. WHATEVER HAPPENED TO HIM STARTED WITH US.
SO NOW HE BLAMES US FOUR. PERHAPS RIGHTLY SO.
SO GO. LET HIM TAKE ME. MAYBE THAT'S THE ONLY WAY.
WHAT ARE YOU TALKING ABOUT? YOU'RE THE SORCERER SUPREME. YOU COULD STOP ALL OF THIS WITH A TWITCH OF YOUR LITTLE FINGER.
YOU MEAN SEND HIM AWAY AGAIN? SO HE CAN RETURN EVEN ANGRIER?
NO. KILL HIM.
AND LOSE MY SOUL FOREVER, ECHO?
NO. THERE IS ANOTHER WAY.
PRAY FOR ME, CHILDREN. FOR I HAVE BEGUN THE INCANTATIONS...

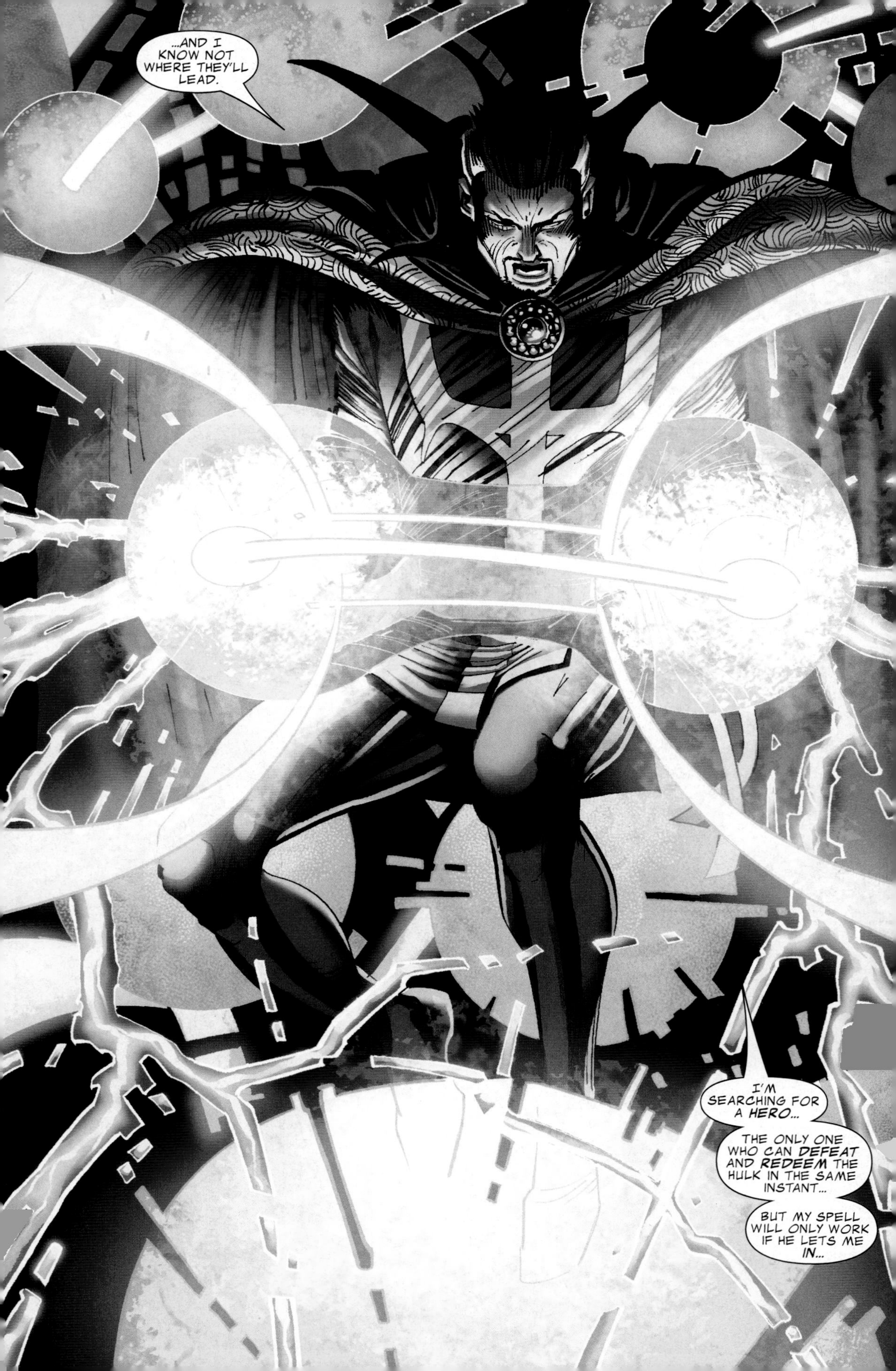

...AND I KNOW NOT WHERE THEY'LL LEAD.
I'M SEARCHING FOR A HERO...
THE ONLY ONE WHO CAN DEFEAT AND REDEEM THE HULK IN THE SAME INSTANT...
BUT MY SPELL WILL ONLY WORK IF HE LETS ME IN...

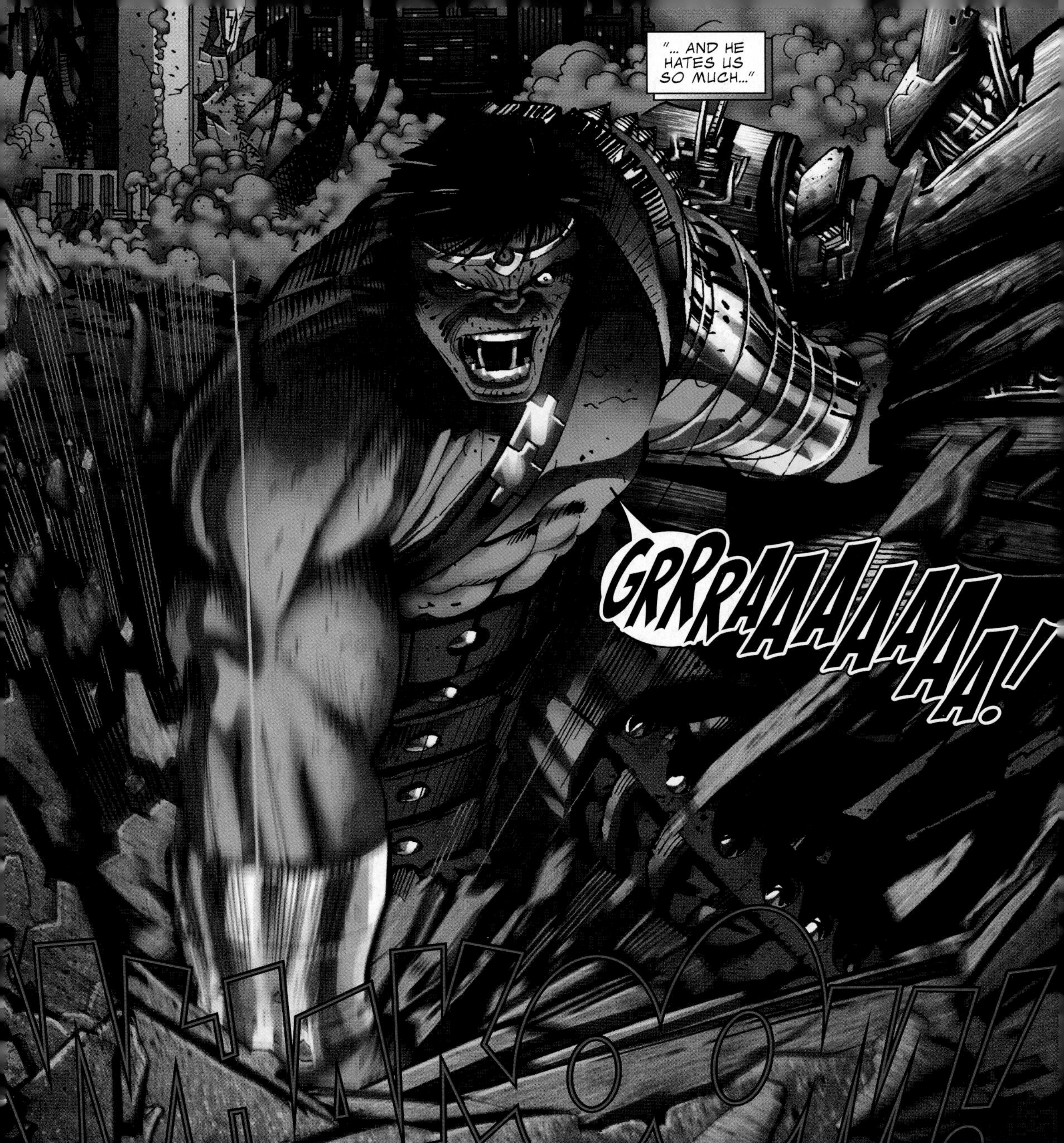
"... AND HE HATES US SO MUCH..."
GRRRAAAAAAAA!
WHAKOOM!

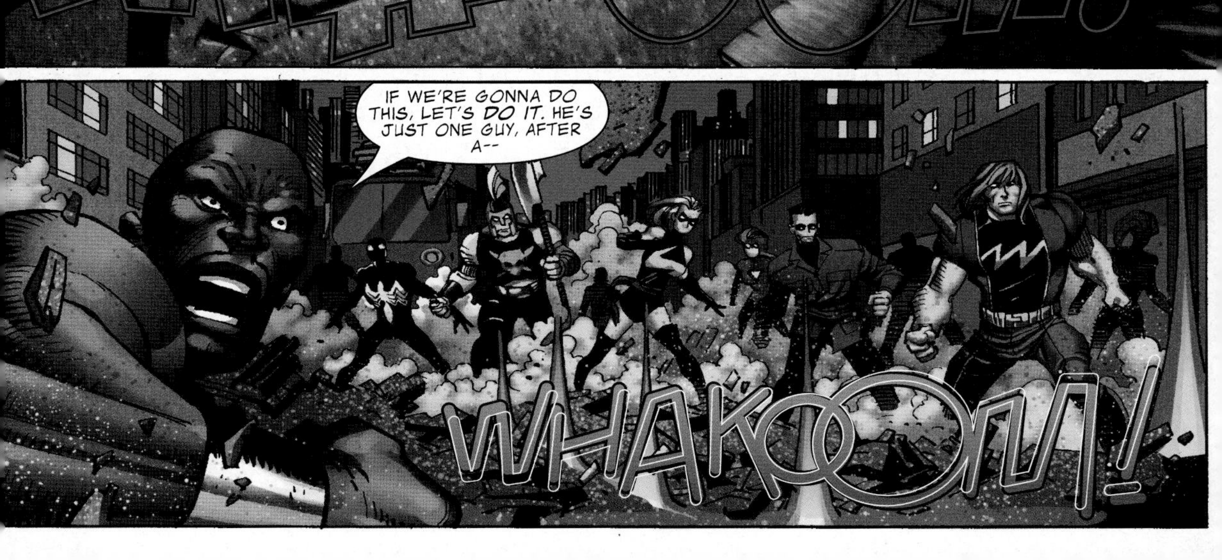
IF WE'RE GONNA DO THIS, LET'S DO IT. HE'S JUST ONE GUY, AFTER A--
WHAKOOM!

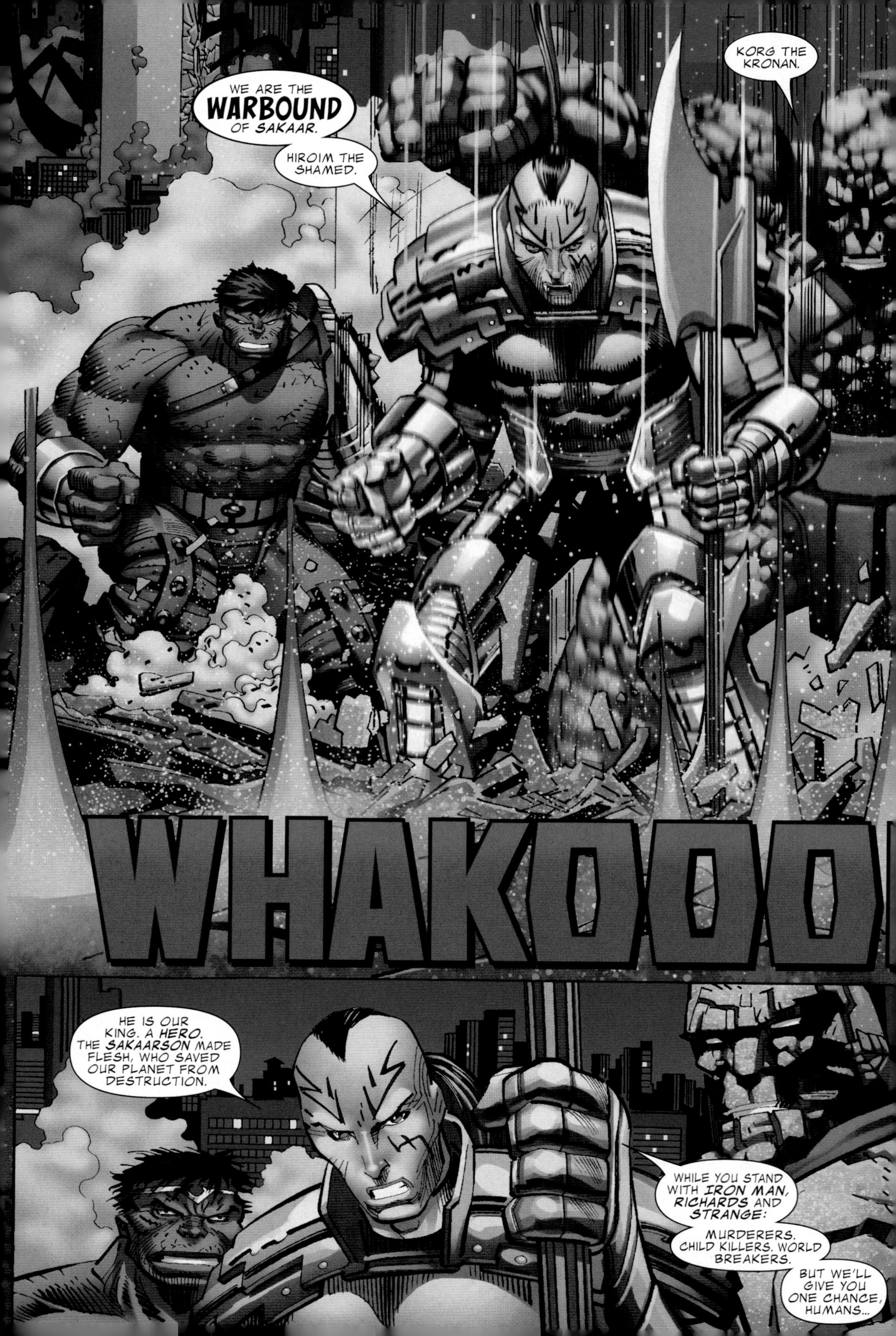
WE ARE THE WARBOUND OF SAKAAR.
HIROIM THE SHAMED.
KORG THE KRONAN.
WHAKOOO
HE IS OUR KING. A HERO. THE SAKAARSON MADE FLESH, WHO SAVED OUR PLANET FROM DESTRUCTION.
WHILE YOU STAND WITH IRON MAN, RICHARDS AND STRANGE:
MURDERERS. CHILD KILLERS. WORLD BREAKERS.
BUT WE'LL GIVE YOU ONE CHANCE, HUMANS...

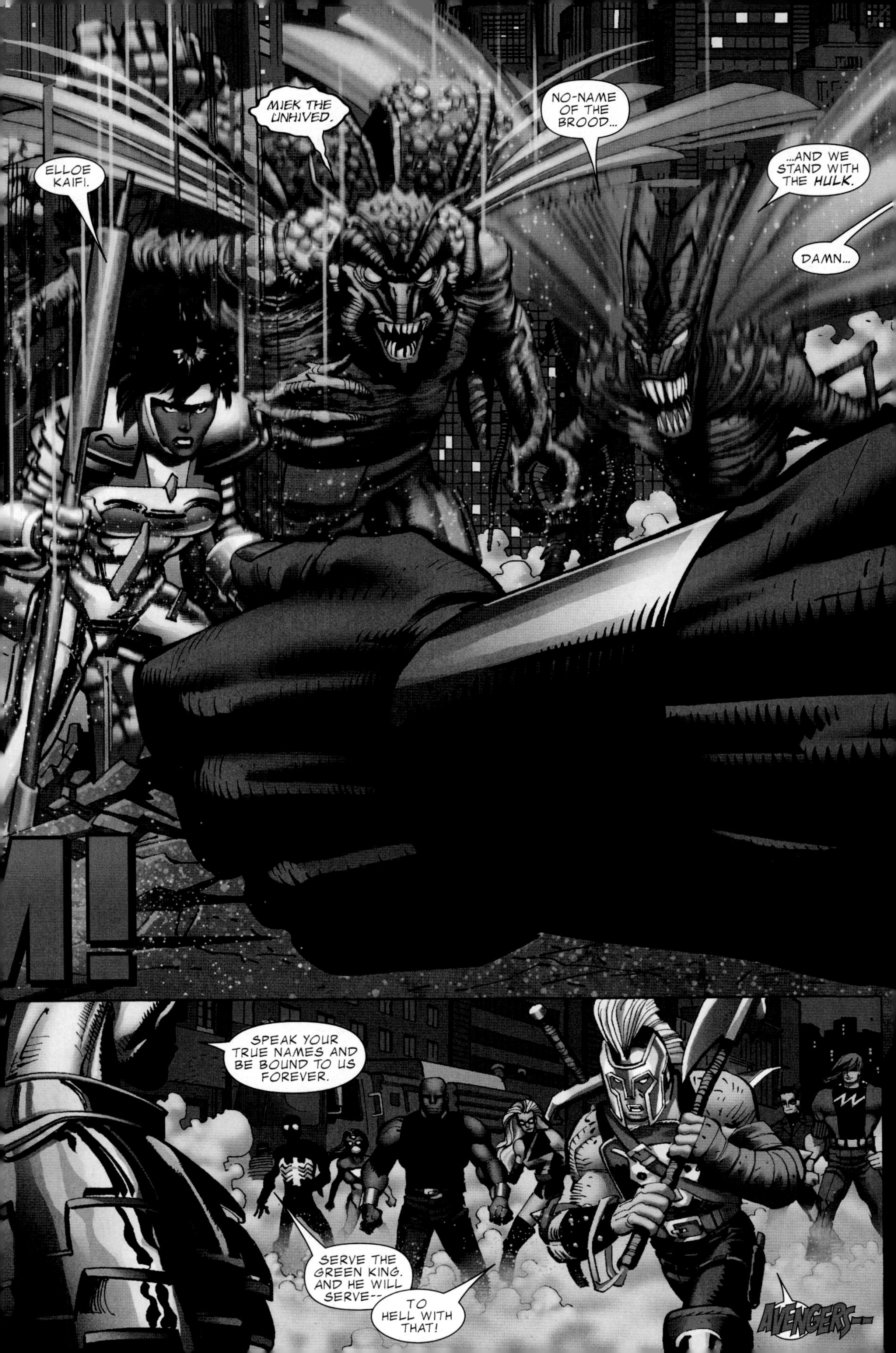
ELLOE KAIFI.
MIEK THE UNHIVED.
NO-NAME OF THE BROOD...
...AND WE STAND WITH THE HULK.
DAMN...
SPEAK YOUR TRUE NAMES AND BE BOUND TO US FOREVER.
SERVE THE GREEN KING. AND HE WILL SERVE--
TO HELL WITH THAT!
AVENGERS--

ATTAA--

CLAMP

WAIT, ARES.

WANT TO **LOSE** THAT HAND, WOMAN?

SHE-HULK. WHAT ARE YOU DOING?

CAREFUL, MS. MARVEL. IRON MAN MAY HAVE GIVEN HER HER POWERS BACK, BUT WE DON'T KNOW WHOSE SIDE SHE'S REALLY ON.

THAT'S YOUR PROBLEM IN A NUTSHELL, SAMSON...

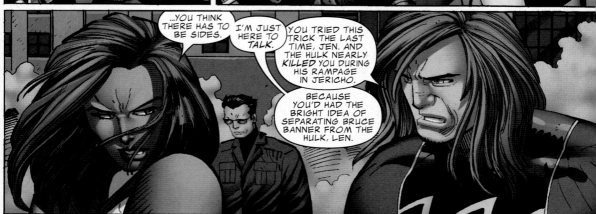

...YOU THINK THERE HAS TO BE SIDES.

I'M JUST HERE TO **TALK.**

YOU TRIED THIS TRICK THE LAST TIME, JEN. AND THE HULK NEARLY **KILLED** YOU DURING HIS RAMPAGE IN JERICHO.

BECAUSE YOU'D HAD THE BRIGHT IDEA OF SEPARATING BRUCE BANNER FROM THE HULK, LEN.

IF MY COUSIN IS IN THERE...

...HE'LL LISTEN TO ME.

SOME MESS, HUH, BRUCE?

LET ME HELP.

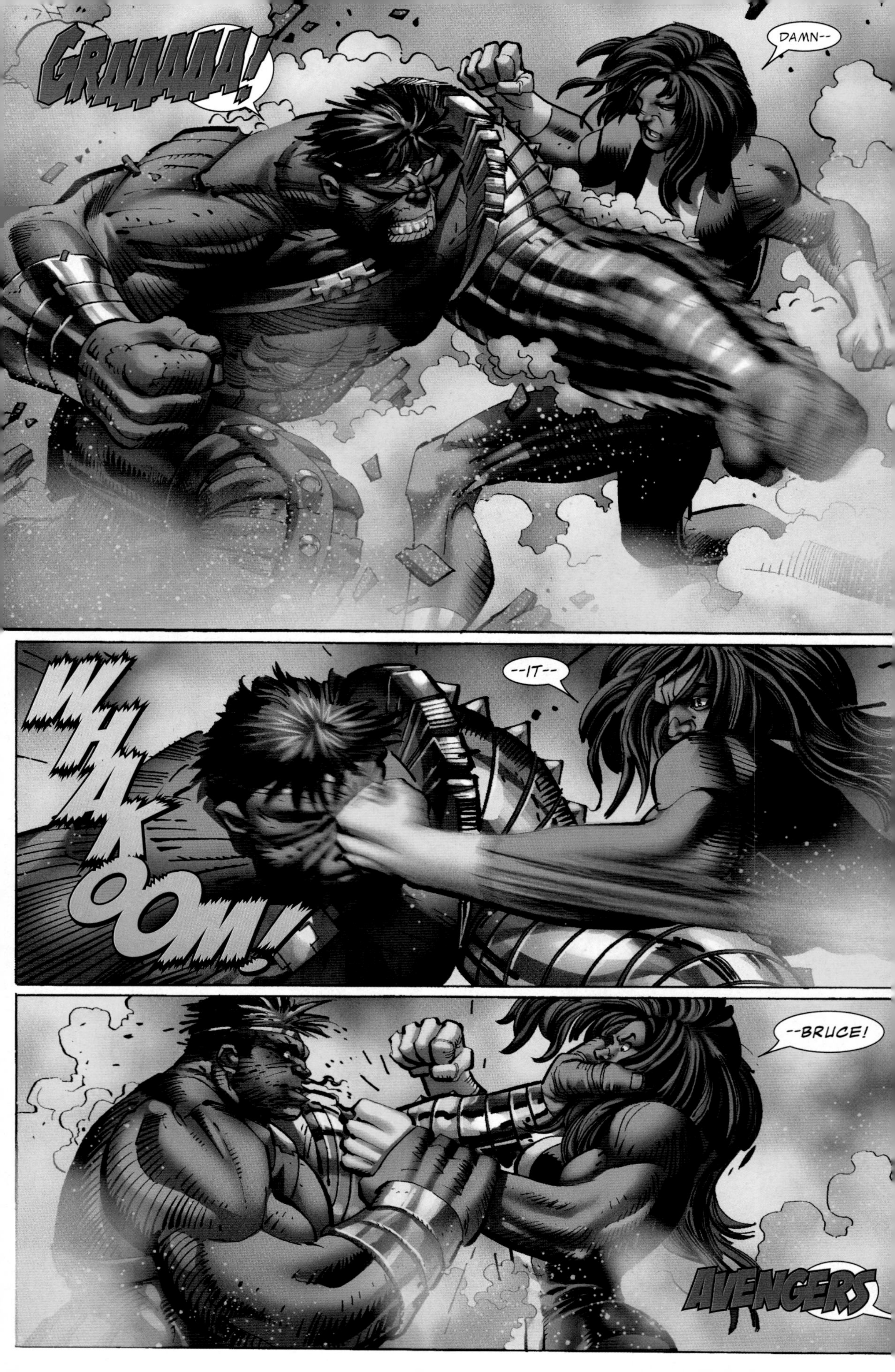

GRAAAAA!
DAMN--
WHAKOOOM!
--IT--
--BRUCE!
AVENGERS

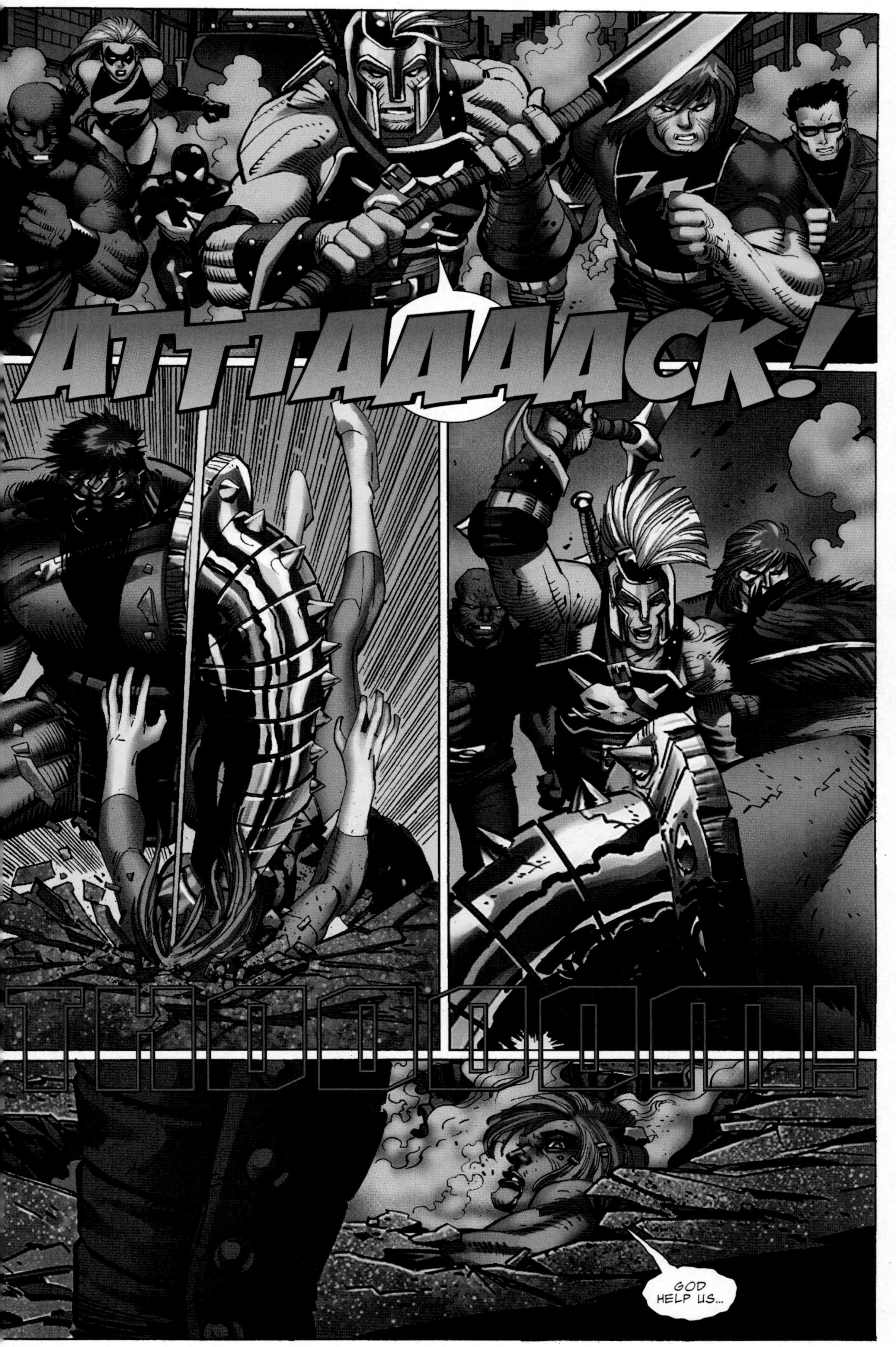
ATTTAAAACK!
THOOOOOOM!
GOD HELP US...

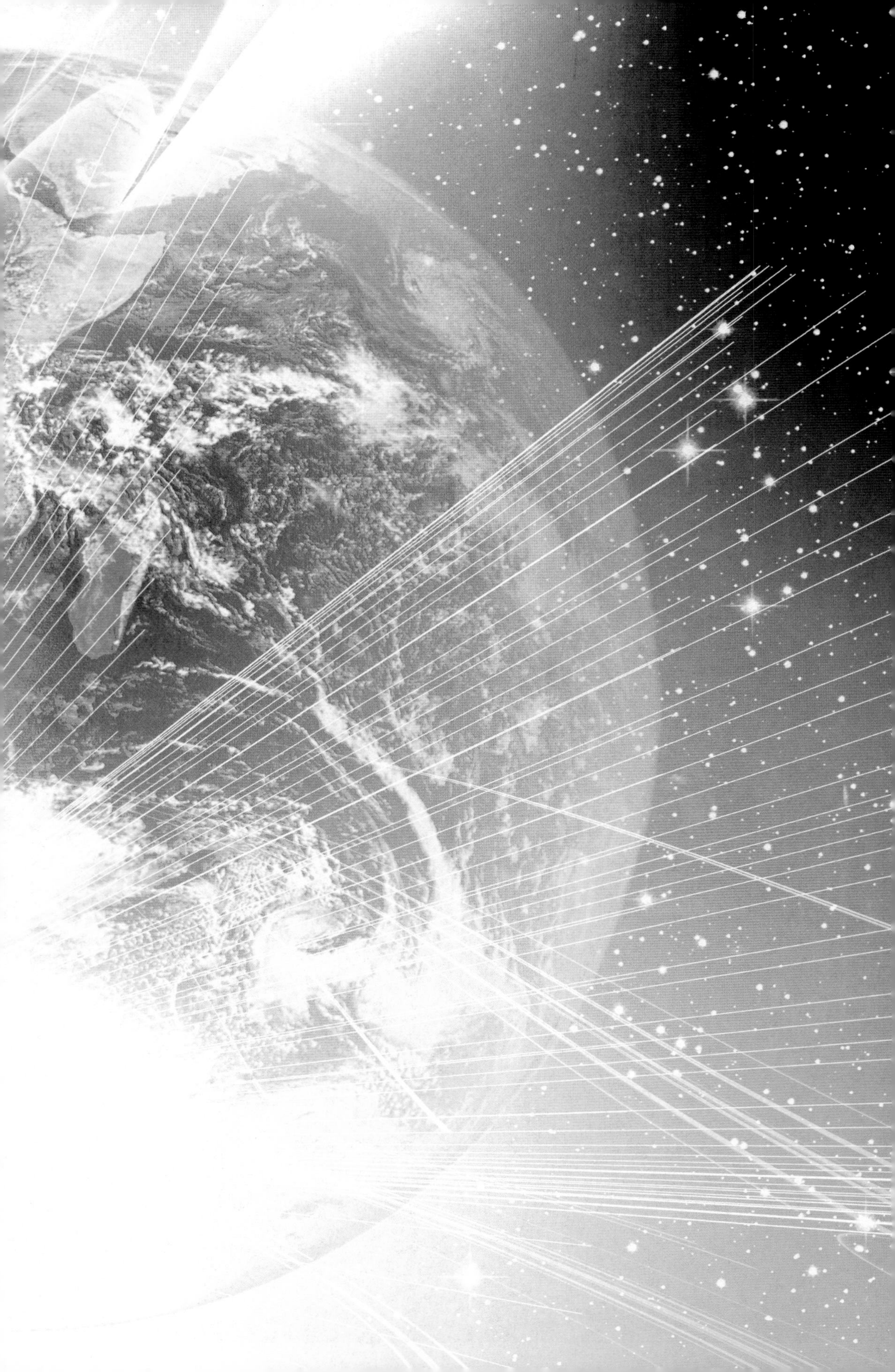

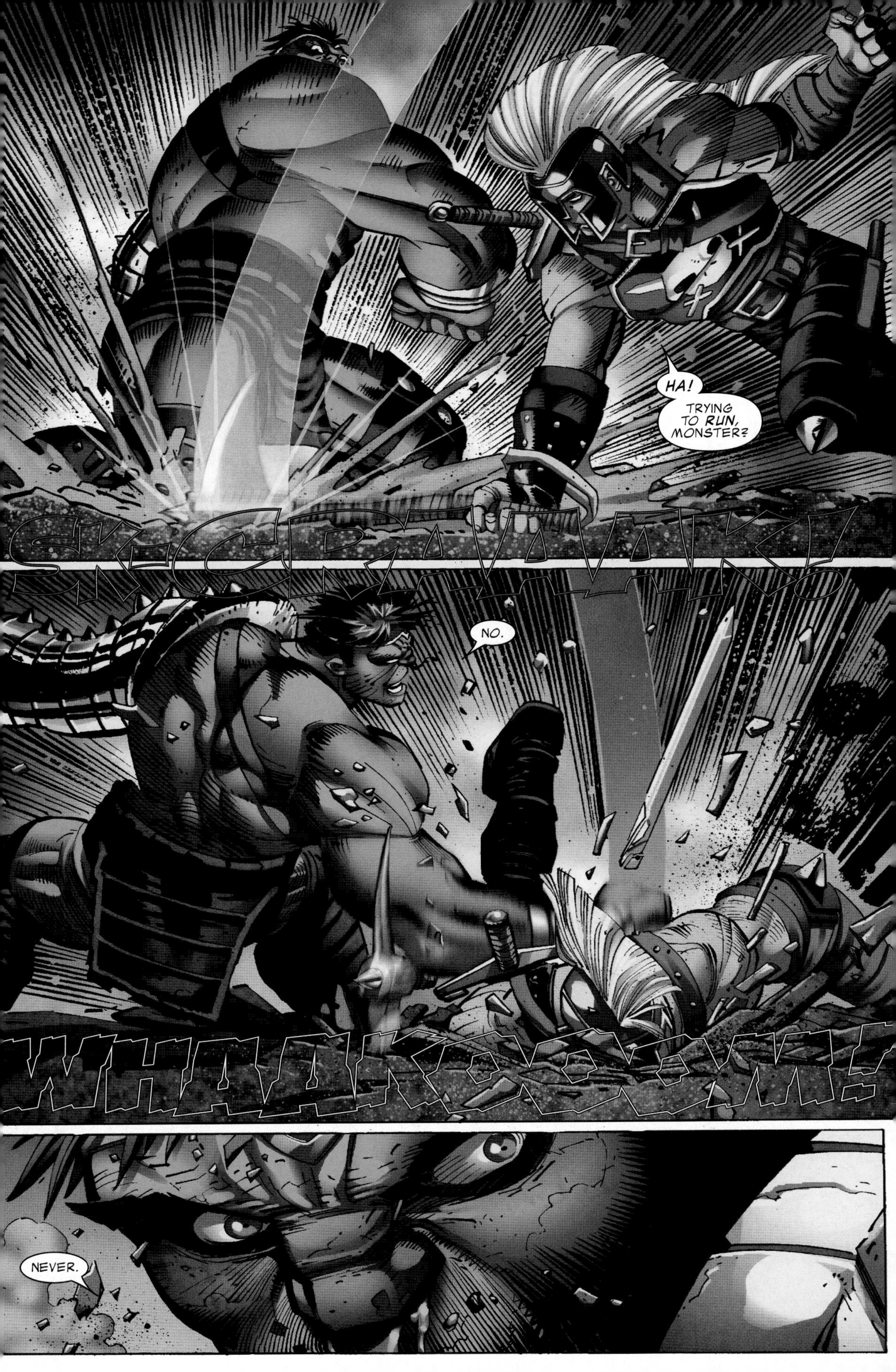
HA! TRYING TO RUN, MONSTER?
NO.
WHAAKOOOM!
NEVER.

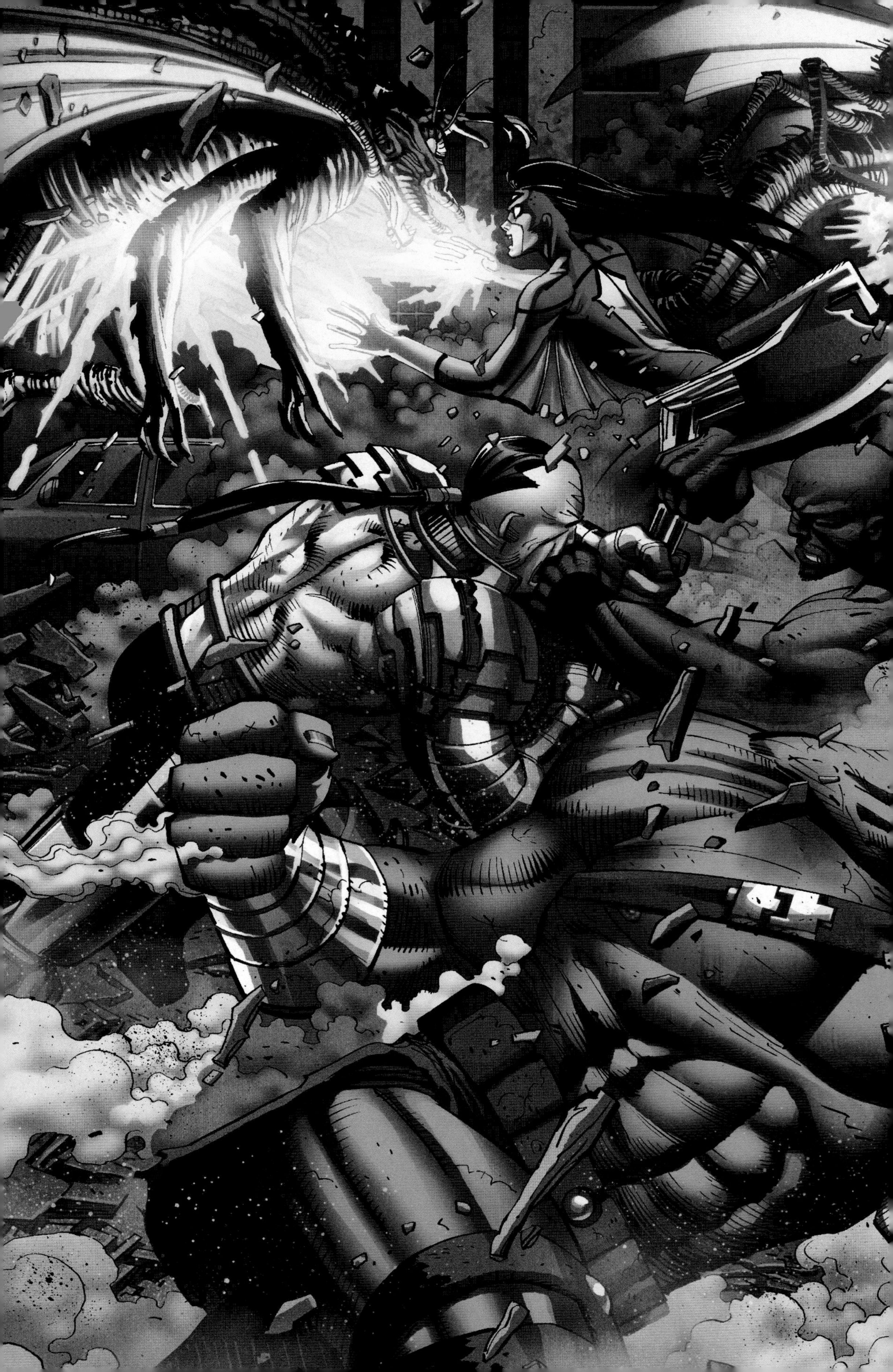

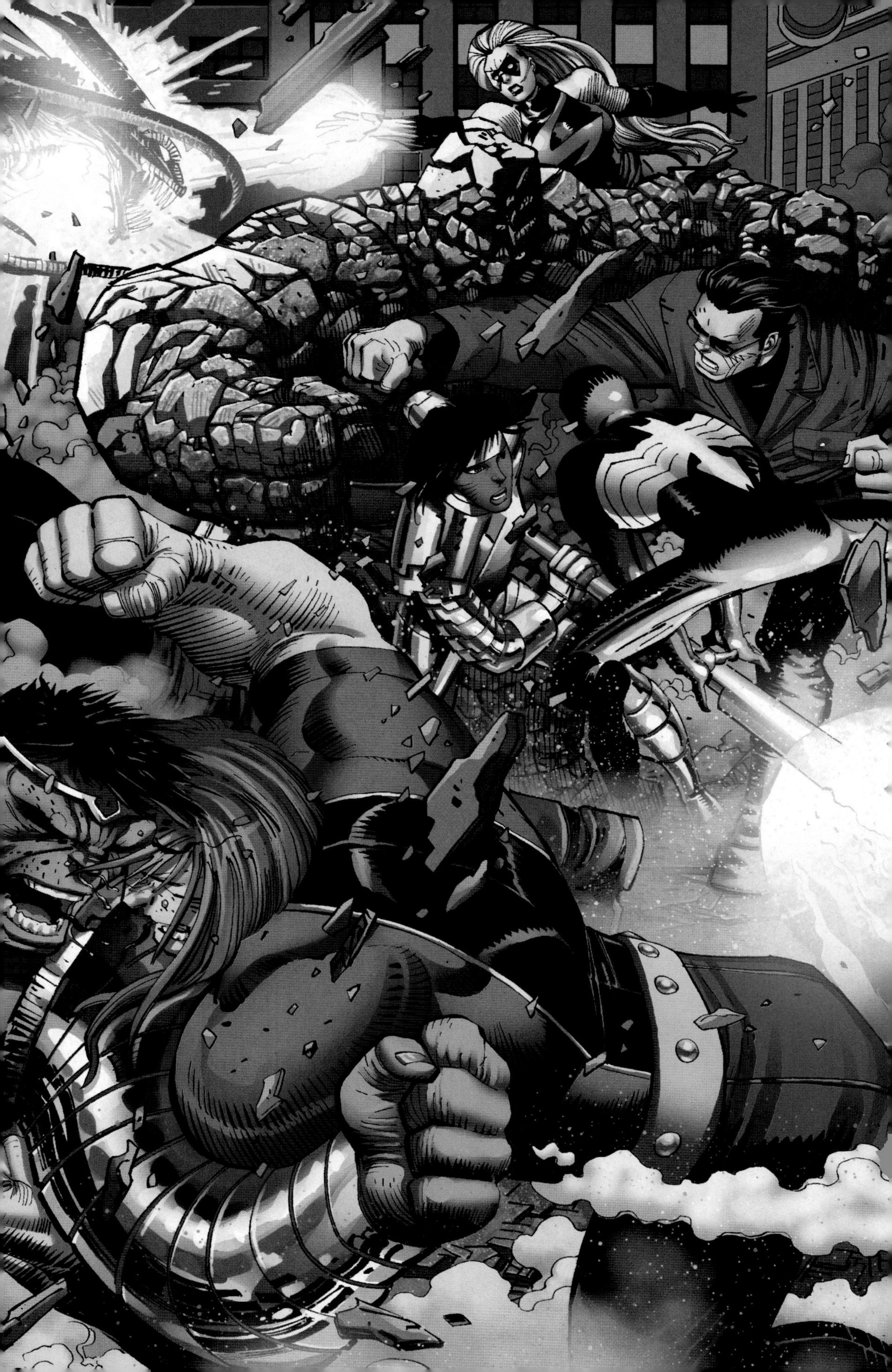

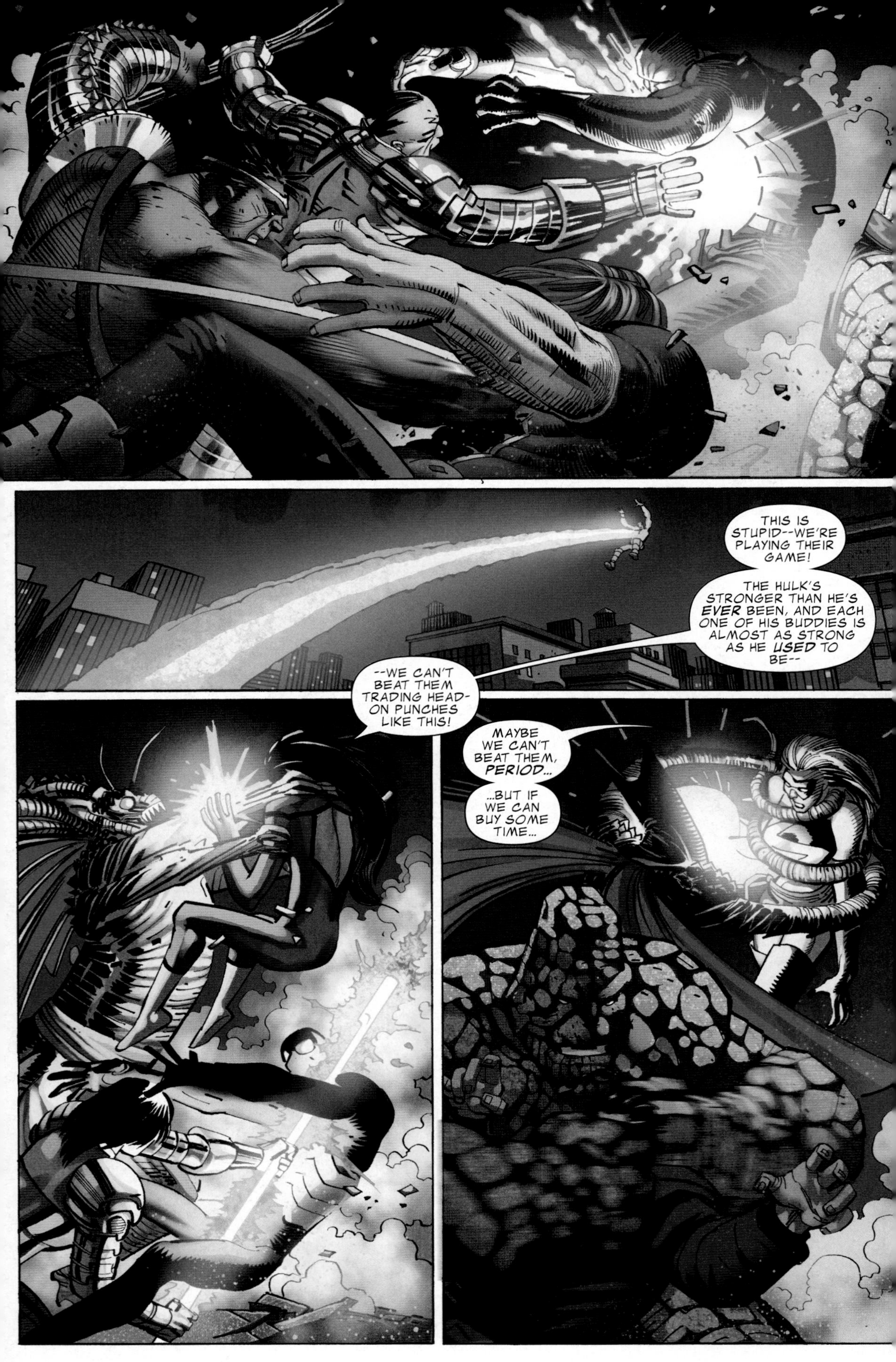

THIS IS STUPID--WE'RE PLAYING THEIR GAME!
THE HULK'S STRONGER THAN HE'S EVER BEEN, AND EACH ONE OF HIS BUDDIES IS ALMOST AS STRONG AS HE USED TO BE--
--WE CAN'T BEAT THEM TRADING HEAD-ON PUNCHES LIKE THIS!
MAYBE WE CAN'T BEAT THEM, PERIOD...
...BUT IF WE CAN BUY SOME TIME...

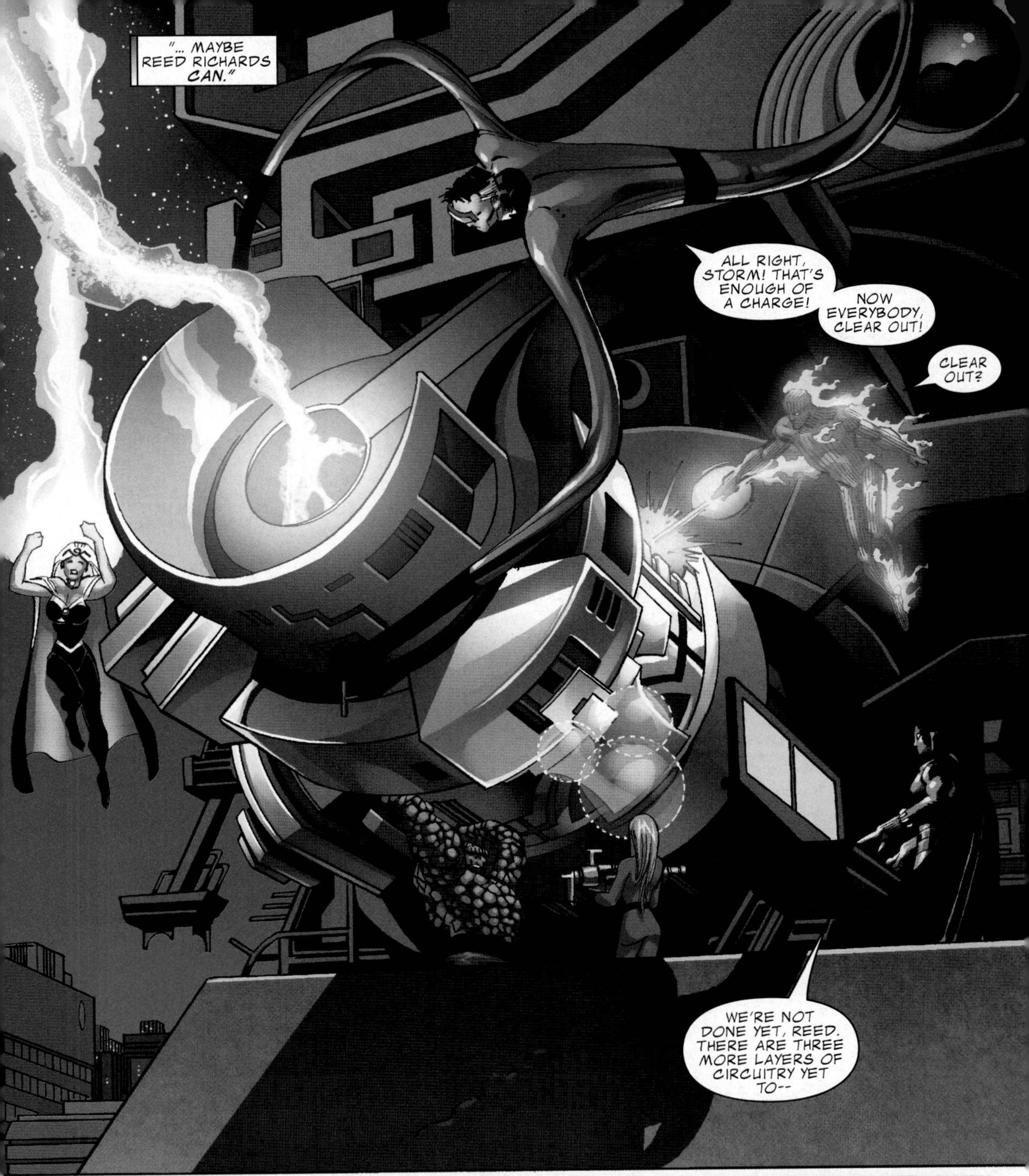
"... MAYBE REED RICHARDS CAN."
ALL RIGHT, STORM! THAT'S ENOUGH OF A CHARGE!
NOW EVERYBODY, CLEAR OUT!
CLEAR OUT?
WE'RE NOT DONE YET, REED. THERE ARE THREE MORE LAYERS OF CIRCUITRY YET TO--

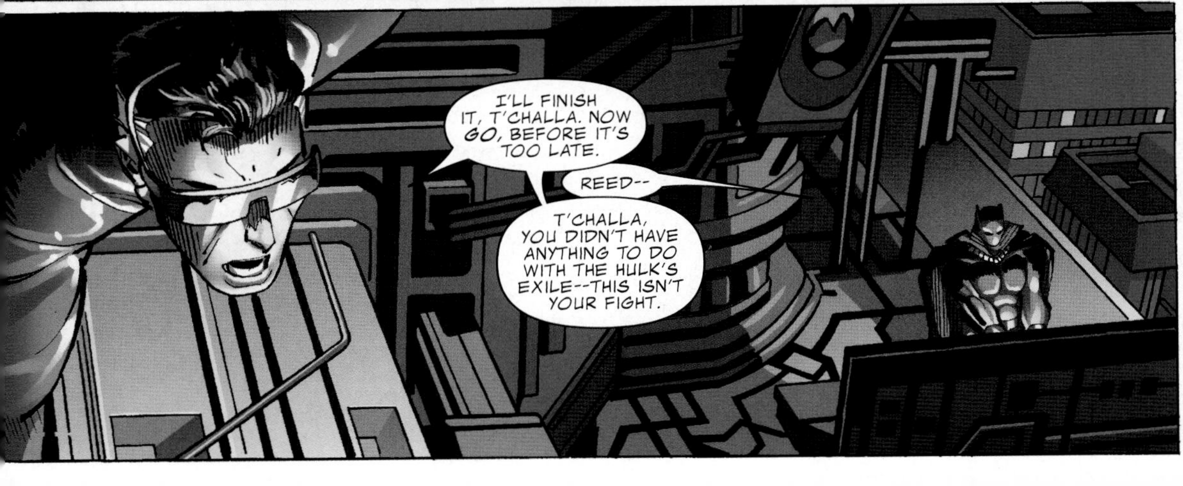
I'LL FINISH IT, T'CHALLA. NOW GO, BEFORE IT'S TOO LATE.
REED--
T'CHALLA, YOU DIDN'T HAVE ANYTHING TO DO WITH THE HULK'S EXILE--THIS ISN'T YOUR FIGHT.

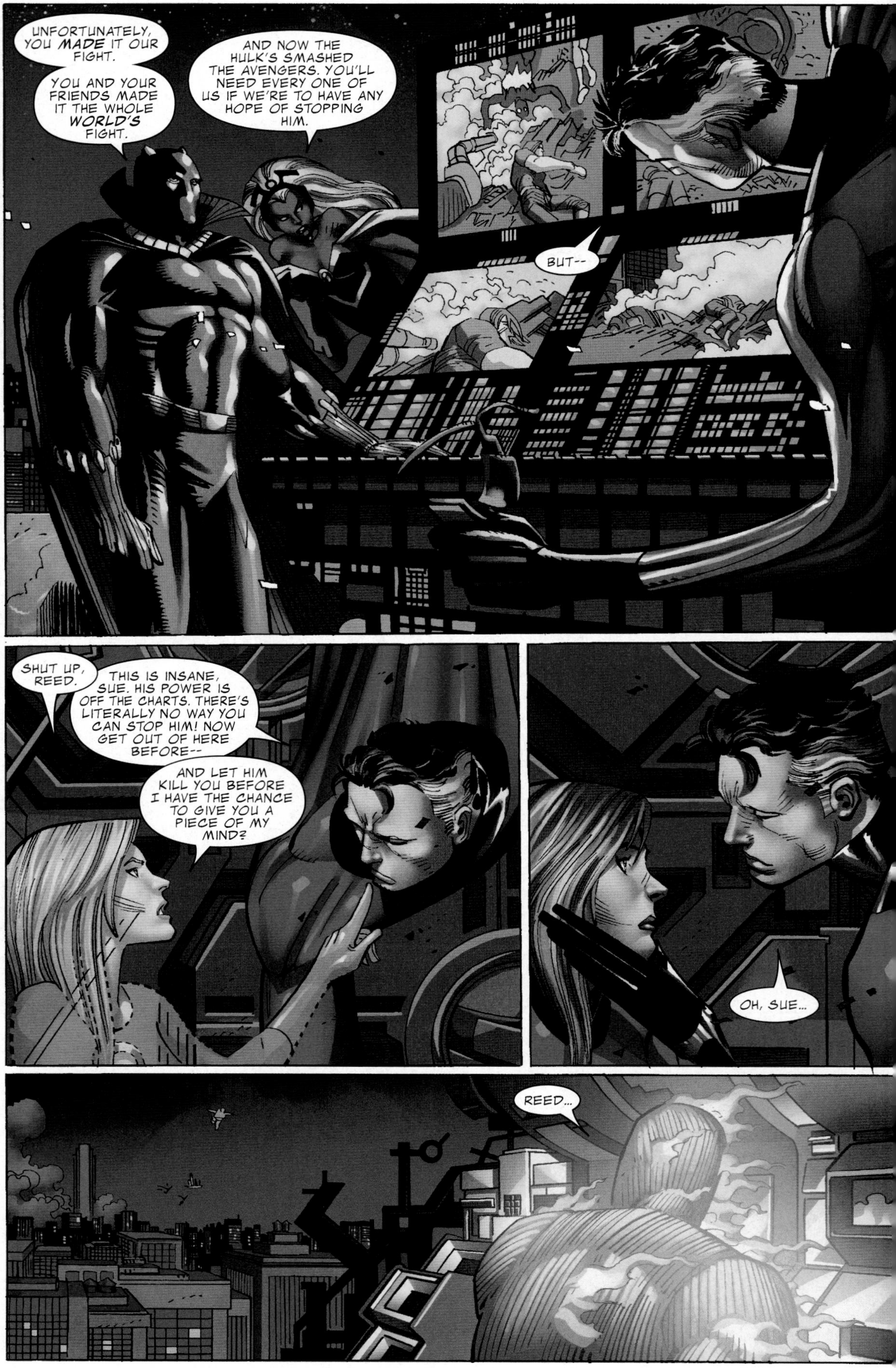
UNFORTUNATELY, YOU MADE IT OUR FIGHT.
YOU AND YOUR FRIENDS MADE IT THE WHOLE WORLD'S FIGHT.
AND NOW THE HULK'S SMASHED THE AVENGERS. YOU'LL NEED EVERY ONE OF US IF WE'RE TO HAVE ANY HOPE OF STOPPING HIM.
BUT--
SHUT UP, REED.
THIS IS INSANE, SUE. HIS POWER IS OFF THE CHARTS. THERE'S LITERALLY NO WAY YOU CAN STOP HIM! NOW GET OUT OF HERE BEFORE--
AND LET HIM KILL YOU BEFORE I HAVE THE CHANCE TO GIVE YOU A PIECE OF MY MIND?
OH, SUE...
REED...

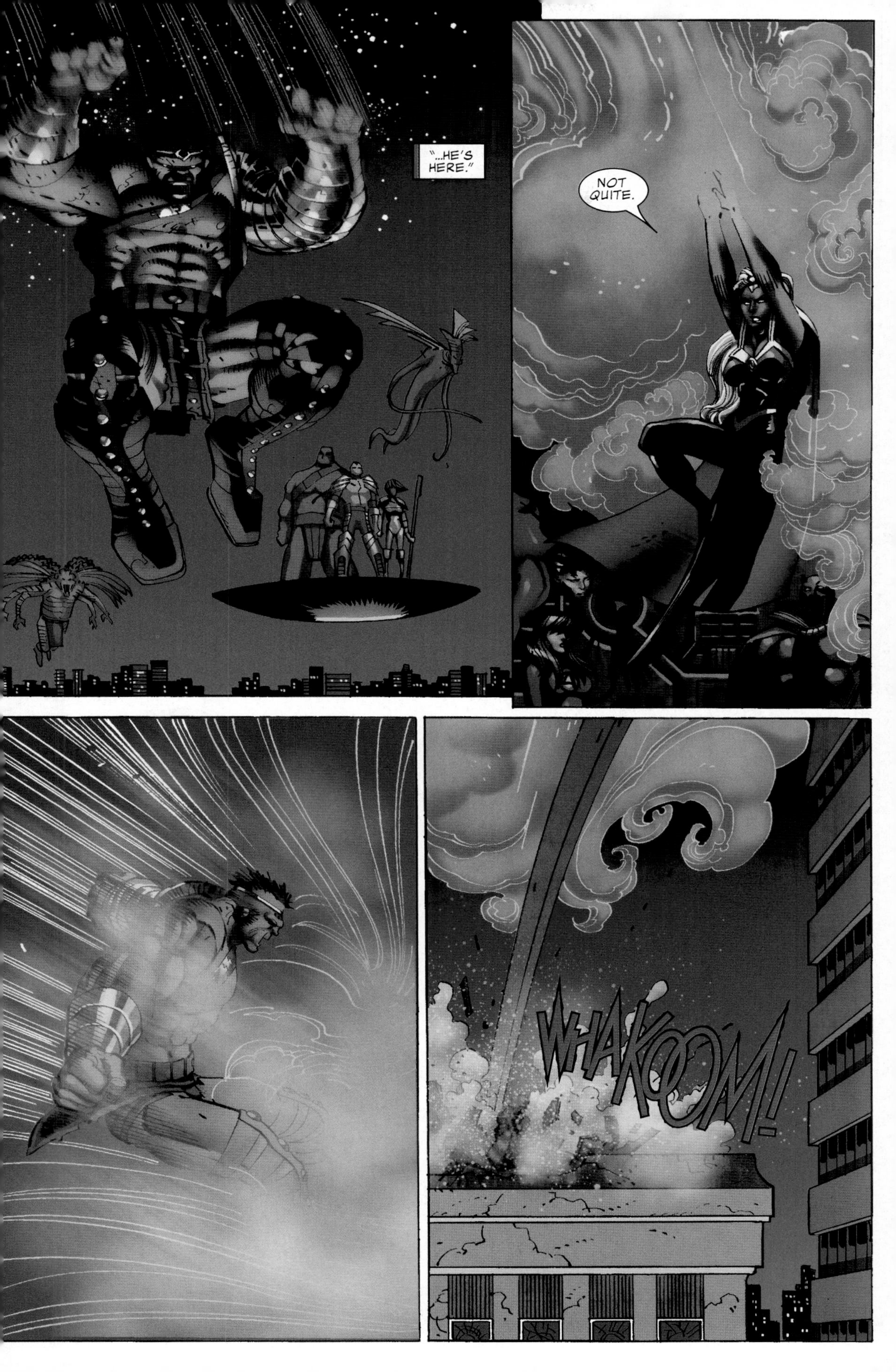
"...HE'S HERE."
NOT QUITE.
WHAKOOM!

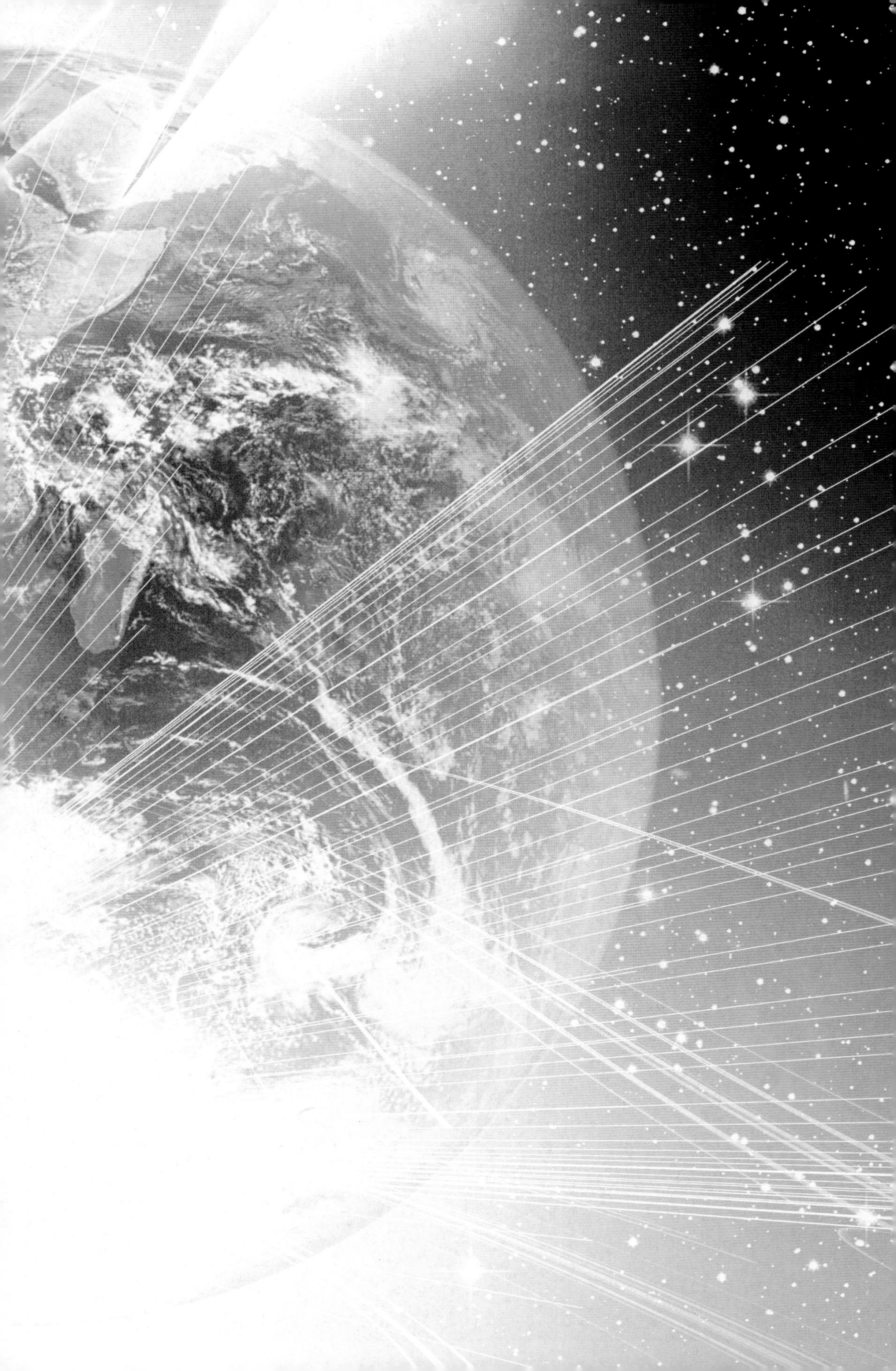

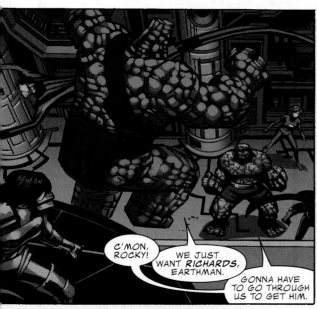

C'MON, ROCKY!

WE JUST WANT *RICHARDS*, EARTHMAN.

GONNA HAVE TO GO THROUGH US TO GET HIM.

SOUNDS LIKE FUN.

GIVE UP, HUMAN. YOU KNOW YOU CAN'T STOP US.

CLEARLY...

...YOU HAVEN'T MET MY WIFE.

HSSSS!

ALL CLEAR, JOHNNY.

HEADS UP, SPORTS FANS--

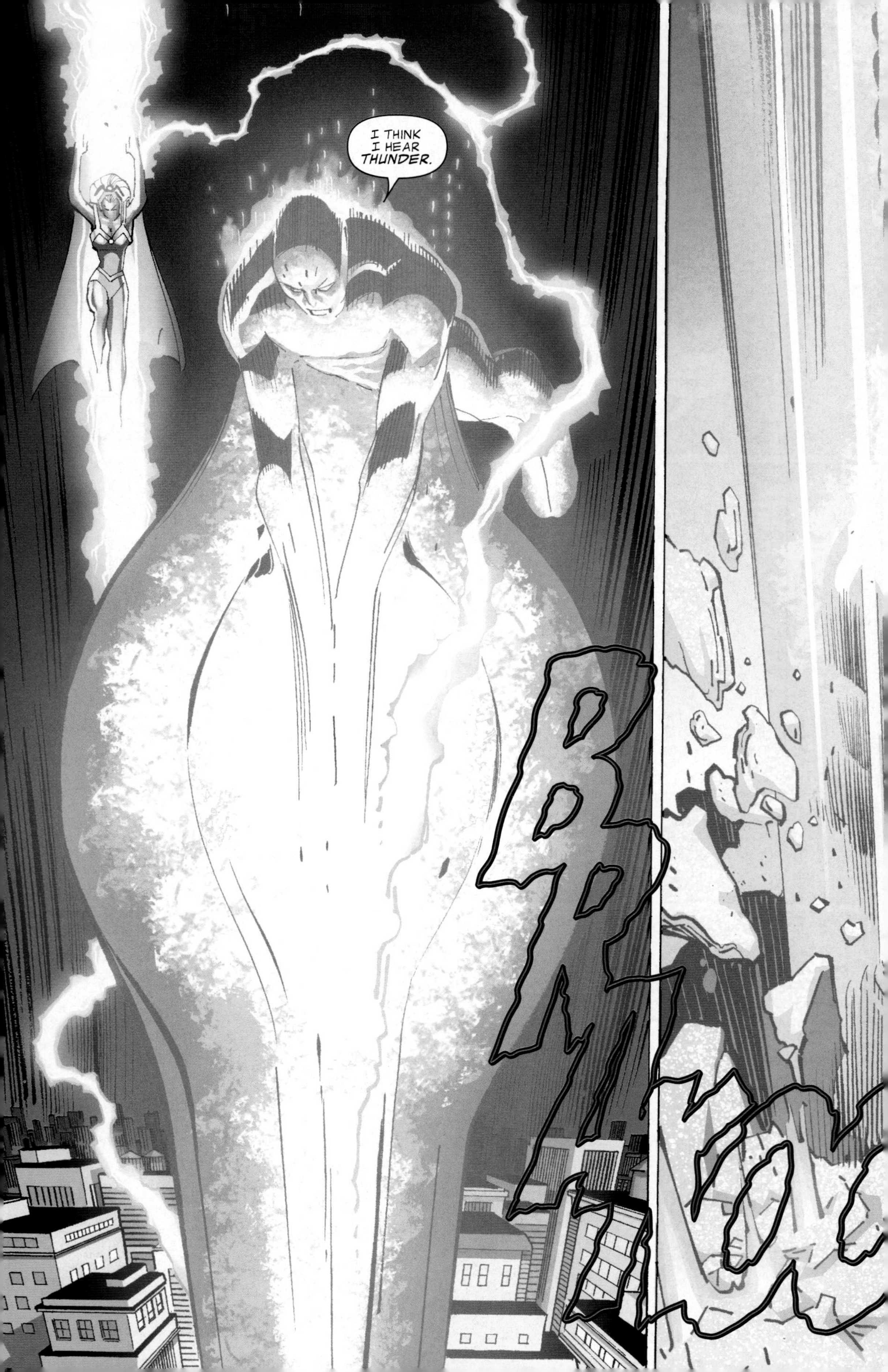
I THINK I HEAR *THUNDER*.

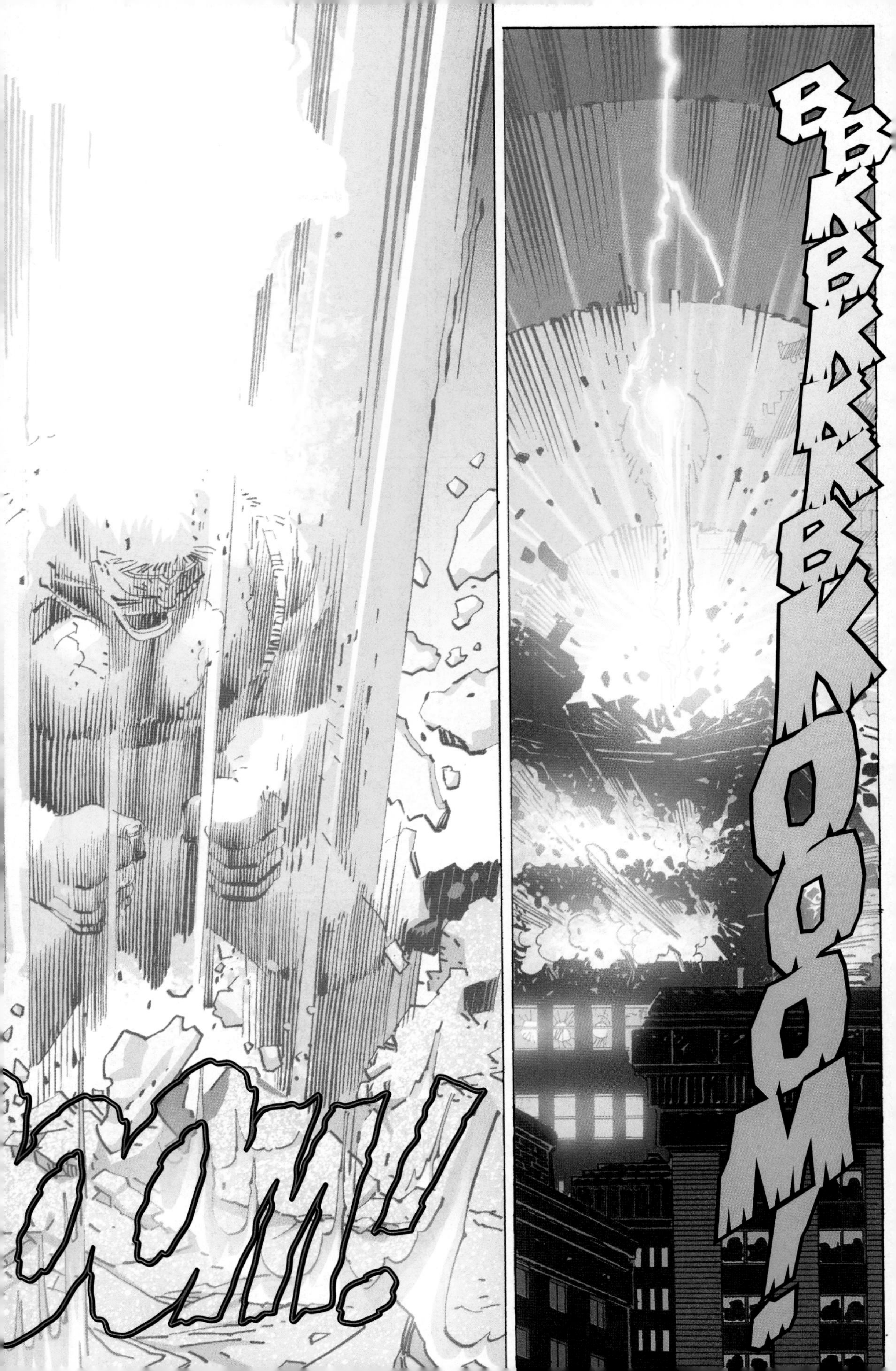
BBKBKKKBKROOOOM!

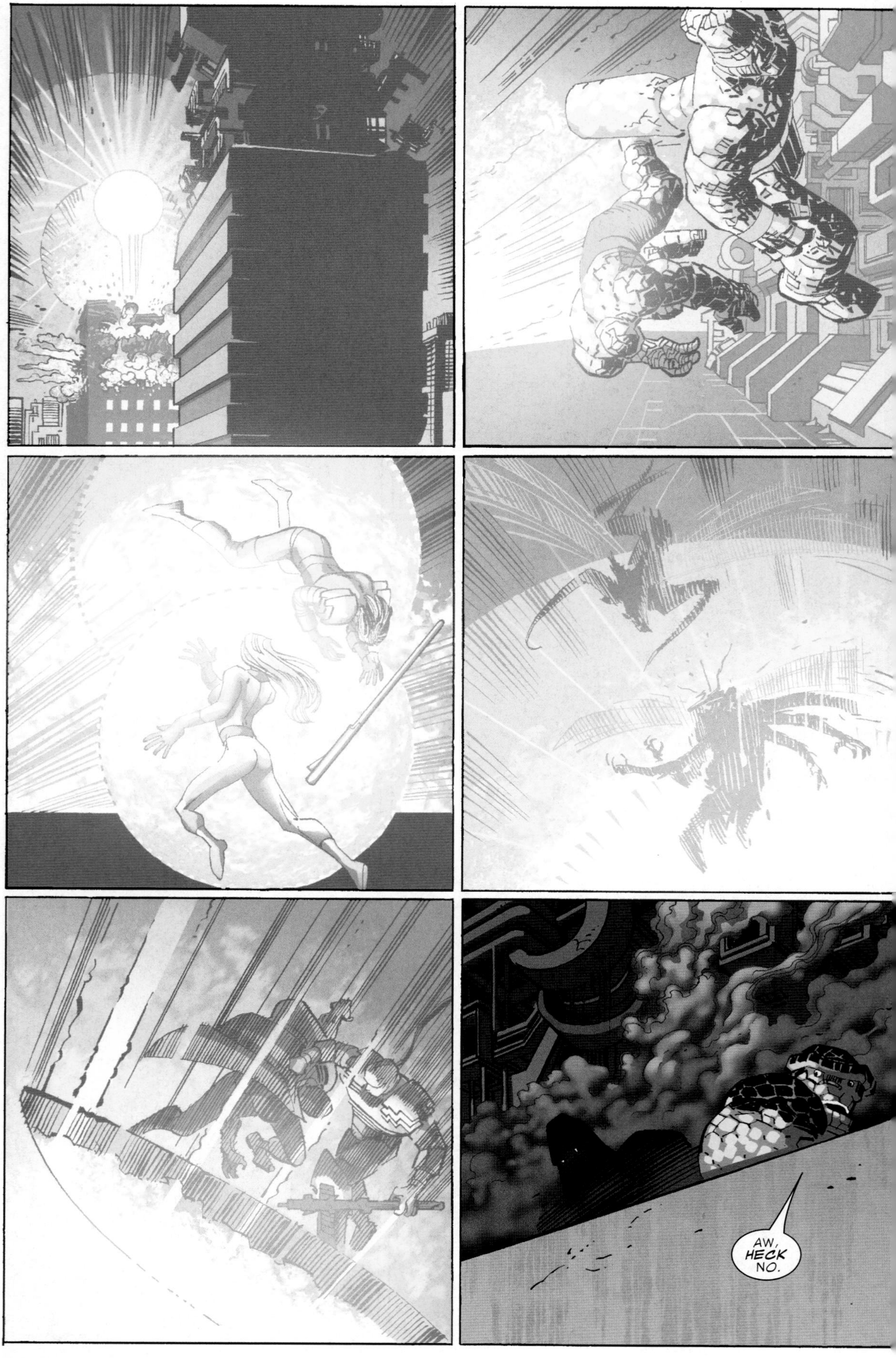
AW, HECK NO.

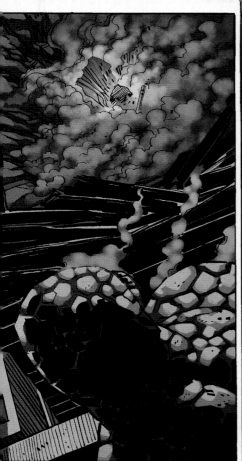

EARTHMAN, WAIT! YOU'VE ALREADY LOST!

PEOPLE BEEN TELLING ME THAT ALL MY LIFE, FELLA.

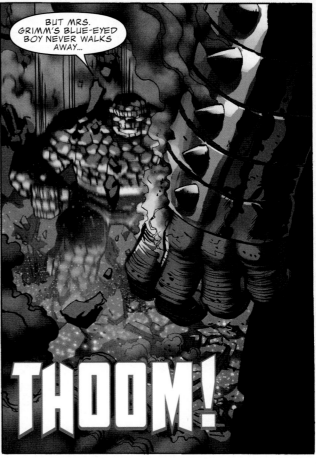

BUT MRS. GRIMM'S BLUE-EYED BOY NEVER WALKS AWAY...

THOOM!

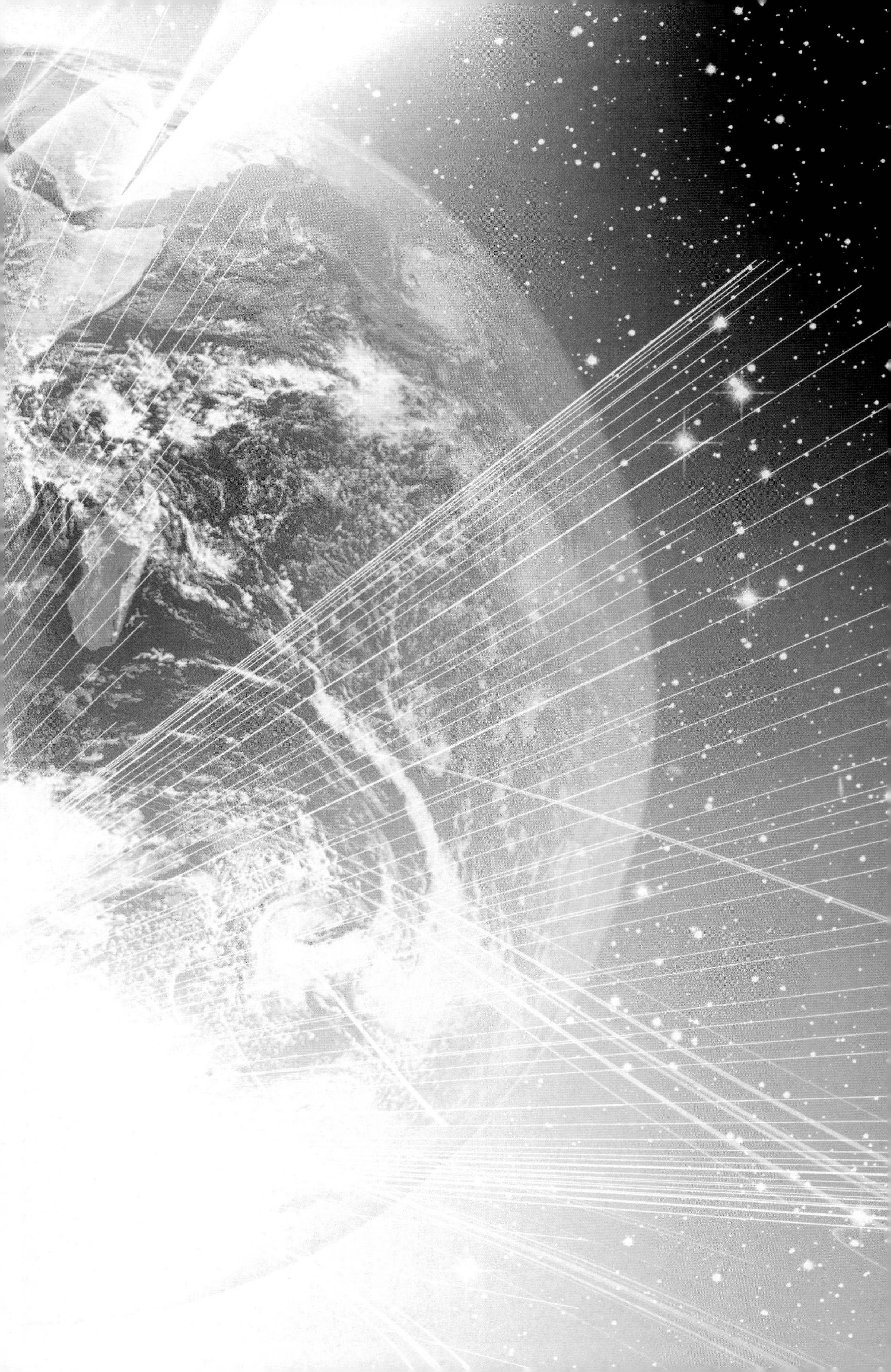

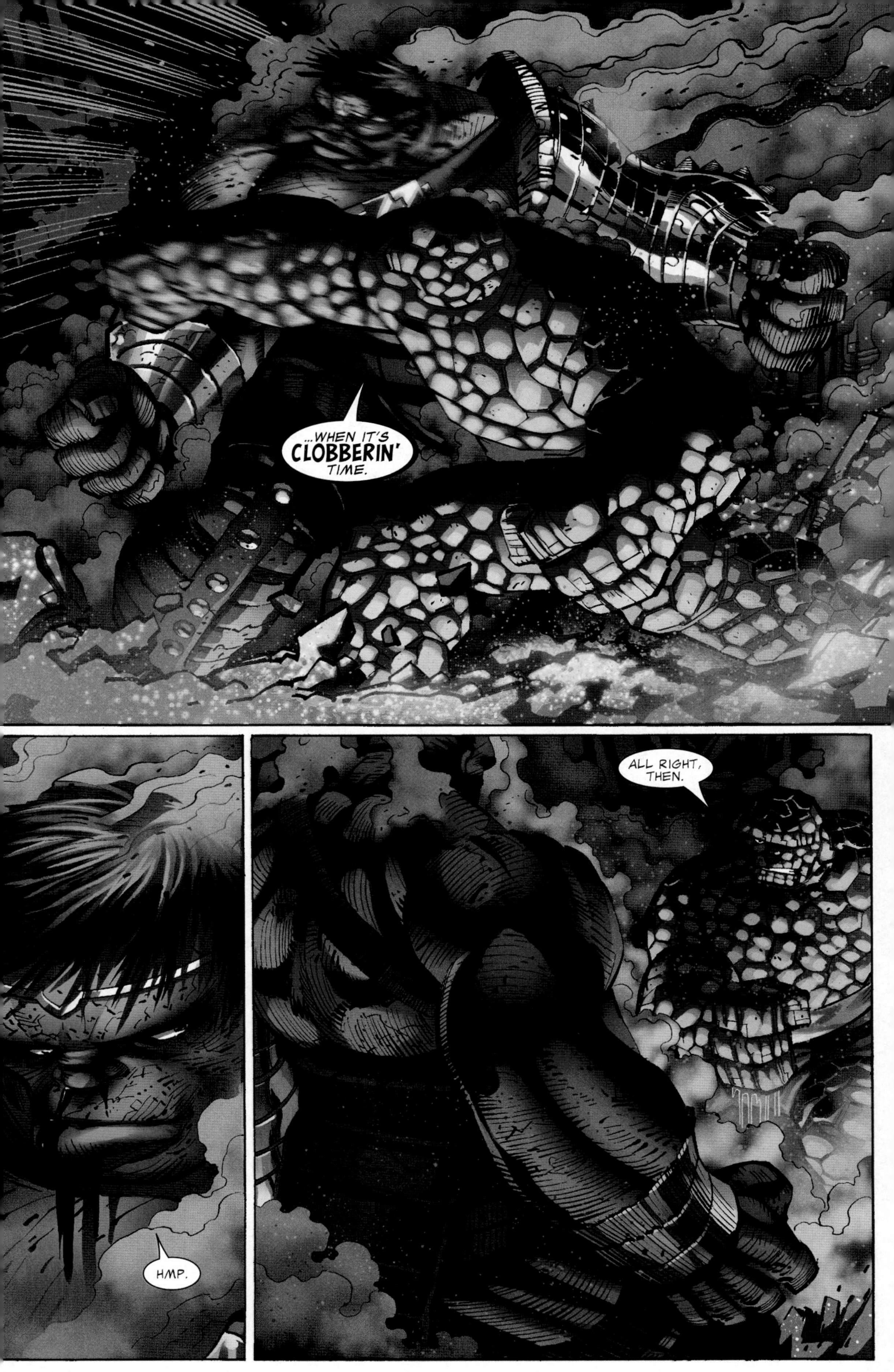

...WHEN IT'S CLOBBERIN' TIME.
HMP.
ALL RIGHT, THEN.

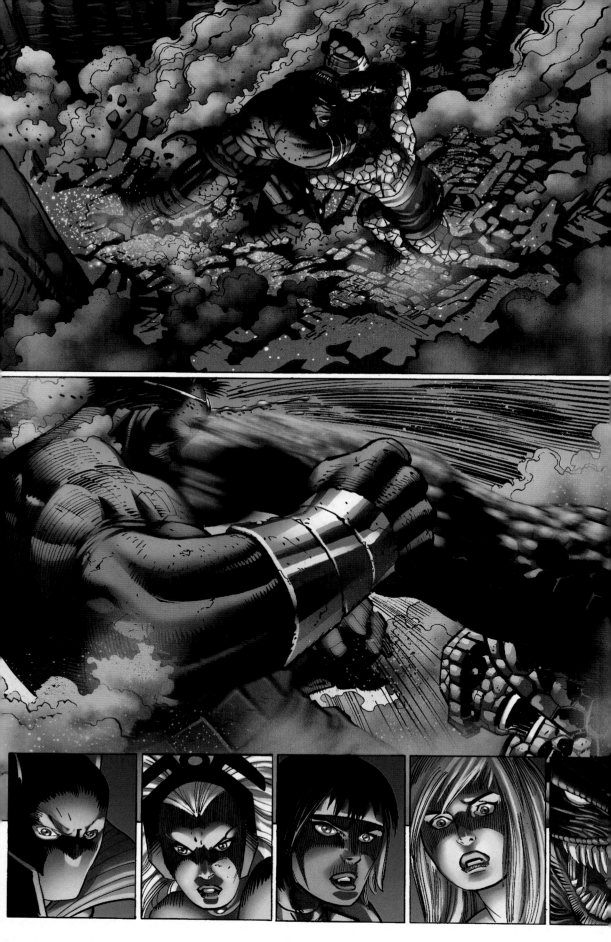

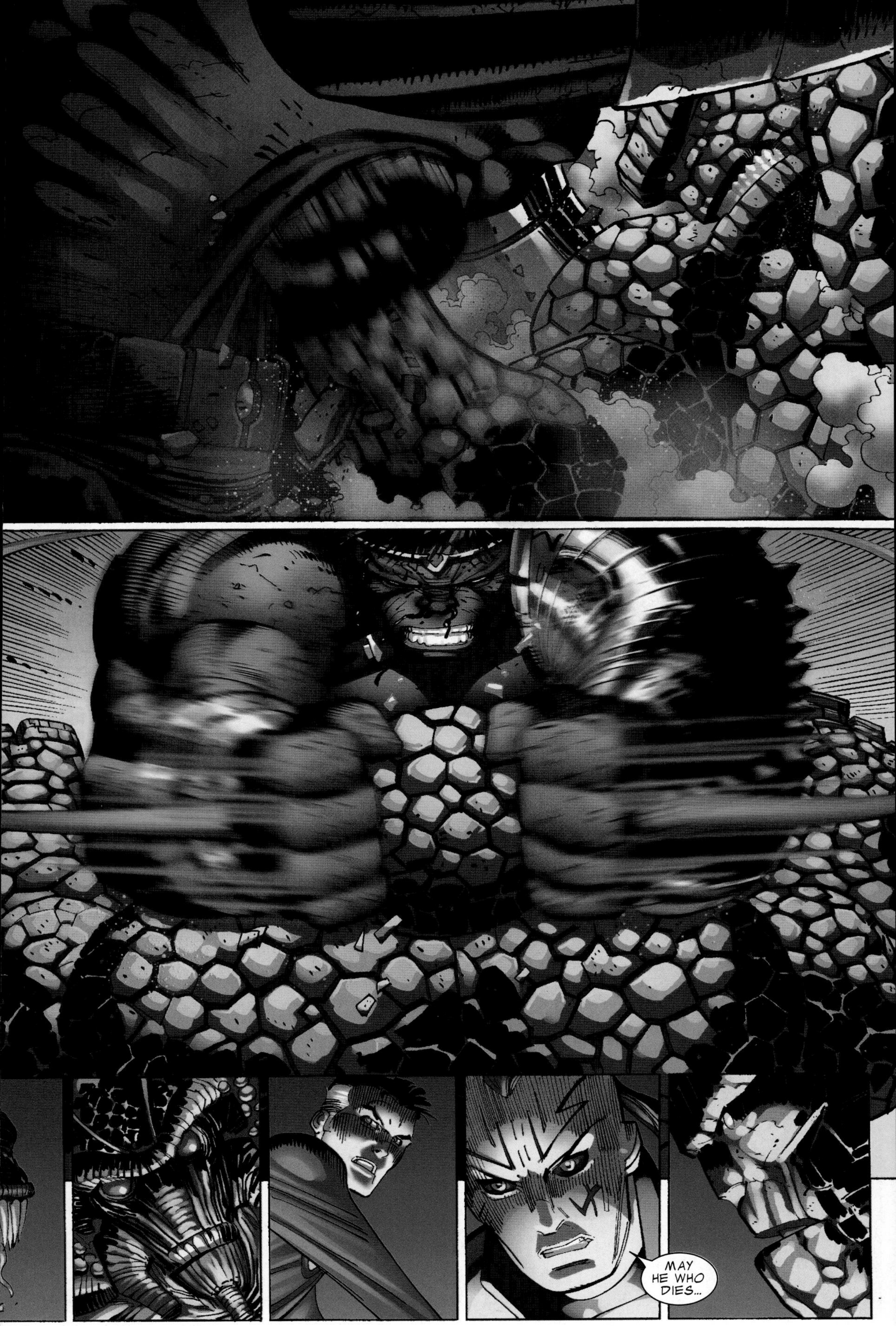
MAY HE WHO DIES...

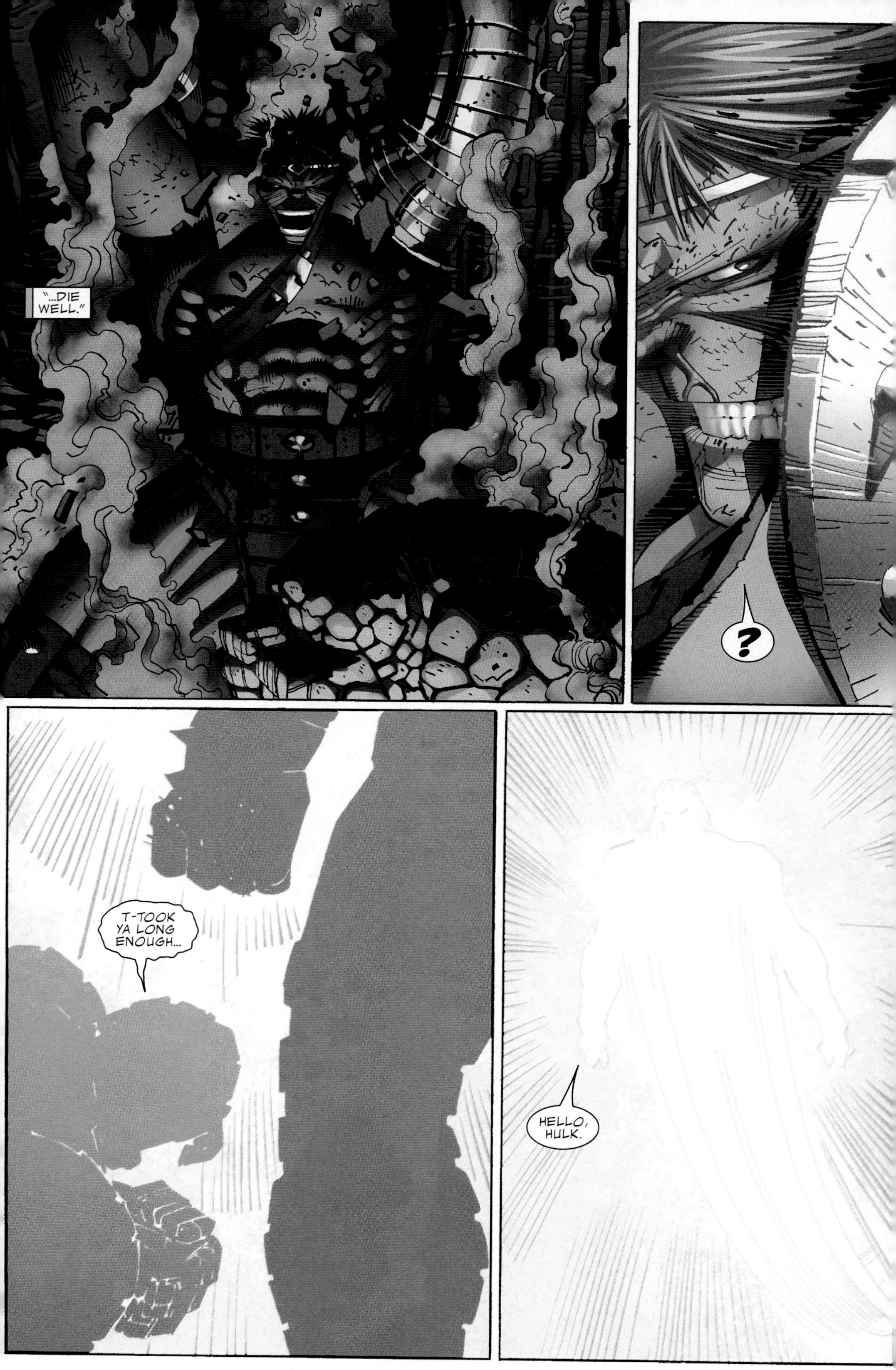
"...DIE WELL."
?
T-TOOK YA LONG ENOUGH...
HELLO, HULK.

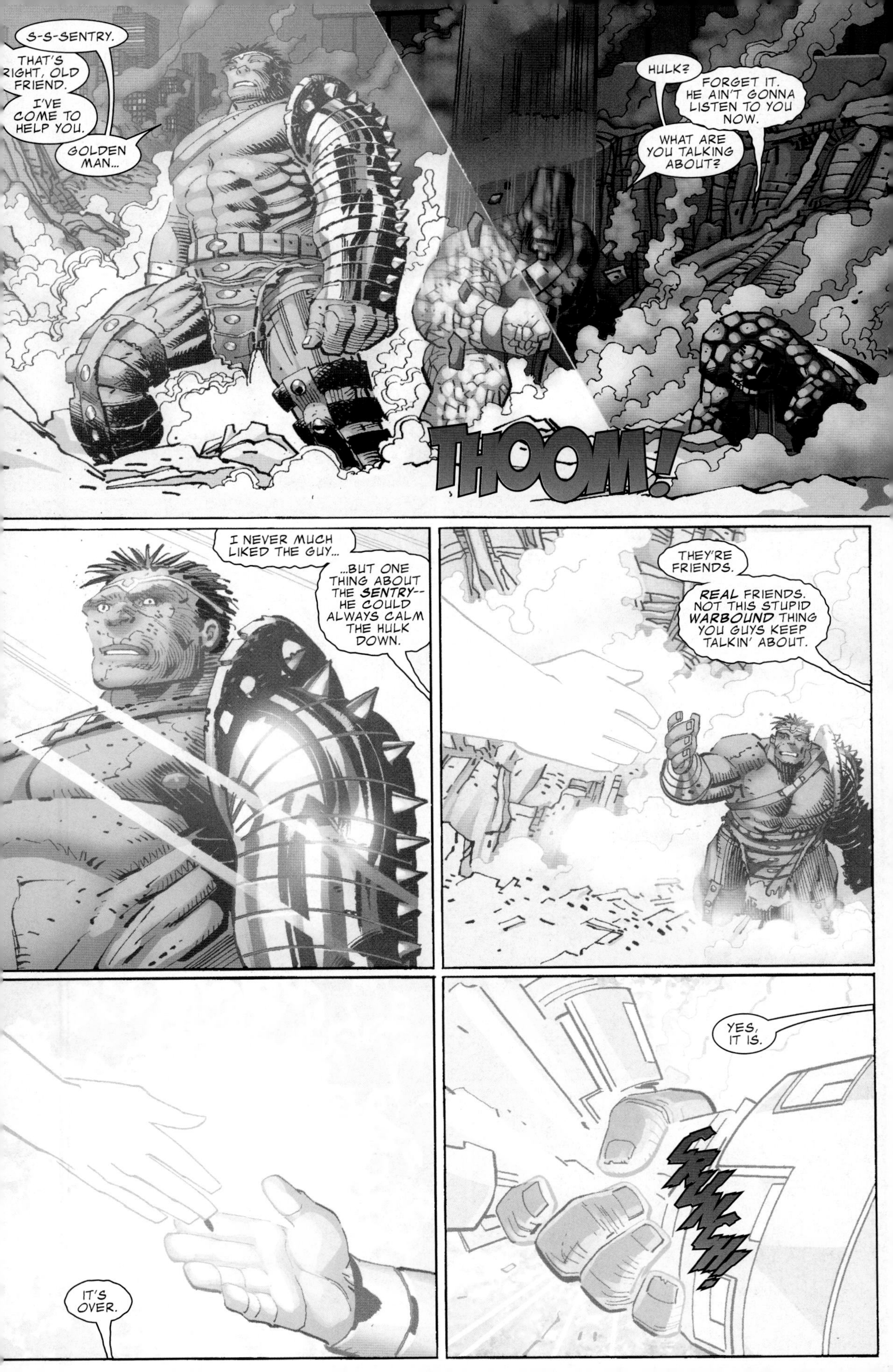
S-S-SENTRY.
THAT'S RIGHT, OLD FRIEND.
I'VE COME TO HELP YOU.
GOLDEN MAN...
HULK?
FORGET IT. HE AIN'T GONNA LISTEN TO YOU NOW.
WHAT ARE YOU TALKING ABOUT?
THOOM!
I NEVER MUCH LIKED THE GUY...
...BUT ONE THING ABOUT THE SENTRY--HE COULD ALWAYS CALM THE HULK DOWN.
THEY'RE FRIENDS.
REAL FRIENDS. NOT THIS STUPID WARBOUND THING YOU GUYS KEEP TALKIN' ABOUT.
IT'S OVER.
YES, IT IS.
CRUNCH!

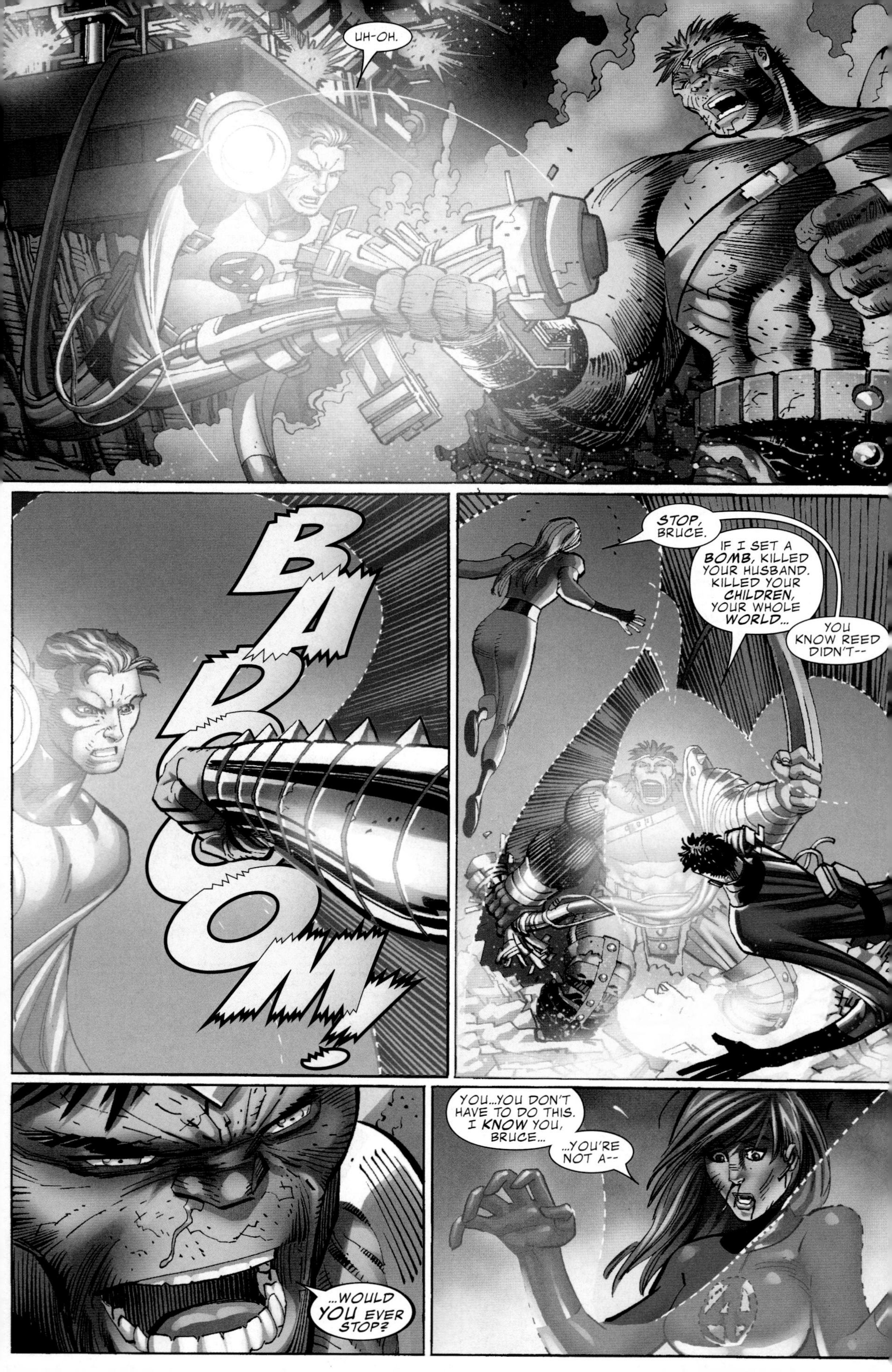
UH-OH.
BADOOOM!
STOP, BRUCE.
IF I SET A BOMB, KILLED YOUR HUSBAND. KILLED YOUR CHILDREN, YOUR WHOLE WORLD...
YOU KNOW REED DIDN'T--
...WOULD YOU EVER STOP?
YOU...YOU DON'T HAVE TO DO THIS. I KNOW YOU, BRUCE...
...YOU'RE NOT A--

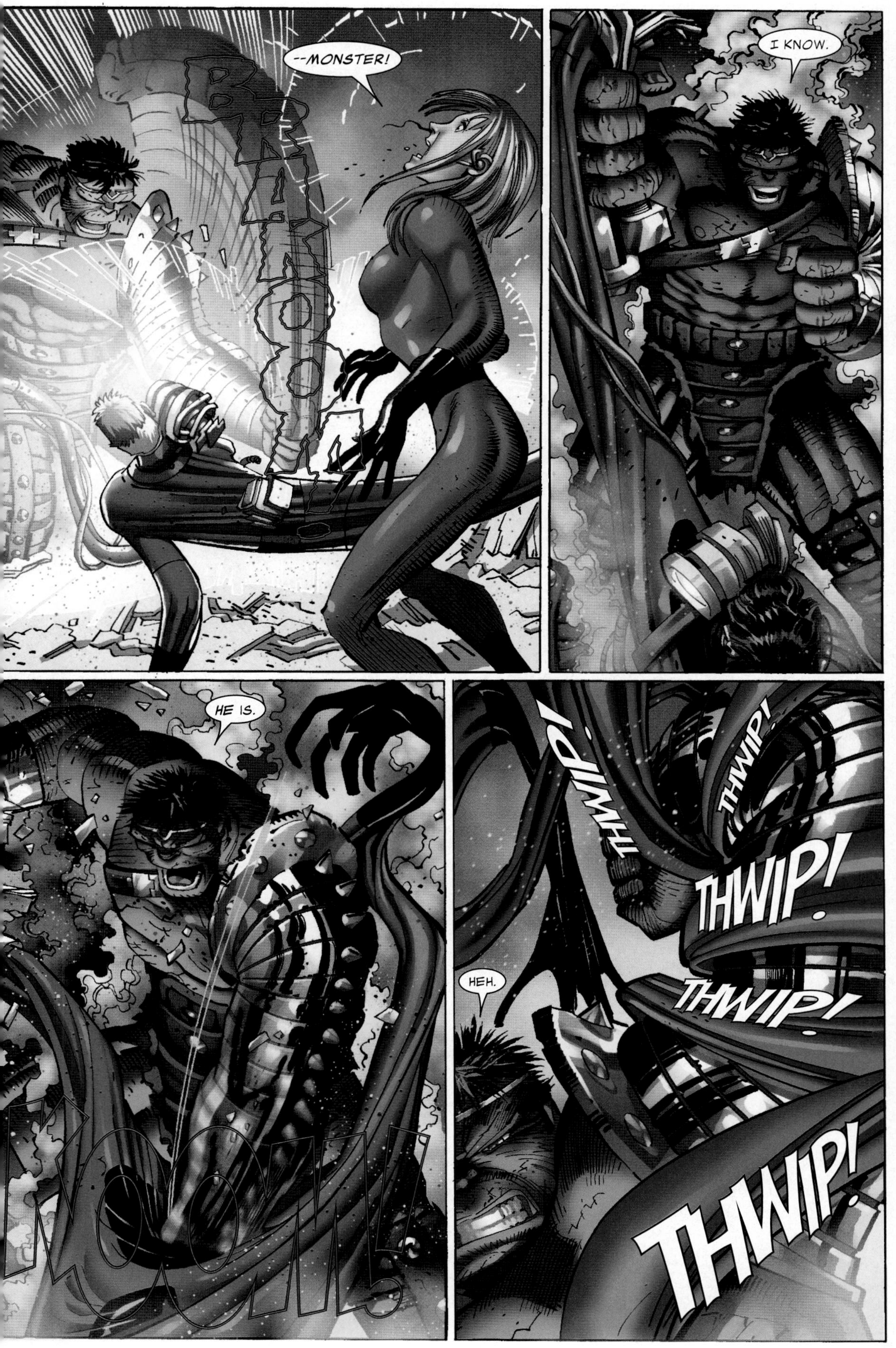
--MONSTER!
I KNOW.
HE IS.
THWIP!
THWIP!
THWIP!
HEH.
THWIP!
THWIP!

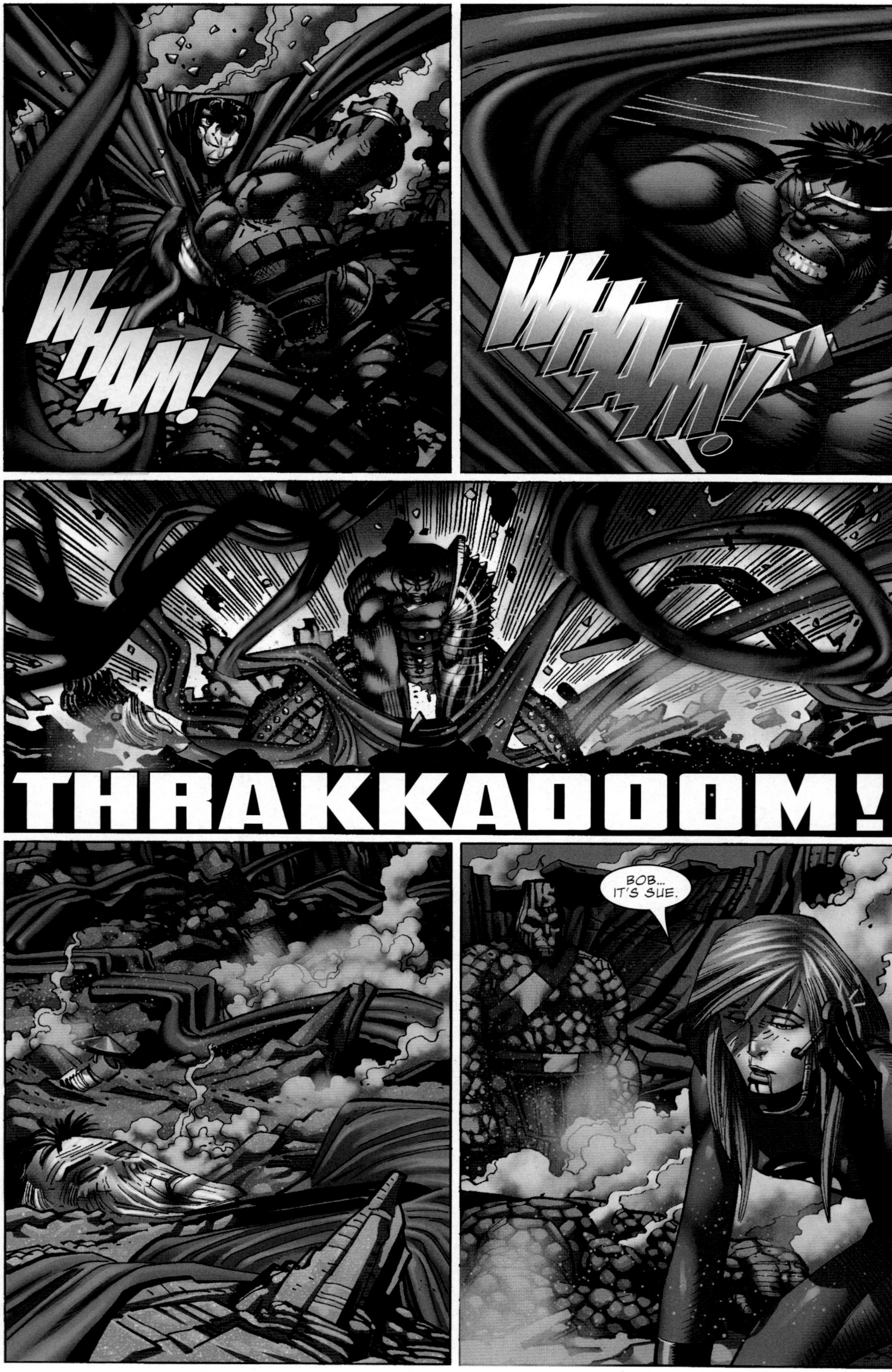
WHAM!
WHAM!
THRAKKADOOOM!
BOB...
IT'S SUE.

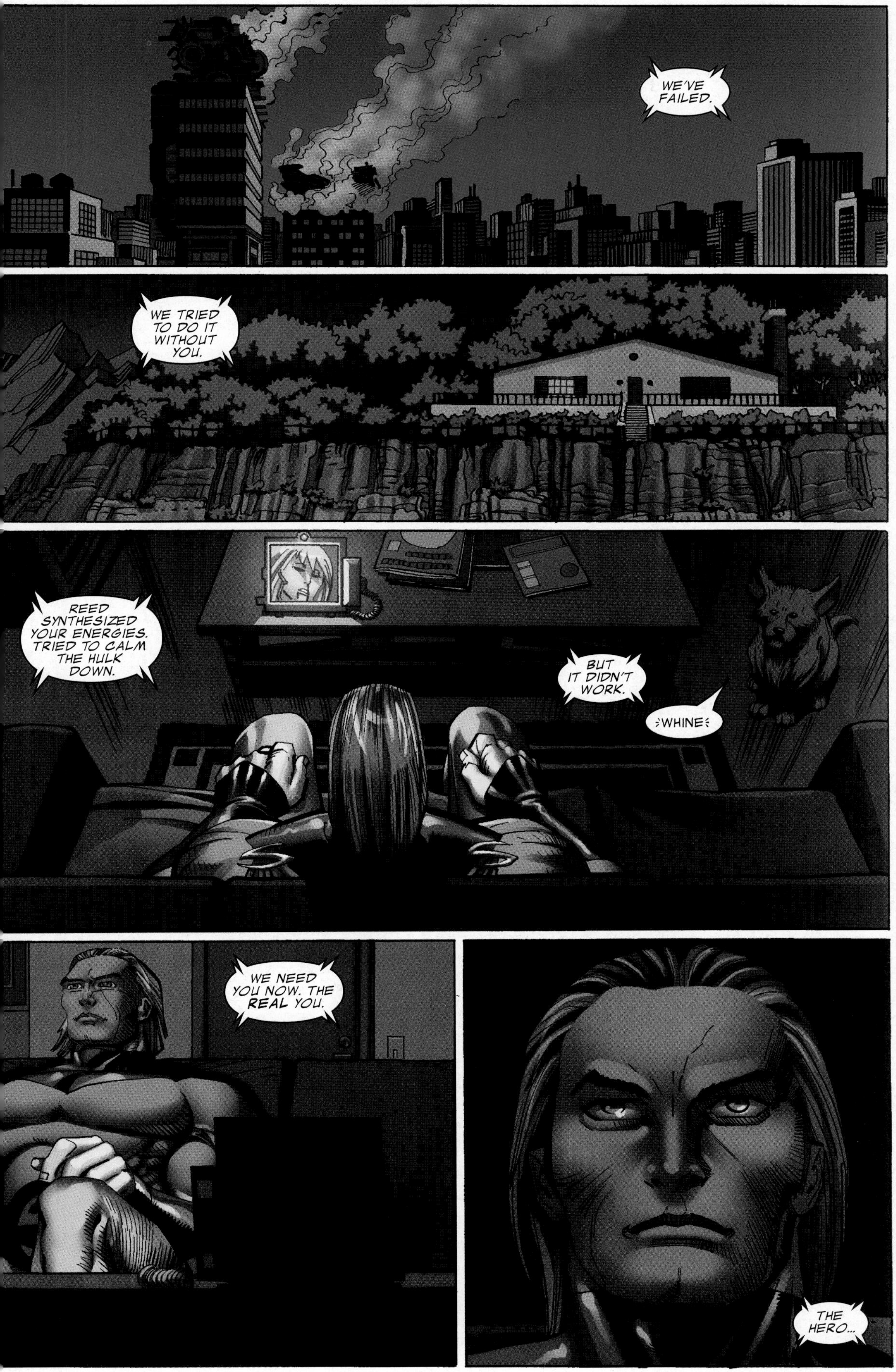
WE'VE FAILED.
WE TRIED TO DO IT WITHOUT YOU.
REED SYNTHESIZED YOUR ENERGIES. TRIED TO CALM THE HULK DOWN.
BUT IT DIDN'T WORK.
WHINE
WE NEED YOU NOW. THE REAL YOU.
THE HERO...

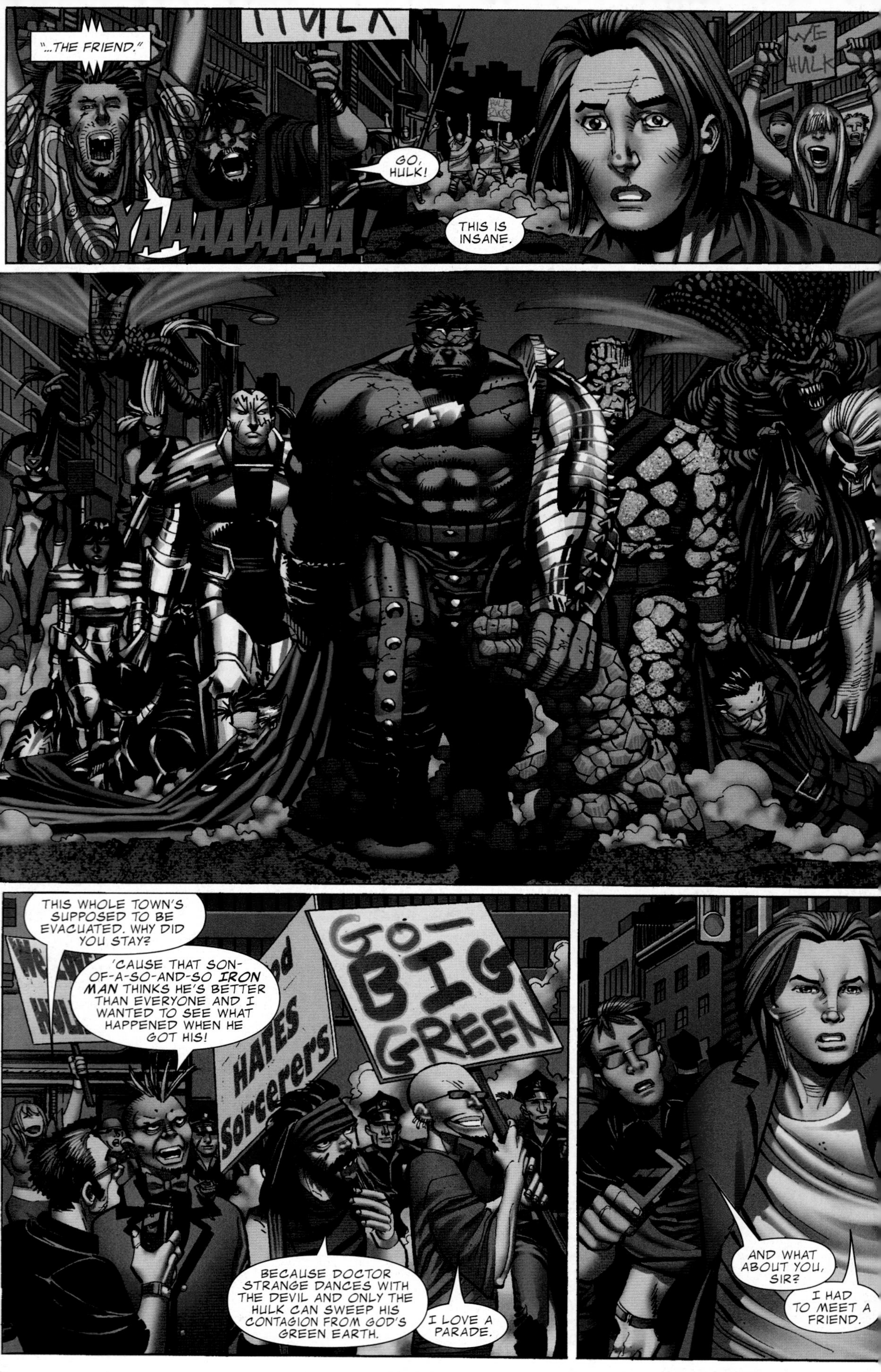

"...THE FRIEND."
HULK
YAAAAAAAA!
GO, HULK!
THIS IS INSANE.
WE ♥ HULK
THIS WHOLE TOWN'S SUPPOSED TO BE EVACUATED. WHY DID YOU STAY?
'CAUSE THAT SON-OF-A-SO-AND-SO **IRON MAN** THINKS HE'S BETTER THAN EVERYONE AND I WANTED TO SEE WHAT HAPPENED WHEN HE GOT HIS!
HATES Sorcerers
GO— BIG GREEN
BECAUSE DOCTOR STRANGE DANCES WITH THE DEVIL AND ONLY THE HULK CAN SWEEP HIS CONTAGION FROM GOD'S GREEN EARTH.
I LOVE A PARADE.
AND WHAT ABOUT YOU, SIR?
I HAD TO MEET A FRIEND.

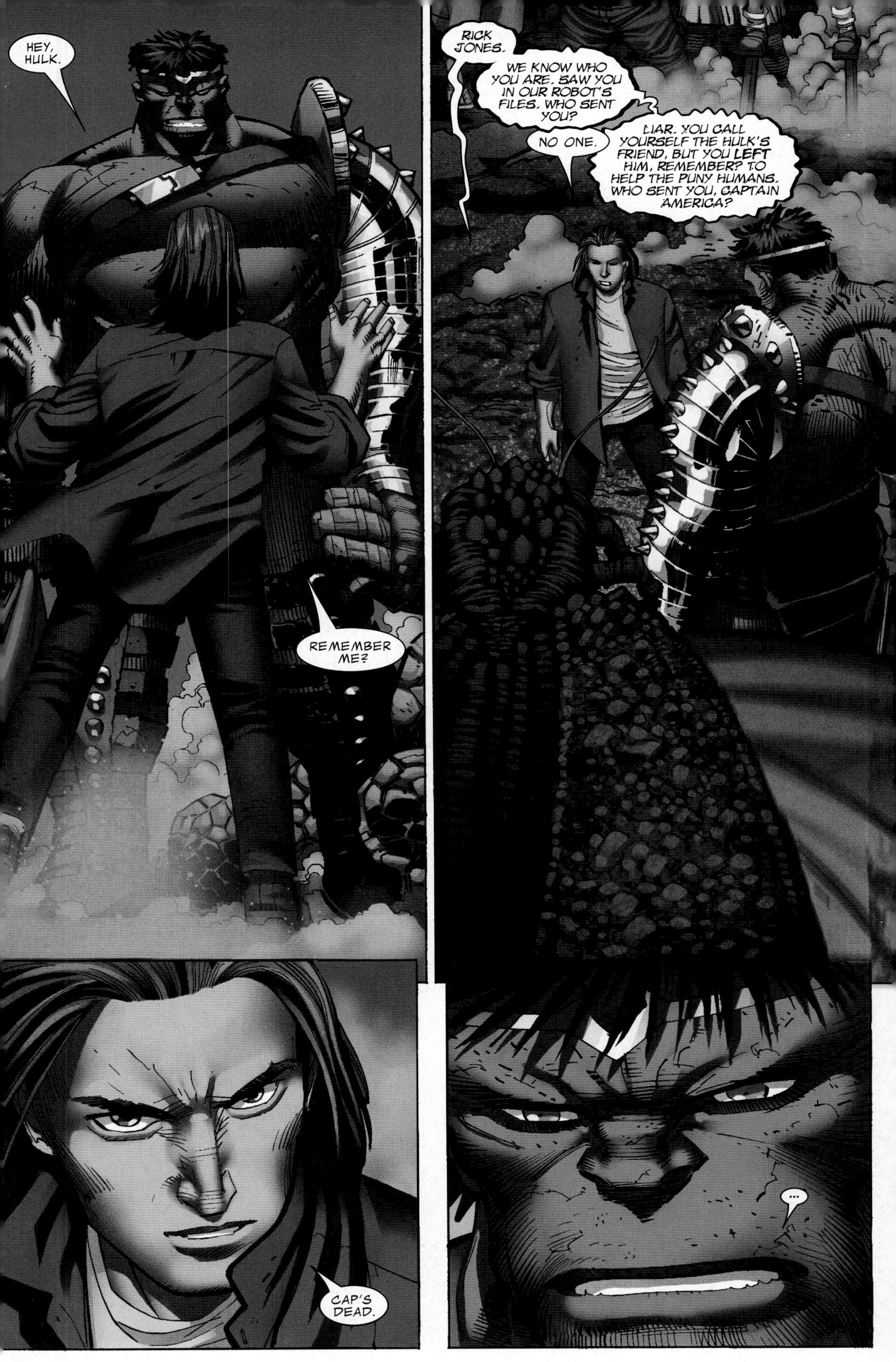
HEY, HULK.
REMEMBER ME?
RICK JONES.
WE KNOW WHO YOU ARE. SAW YOU IN OUR ROBOT'S FILES. WHO SENT YOU?
NO ONE.
LIAR. YOU CALL YOURSELF THE HULK'S FRIEND, BUT YOU LEFT HIM, REMEMBER? TO HELP THE PUNY HUMANS. WHO SENT YOU, CAPTAIN AMERICA?
CAP'S DEAD.
...

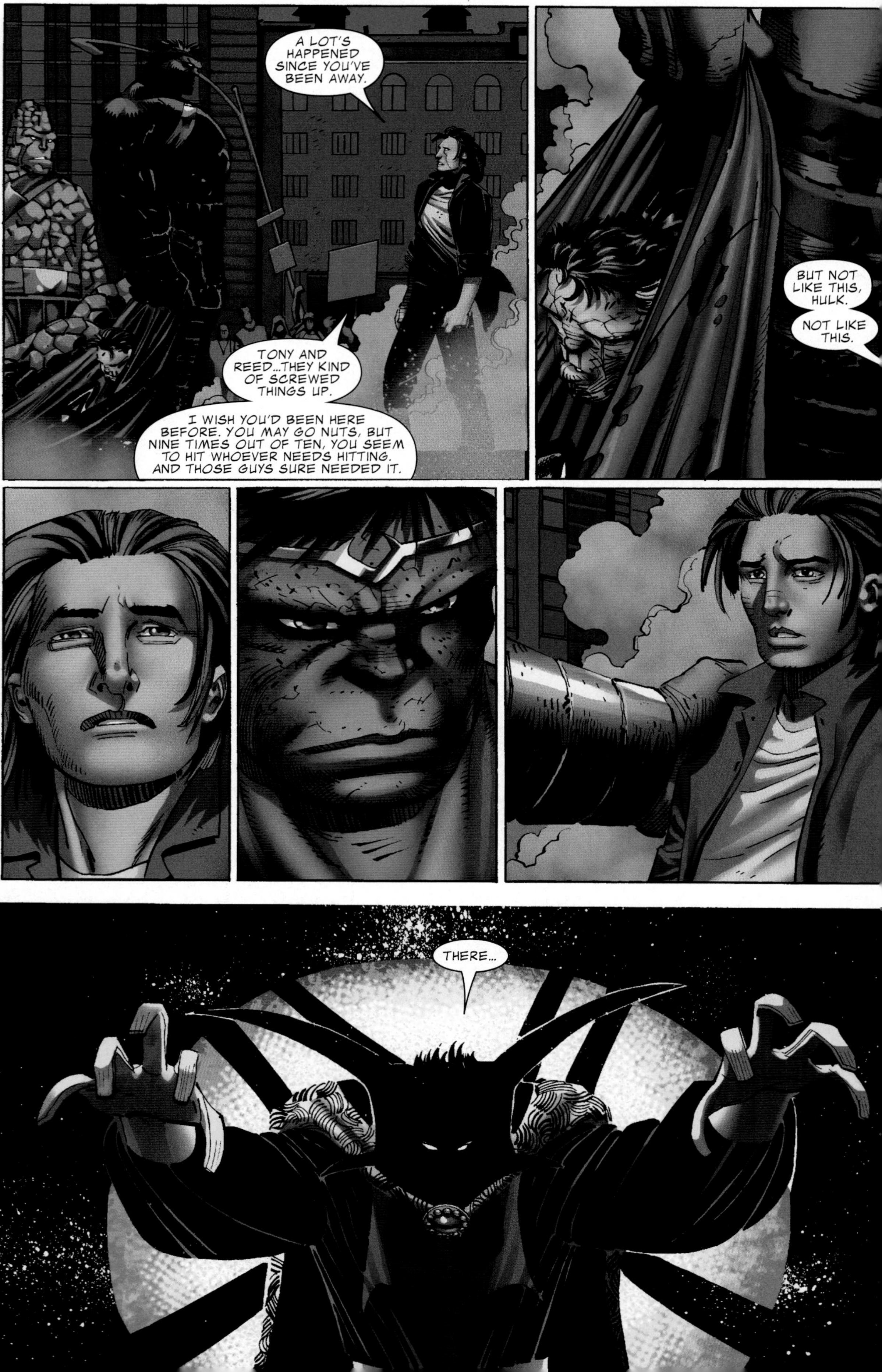
A LOT'S HAPPENED SINCE YOU'VE BEEN AWAY.
TONY AND REED...THEY KIND OF SCREWED THINGS UP.
I WISH YOU'D BEEN HERE BEFORE. YOU MAY GO NUTS, BUT NINE TIMES OUT OF TEN, YOU SEEM TO HIT WHOEVER NEEDS HITTING. AND THOSE GUYS SURE NEEDED IT.
BUT NOT LIKE THIS, HULK.
NOT LIKE THIS.
THERE...

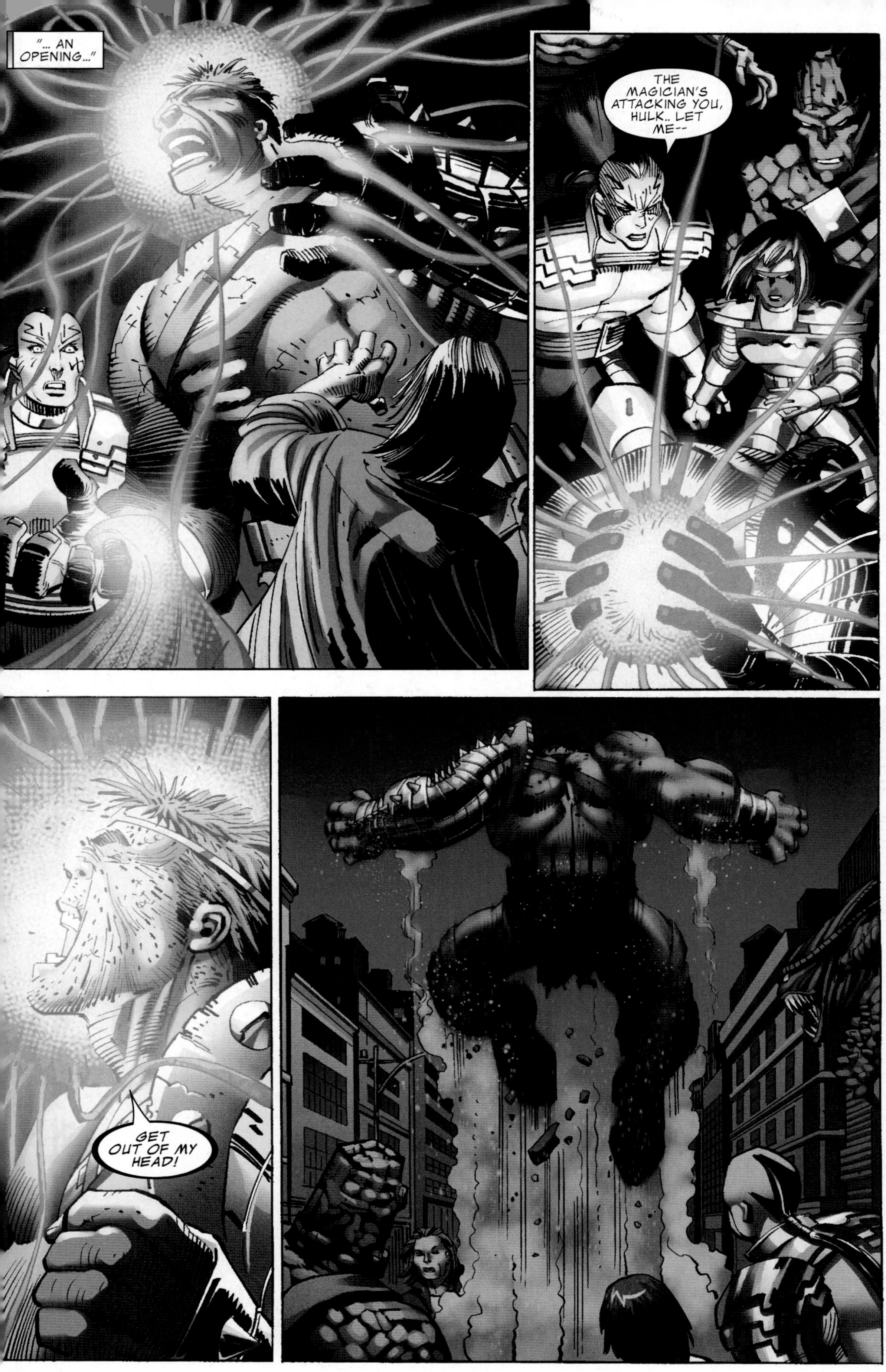
"... AN OPENING..."
THE MAGICIAN'S ATTACKING YOU, HULK.. LET ME--
GET OUT OF MY HEAD!

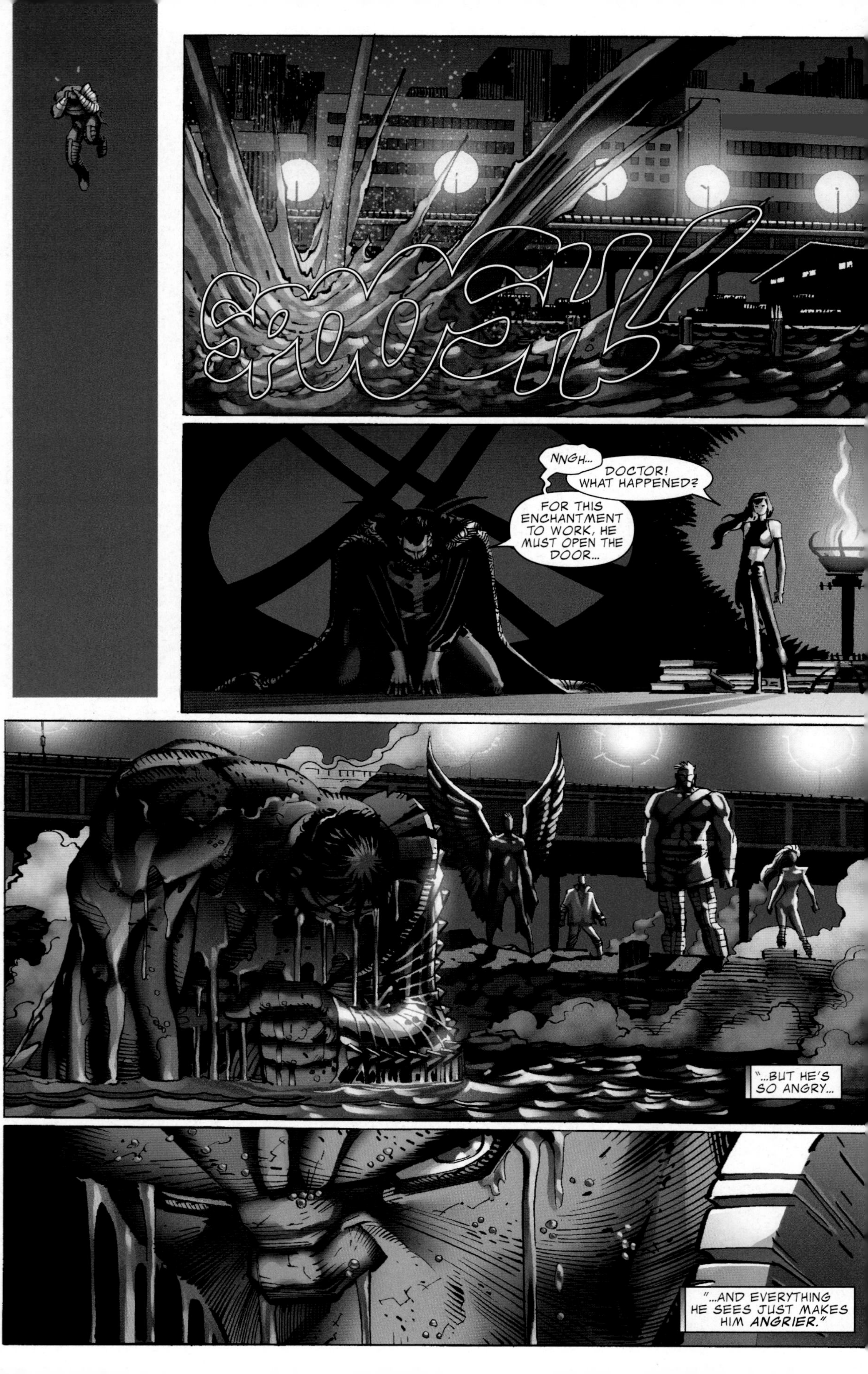
SPLOOSH!
NNGH...
DOCTOR! WHAT HAPPENED?
FOR THIS ENCHANTMENT TO WORK, HE MUST OPEN THE DOOR...
"...BUT HE'S SO ANGRY...
"...AND EVERYTHING HE SEES JUST MAKES HIM ANGRIER."

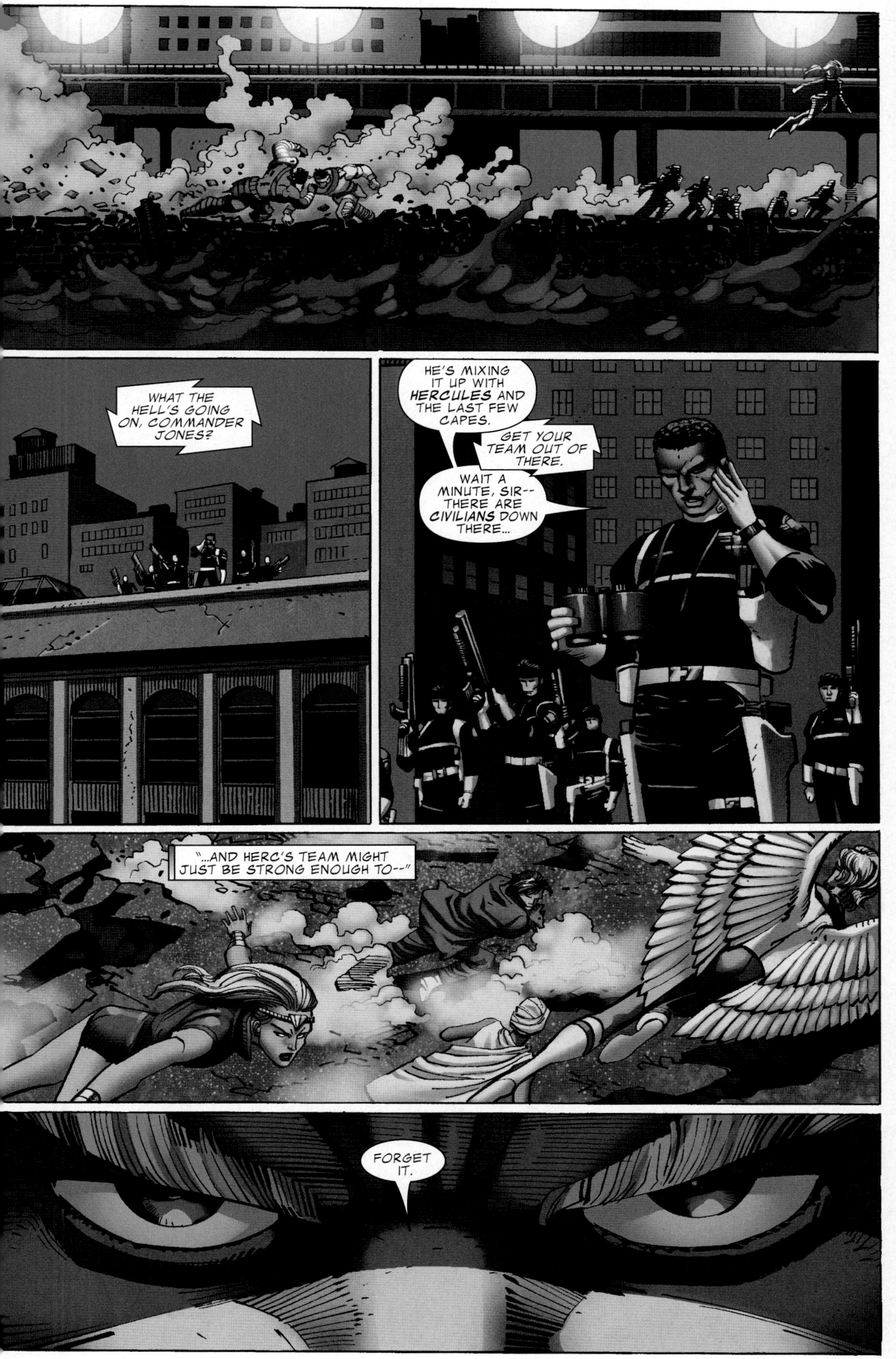
WHAT THE HELL'S GOING ON, COMMANDER JONES?
HE'S MIXING IT UP WITH HERCULES AND THE LAST FEW CAPES.
GET YOUR TEAM OUT OF THERE.
WAIT A MINUTE, SIR-- THERE ARE CIVILIANS DOWN THERE...
"...AND HERC'S TEAM MIGHT JUST BE STRONG ENOUGH TO--"
FORGET IT.

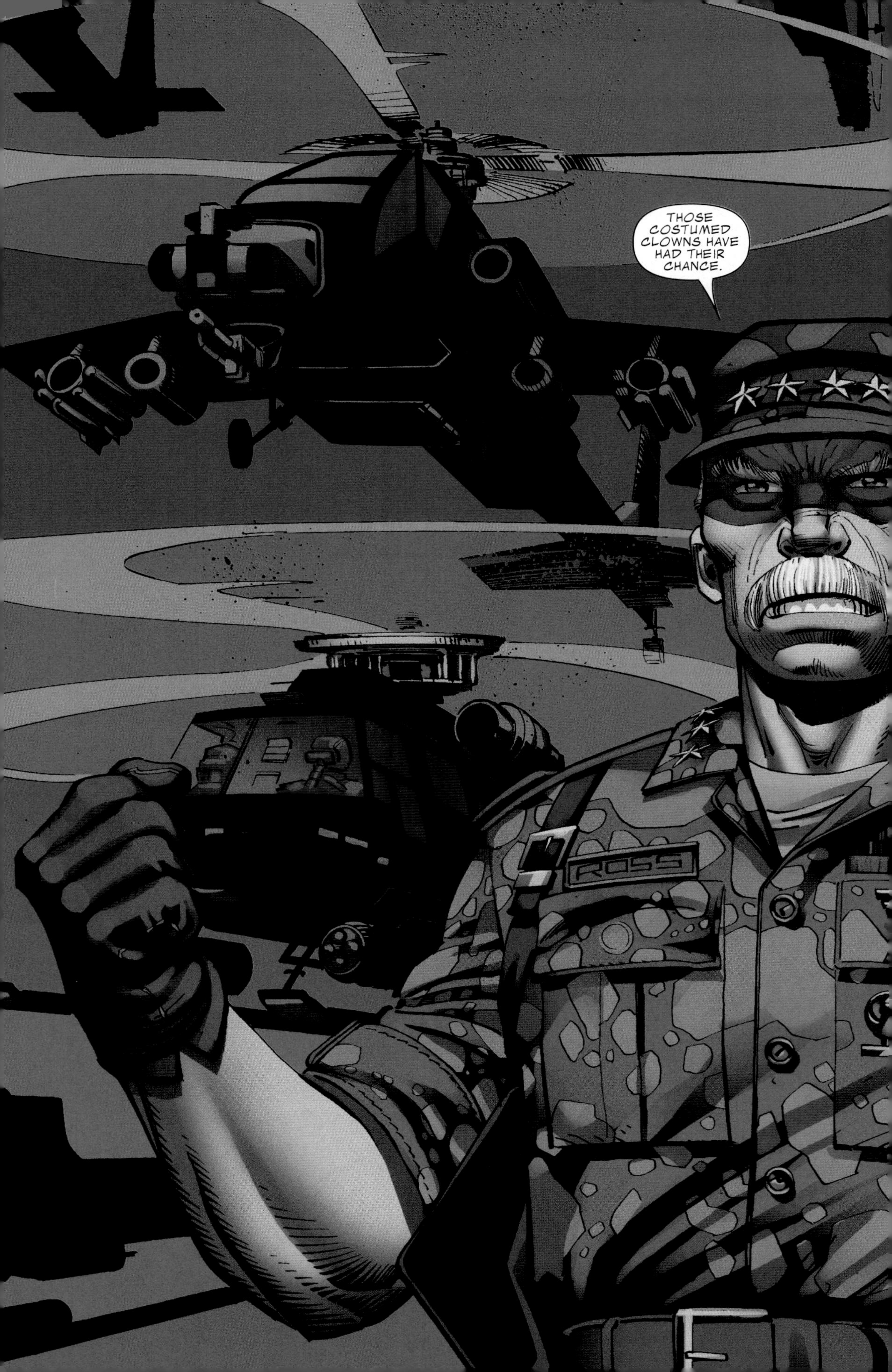
THOSE COSTUMED CLOWNS HAVE HAD THEIR CHANCE.
ROSS

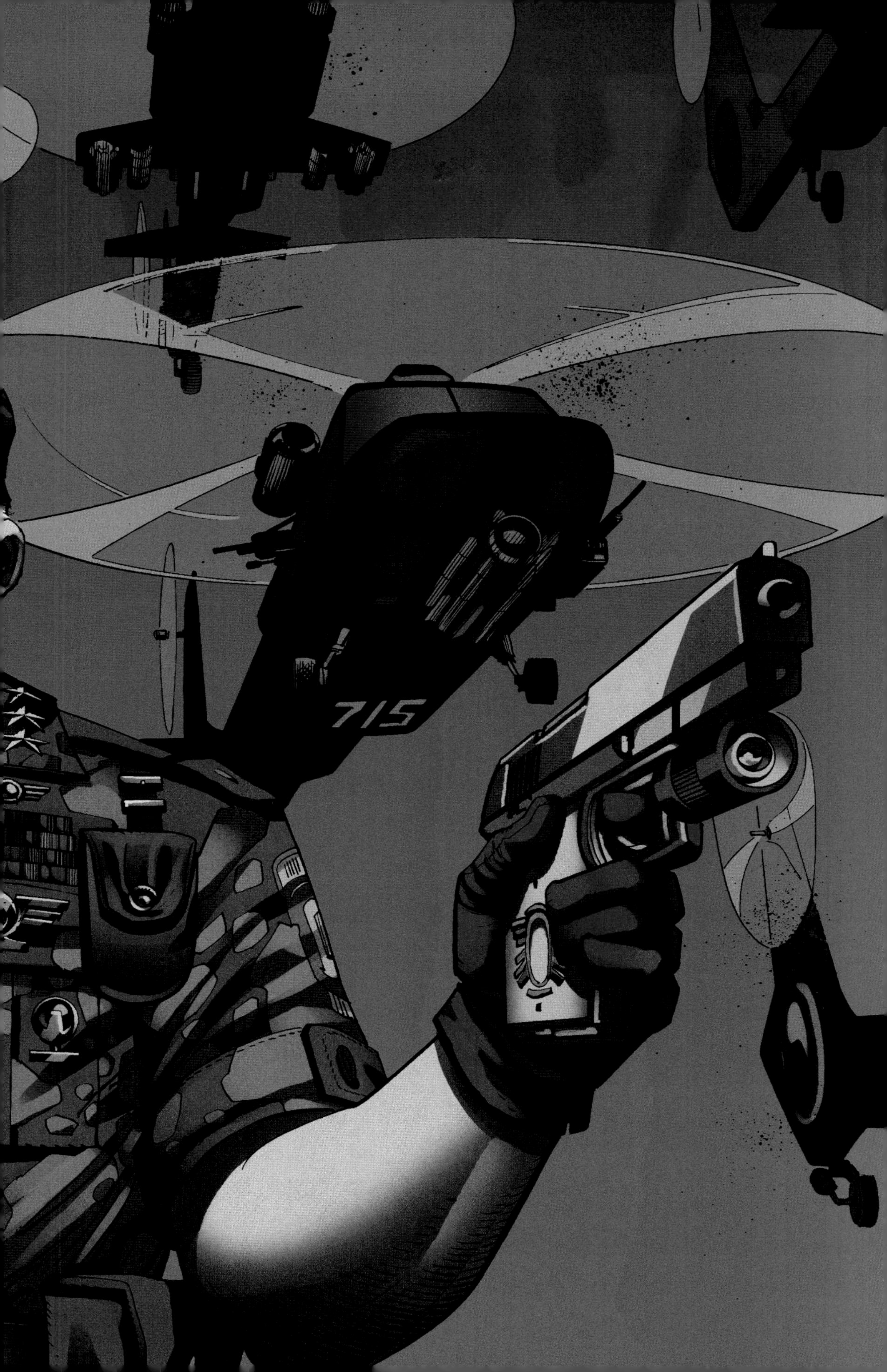
715

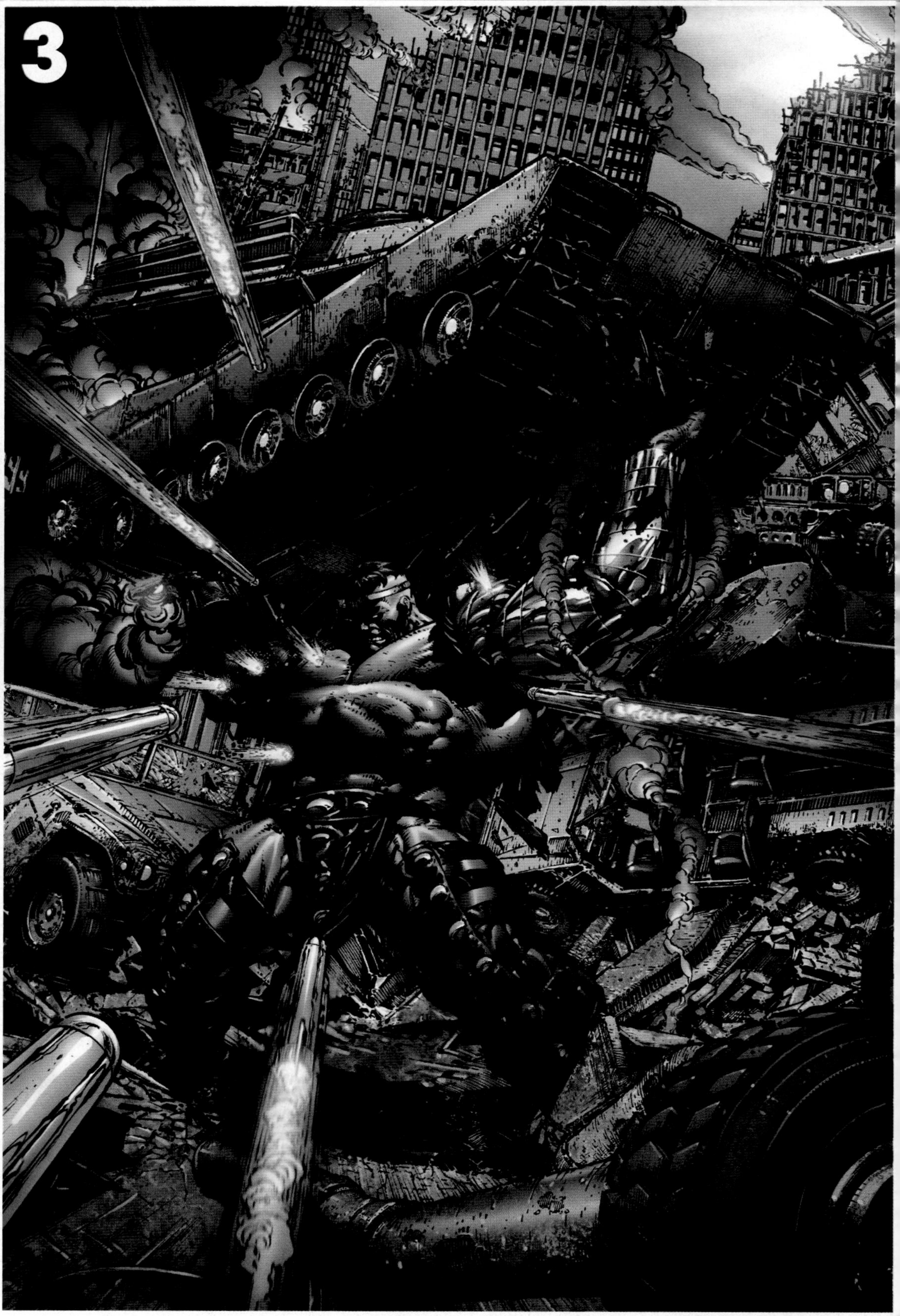
3

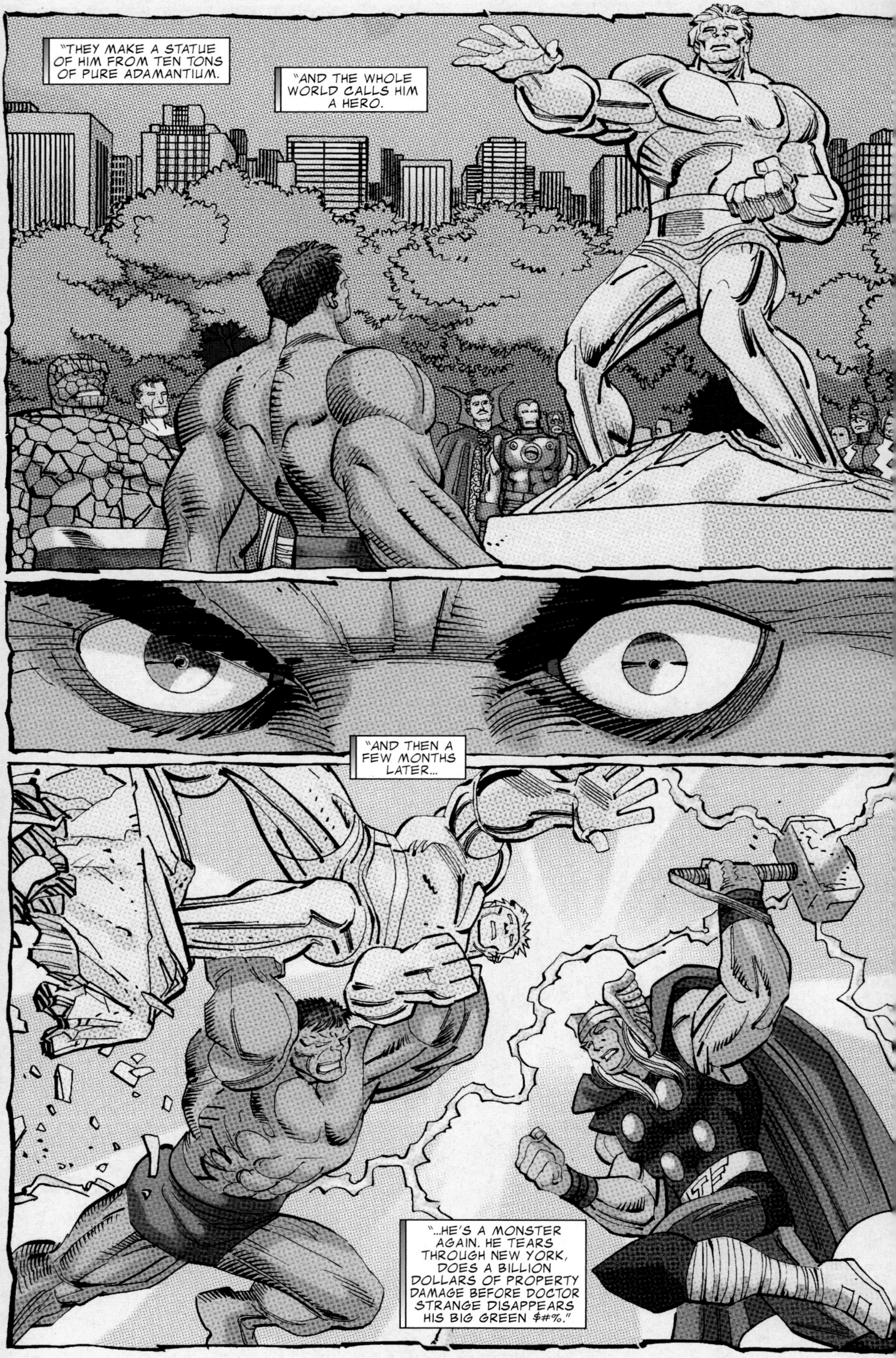
"THEY MAKE A STATUE OF HIM FROM TEN TONS OF PURE ADAMANTIUM.
"AND THE WHOLE WORLD CALLS HIM A HERO.
"AND THEN A FEW MONTHS LATER...
"...HE'S A MONSTER AGAIN. HE TEARS THROUGH NEW YORK, DOES A BILLION DOLLARS OF PROPERTY DAMAGE BEFORE DOCTOR STRANGE DISAPPEARS HIS BIG GREEN $#%."

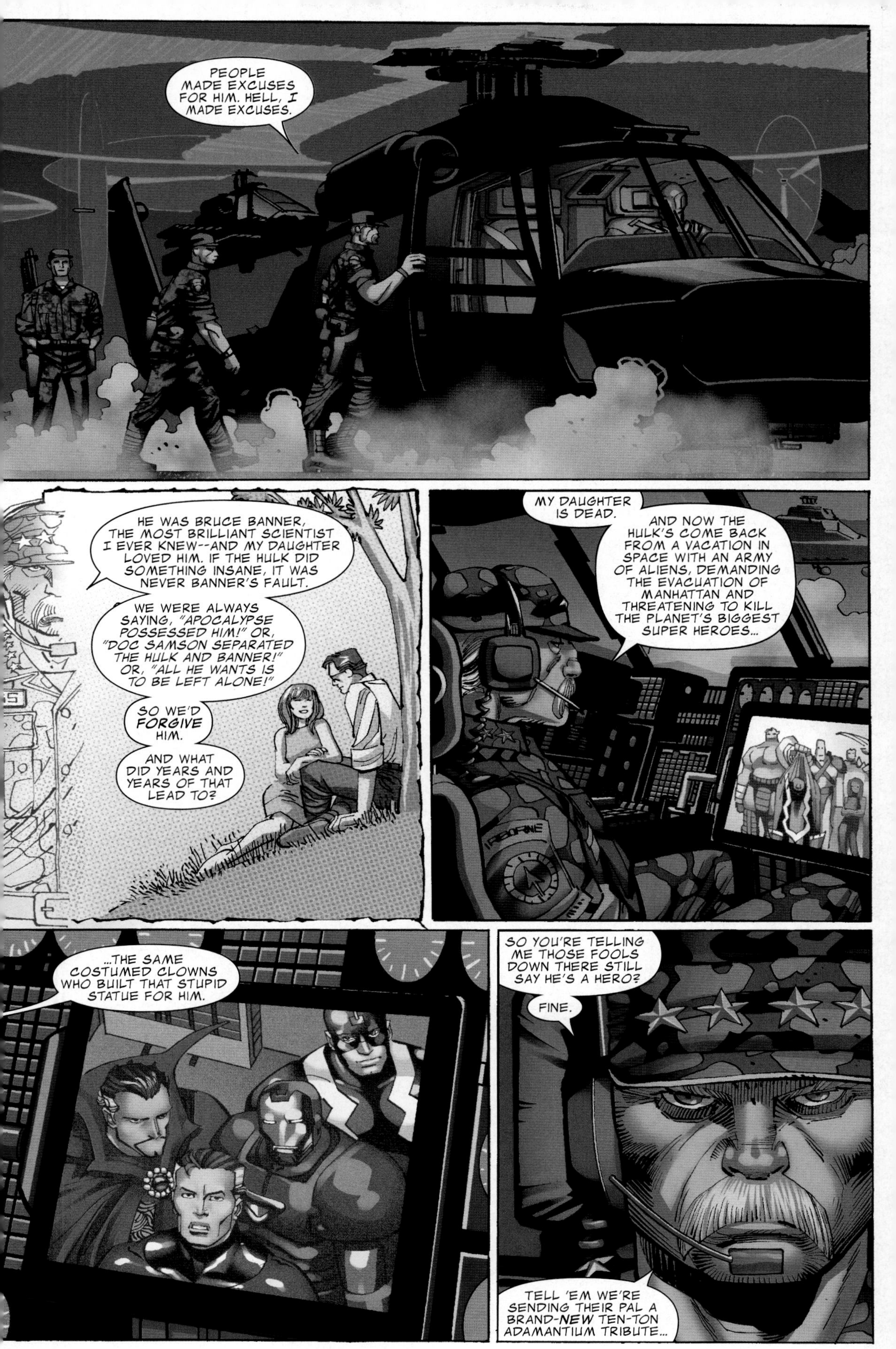
PEOPLE MADE EXCUSES FOR HIM. HELL, I MADE EXCUSES.
HE WAS BRUCE BANNER, THE MOST BRILLIANT SCIENTIST I EVER KNEW--AND MY DAUGHTER LOVED HIM. IF THE HULK DID SOMETHING INSANE, IT WAS NEVER BANNER'S FAULT.
WE WERE ALWAYS SAYING, "APOCALYPSE POSSESSED HIM!" OR, "DOC SAMSON SEPARATED THE HULK AND BANNER!" OR, "ALL HE WANTS IS TO BE LEFT ALONE!"
SO WE'D *FORGIVE* HIM.
AND WHAT DID YEARS AND YEARS OF THAT LEAD TO?
MY DAUGHTER IS DEAD.
AND NOW THE HULK'S COME BACK FROM A VACATION IN SPACE WITH AN ARMY OF ALIENS, DEMANDING THE EVACUATION OF MANHATTAN AND THREATENING TO KILL THE PLANET'S BIGGEST SUPER HEROES...
...THE SAME COSTUMED CLOWNS WHO BUILT THAT STUPID STATUE FOR HIM.
SO YOU'RE TELLING ME THOSE FOOLS DOWN THERE STILL SAY HE'S A HERO?
FINE.
TELL 'EM WE'RE SENDING THEIR PAL A BRAND-*NEW* TEN-TON ADAMANTIUM TRIBUTE...

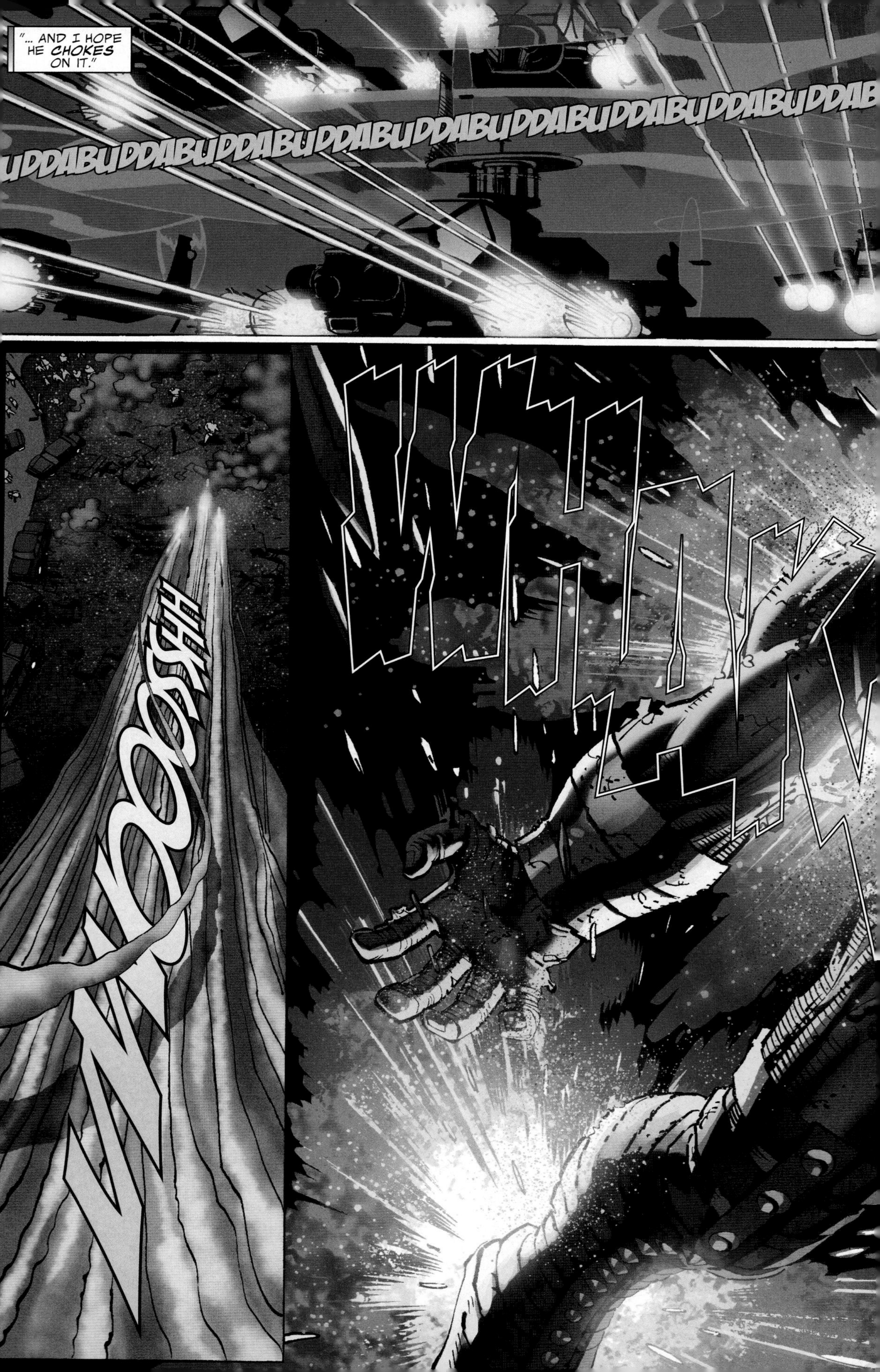
"... AND I HOPE HE CHOKES ON IT."
UDDABUDDABUDDABUDDABUDDABUDDABUDDAB

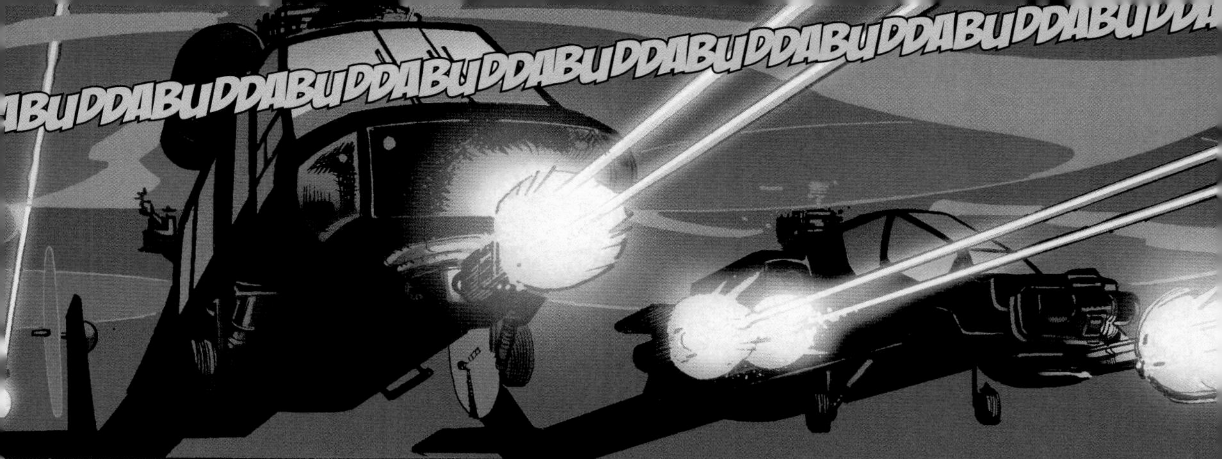
ABUDDABUDDABUDDABUDDABUDDABUDDABUDDABUDDA

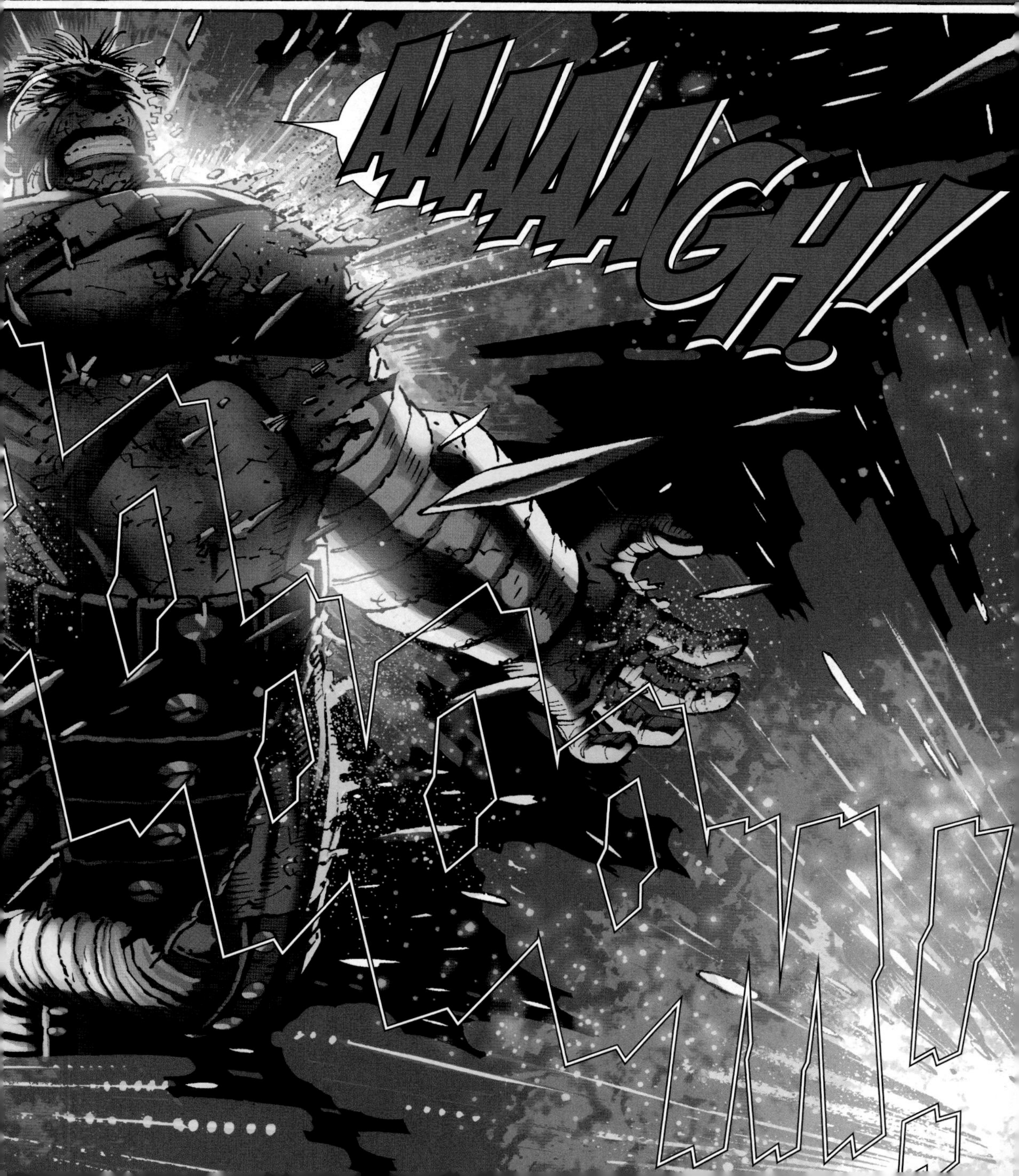
AAAAAAGH!

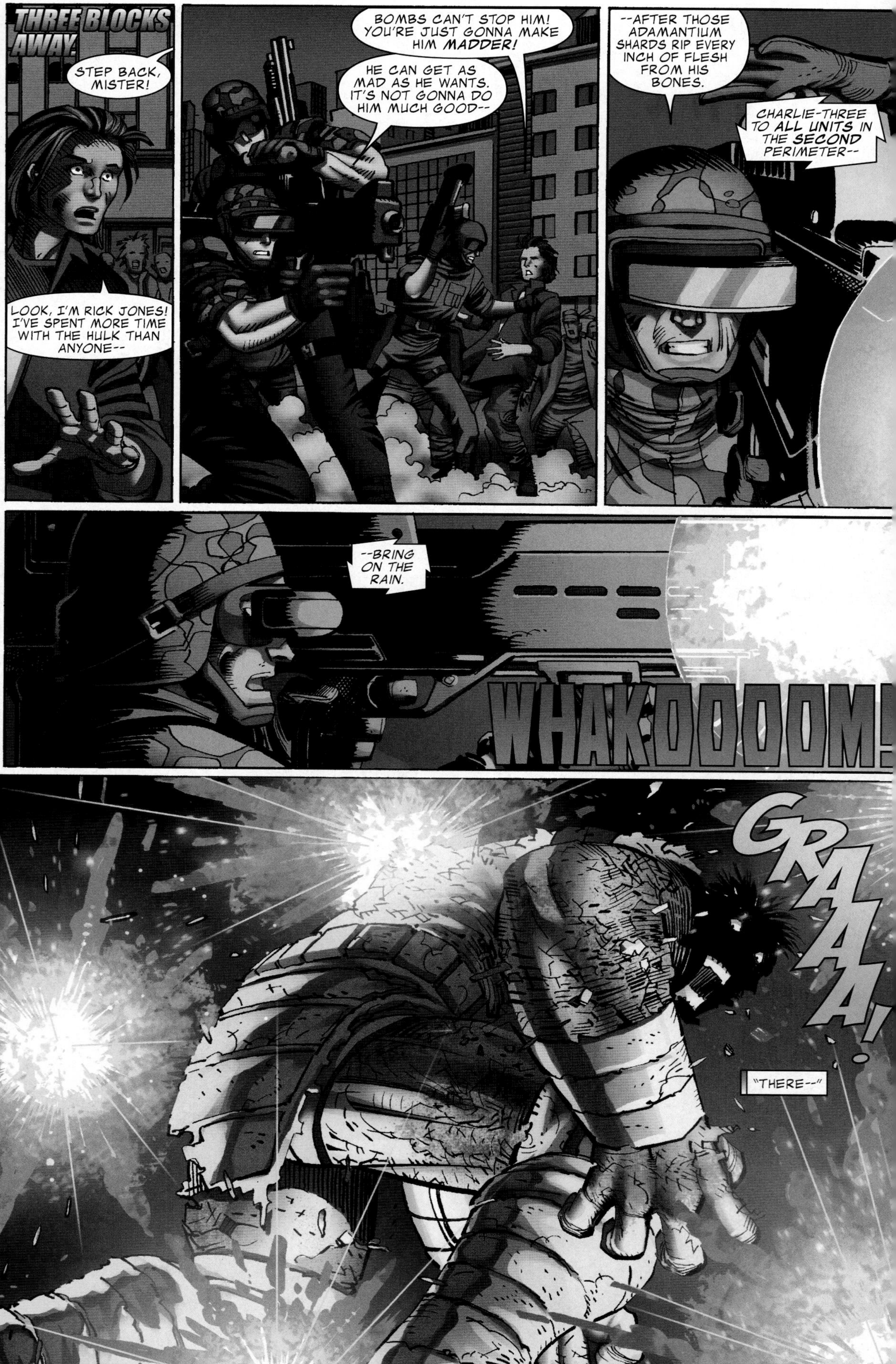
THREE BLOCKS AWAY.
STEP BACK, MISTER!
LOOK, I'M RICK JONES! I'VE SPENT MORE TIME WITH THE HULK THAN ANYONE--
BOMBS CAN'T STOP HIM! YOU'RE JUST GONNA MAKE HIM MADDER!
HE CAN GET AS MAD AS HE WANTS. IT'S NOT GONNA DO HIM MUCH GOOD--
--AFTER THOSE ADAMANTIUM SHARDS RIP EVERY INCH OF FLESH FROM HIS BONES.
CHARLIE-THREE TO ALL UNITS IN THE SECOND PERIMETER--
--BRING ON THE RAIN.
WHAKOOOOM!
GRAAAA!
"THERE--"

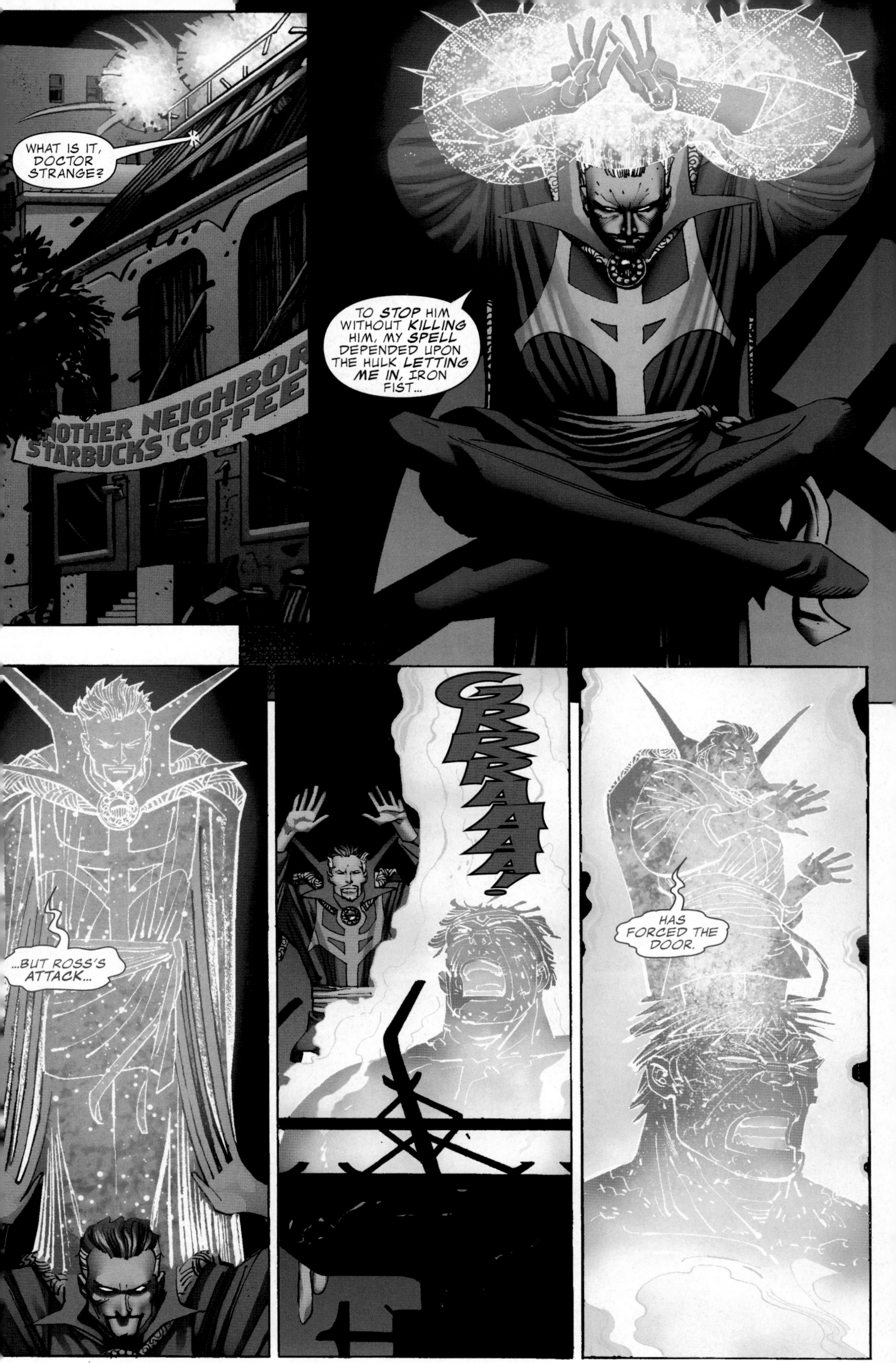

WHAT IS IT, DOCTOR STRANGE?
NOTHER NEIGHBOR
STARBUCKS COFFEE
TO STOP HIM WITHOUT KILLING HIM, MY SPELL DEPENDED UPON THE HULK LETTING ME IN, IRON FIST...
...BUT ROSS'S ATTACK...
GRRAAAA!
HAS FORCED THE DOOR.

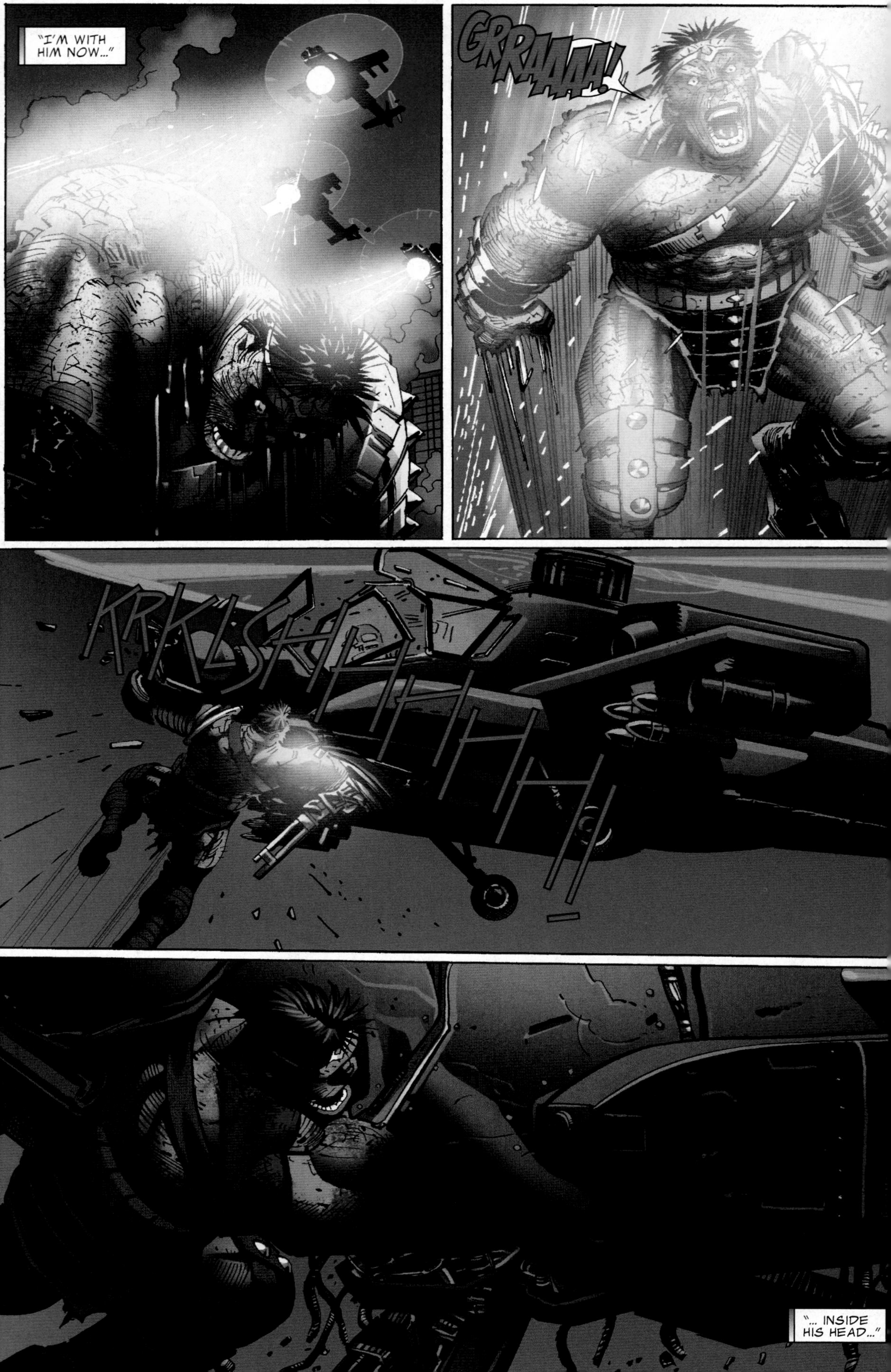
"I'M WITH HIM NOW..."
GRRAAAAA!
KRKLSHHHHHHH!
"... INSIDE HIS HEAD..."

COME ALONG, BRUCE.

NNNGH...

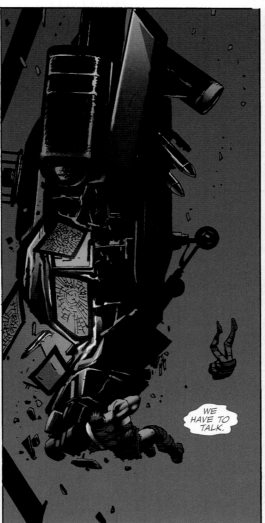

WE HAVE TO TALK.

HE'S-- HE'S STOPPED FIGHTING!

"HE'S GOING DOWN!"

SKRAKOOOOM!

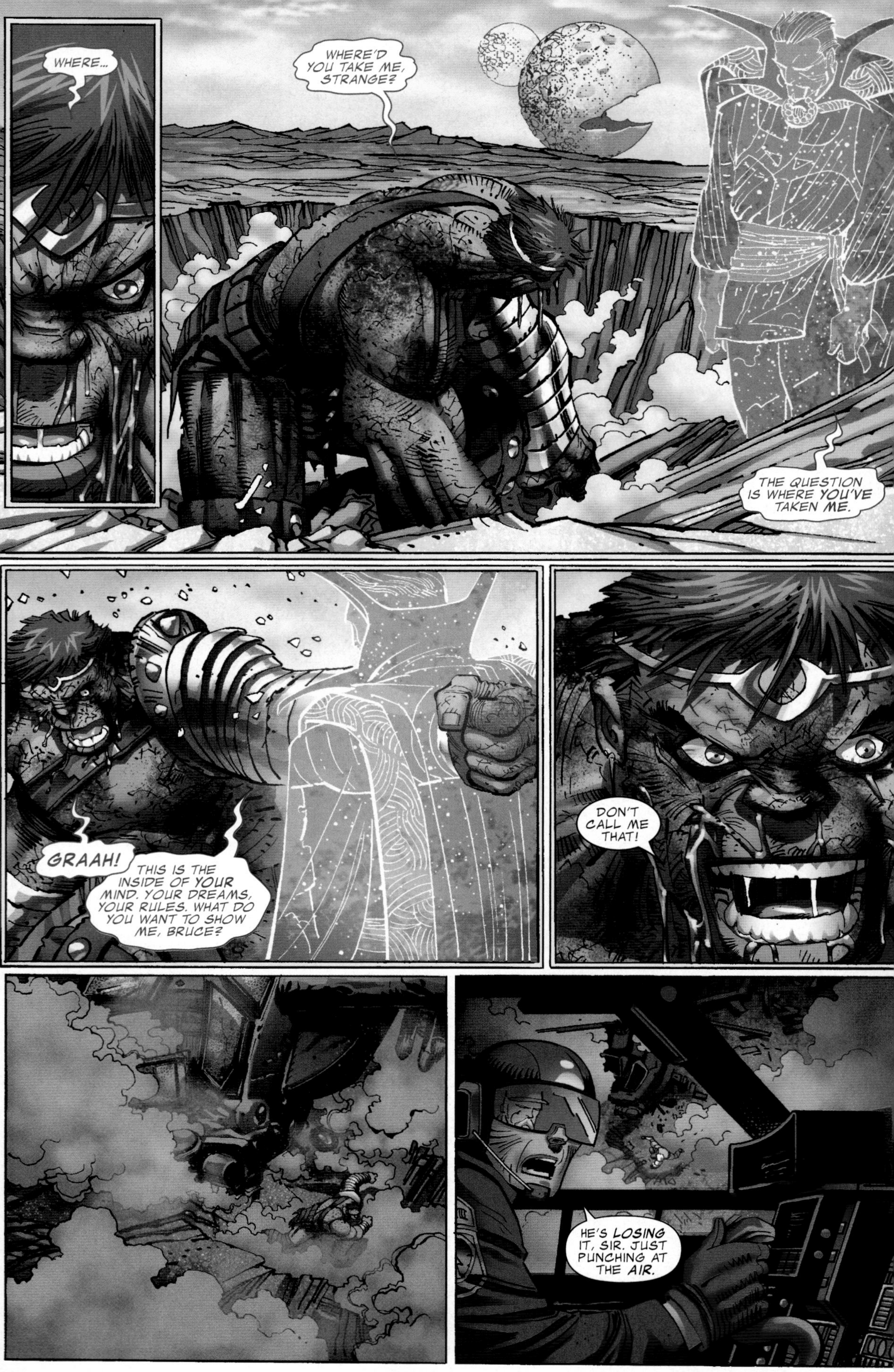
WHERE...
WHERE'D YOU TAKE ME, STRANGE?
THE QUESTION IS WHERE YOU'VE TAKEN ME.
GRAAH!
THIS IS THE INSIDE OF YOUR MIND. YOUR DREAMS, YOUR RULES. WHAT DO YOU WANT TO SHOW ME, BRUCE?
DON'T CALL ME THAT!
HE'S LOSING IT, SIR. JUST PUNCHING AT THE AIR.

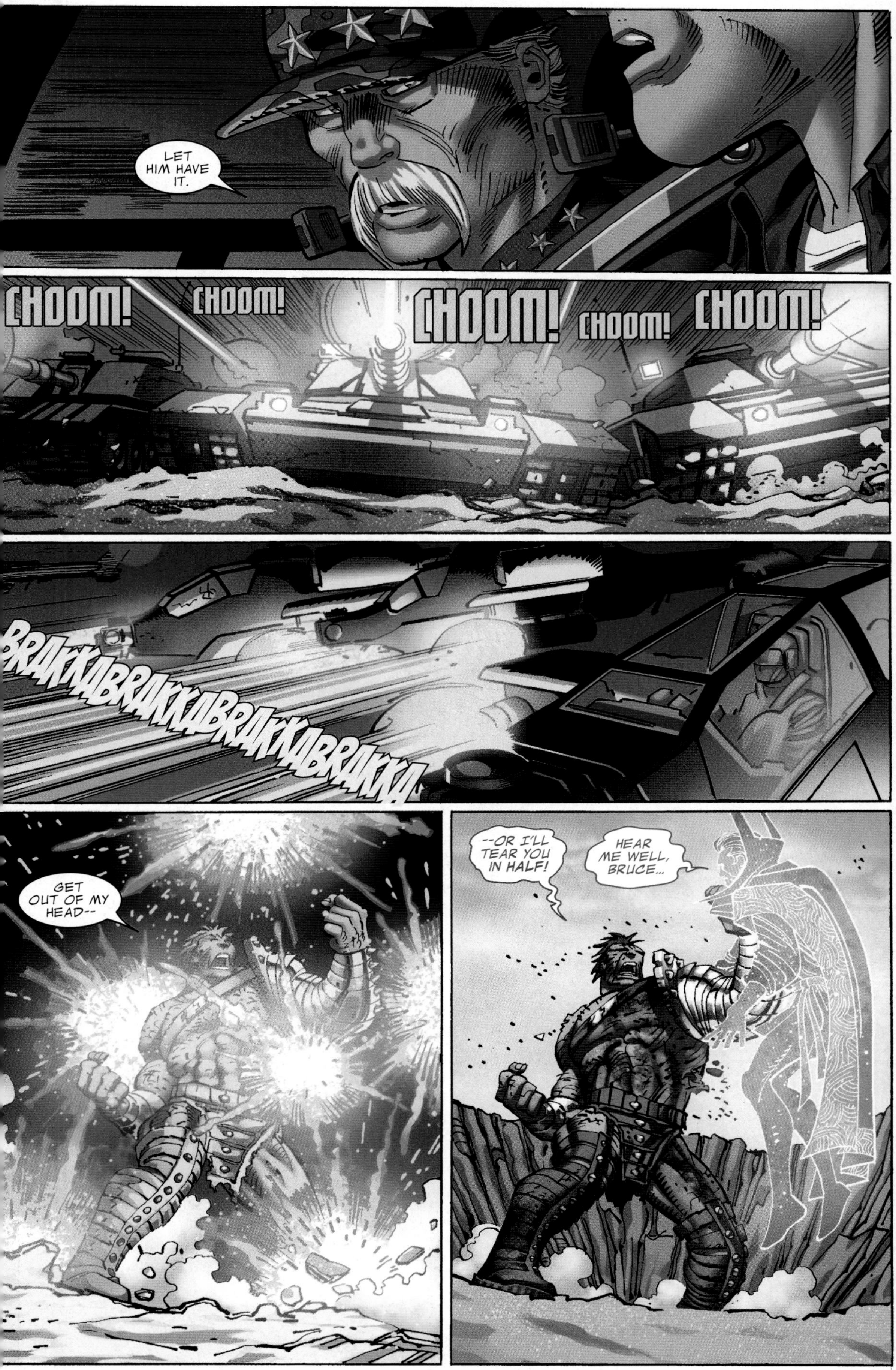
LET HIM HAVE IT.
CHOOM!
CHOOM!
CHOOM!
CHOOM!
CHOOM!
BRAKKABRAKKABRAKKABRAKKA
GET OUT OF MY HEAD--
--OR I'LL TEAR YOU IN HALF!
HEAR ME WELL, BRUCE...

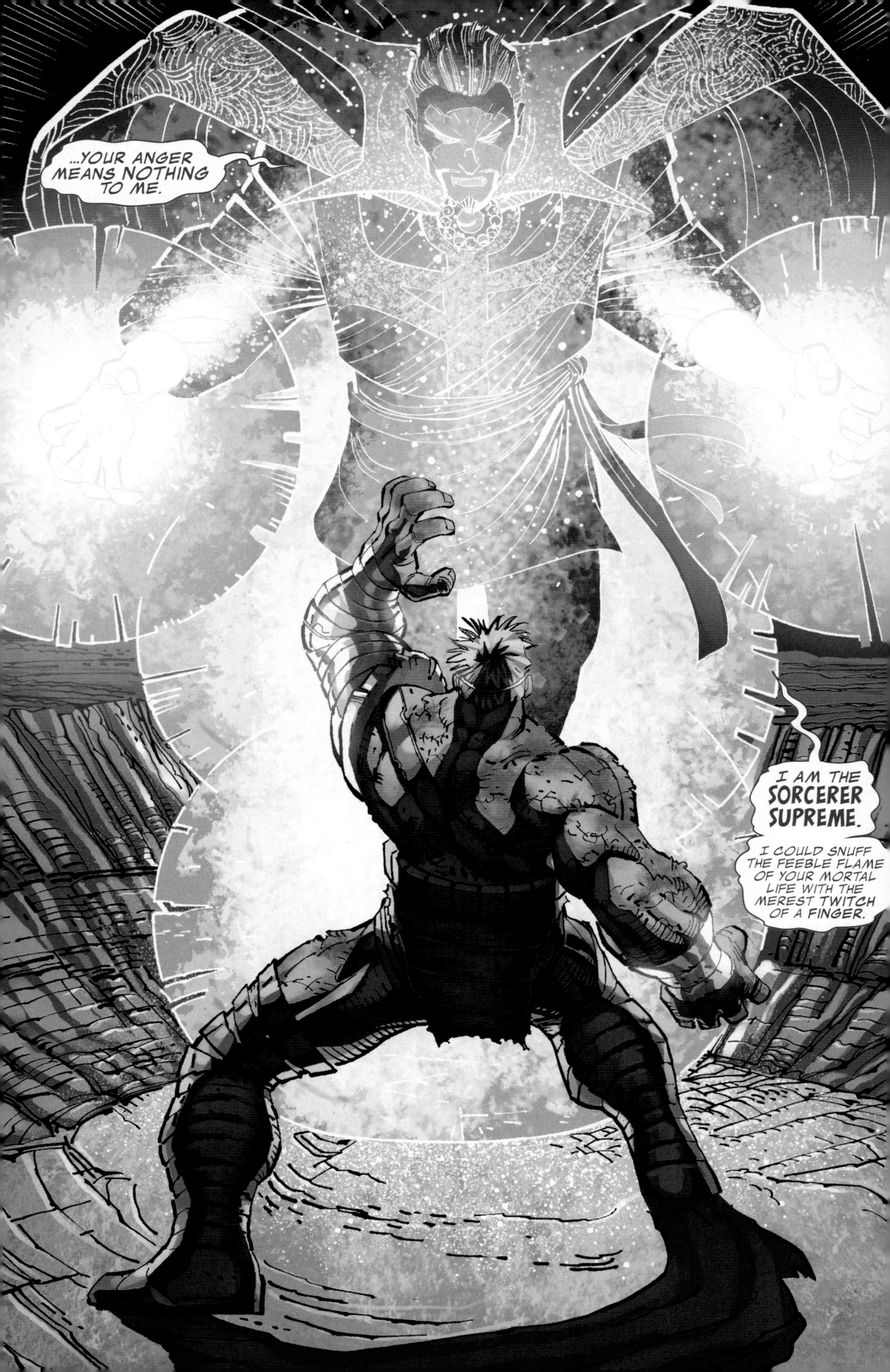
...YOUR ANGER MEANS NOTHING TO ME.
I AM THE SORCERER SUPREME.
I COULD SNUFF THE FEEBLE FLAME OF YOUR MORTAL LIFE WITH THE MEREST TWITCH OF A FINGER.

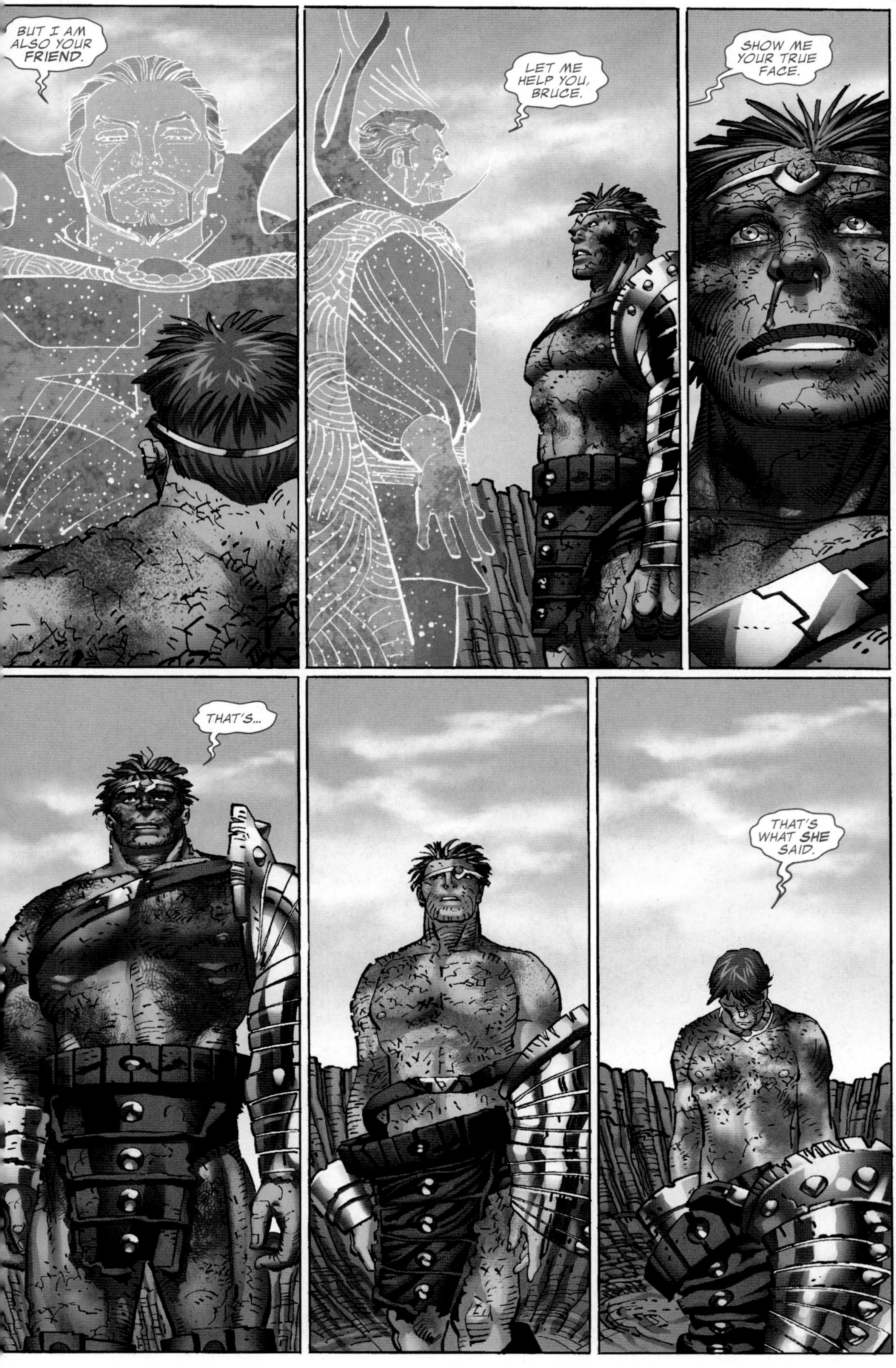
BUT I AM ALSO YOUR FRIEND.
LET ME HELP YOU, BRUCE.
SHOW ME YOUR TRUE FACE.
THAT'S...
THAT'S WHAT SHE SAID.

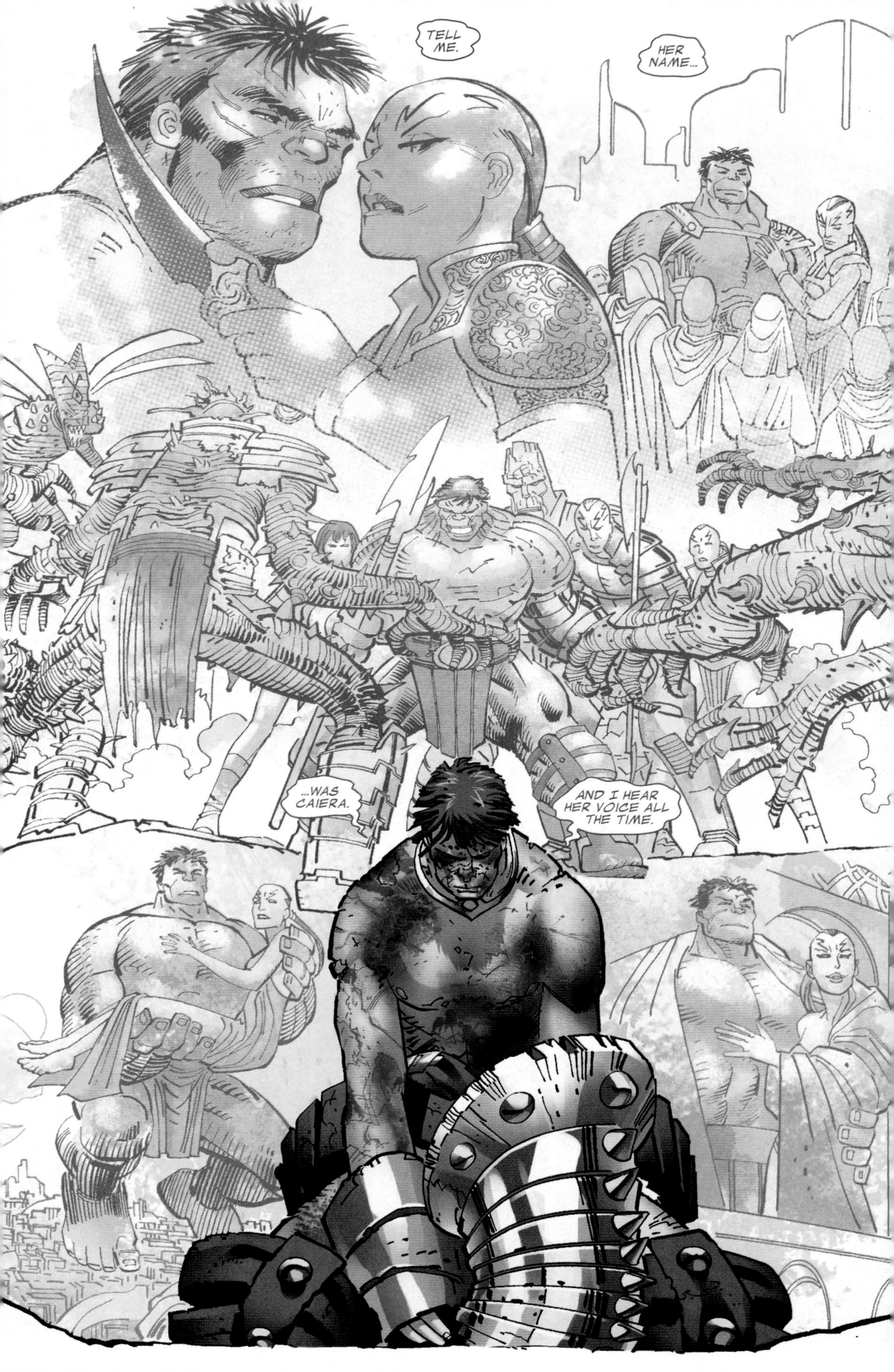
TELL ME.
HER NAME...
...WAS CAIERA.
AND I HEAR HER VOICE ALL THE TIME.

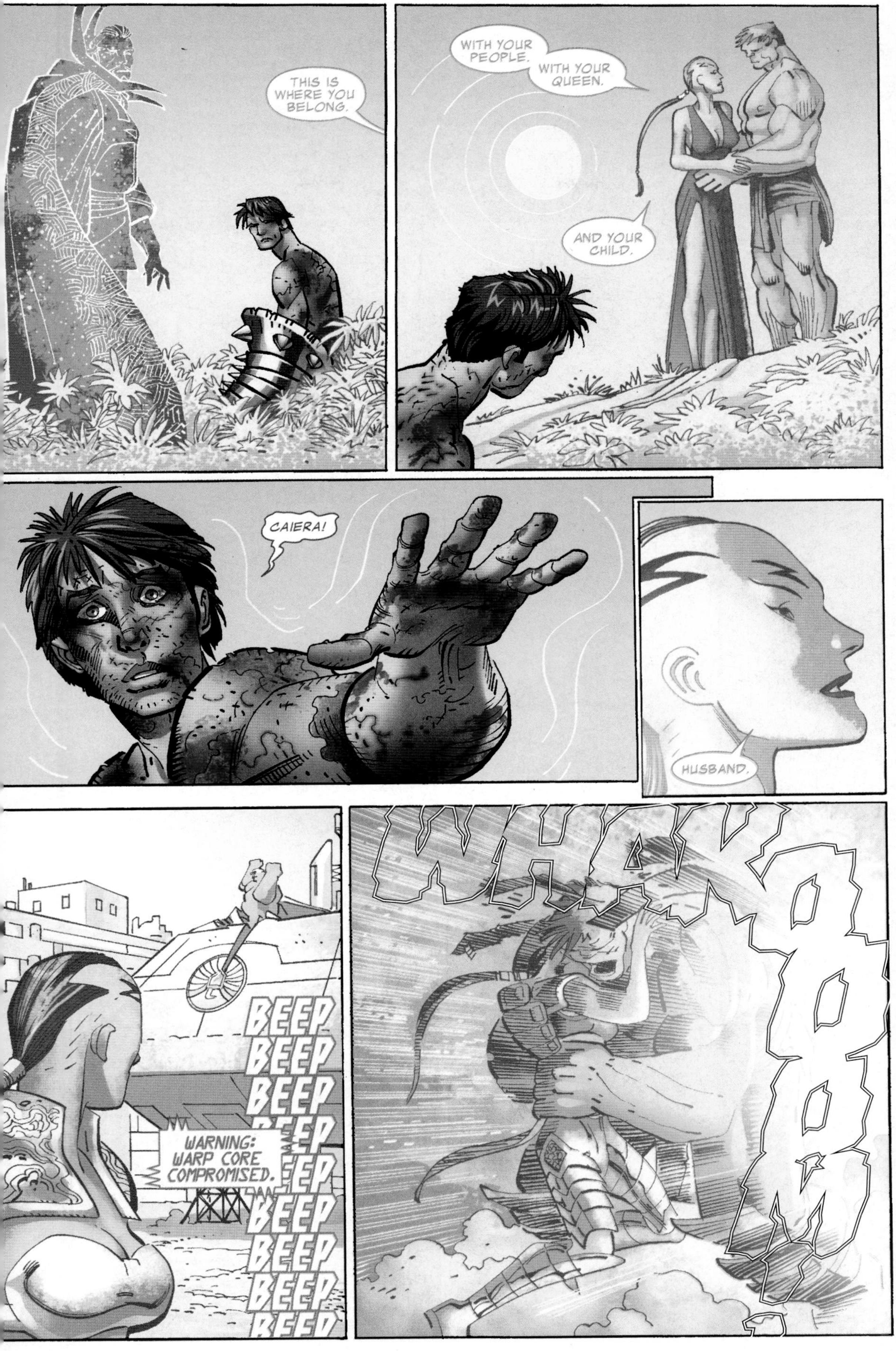
THIS IS WHERE YOU BELONG.
WITH YOUR PEOPLE.
WITH YOUR QUEEN.
AND YOUR CHILD.
CAIERA!
HUSBAND.
BEEP BEEP BEEP BEEP BEEP BEEP BEEP BEEP BEEP BEEP
WARNING: WARP CORE COMPROMISED.

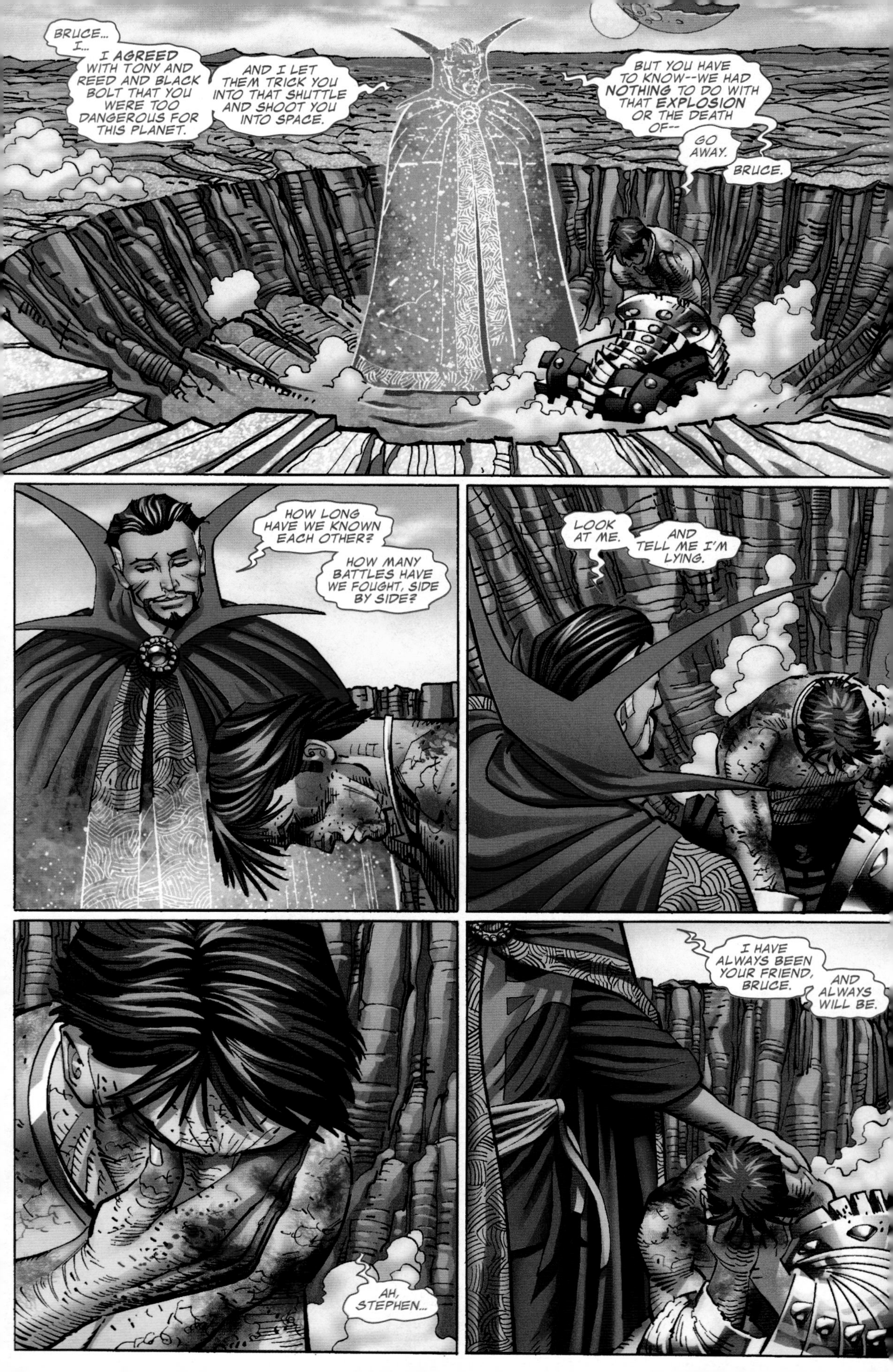
BRUCE... I...
I AGREED WITH TONY AND REED AND BLACK BOLT THAT YOU WERE TOO DANGEROUS FOR THIS PLANET.
AND I LET THEM TRICK YOU INTO THAT SHUTTLE AND SHOOT YOU INTO SPACE.
BUT YOU HAVE TO KNOW--WE HAD NOTHING TO DO WITH THAT EXPLOSION OR THE DEATH OF--
GO AWAY.
BRUCE.
HOW LONG HAVE WE KNOWN EACH OTHER?
HOW MANY BATTLES HAVE WE FOUGHT, SIDE BY SIDE?
LOOK AT ME.
AND TELL ME I'M LYING.
AH, STEPHEN...
I HAVE ALWAYS BEEN YOUR FRIEND, BRUCE.
AND ALWAYS WILL BE.

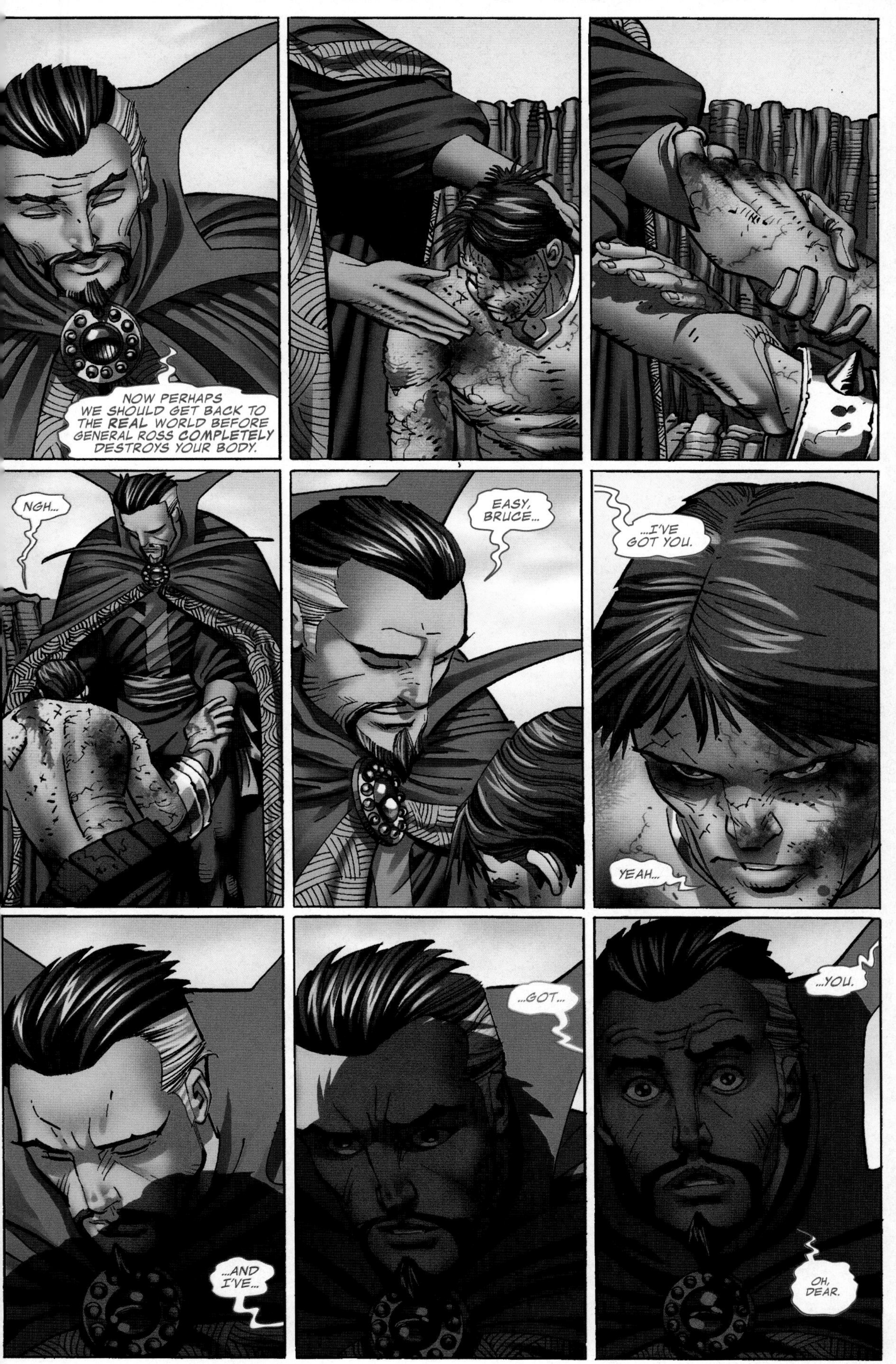
NOW PERHAPS WE SHOULD GET BACK TO THE REAL WORLD BEFORE GENERAL ROSS COMPLETELY DESTROYS YOUR BODY.
NGH...
EASY, BRUCE...
...I'VE GOT YOU.
YEAH...
...AND I'VE...
...GOT...
...YOU.
OH, DEAR.

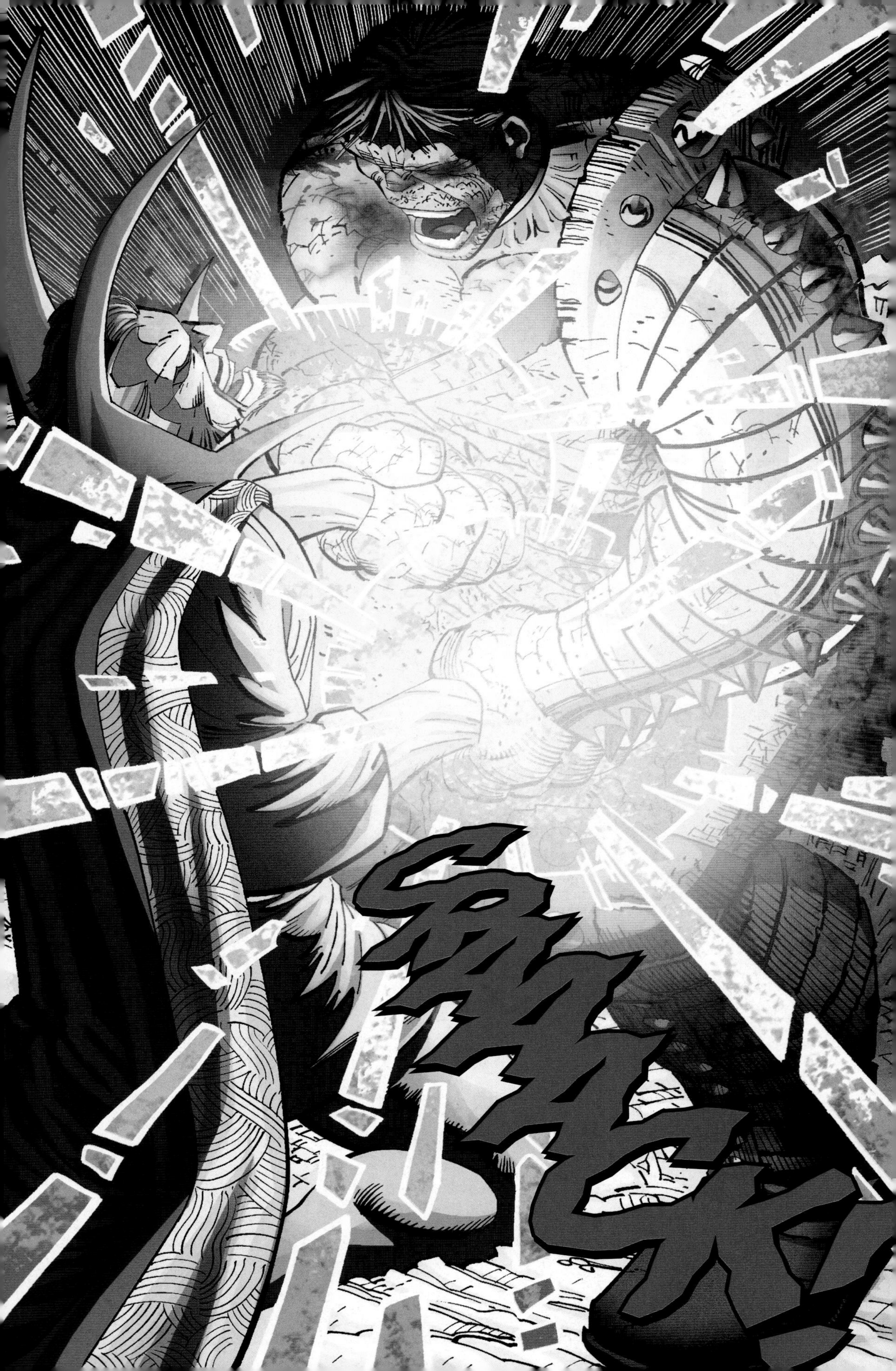
CRAACK!

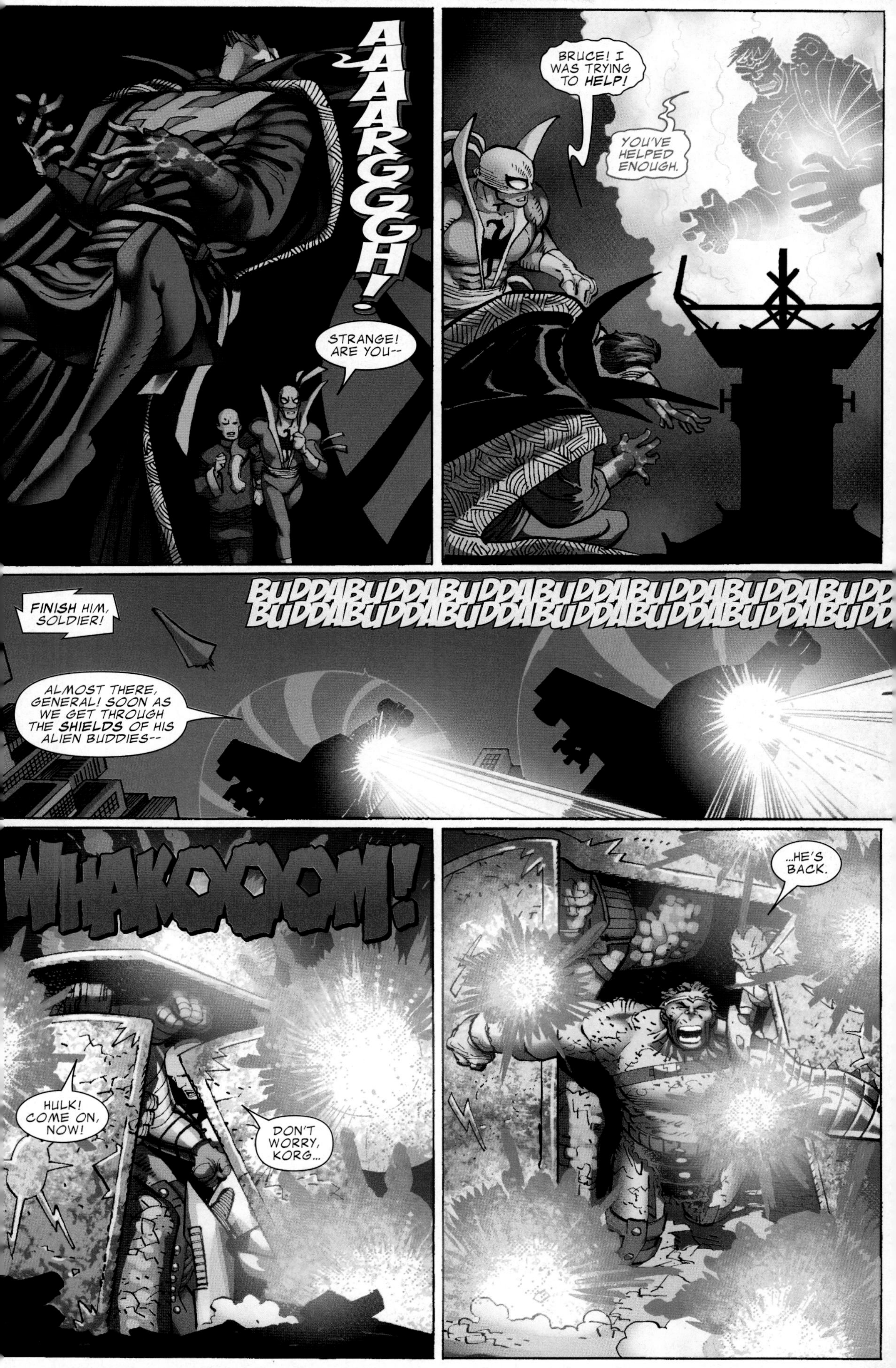
AAAARGGGH!
STRANGE! ARE YOU--
BRUCE! I WAS TRYING TO HELP!
YOU'VE HELPED ENOUGH.
BUDDABUDDABUDDABUDDABUDDABUDDABUDDABUDD
BUDDABUDDABUDDABUDDABUDDABUDDABUDDABUDD
FINISH HIM, SOLDIER!
ALMOST THERE, GENERAL! SOON AS WE GET THROUGH THE SHIELDS OF HIS ALIEN BUDDIES--
WHAKOOOM!
HULK! COME ON, NOW!
DON'T WORRY, KORG...
...HE'S BACK.

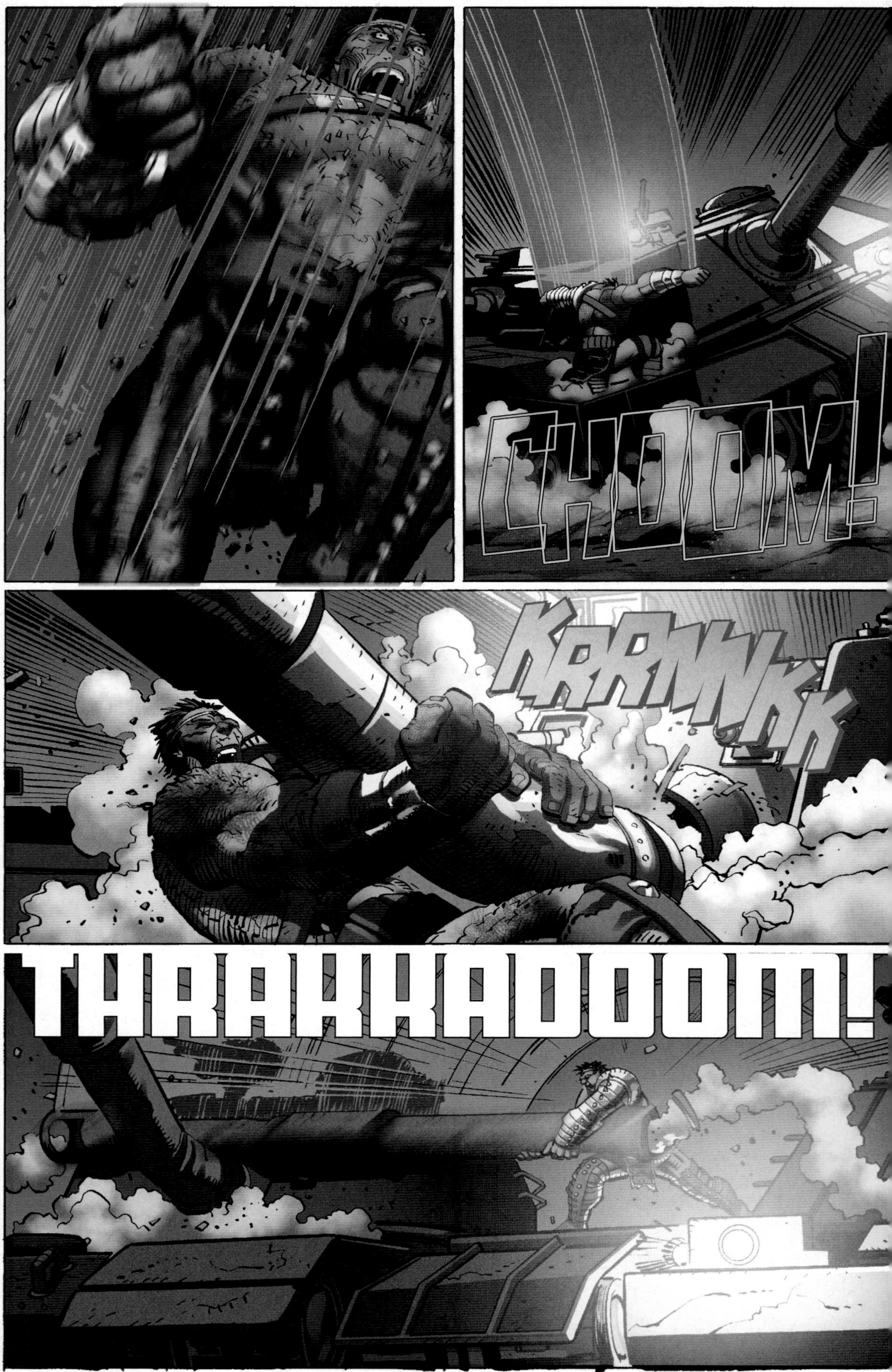
CHOOOM!
KRRNNKK
THRAKKADOOOM!

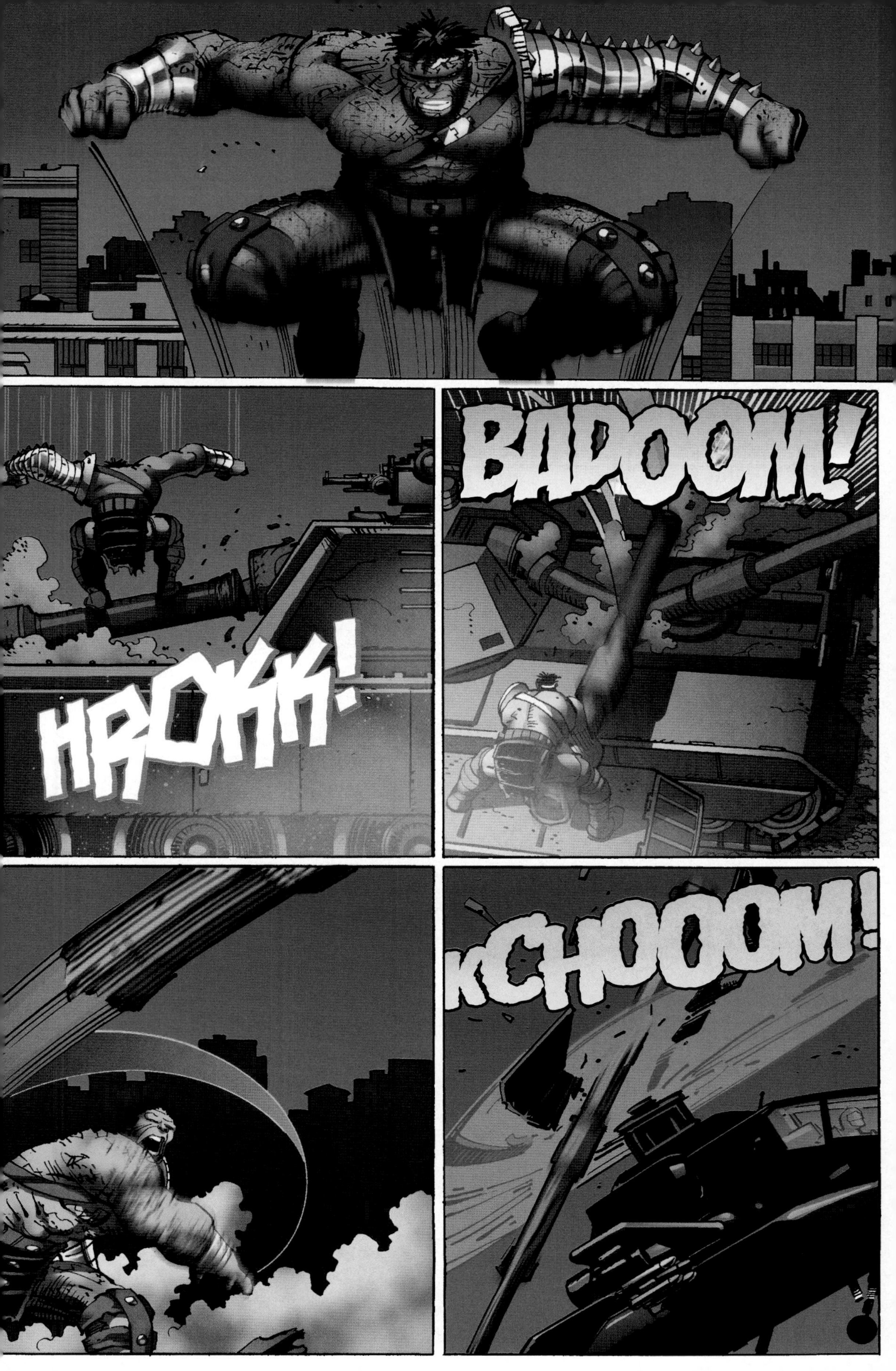
HROKK!
BADOOM!
KCHOOOM!

CHOOM!
CHOOM!

SKROOM!!

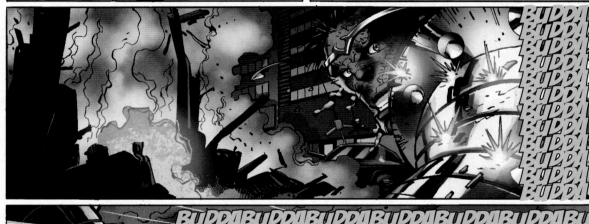

BUDDA
BUDDA
BUDDA
BUDDA
BUDDA
BUDDA
BUDDA
BUDDA
BUDDA
BUDDA

BUDDABUDDABUDDABUDDABUDDABUDDABU
BUDDABUDDABUDDABUDDABUDDABUDDABU

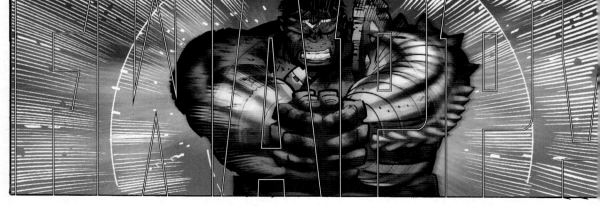

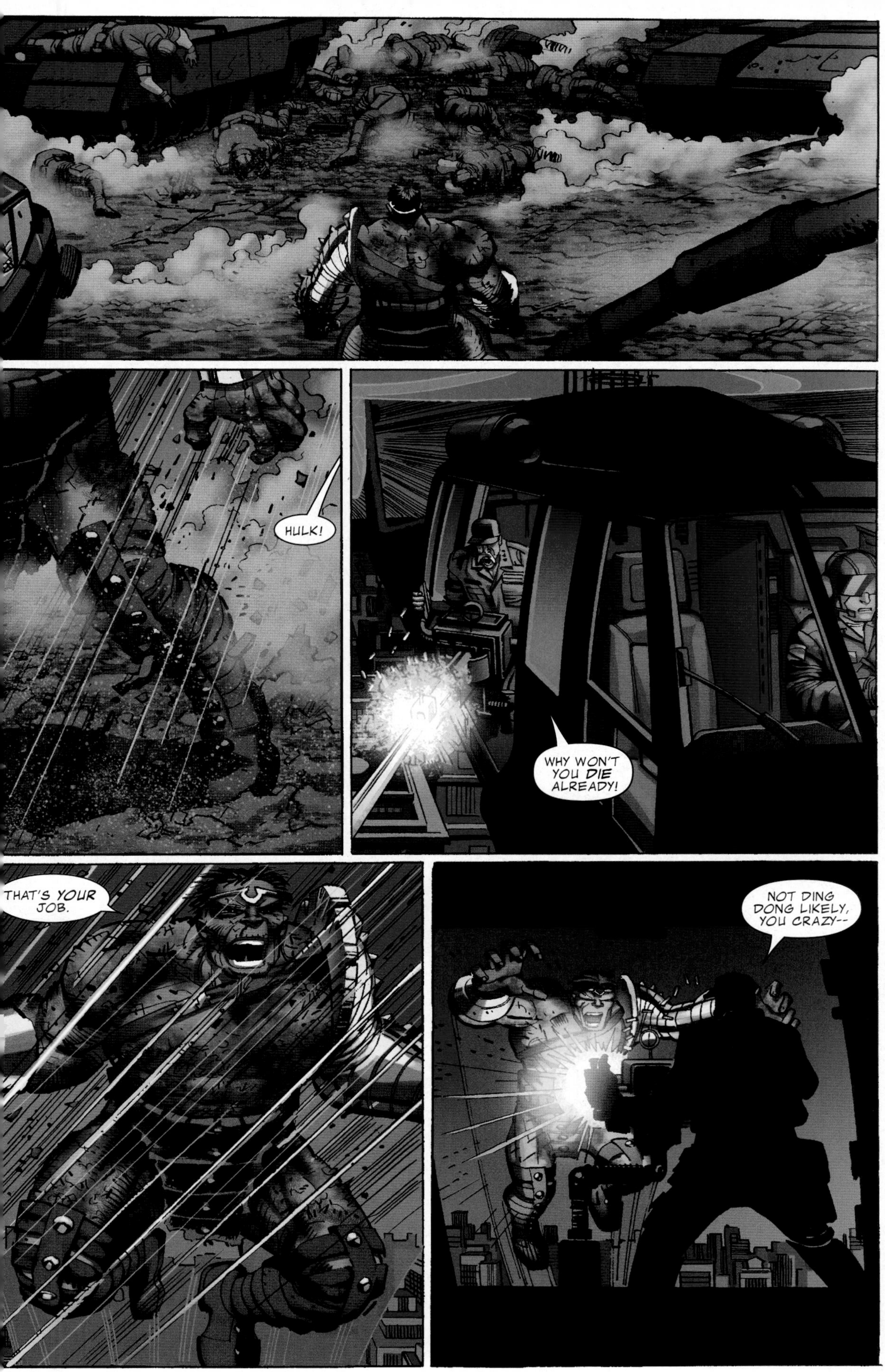
HULK!
WHY WON'T YOU DIE ALREADY!
THAT'S YOUR JOB.
NOT DING DONG LIKELY, YOU CRAZY--

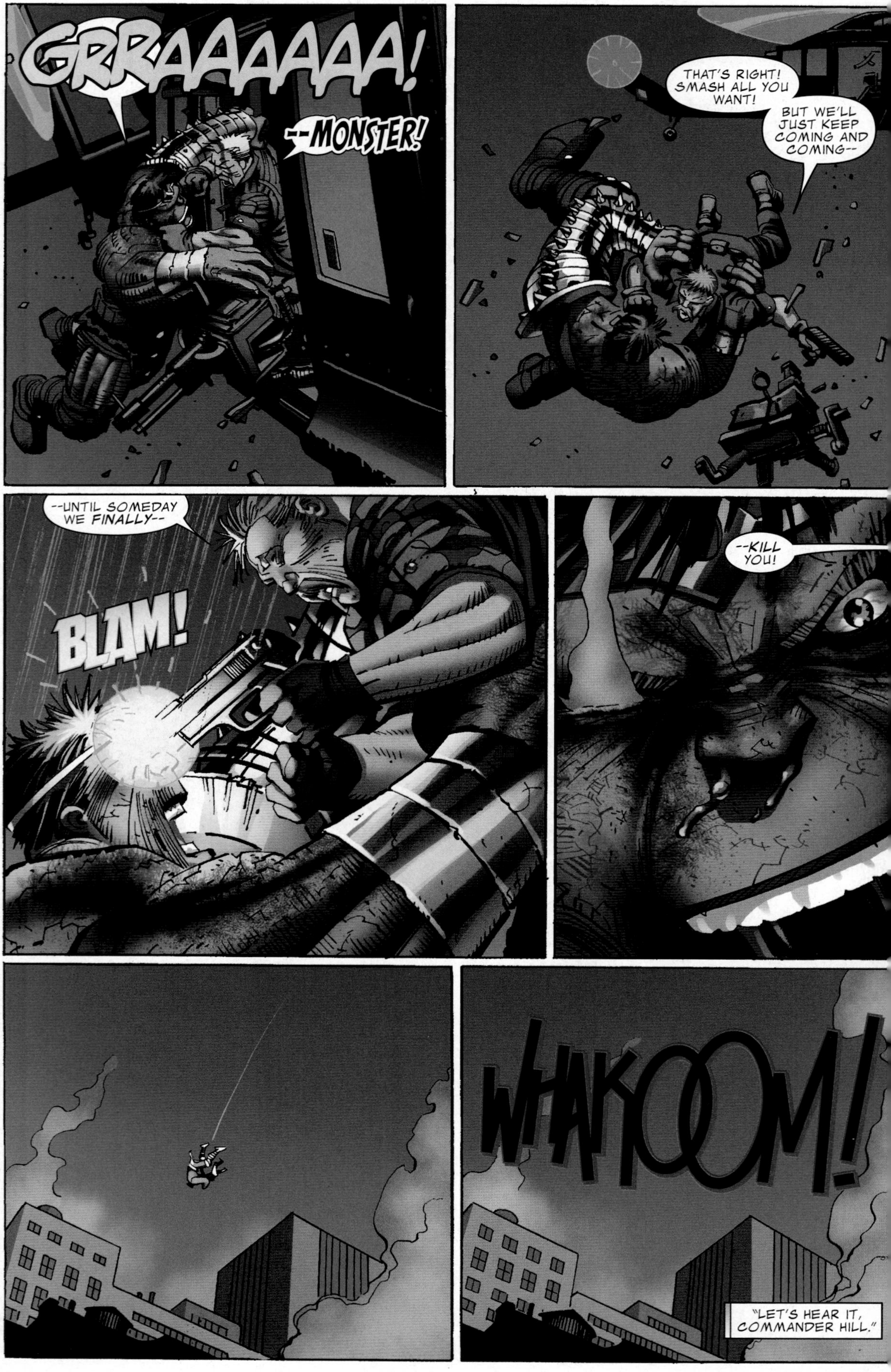
GRRAAAAAA!
--MONSTER!
THAT'S RIGHT! SMASH ALL YOU WANT!
BUT WE'LL JUST KEEP COMING AND COMING--
--UNTIL SOMEDAY WE FINALLY--
BLAM!
--KILL YOU!
WHAKOOM!
"LET'S HEAR IT, COMMANDER HILL."

ROSS IS DOWN. THERE'S ONLY ONE OPTION LEFT.

NUKES?

NO, SIR. EVERY SCIENTIST ON THE PAYROLL SAYS THAT WOULD ONLY MAKE THE HULK *STRONGER*.

IT'S TIME TO APPEAL TO A *HIGHER* POWER...

"... PLEASE REMEMBER, SIR, WE NEED YOU TO STAY ON *SCRIPT*. THE SENTRY'S THE MOST *POWERFUL* SUPER HERO ON THE PLANET..."

"...BUT HE'S ALSO AN AGORAPHOBIC SCHIZOPHRENIC.

"HE'S SCARED OF THE WORLD. TERRIFIED OF *HIMSELF*. HE NEEDS TO BE REASSURED EVERY STEP OF THE WAY THAT WHAT WE WANT HIM TO DO IS THE *RIGHT* THING TO DO."

MR. REYNOLDS. THIS IS YOUR PRESIDENT SPEAKING.

AND I'VE GOT A JOB FOR YOU.

THE HEROES NEED YOUR HELP.

THEY'RE YOUR *FRIENDS*. AND THEY *BELIEVE* IN YOU. JUST LIKE I DO.

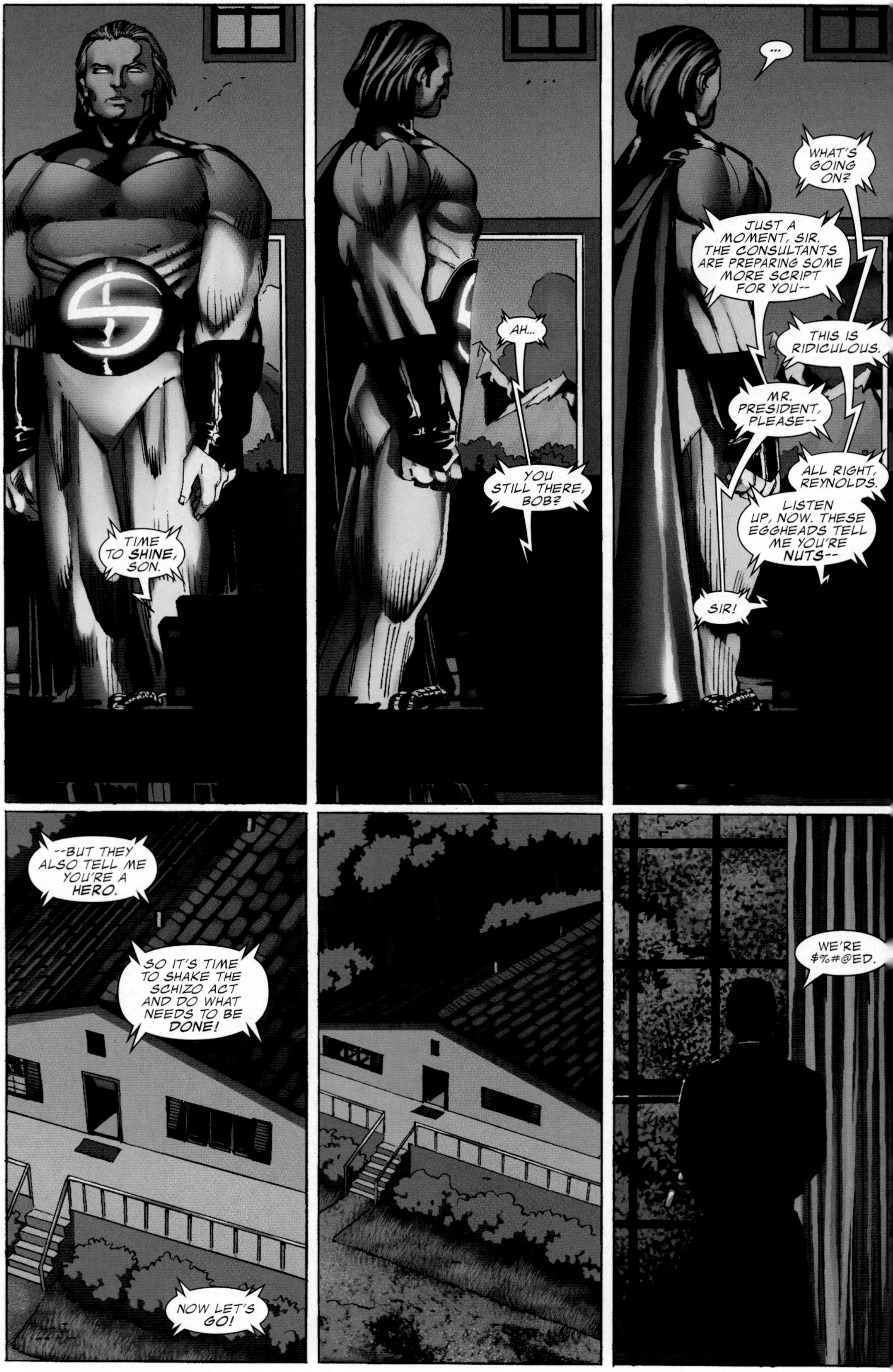

TIME TO SHINE, SON.
...
AH...
YOU STILL THERE, BOB?
...
WHAT'S GOING ON?
JUST A MOMENT, SIR. THE CONSULTANTS ARE PREPARING SOME MORE SCRIPT FOR YOU--
THIS IS RIDICULOUS.
MR. PRESIDENT, PLEASE--
ALL RIGHT, REYNOLDS.
LISTEN UP, NOW. THESE EGGHEADS TELL ME YOU'RE NUTS--
SIR!
--BUT THEY ALSO TELL ME YOU'RE A HERO.
SO IT'S TIME TO SHAKE THE SCHIZO ACT AND DO WHAT NEEDS TO BE DONE!
NOW LET'S GO!
WE'RE $%#@ED.

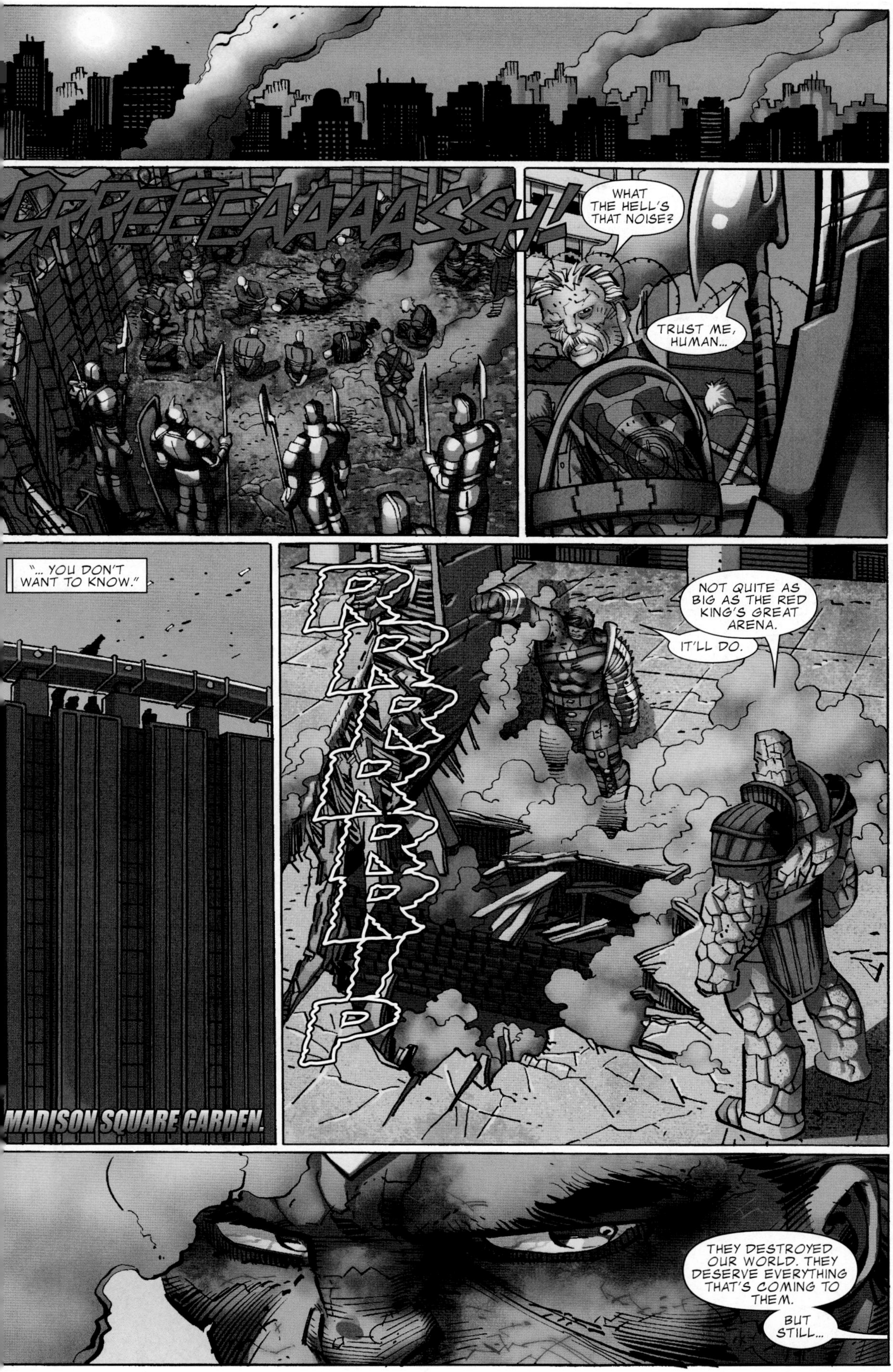

SKRREEEAAAAASSH!
WHAT THE HELL'S THAT NOISE?
TRUST ME, HUMAN...
"... YOU DON'T WANT TO KNOW."
MADISON SQUARE GARDEN.
NOT QUITE AS BIG AS THE RED KING'S GREAT ARENA.
IT'LL DO.
THEY DESTROYED OUR WORLD. THEY DESERVE EVERYTHING THAT'S COMING TO THEM.
BUT STILL...

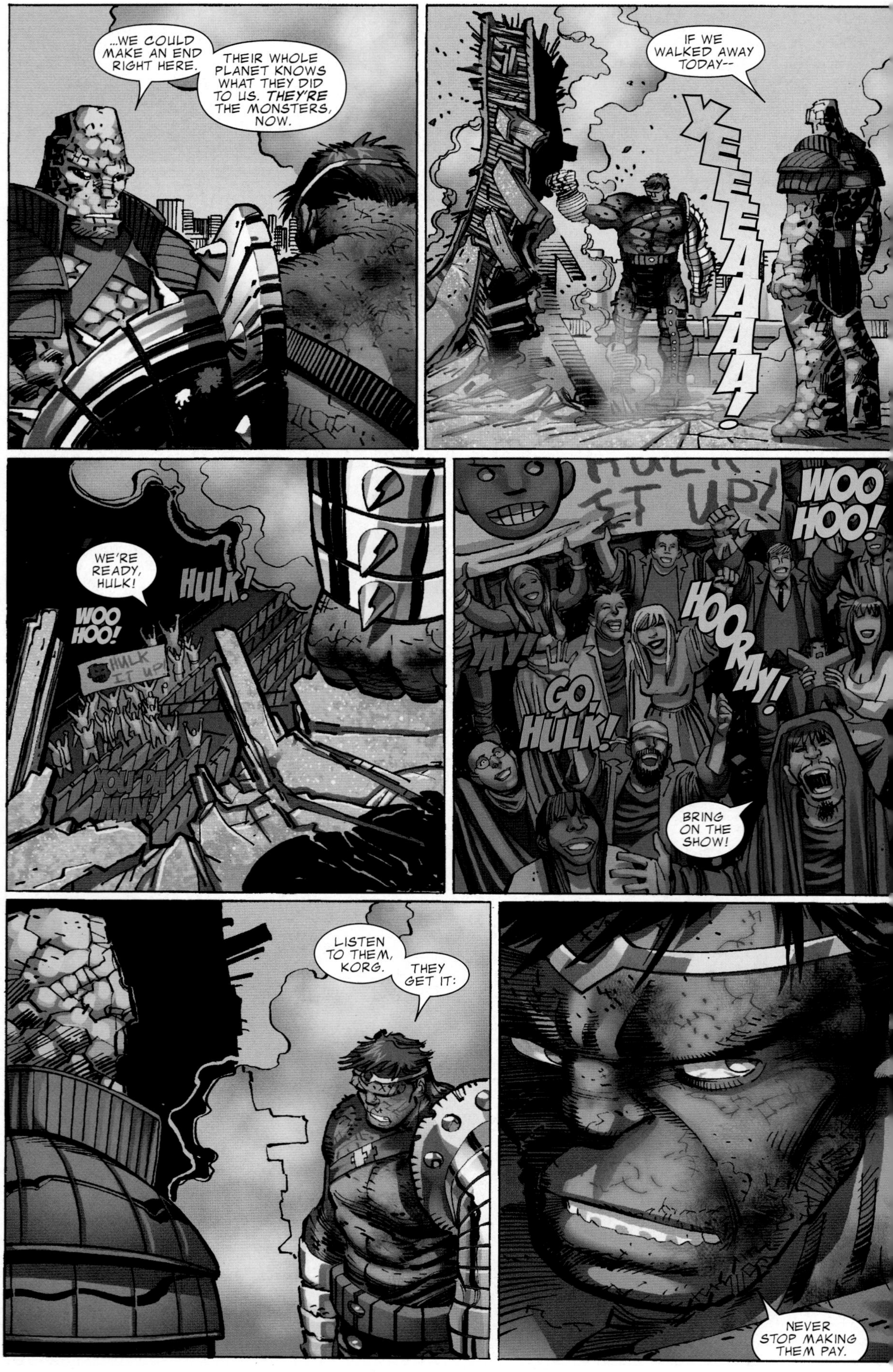
...WE COULD MAKE AN END RIGHT HERE.
THEIR WHOLE PLANET KNOWS WHAT THEY DID TO US. THEY'RE THE MONSTERS, NOW.
IF WE WALKED AWAY TODAY--
YEEEAAAAA!
WE'RE READY, HULK!
HULK!
WOO HOO!
HULK IT UP!
YOU DA MAN!
WOO HOO!
HOORAY!
YAY!
GO, HULK!
BRING ON THE SHOW!
LISTEN TO THEM, KORG.
THEY GET IT:
NEVER STOP MAKING THEM PAY.

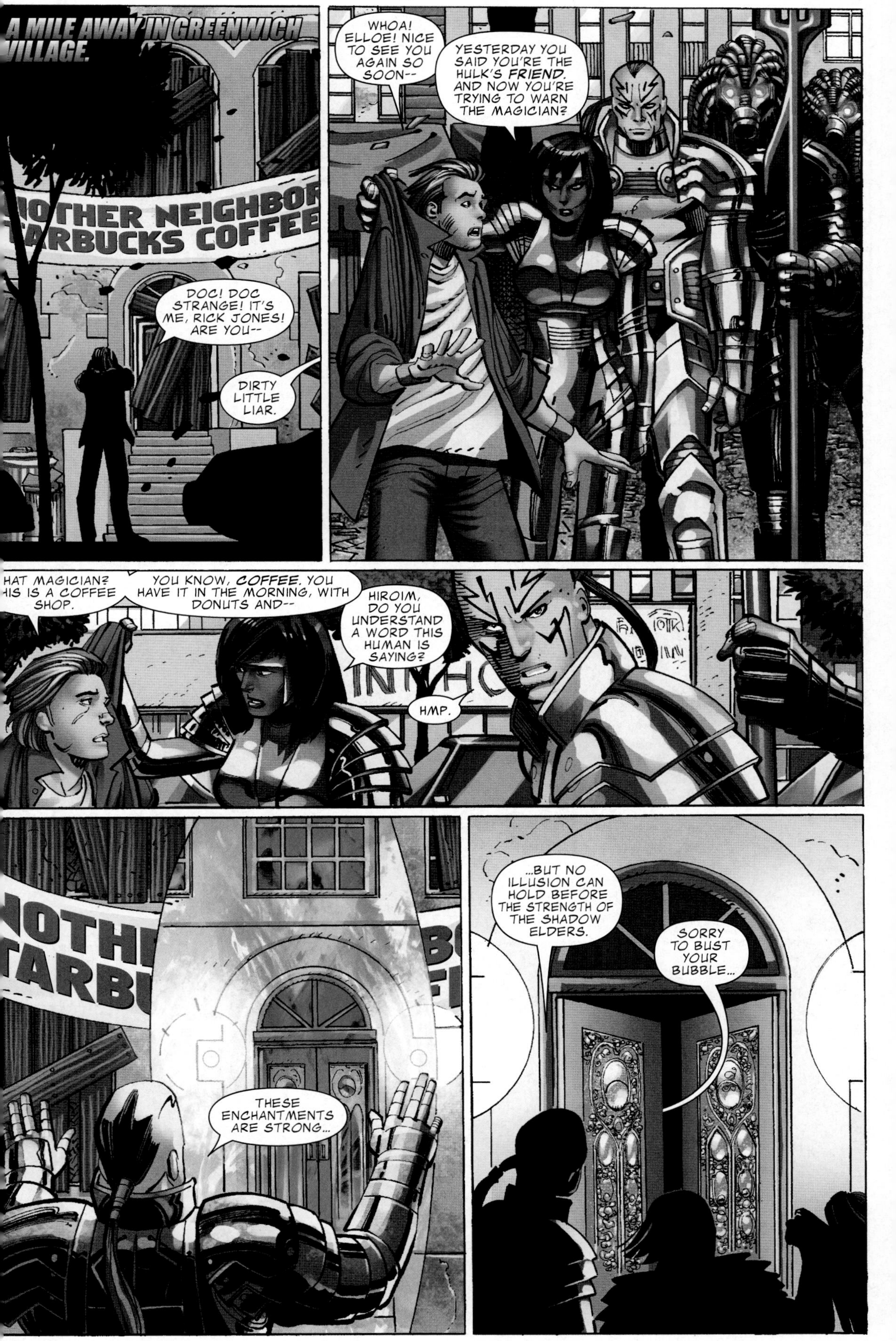
A MILE AWAY IN GREENWICH VILLAGE.
NOTHER NEIGHBOR
TARBUCKS COFFEE
DOC! DOC STRANGE! IT'S ME, RICK JONES! ARE YOU--
DIRTY LITTLE LIAR.
WHOA! ELLOE! NICE TO SEE YOU AGAIN SO SOON--
YESTERDAY YOU SAID YOU'RE THE HULK'S FRIEND. AND NOW YOU'RE TRYING TO WARN THE MAGICIAN?
HAT MAGICIAN? HIS IS A COFFEE SHOP.
YOU KNOW, COFFEE. YOU HAVE IT IN THE MORNING, WITH DONUTS AND--
HIROIM, DO YOU UNDERSTAND A WORD THIS HUMAN IS SAYING?
HMP.
THESE ENCHANTMENTS ARE STRONG...
...BUT NO ILLUSION CAN HOLD BEFORE THE STRENGTH OF THE SHADOW ELDERS.
SORRY TO BUST YOUR BUBBLE...

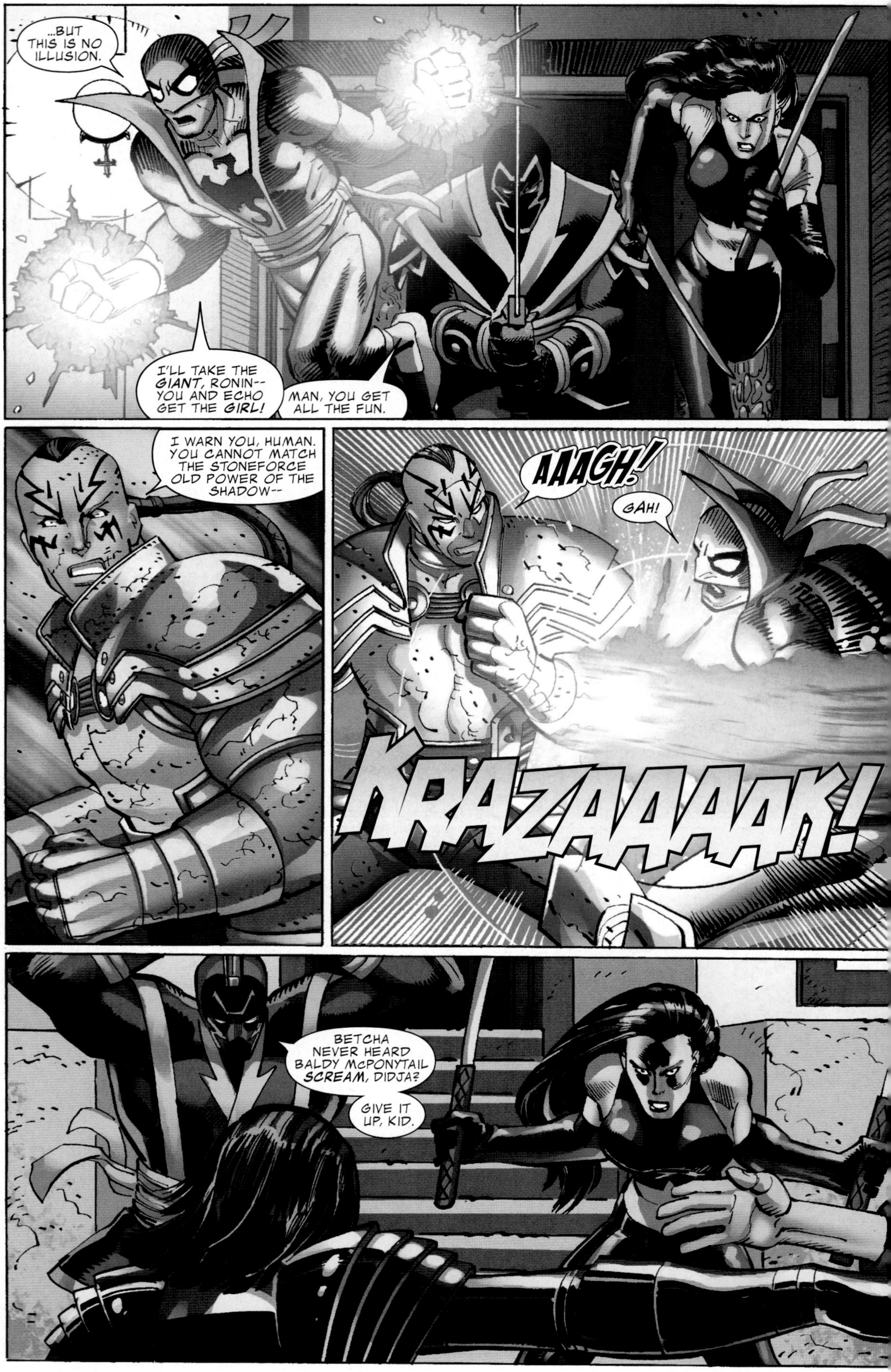
...BUT THIS IS NO ILLUSION.
I'LL TAKE THE GIANT, RONIN-- YOU AND ECHO GET THE GIRL!
MAN, YOU GET ALL THE FUN.
I WARN YOU, HUMAN. YOU CANNOT MATCH THE STONEFORCE OLD POWER OF THE SHADOW--
AAAGH!
GAH!
KRAZAAAAK!
BETCHA NEVER HEARD BALDY McPONYTAIL SCREAM, DIDJA?
GIVE IT UP, KID.

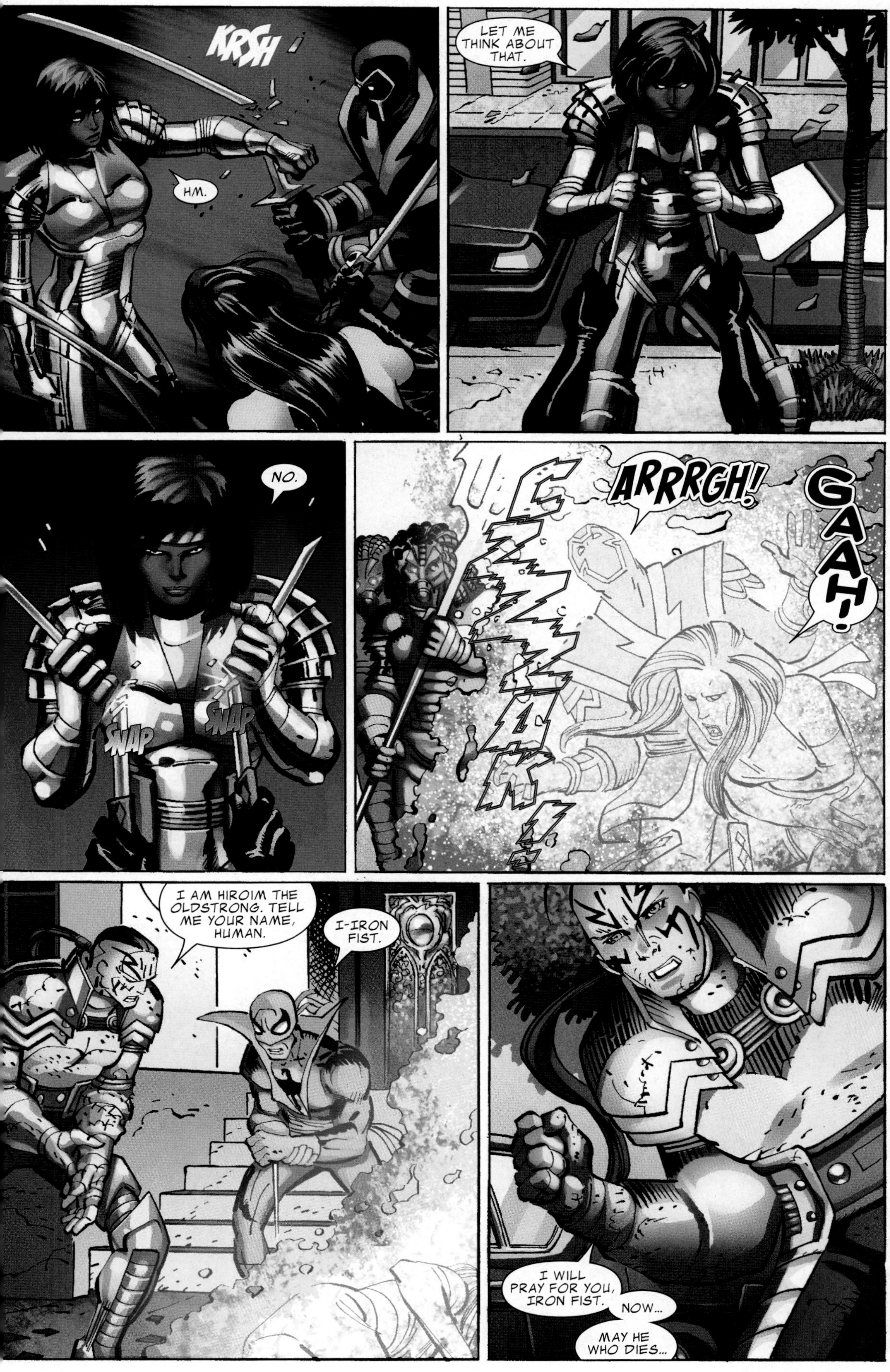
KRSH
HM.
LET ME THINK ABOUT THAT.
NO.
SNAP
SNAP
ARRRGH!
GAAH!
I AM HIROIM THE OLDSTRONG. TELL ME YOUR NAME, HUMAN.
I-IRON FIST.
I WILL PRAY FOR YOU, IRON FIST.
NOW...
MAY HE WHO DIES...

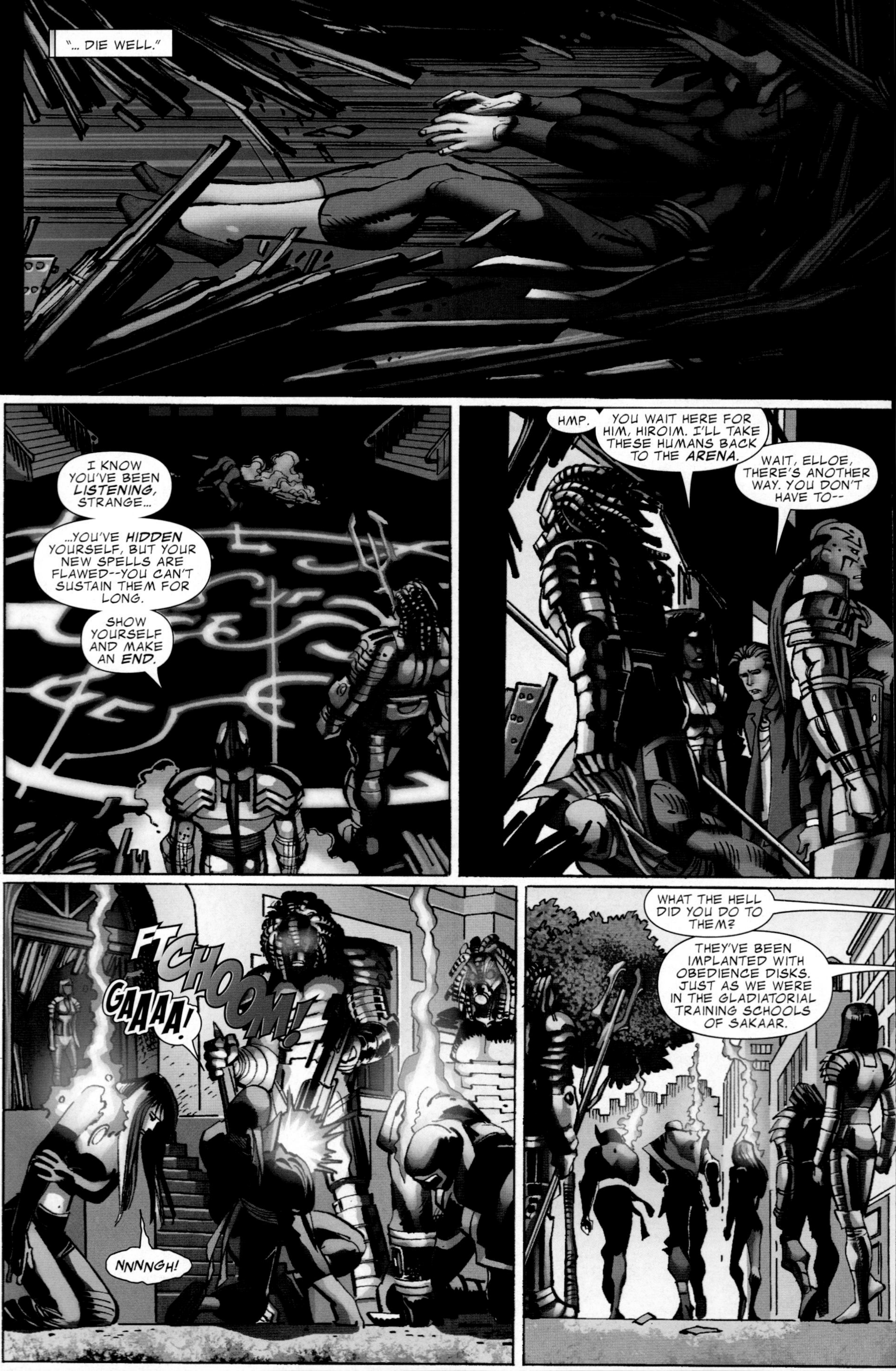
"... DIE WELL."
I KNOW YOU'VE BEEN LISTENING, STRANGE...
...YOU'VE HIDDEN YOURSELF, BUT YOUR NEW SPELLS ARE FLAWED--YOU CAN'T SUSTAIN THEM FOR LONG.
SHOW YOURSELF AND MAKE AN END.
HMP.
YOU WAIT HERE FOR HIM, HIROIM. I'LL TAKE THESE HUMANS BACK TO THE ARENA.
WAIT, ELLOE, THERE'S ANOTHER WAY. YOU DON'T HAVE TO--
FTCHOOM!
GAAAA!
NNNNGH!
WHAT THE HELL DID YOU DO TO THEM?
THEY'VE BEEN IMPLANTED WITH OBEDIENCE DISKS. JUST AS WE WERE IN THE GLADIATORIAL TRAINING SCHOOLS OF SAKAAR.

HIROIM...YOU SAID YOU WERE A PRIEST. YOU KNOW THIS IS WRONG.

OF COURSE IT IS, RICK JONES.

AND SOME DAY WE WARBOUND WILL PAY FOR THE RAGE IN OUR HEARTS.

BUT FIRST...

"...WE'LL MAKE *YOU* PAY."

DOCTOR! YOU HAVE TO LET ME LOOK AT YOUR HANDS!

THERE'S NO TIME, WONG. I CAN *HEAR* THE SHADOW PRIEST--HE'S *BURNING* THROUGH THE SPELLS THAT HIDE US, AND WITH THESE BROKEN HANDS...

...I CAN'T DO A THING TO STOP HIM.

BRUCE. YOU'RE REALLY GOING TO KILL THEM ALL, AREN'T YOU?

NO. YOU *KNOW* BANNER. HE WOULDN'T--

YOU DIDN'T *SEE* HIM, WONG. YOU DIDN'T FEEL HIS *RAGE.* IT'S BEYOND ANYTHING I EVER...

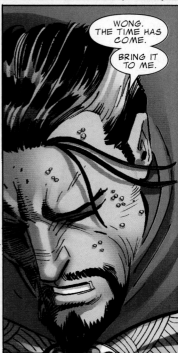

WONG. THE TIME HAS COME.

BRING IT TO ME.

NO, DOCTOR. YOU CAN'T.

I CAN. AND MUST.

NOW BRING ME THE *BOX.*

SKRRRREEEE!

DOCTOR... THE WALLS...

THE SHADOW PRIEST COMES. SO YOU MUST *GO.* AS FAST AND FAR AS YOU CAN.

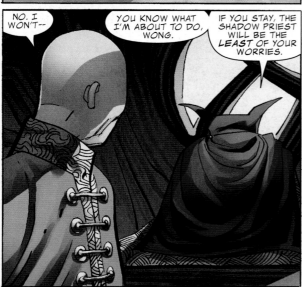

NO. I WON'T--

YOU KNOW WHAT I'M ABOUT TO DO, WONG.

IF YOU STAY, THE SHADOW PRIEST WILL BE THE *LEAST* OF YOUR WORRIES.

IN THE NAME OF THE ETERNAL...

BY THE RINGS OF RAGGADORR...

THOUGH HIS SPIRIT BE INFERNAL...

ZOM MUST LIVE ONCE MORE.

AND MAY HE WHO DIES...

...DIE WELL.

SKRRASH!

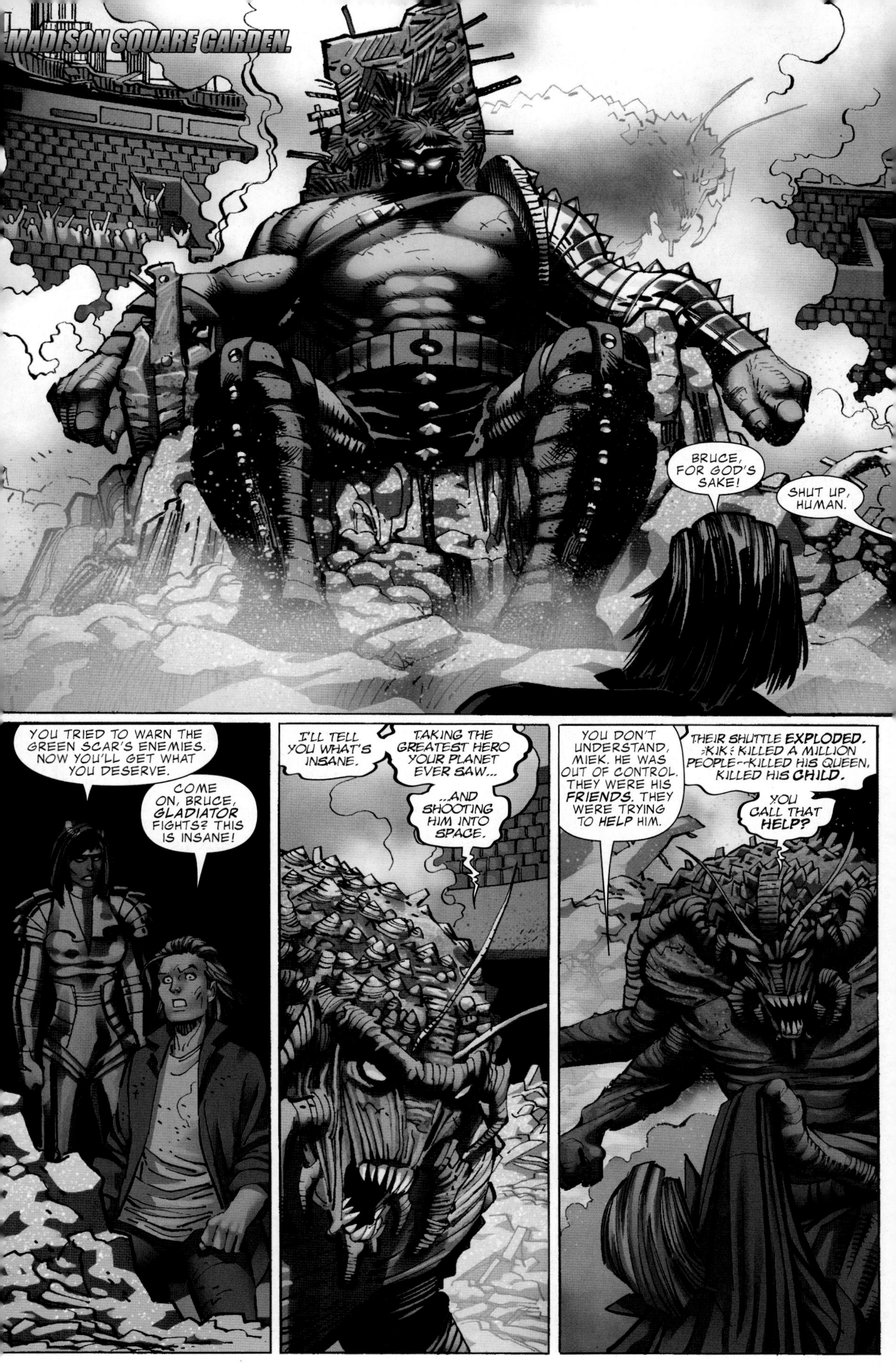
MADISON SQUARE GARDEN.
BRUCE, FOR GOD'S SAKE!
SHUT UP, HUMAN.
YOU TRIED TO WARN THE GREEN SCAR'S ENEMIES. NOW YOU'LL GET WHAT YOU DESERVE.
COME ON, BRUCE, GLADIATOR FIGHTS? THIS IS INSANE!
I'LL TELL YOU WHAT'S INSANE.
TAKING THE GREATEST HERO YOUR PLANET EVER SAW...
...AND SHOOTING HIM INTO SPACE.
YOU DON'T UNDERSTAND, MIEK. HE WAS OUT OF CONTROL. THEY WERE HIS FRIENDS. THEY WERE TRYING TO HELP HIM.
THEIR SHUTTLE EXPLODED. KIK KILLED A MILLION PEOPLE--KILLED HIS QUEEN, KILLED HIS CHILD.
YOU CALL THAT HELP?

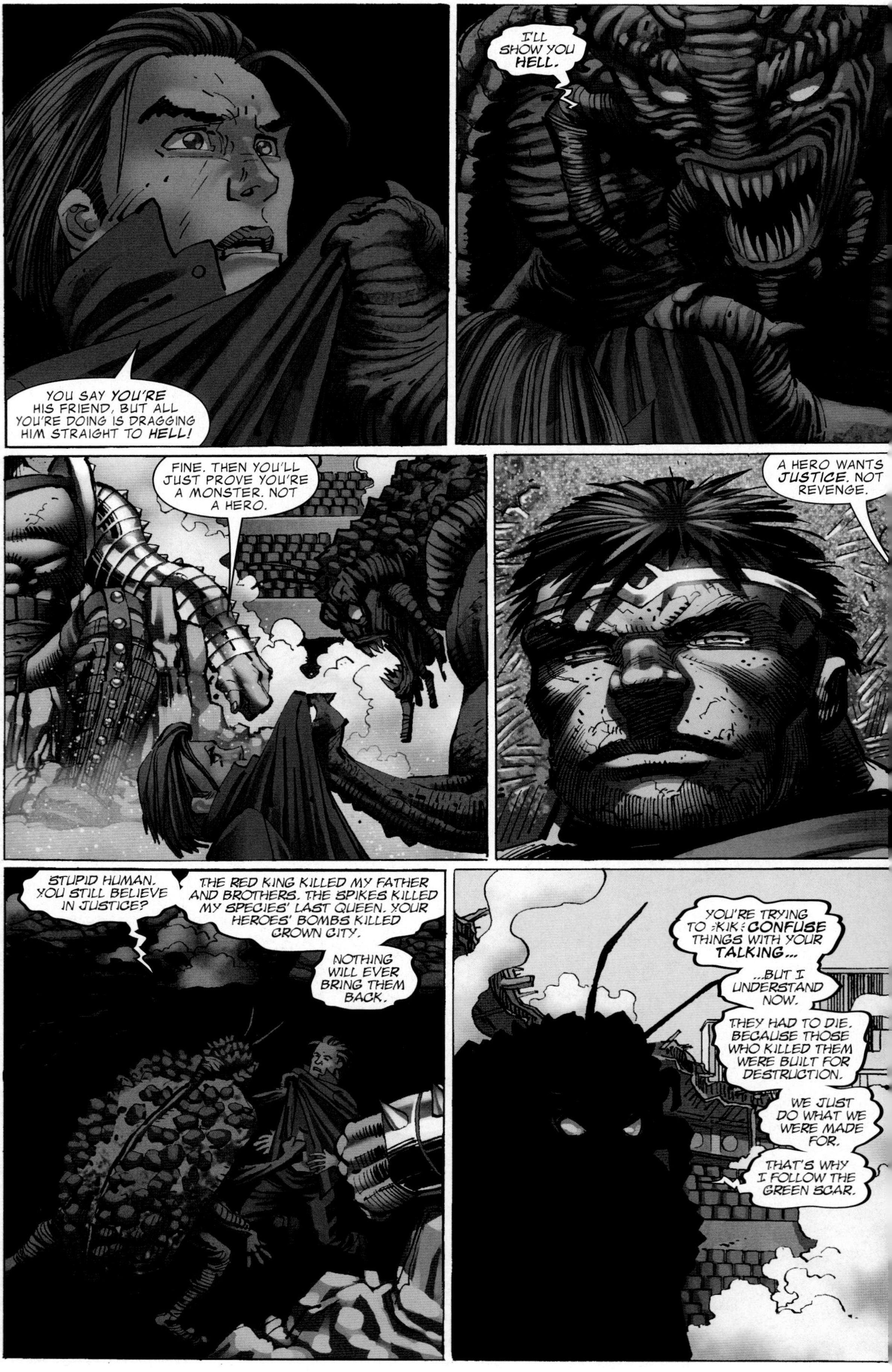
YOU SAY YOU'RE HIS FRIEND, BUT ALL YOU'RE DOING IS DRAGGING HIM STRAIGHT TO HELL!
I'LL SHOW YOU HELL.
FINE. THEN YOU'LL JUST PROVE YOU'RE A MONSTER. NOT A HERO.
A HERO WANTS JUSTICE. NOT REVENGE.
STUPID HUMAN. YOU STILL BELIEVE IN JUSTICE?
THE RED KING KILLED MY FATHER AND BROTHERS. THE SPIKES KILLED MY SPECIES' LAST QUEEN. YOUR HEROES' BOMBS KILLED CROWN CITY.
NOTHING WILL EVER BRING THEM BACK.
YOU'RE TRYING TO :KIK: CONFUSE THINGS WITH YOUR TALKING...
...BUT I UNDERSTAND NOW.
THEY HAD TO DIE. BECAUSE THOSE WHO KILLED THEM WERE BUILT FOR DESTRUCTION.
WE JUST DO WHAT WE WERE MADE FOR.
THAT'S WHY I FOLLOW THE GREEN SCAR.

...BECAUSE HE IS THE WORLDBREAKER.

SO COME, LITTLE HUMAN. IT'S TIME TO MAKE AN END TO--

WHAKOOM!

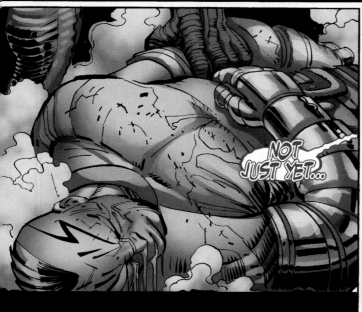

NOT JUST YET...

...FIRST...

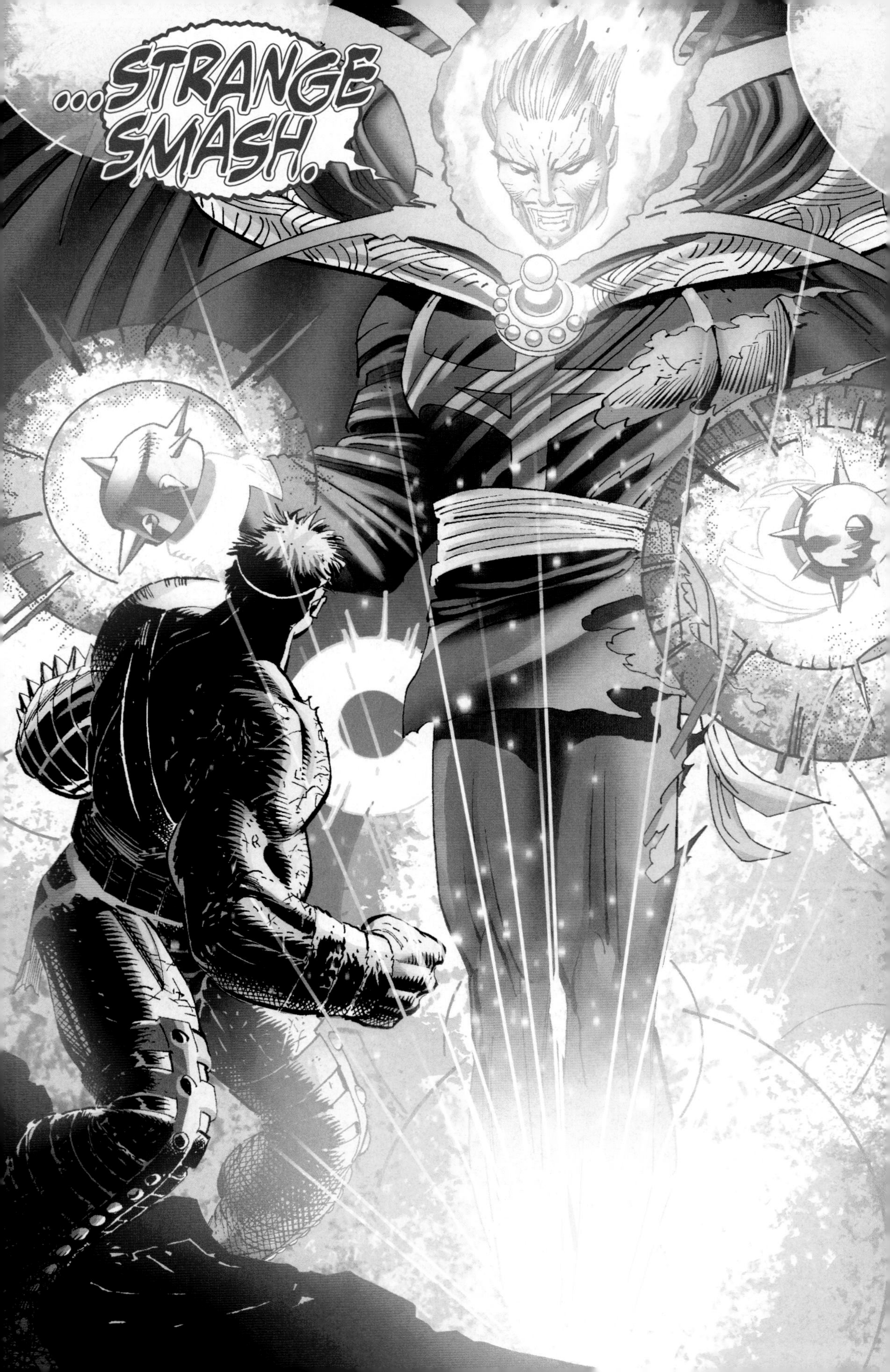
...STRANGE SMASH.

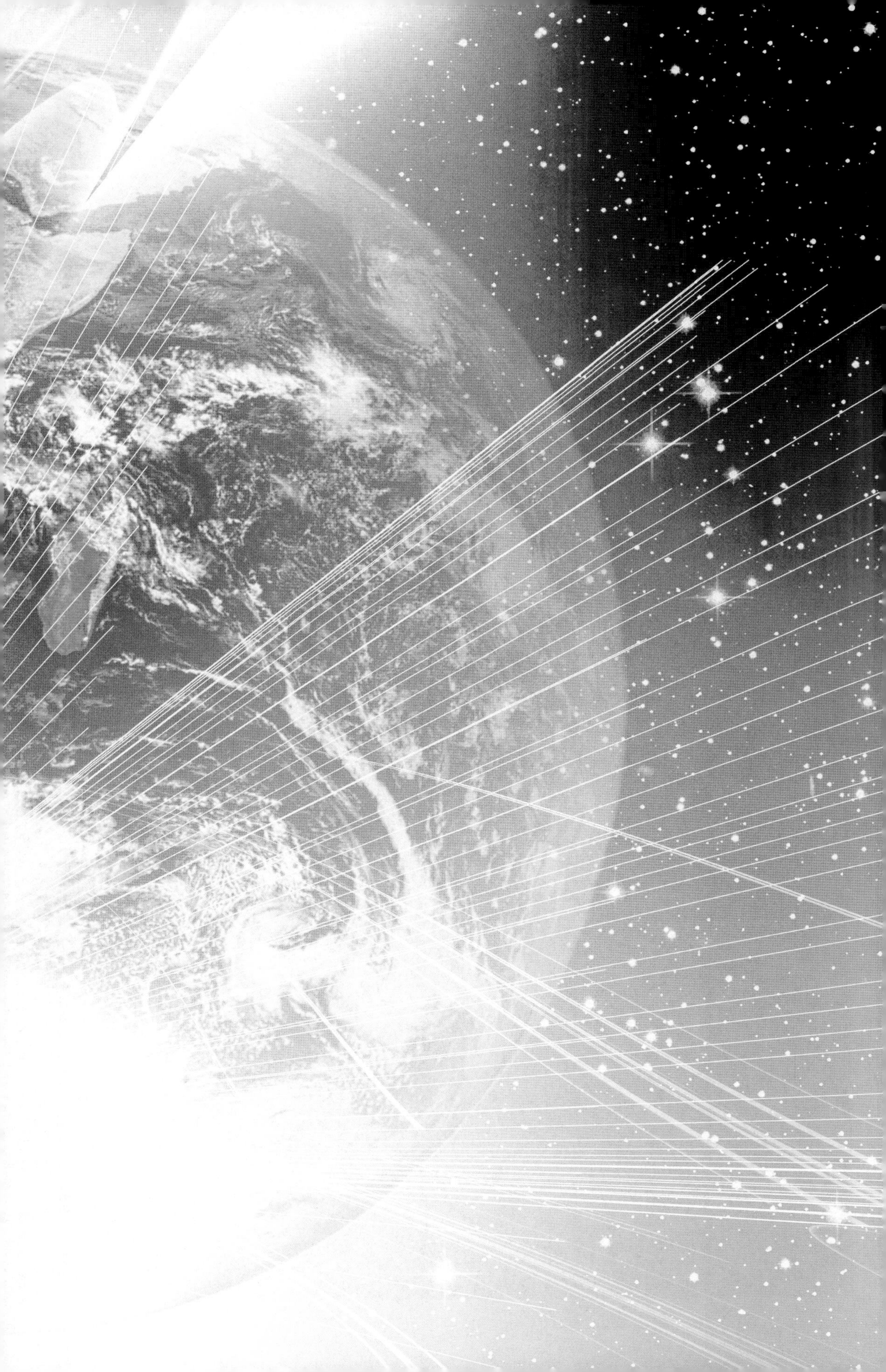

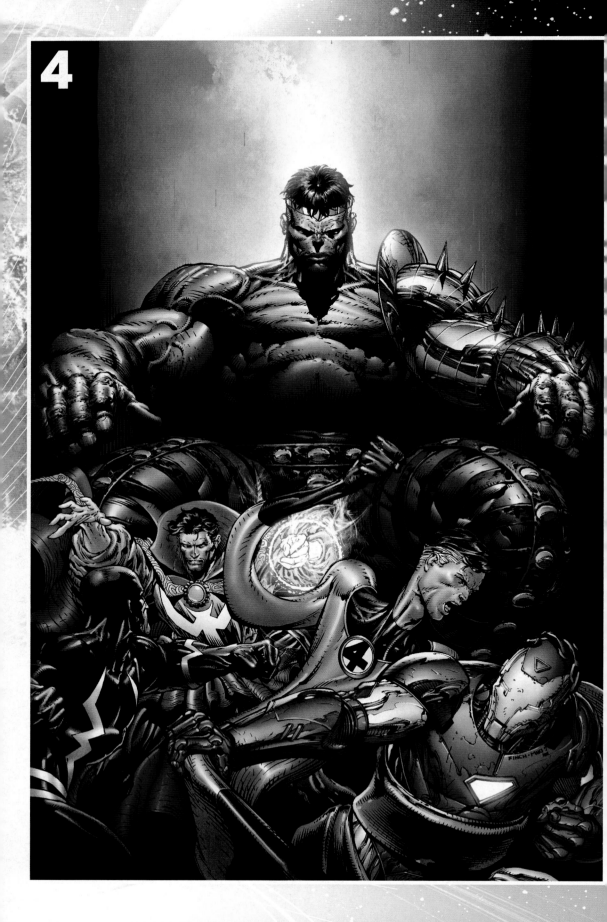

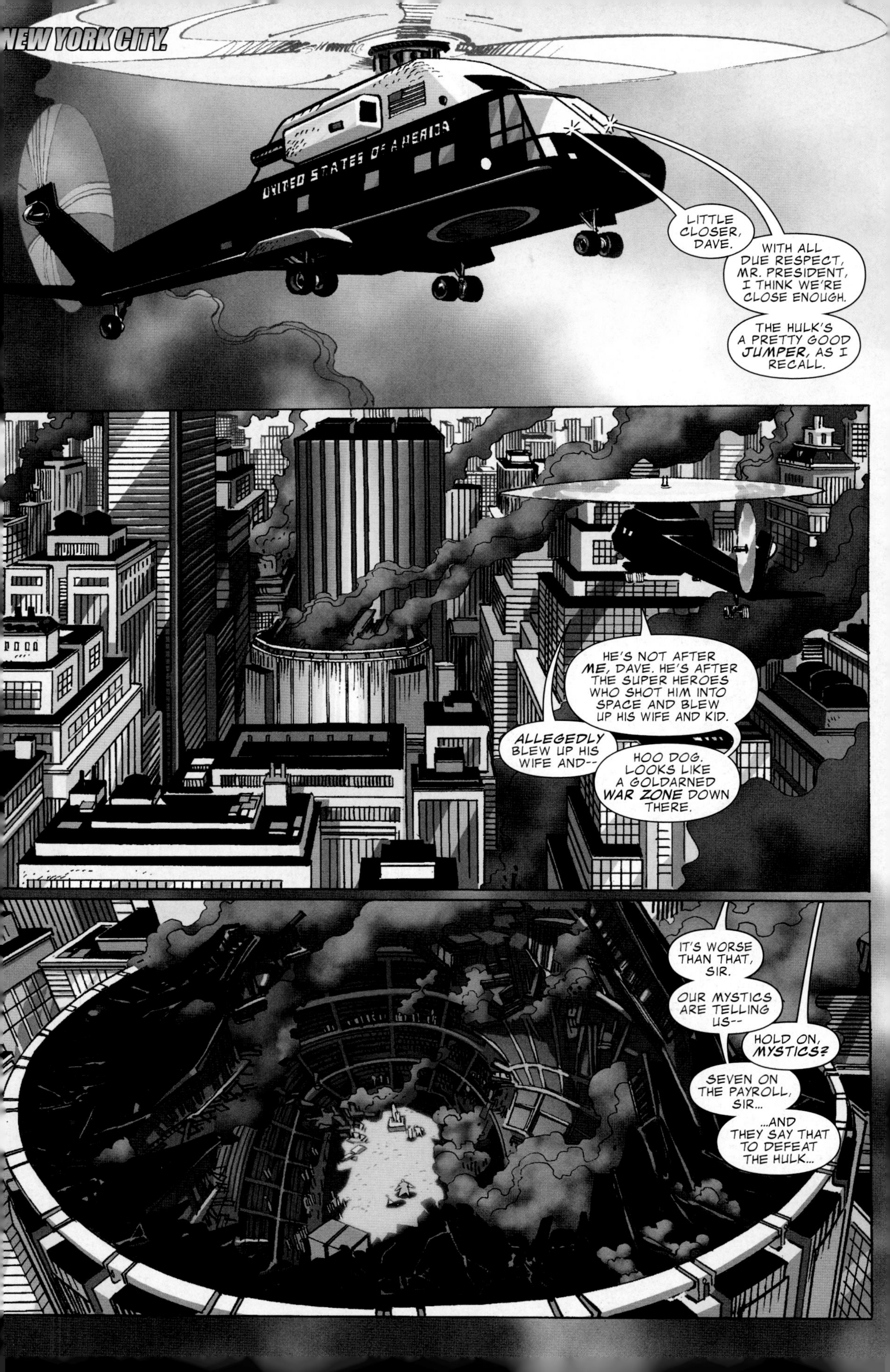
NEW YORK CITY.
UNITED STATES OF AMERICA
LITTLE CLOSER, DAVE.
WITH ALL DUE RESPECT, MR. PRESIDENT, I THINK WE'RE CLOSE ENOUGH.
THE HULK'S A PRETTY GOOD JUMPER, AS I RECALL.
HE'S NOT AFTER ME, DAVE. HE'S AFTER THE SUPER HEROES WHO SHOT HIM INTO SPACE AND BLEW UP HIS WIFE AND KID.
ALLEGEDLY BLEW UP HIS WIFE AND--
HOO DOG. LOOKS LIKE A GOLDARNED WAR ZONE DOWN THERE.
IT'S WORSE THAN THAT, SIR.
OUR MYSTICS ARE TELLING US--
HOLD ON, MYSTICS?
SEVEN ON THE PAYROLL, SIR...
...AND THEY SAY THAT TO DEFEAT THE HULK...

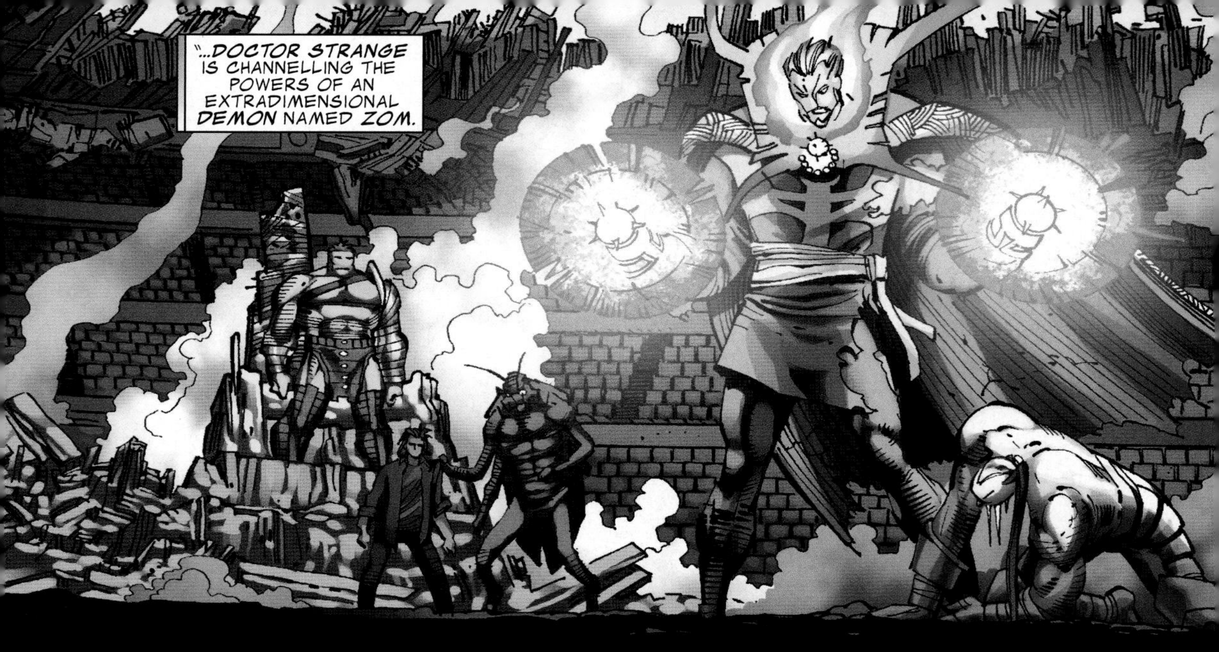
"...DOCTOR STRANGE IS CHANNELLING THE POWERS OF AN EXTRADIMENSIONAL DEMON NAMED ZOM.

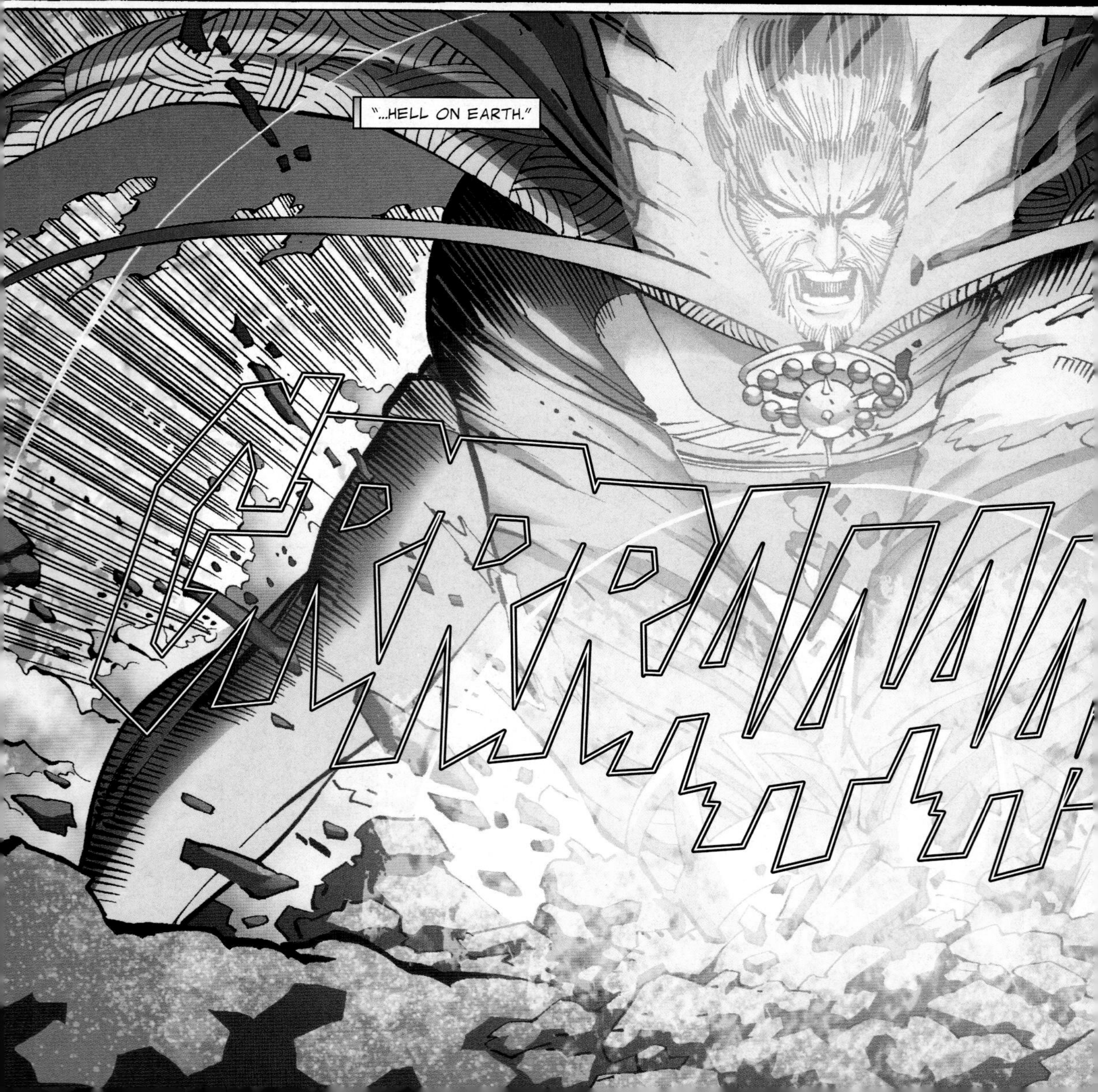
"...HELL ON EARTH."

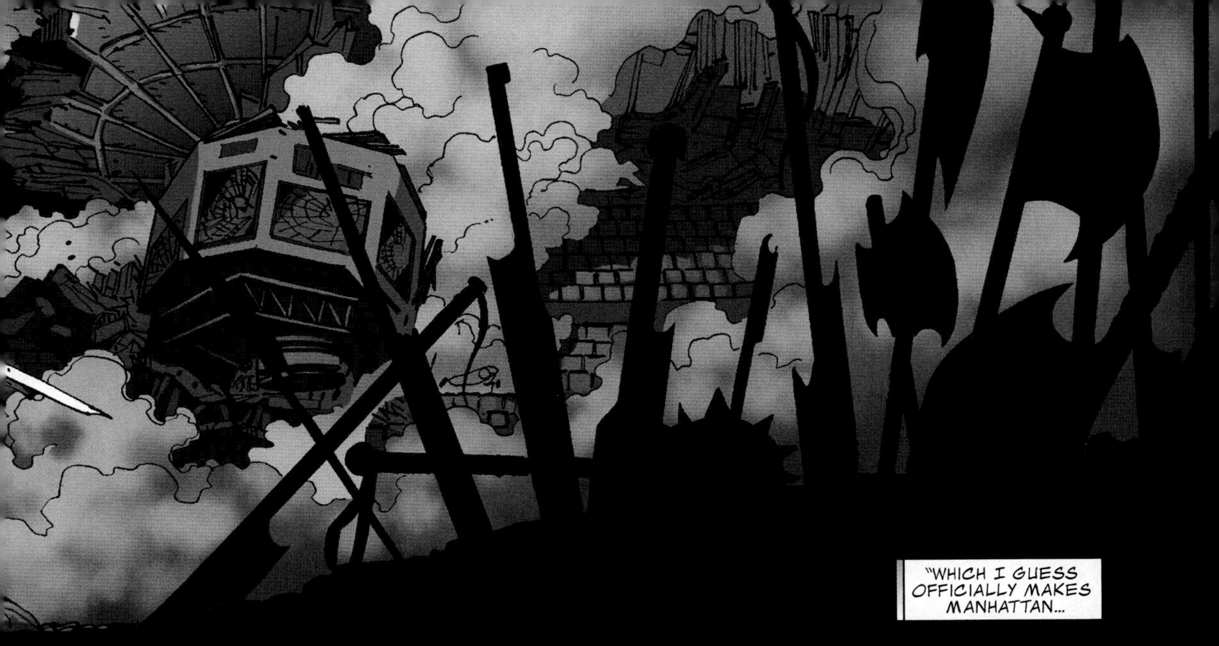
"WHICH I GUESS
OFFICIALLY MAKES
MANHATTAN...

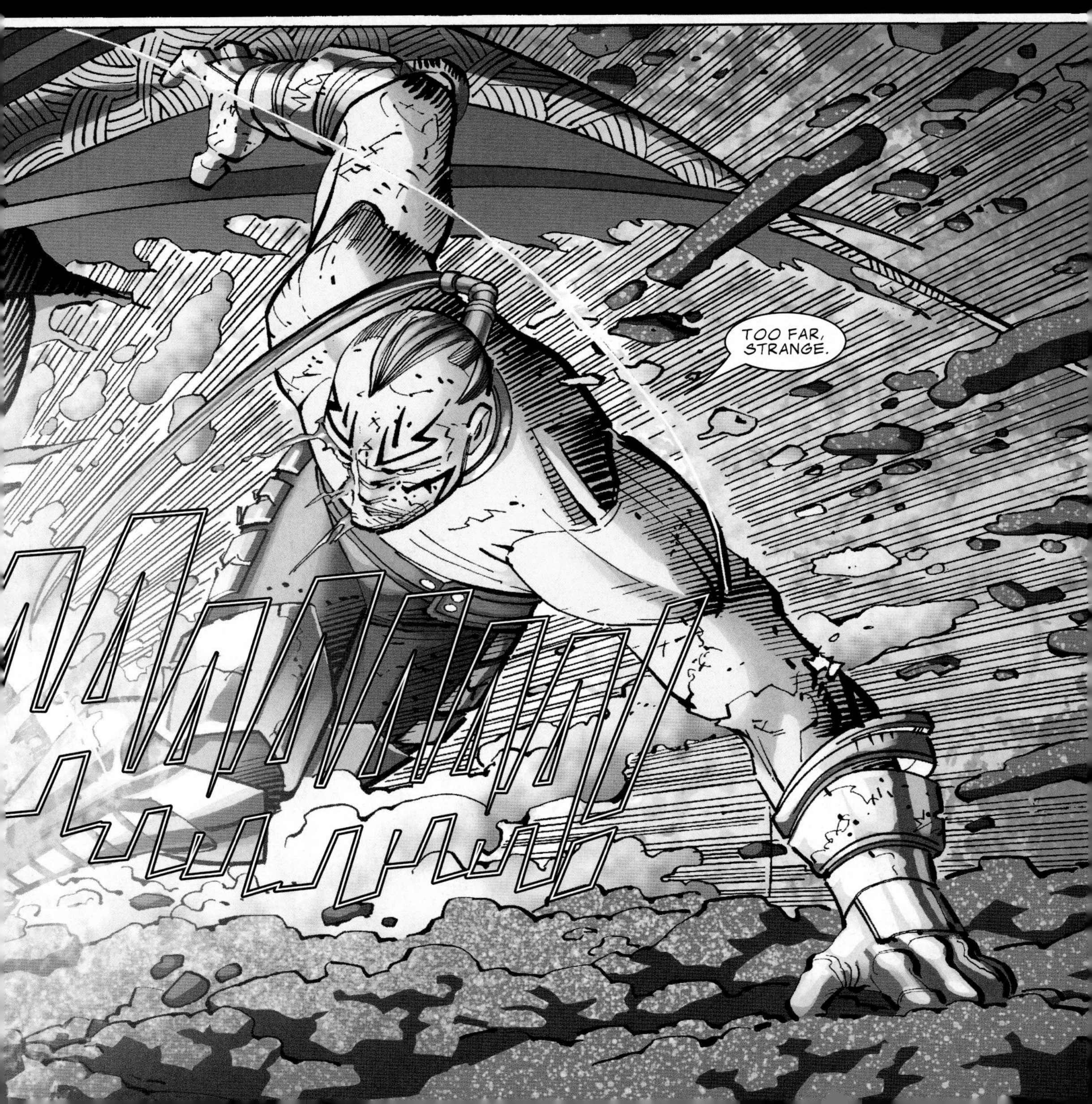
TOO FAR,
STRANGE.

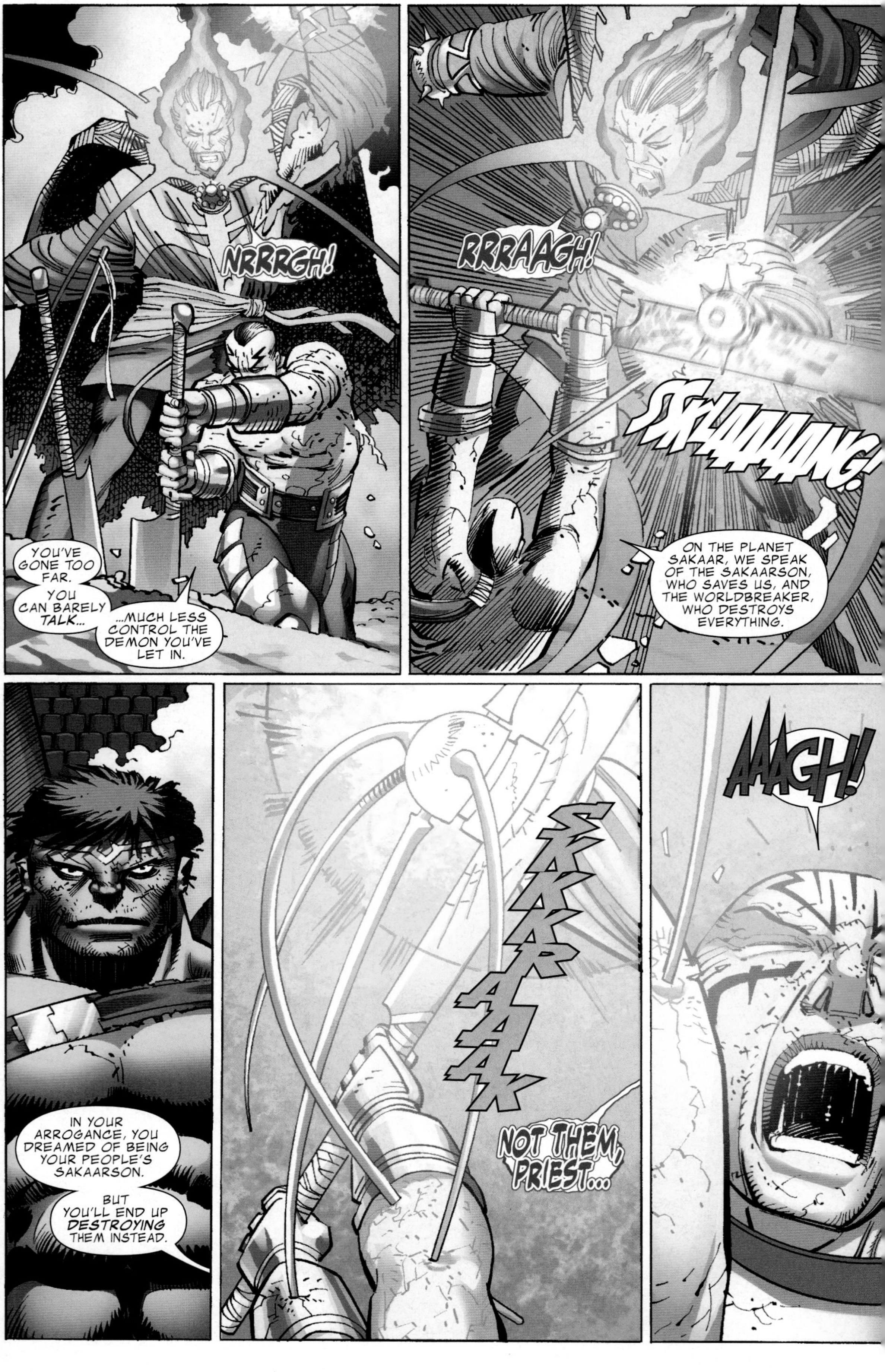
NRRRGH!
YOU'VE GONE TOO FAR.
YOU CAN BARELY TALK...
...MUCH LESS CONTROL THE DEMON YOU'VE LET IN.
RRRAAGH!
SKLAAAAANG!
ON THE PLANET SAKAAR, WE SPEAK OF THE SAKAARSON, WHO SAVES US, AND THE WORLDBREAKER, WHO DESTROYS EVERYTHING.
IN YOUR ARROGANCE, YOU DREAMED OF BEING YOUR PEOPLE'S SAKAARSON.
BUT YOU'LL END UP DESTROYING THEM INSTEAD.
SKKRAAAK
NOT THEM, PRIEST...
AAAGH!

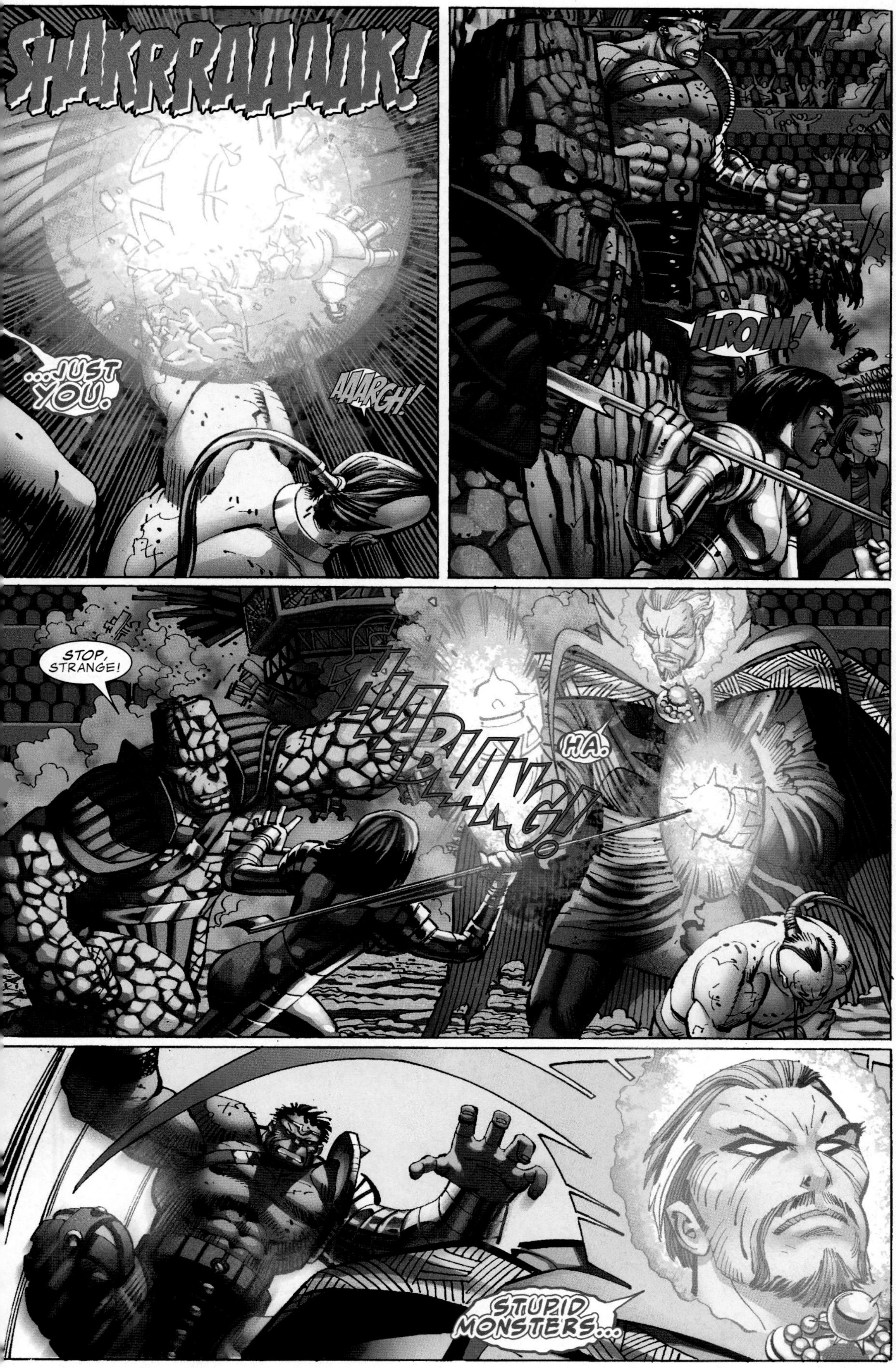
SHAKRRAAAAK!
...JUST YOU.
AAARGH!
HIROIM!
STOP, STRANGE!
THUDUNG!
HA.
STUPID MONSTERS...

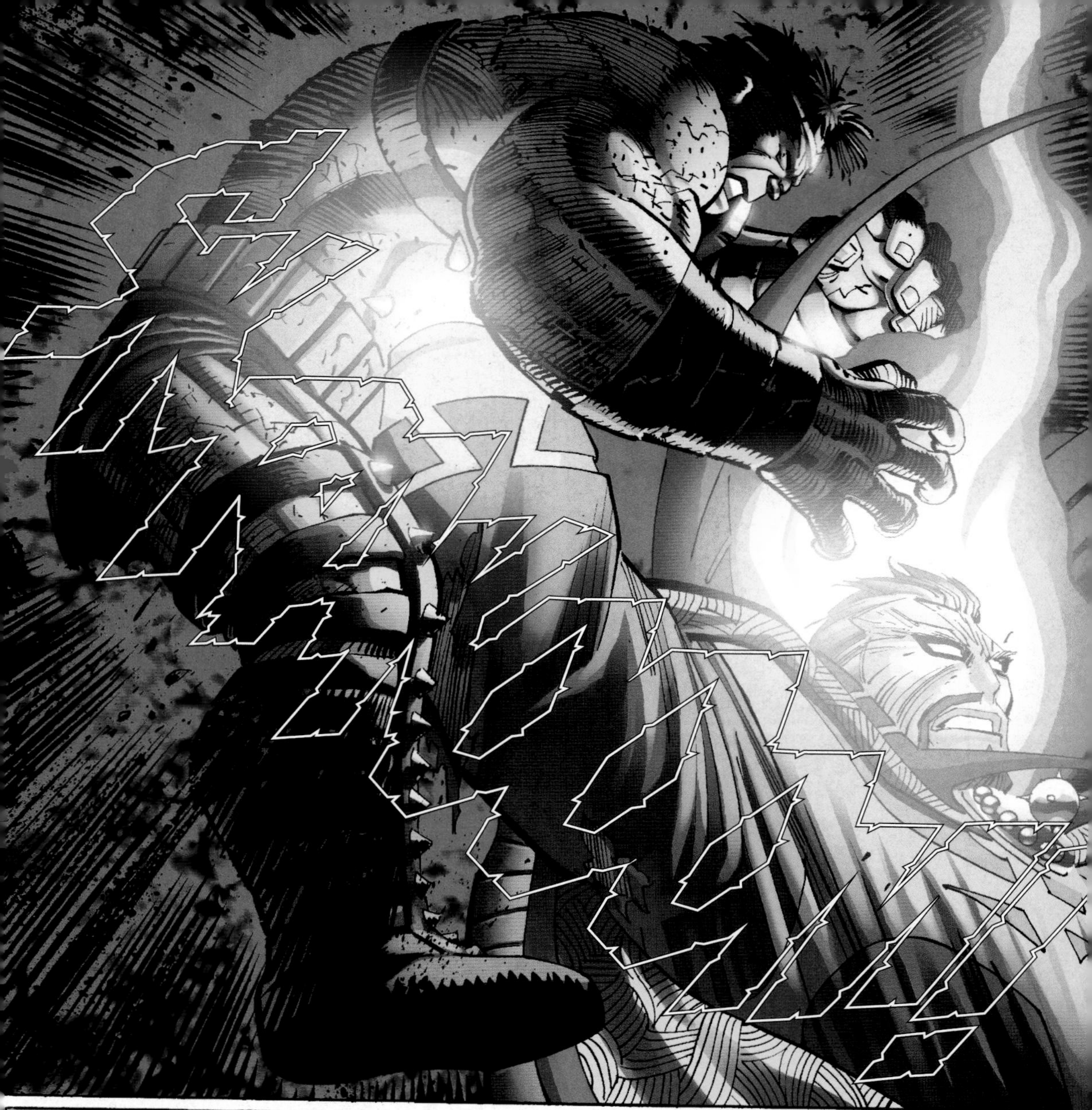

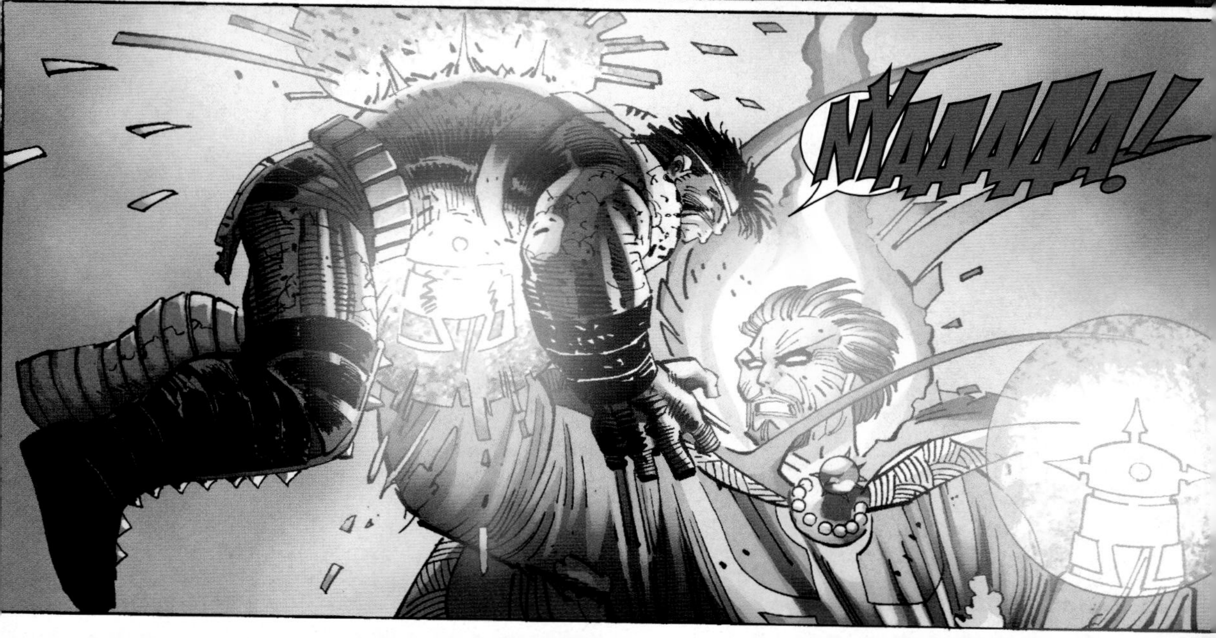
NYAAAAAA!!

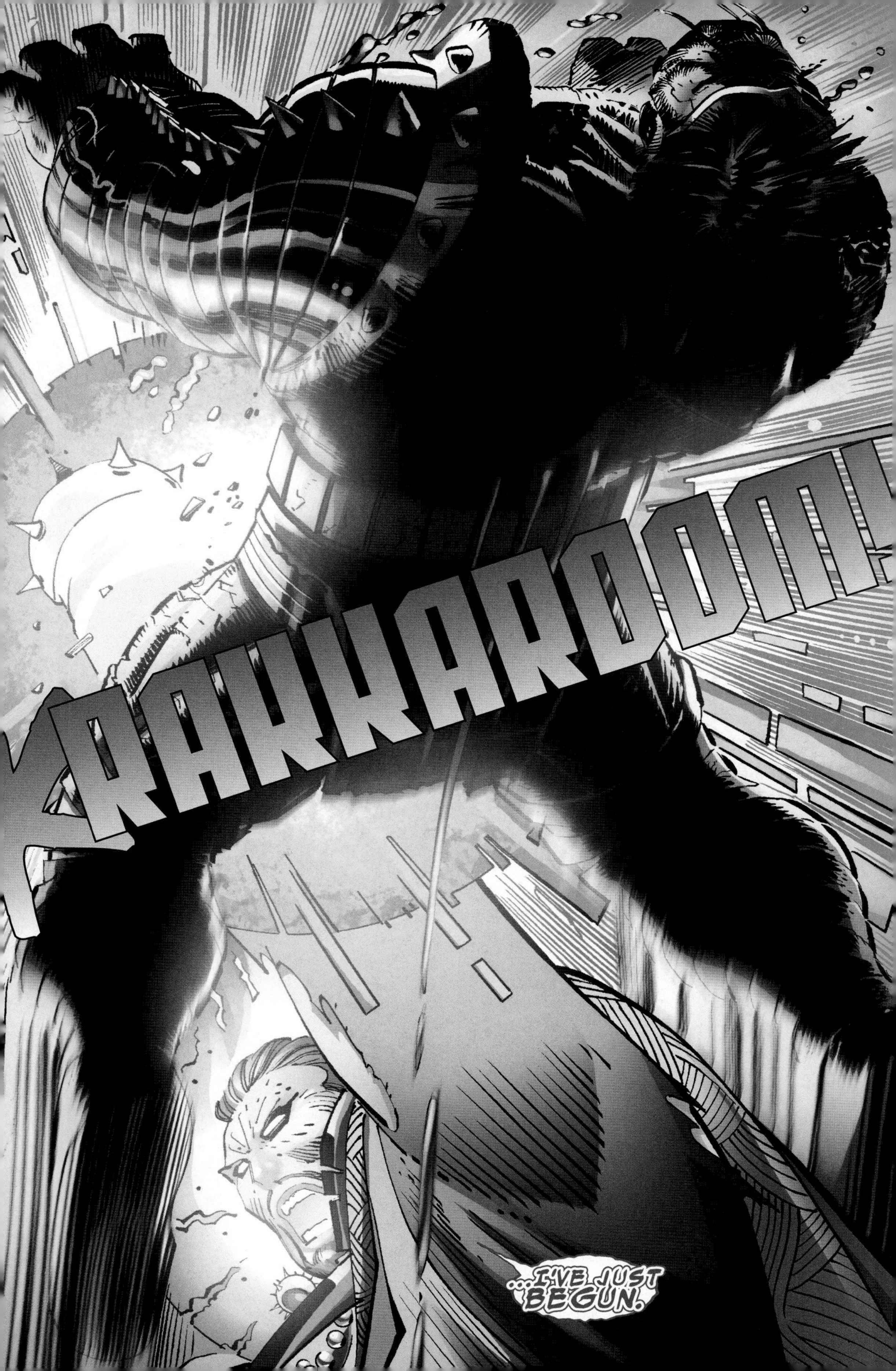
KRAKKAROOOM!
...I'VE JUST BEGUN.

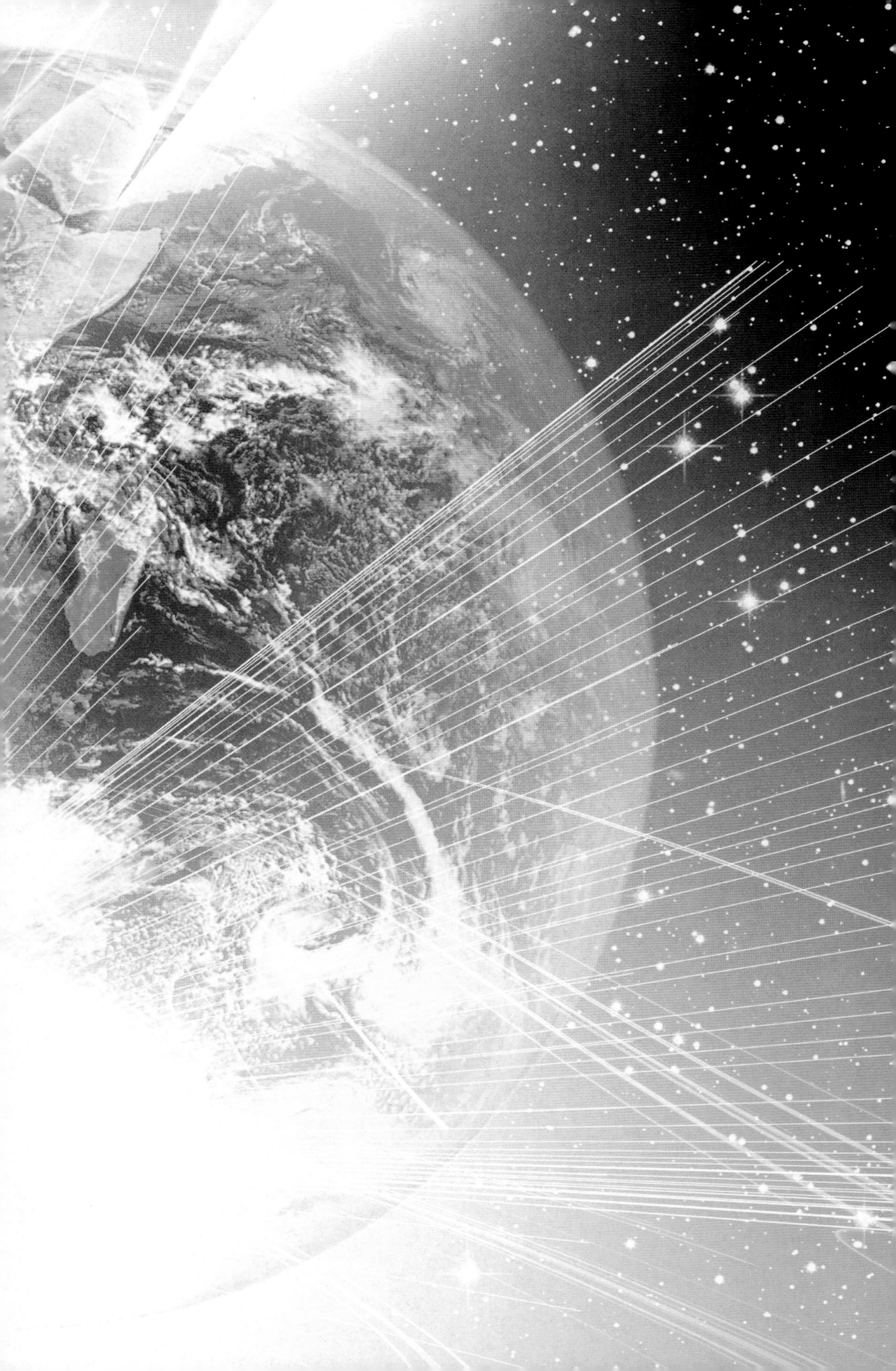

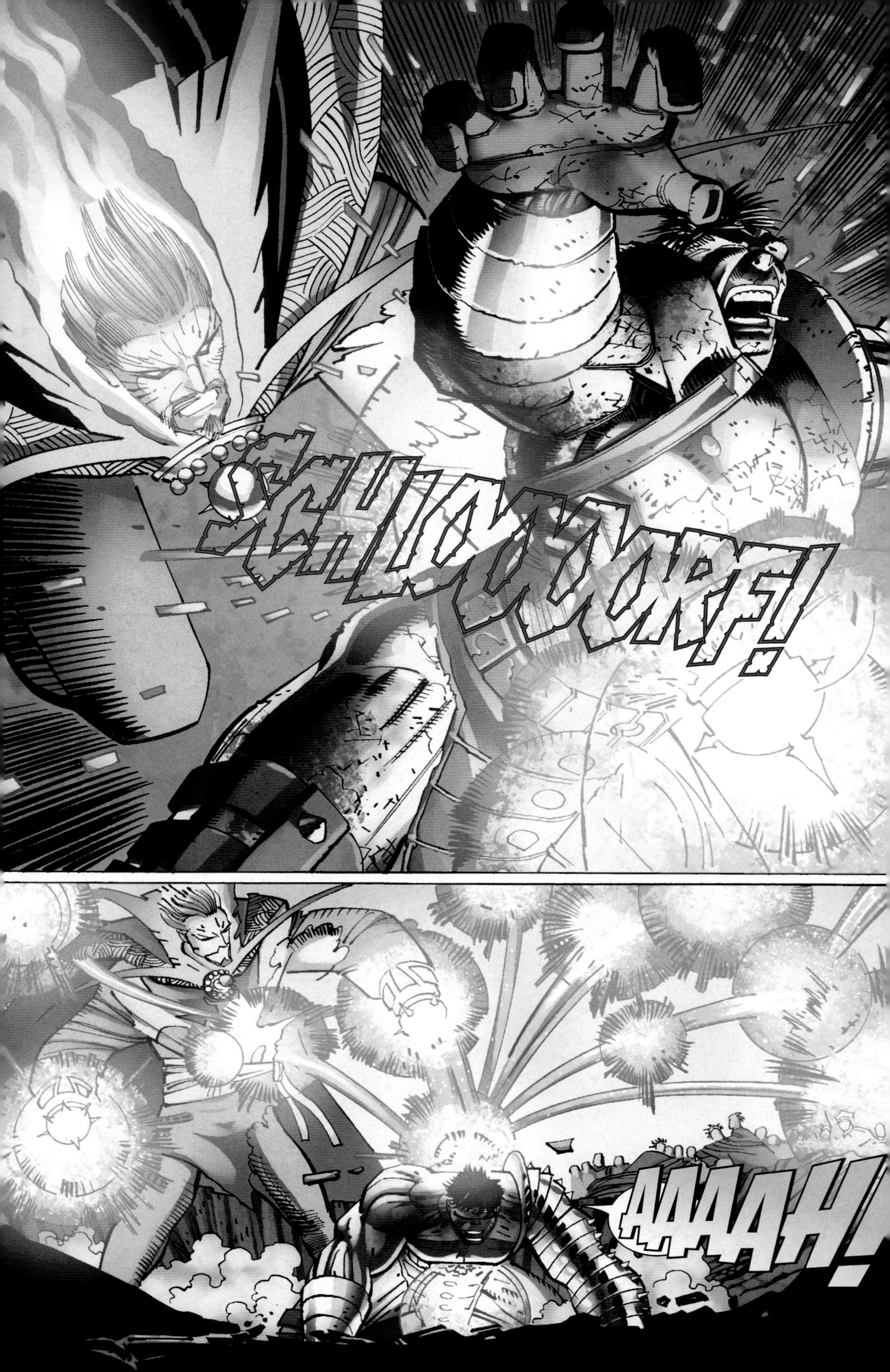
SCHLOOOORF!
AAAAH!

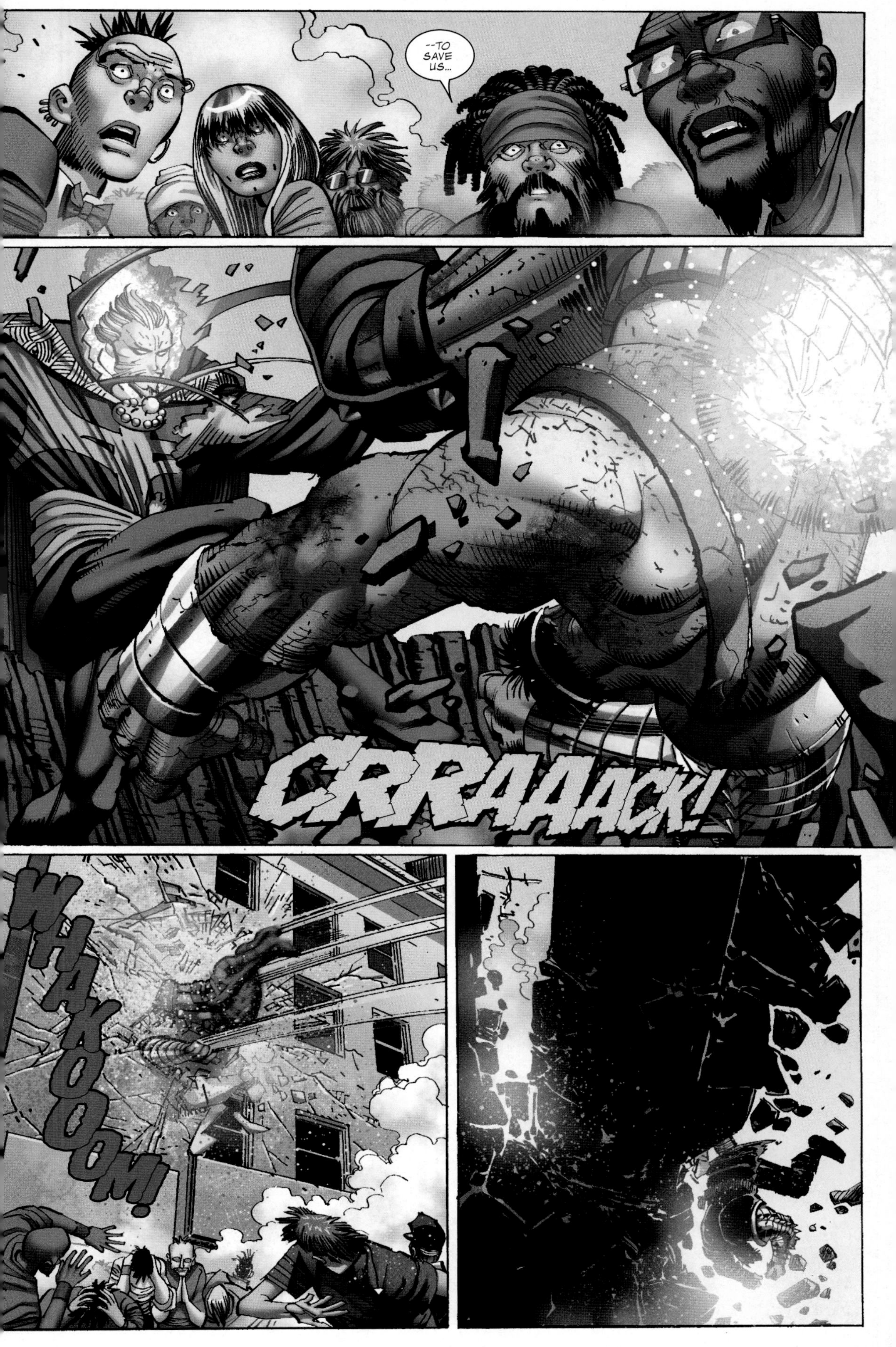
--TO SAVE US...
CRRAAAACK!
WHAKOOOOM!

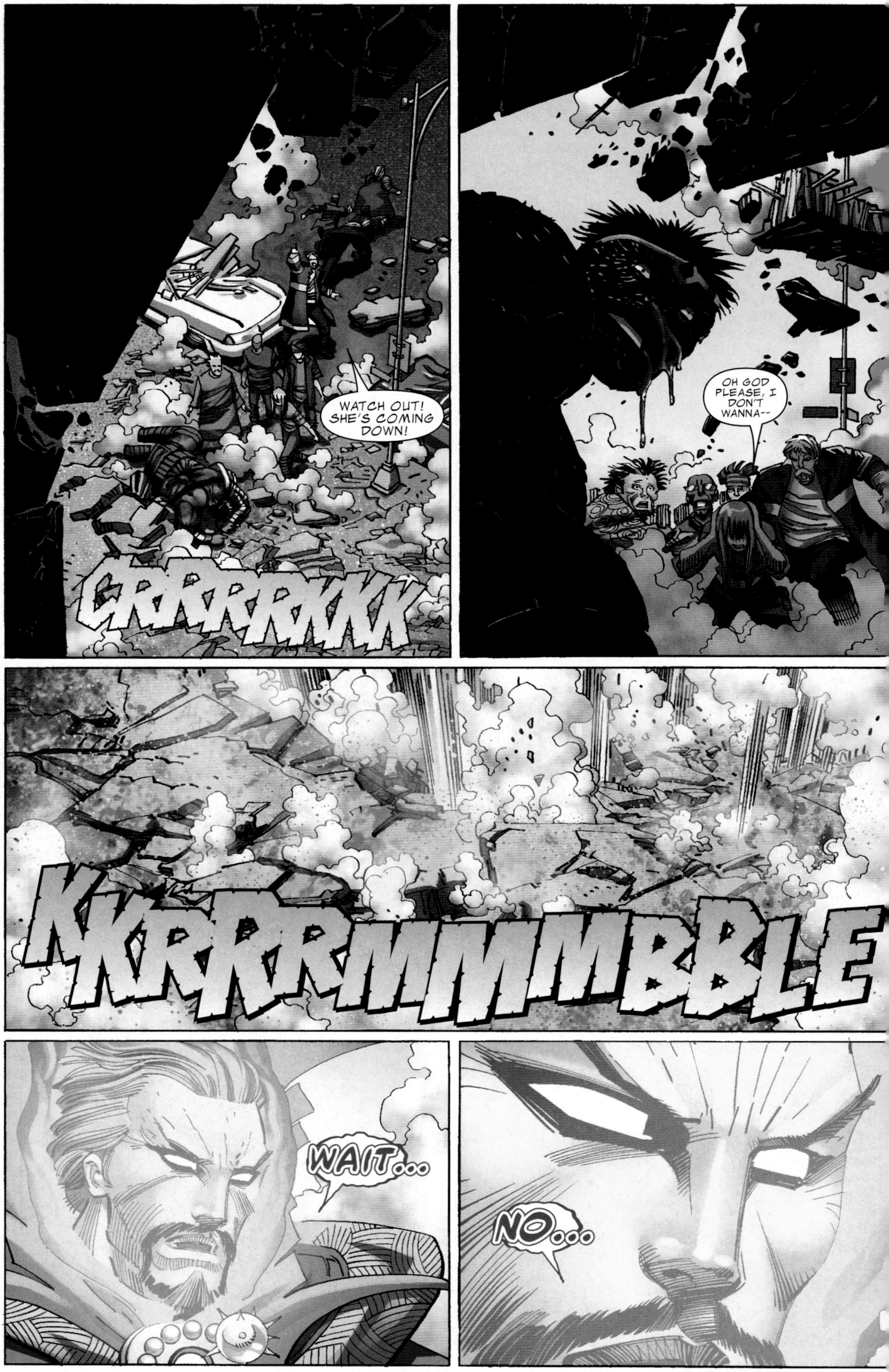
WATCH OUT! SHE'S COMING DOWN!
CRKRRRKKK
OH GOD PLEASE, I DON'T WANNA--
KKRRRMMMMBBLE
WAIT...
NO...

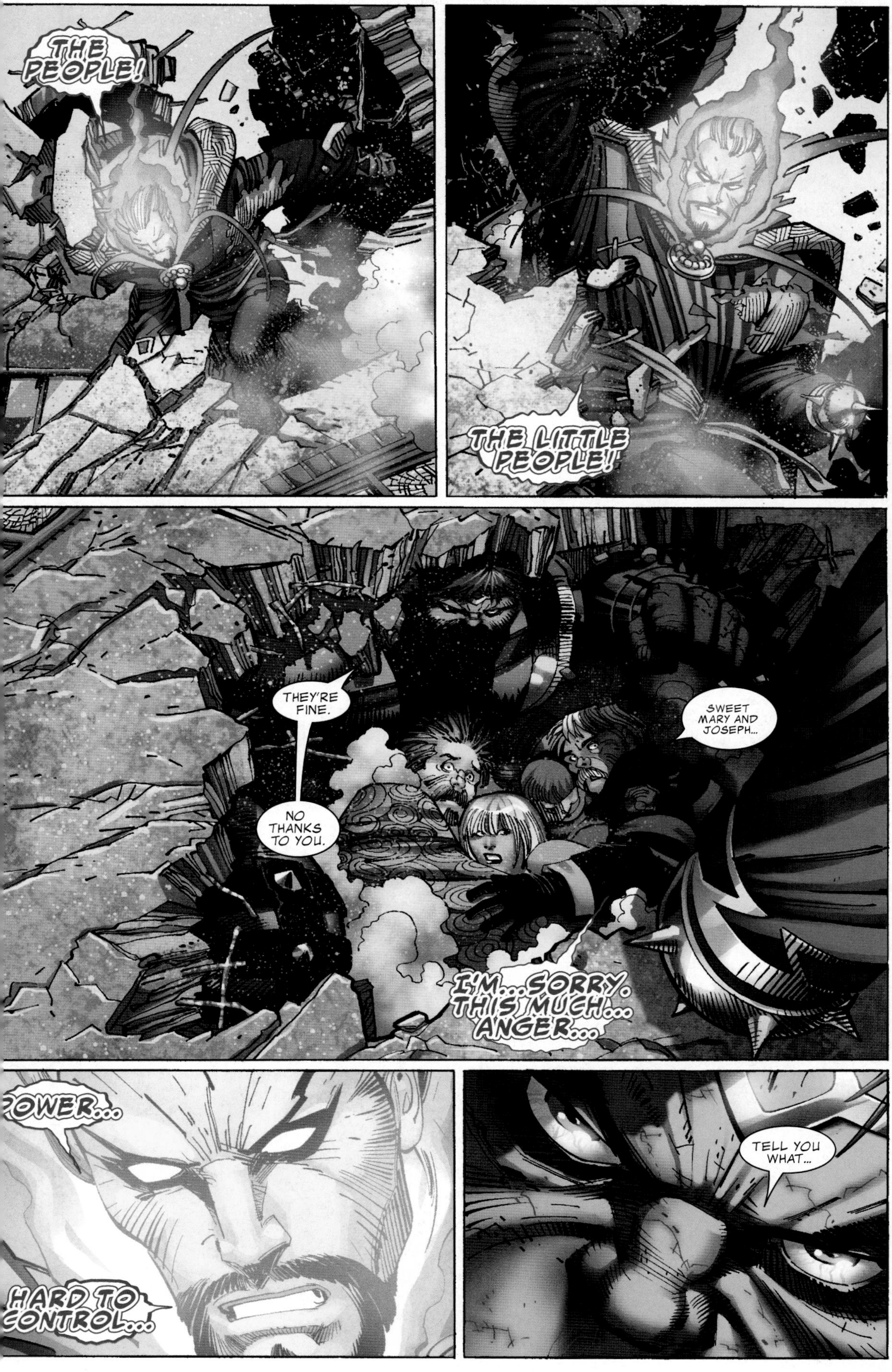
THE PEOPLE!
THE LITTLE PEOPLE!!
THEY'RE FINE.
NO THANKS TO YOU.
SWEET MARY AND JOSEPH...
I'M... SORRY. THIS MUCH... ANGER...
POWER...
HARD TO CONTROL...
TELL YOU WHAT...

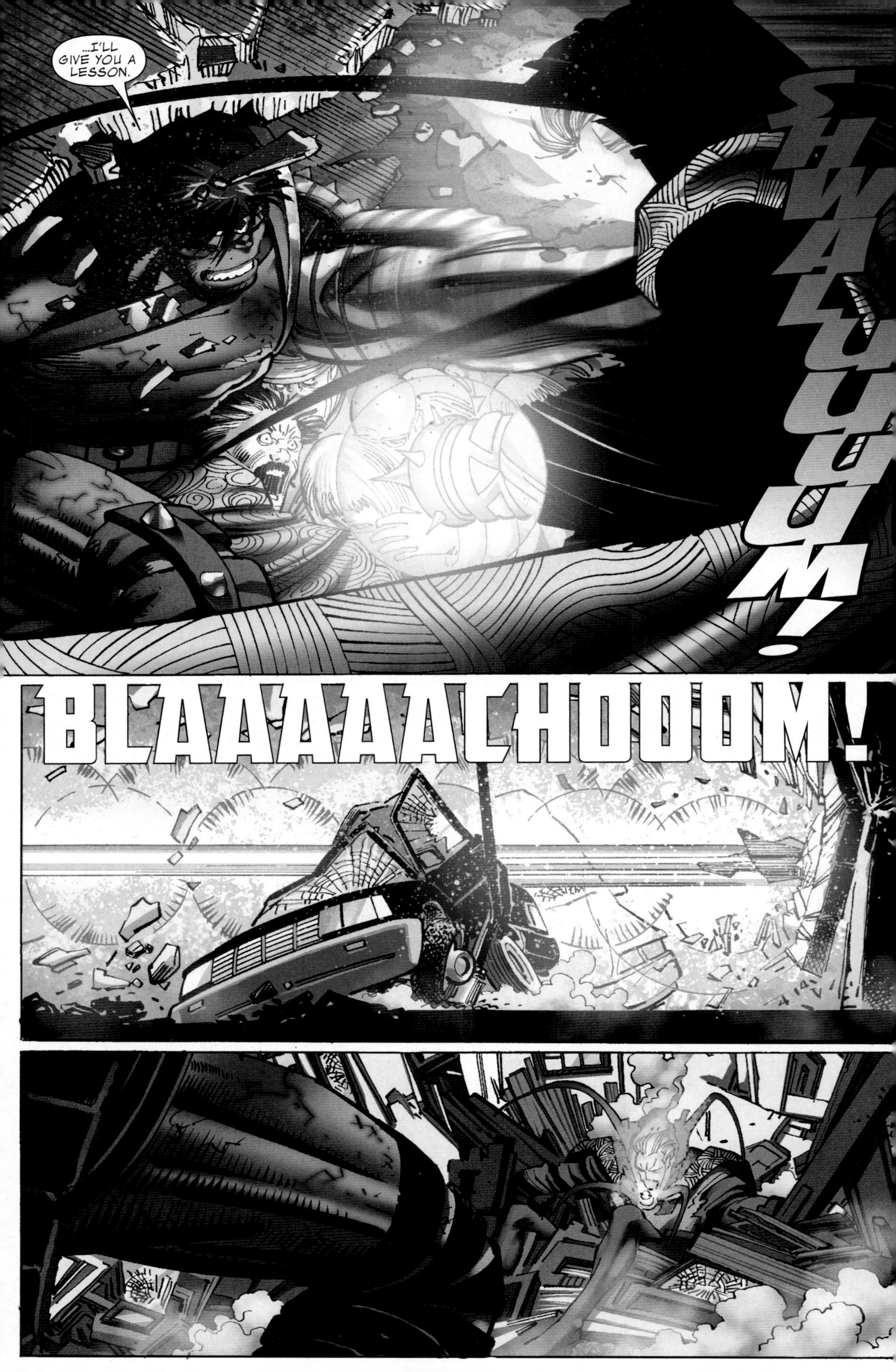
...I'LL GIVE YOU A LESSON.
SHWAUUUUM!
BLAAAAACHOOOM!

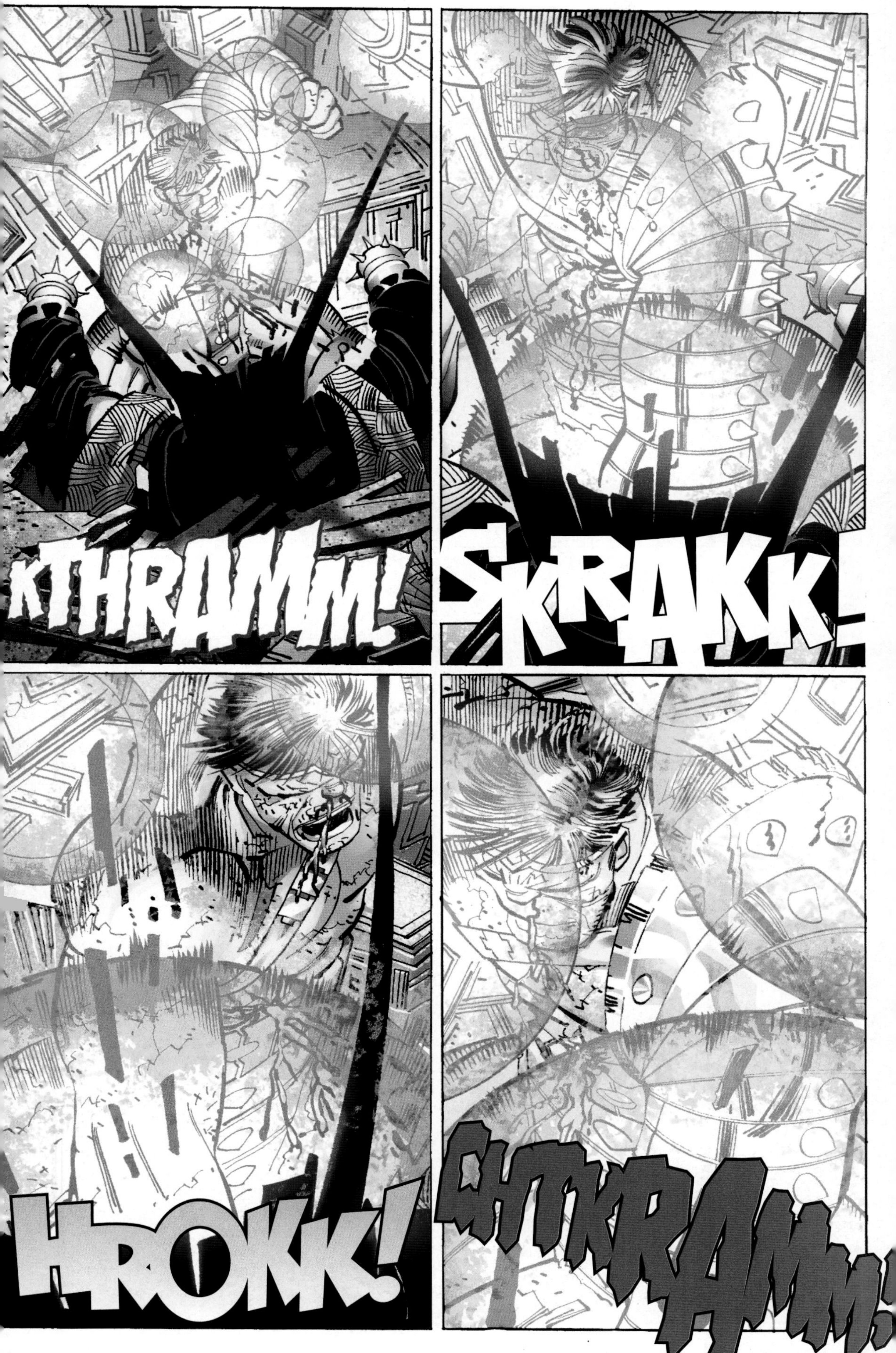

KTHRAMM!
SKRAKK!
HROKK!
CHTKRAMM!

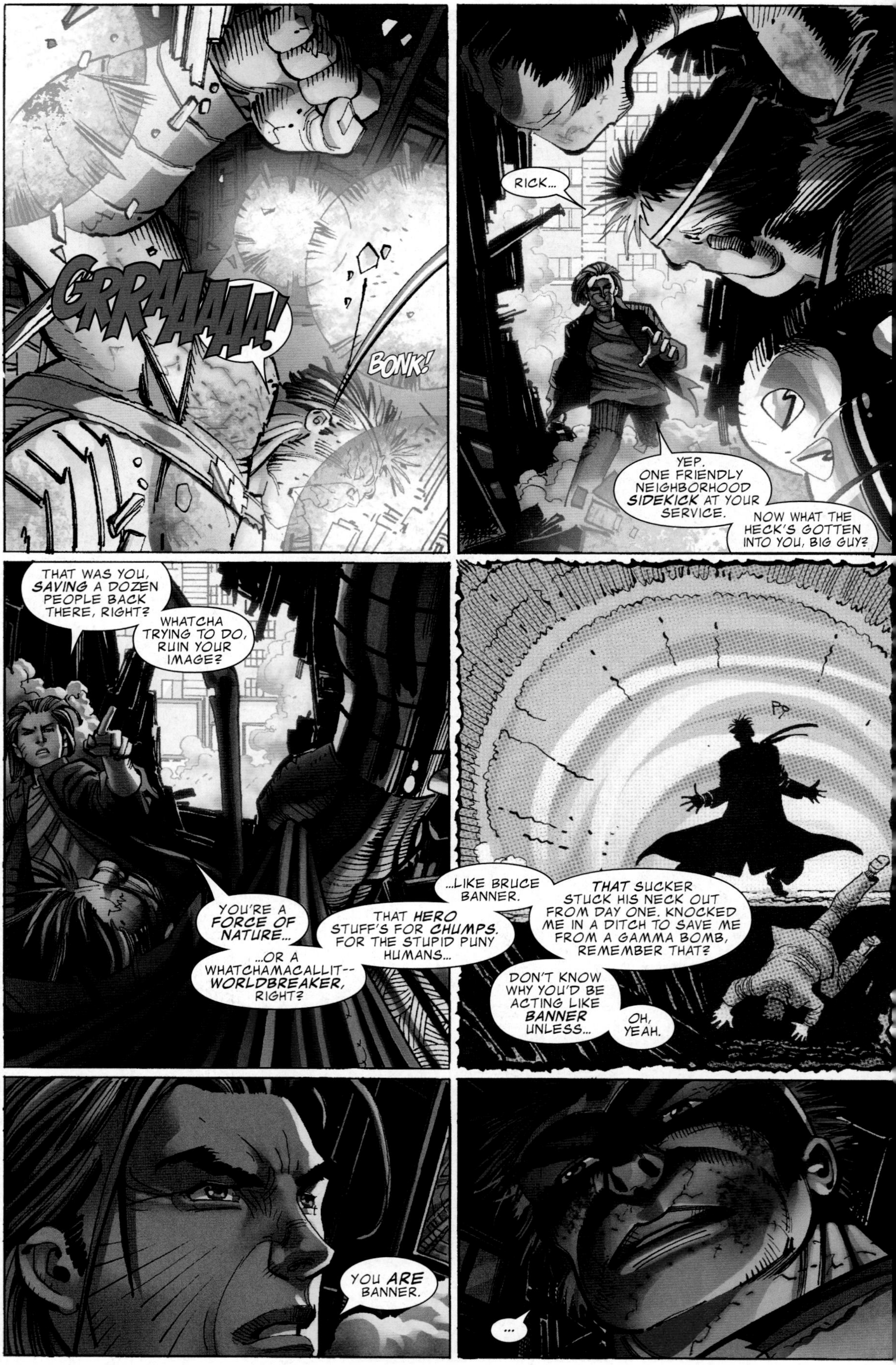
GRRAAAAAA!
BONK!
RICK...
YEP. ONE FRIENDLY NEIGHBORHOOD SIDEKICK AT YOUR SERVICE.
NOW WHAT THE HECK'S GOTTEN INTO YOU, BIG GUY?
THAT WAS YOU, SAVING A DOZEN PEOPLE BACK THERE, RIGHT?
WHATCHA TRYING TO DO, RUIN YOUR IMAGE?
YOU'RE A FORCE OF NATURE...
...OR A WHATCHAMACALLIT--WORLDBREAKER, RIGHT?
THAT HERO STUFF'S FOR CHUMPS. FOR THE STUPID PUNY HUMANS...
...LIKE BRUCE BANNER.
THAT SUCKER STUCK HIS NECK OUT FROM DAY ONE. KNOCKED ME IN A DITCH TO SAVE ME FROM A GAMMA BOMB, REMEMBER THAT?
DON'T KNOW WHY YOU'D BE ACTING LIKE BANNER UNLESS...
OH, YEAH.
YOU ARE BANNER.
...

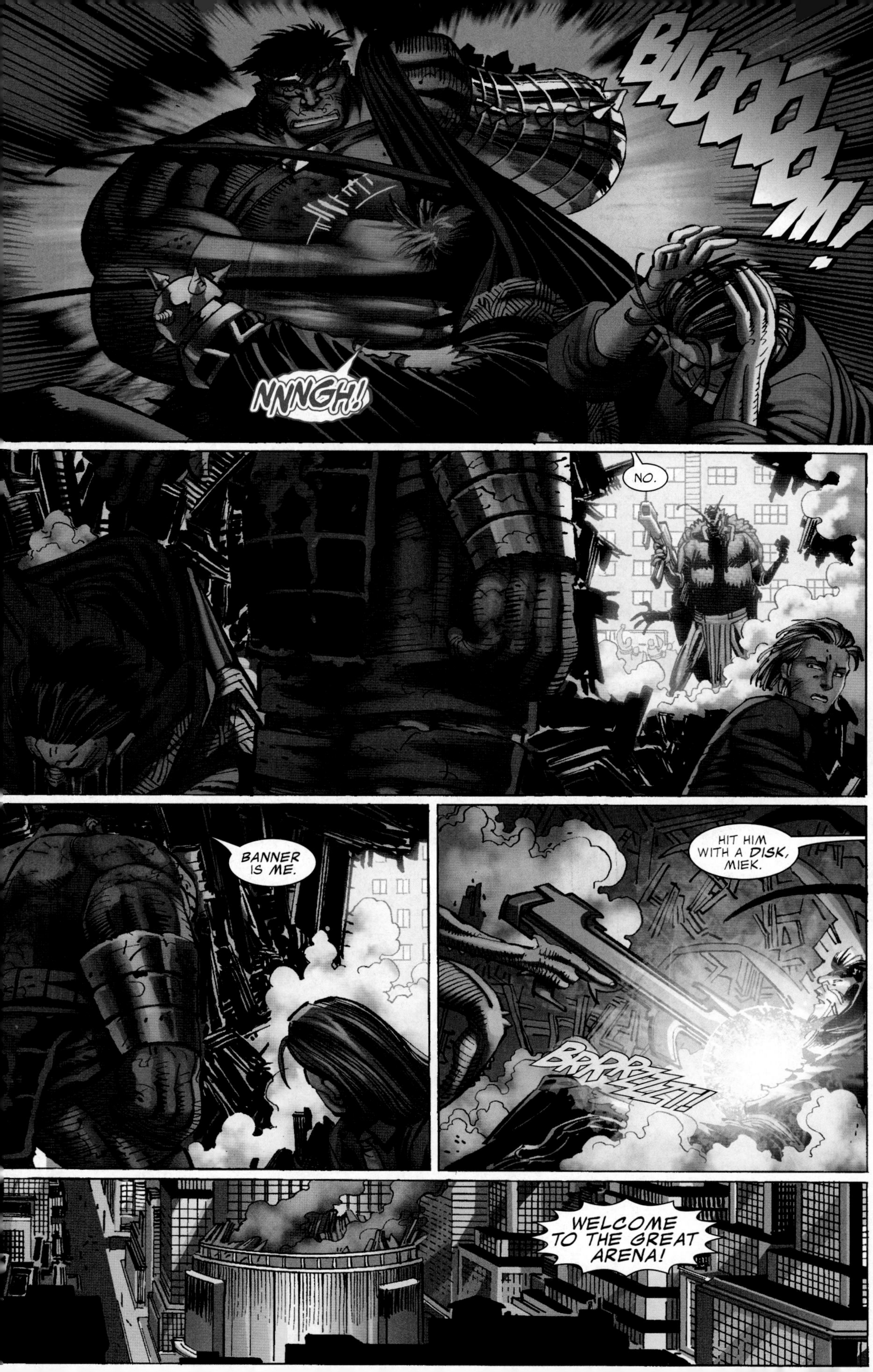
BADOOOM!
NNNGH!
NO.
BANNER IS ME.
HIT HIM WITH A DISK, MIEK.
BRRRZZZT!
WELCOME TO THE GREAT ARENA!

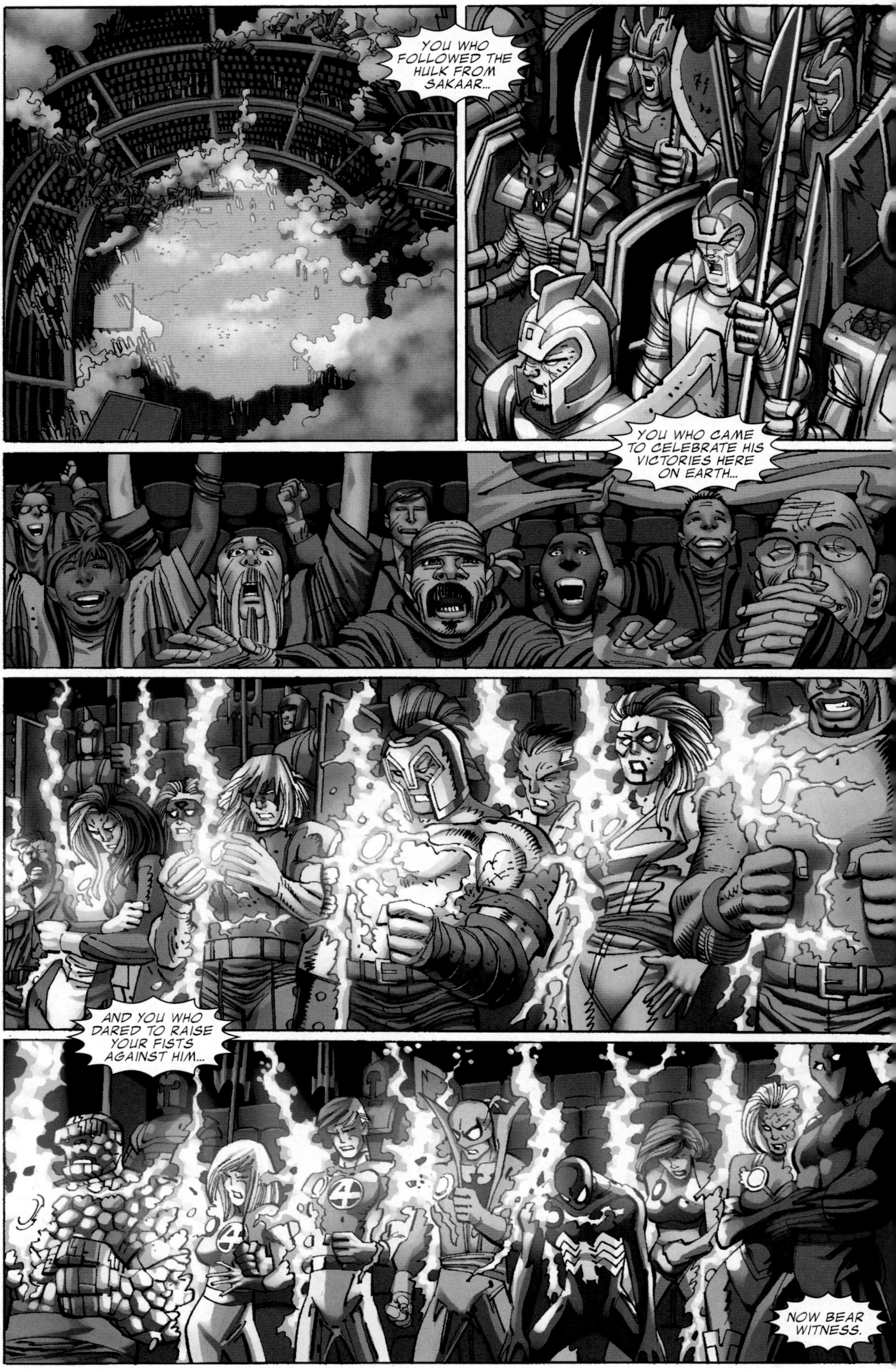
YOU WHO FOLLOWED THE HULK FROM SAKAAR...
YOU WHO CAME TO CELEBRATE HIS VICTORIES HERE ON EARTH...
AND YOU WHO DARED TO RAISE YOUR FISTS AGAINST HIM...
NOW BEAR WITNESS.

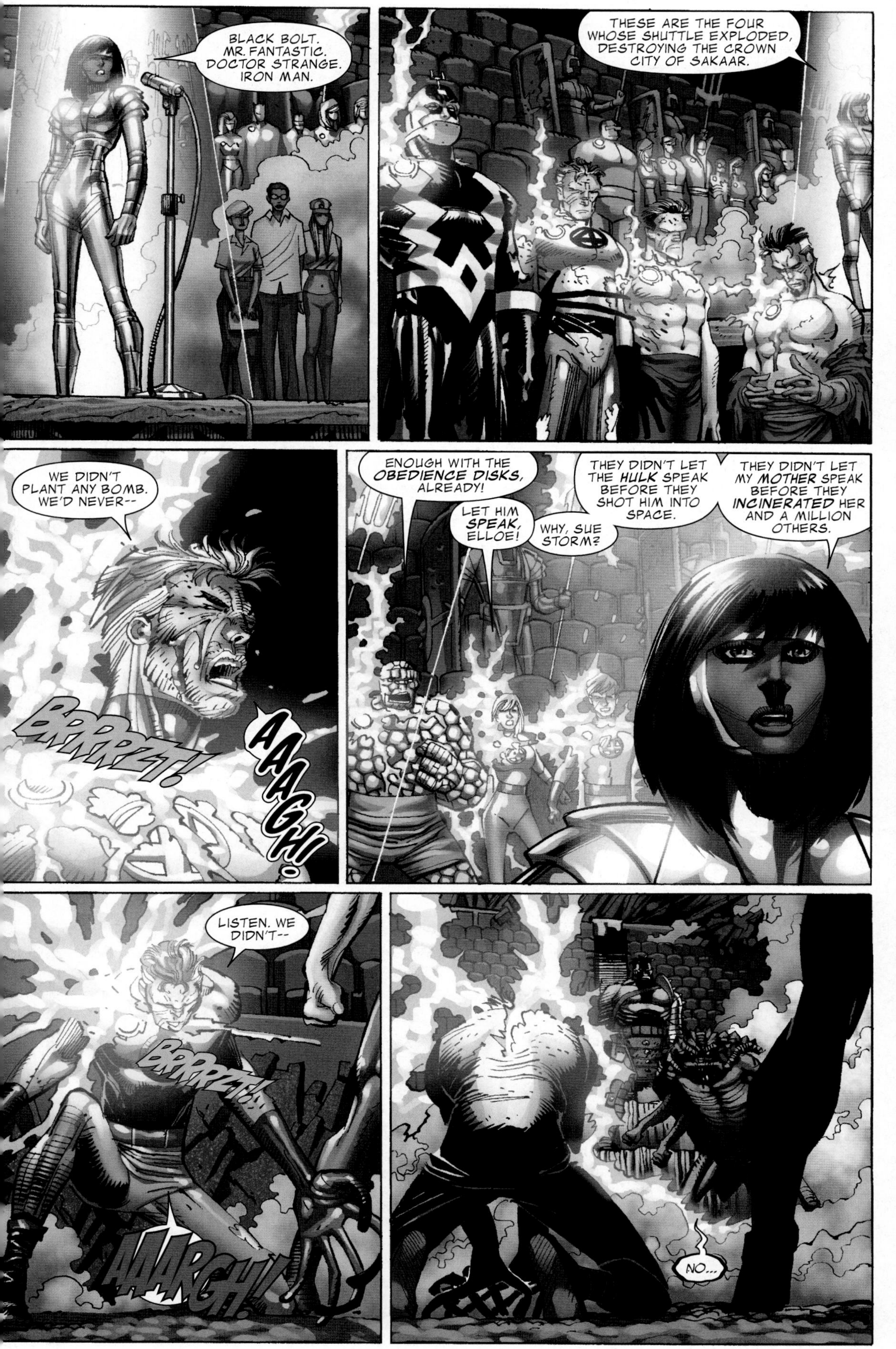
BLACK BOLT. MR. FANTASTIC. DOCTOR STRANGE. IRON MAN.
THESE ARE THE FOUR WHOSE SHUTTLE EXPLODED, DESTROYING THE CROWN CITY OF SAKAAR.
WE DIDN'T PLANT ANY BOMB. WE'D NEVER--
BRRRRZZT!
AAAGH!
ENOUGH WITH THE OBEDIENCE DISKS, ALREADY!
LET HIM SPEAK, ELLOE!
WHY, SUE STORM?
THEY DIDN'T LET THE HULK SPEAK BEFORE THEY SHOT HIM INTO SPACE.
THEY DIDN'T LET MY MOTHER SPEAK BEFORE THEY INCINERATED HER AND A MILLION OTHERS.
LISTEN. WE DIDN'T--
BRRRZZT!
AAARGH!
NO...

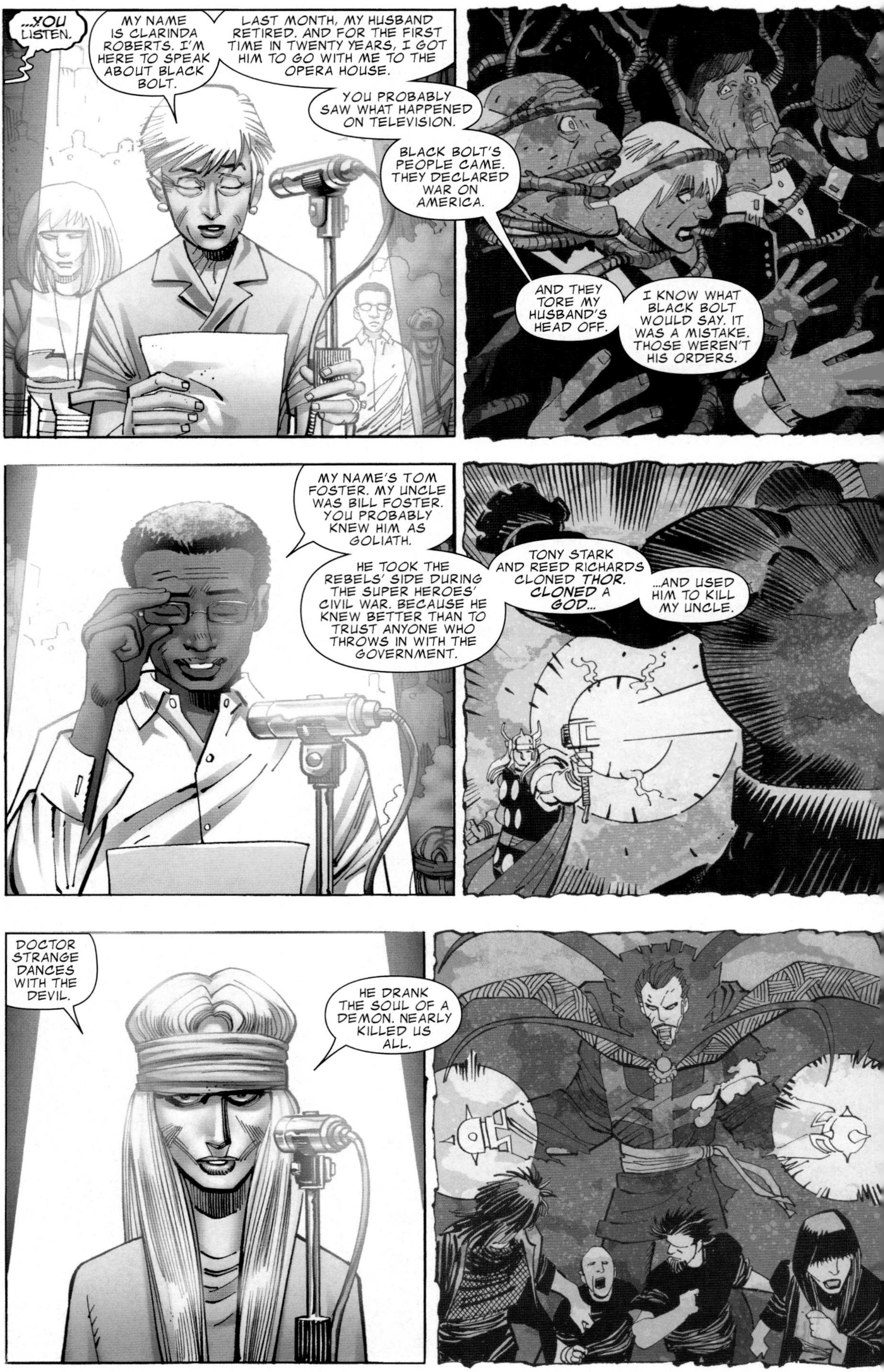
...YOU LISTEN.
MY NAME IS CLARINDA ROBERTS. I'M HERE TO SPEAK ABOUT BLACK BOLT.
LAST MONTH, MY HUSBAND RETIRED. AND FOR THE FIRST TIME IN TWENTY YEARS, I GOT HIM TO GO WITH ME TO THE OPERA HOUSE.
YOU PROBABLY SAW WHAT HAPPENED ON TELEVISION.
BLACK BOLT'S PEOPLE CAME. THEY DECLARED WAR ON AMERICA.
AND THEY TORE MY HUSBAND'S HEAD OFF.
I KNOW WHAT BLACK BOLT WOULD SAY. IT WAS A MISTAKE. THOSE WEREN'T HIS ORDERS.
MY NAME'S TOM FOSTER. MY UNCLE WAS BILL FOSTER. YOU PROBABLY KNEW HIM AS GOLIATH.
HE TOOK THE REBELS' SIDE DURING THE SUPER HEROES' CIVIL WAR. BECAUSE HE KNEW BETTER THAN TO TRUST ANYONE WHO THROWS IN WITH THE GOVERNMENT.
TONY STARK AND REED RICHARDS CLONED *THOR. CLONED* A *GOD*...
...AND USED HIM TO KILL MY UNCLE.
DOCTOR STRANGE DANCES WITH THE DEVIL.
HE DRANK THE SOUL OF A DEMON. NEARLY KILLED US ALL.

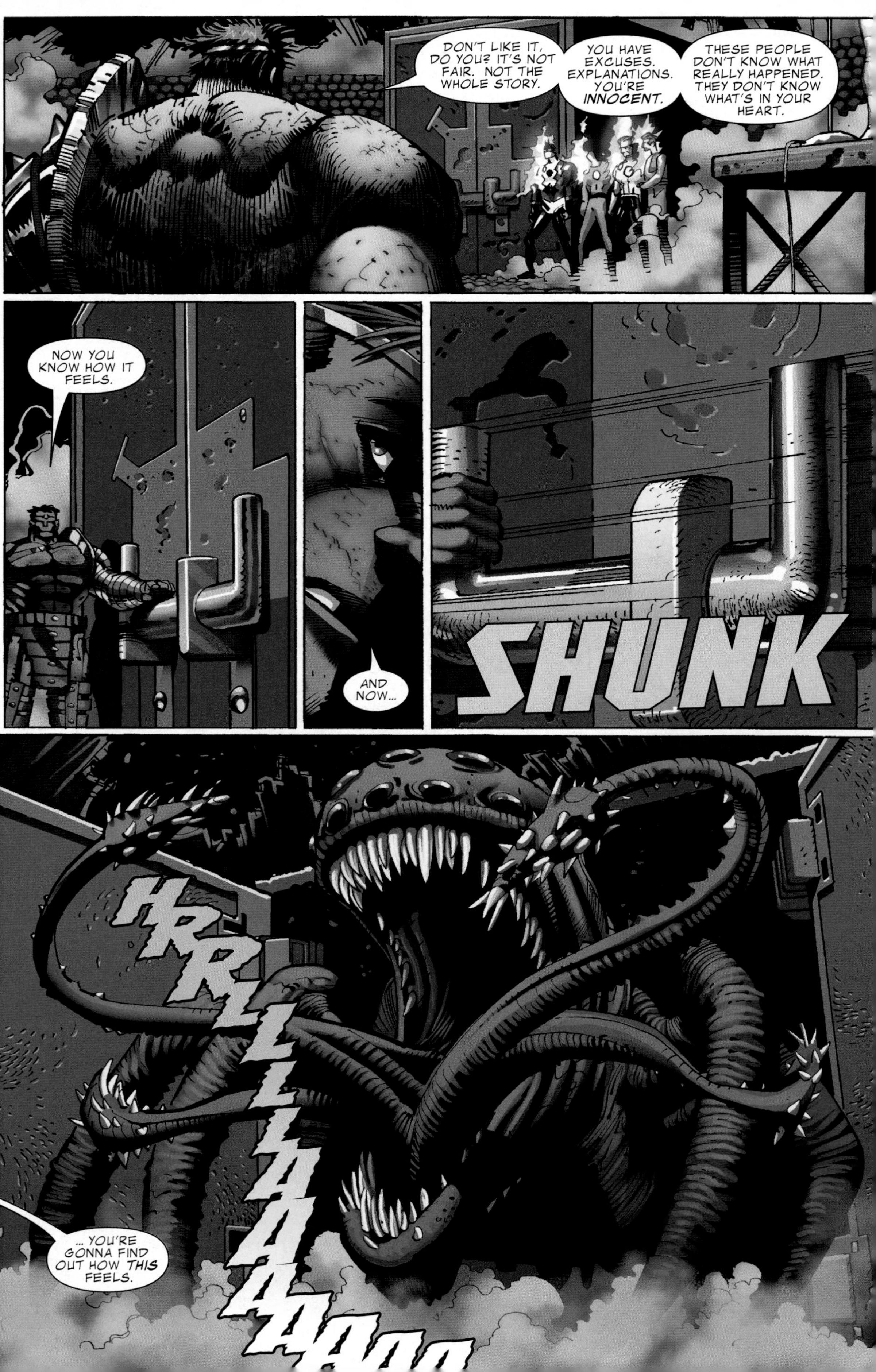
DON'T LIKE IT, DO YOU? IT'S NOT FAIR. NOT THE WHOLE STORY.
YOU HAVE EXCUSES. EXPLANATIONS. YOU'RE INNOCENT.
THESE PEOPLE DON'T KNOW WHAT REALLY HAPPENED. THEY DON'T KNOW WHAT'S IN YOUR HEART.
NOW YOU KNOW HOW IT FEELS.
AND NOW...
SHUNK
HRRLLAAAAAA
... YOU'RE GONNA FIND OUT HOW THIS FEELS.

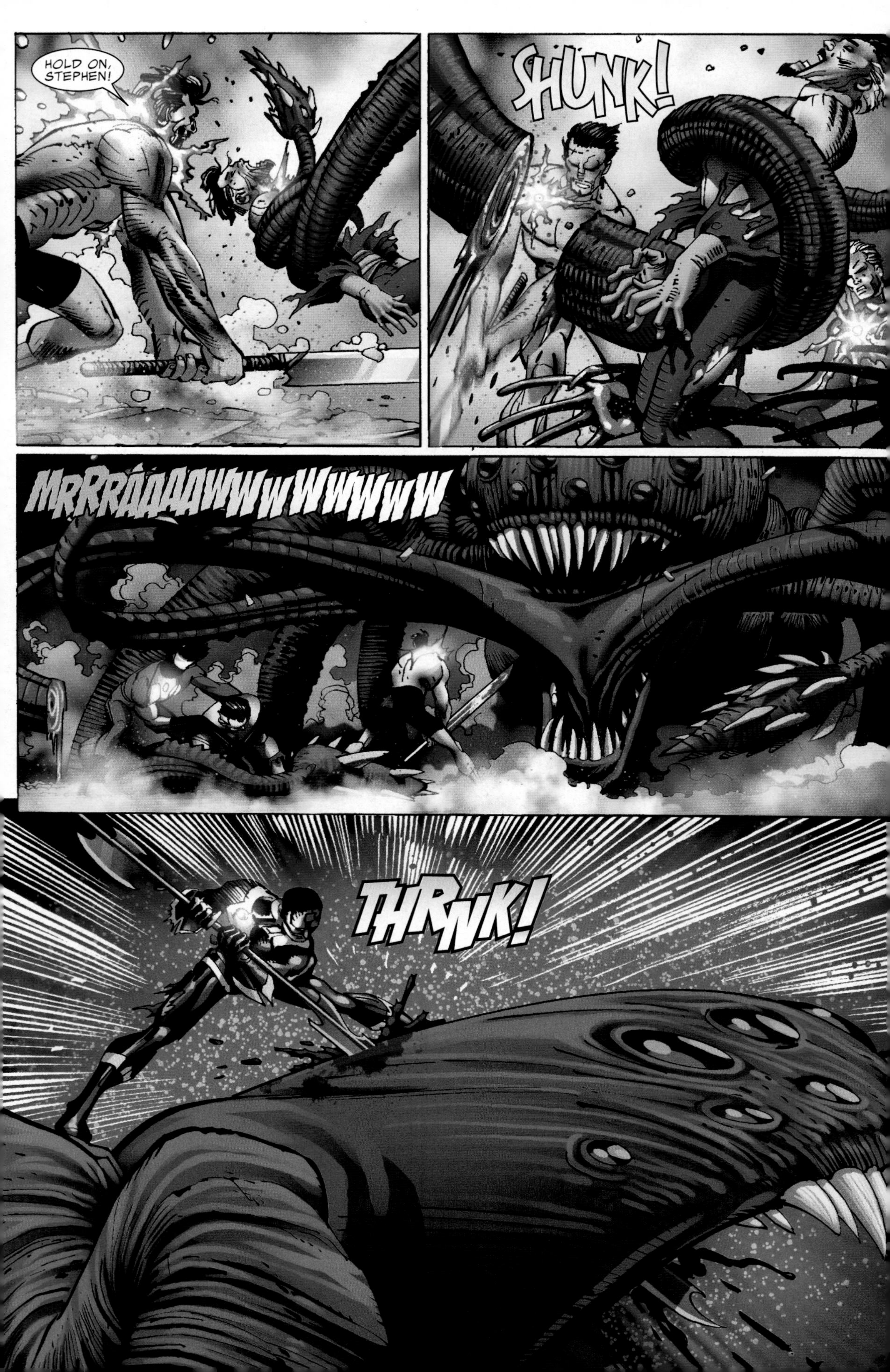
HOLD ON, STEPHEN!
SHUNK!
MRRRAAAAWWWWWWWWW
THRNK!

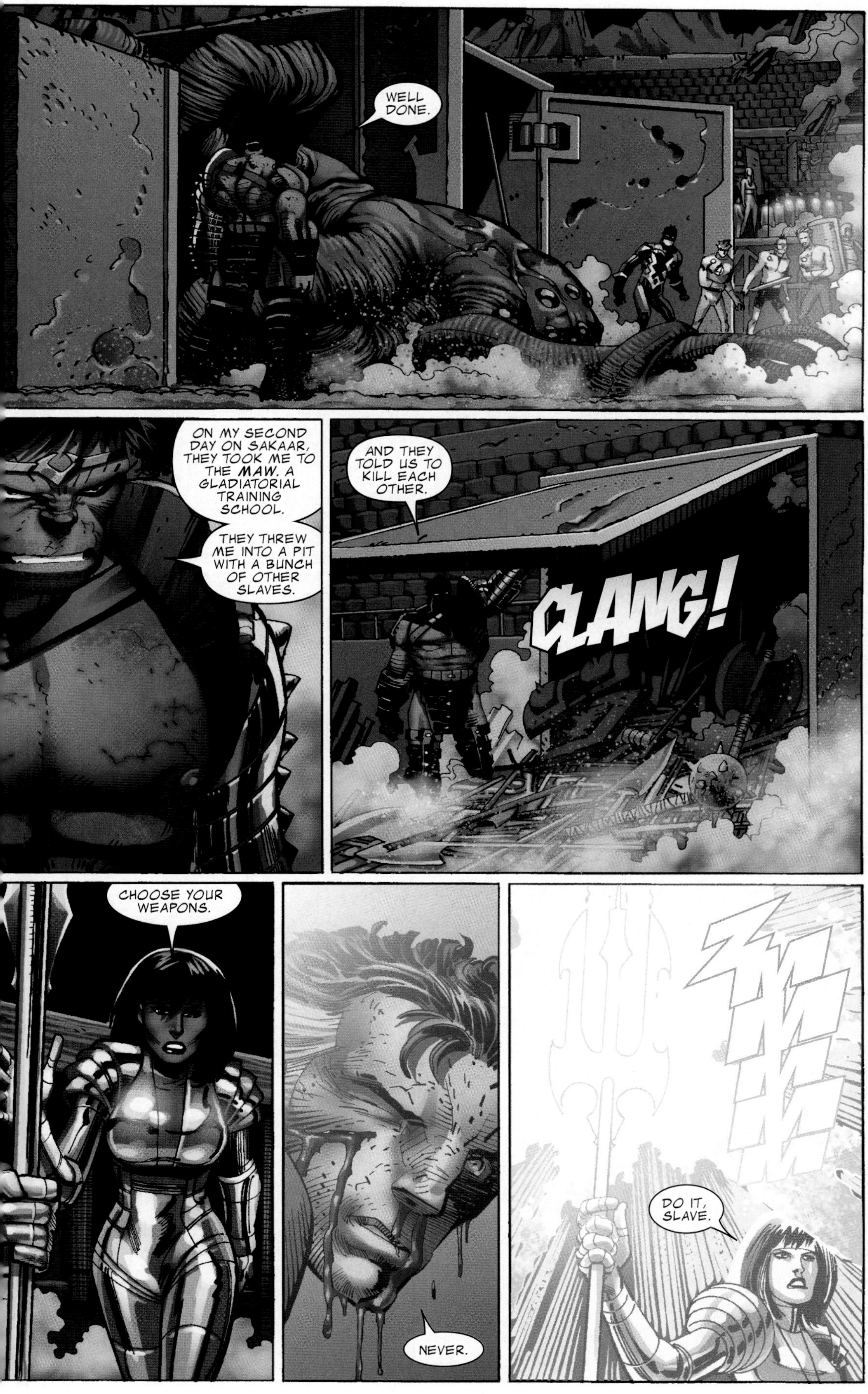
WELL DONE.
ON MY SECOND DAY ON SAKAAR, THEY TOOK ME TO THE MAW. A GLADIATORIAL TRAINING SCHOOL.
THEY THREW ME INTO A PIT WITH A BUNCH OF OTHER SLAVES.
AND THEY TOLD US TO KILL EACH OTHER.
CLANG!
CHOOSE YOUR WEAPONS.
NEVER.
DO IT, SLAVE.

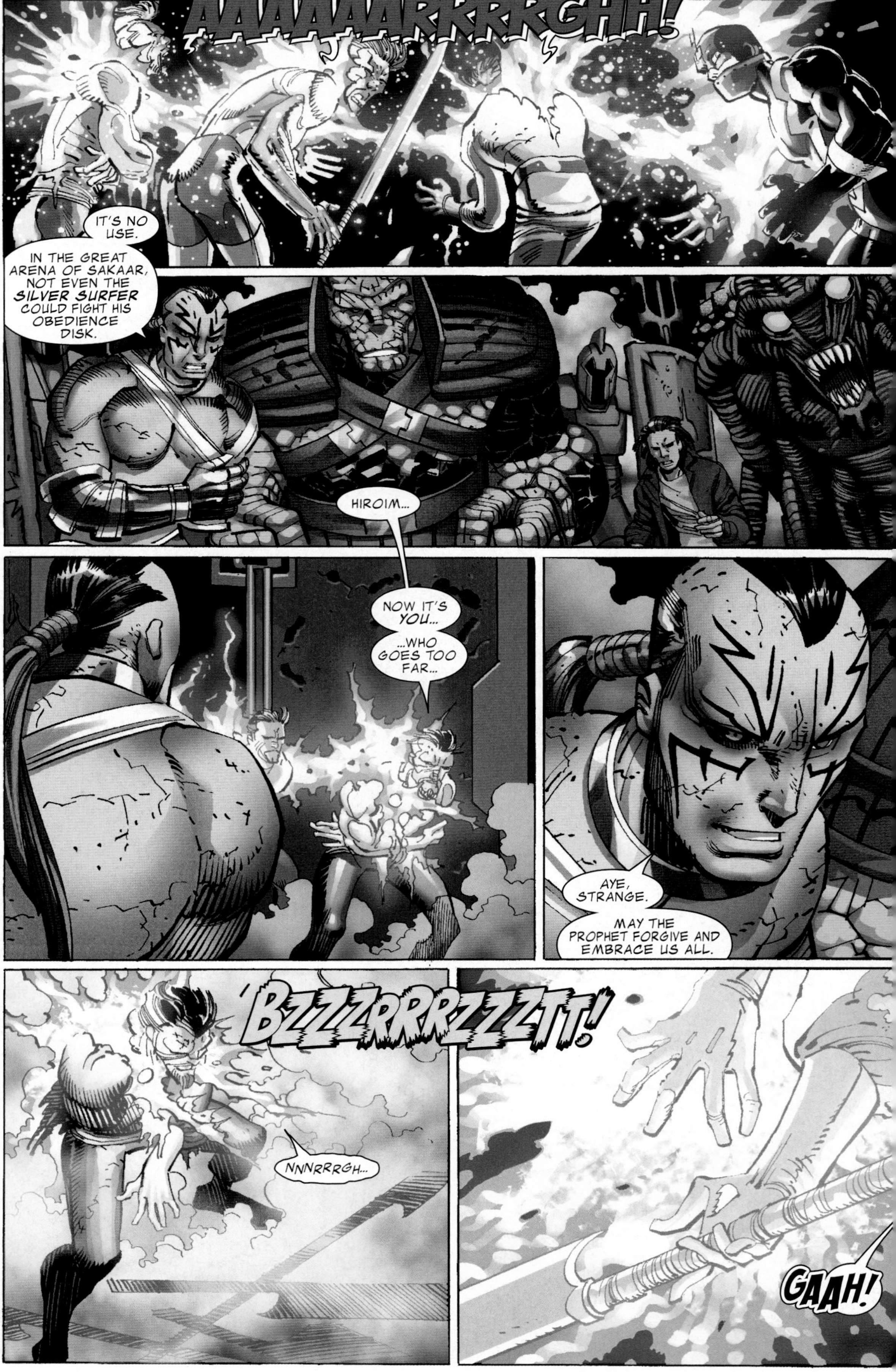
AAAAAARRRRGHH!
IT'S NO USE.
IN THE GREAT ARENA OF SAKAAR, NOT EVEN THE SILVER SURFER COULD FIGHT HIS OBEDIENCE DISK.
HIROIM...
NOW IT'S YOU...
...WHO GOES TOO FAR...
AYE, STRANGE.
MAY THE PROPHET FORGIVE AND EMBRACE US ALL.
BZZZRRRZZZTT!
NNNRRRGH...
GAAH!

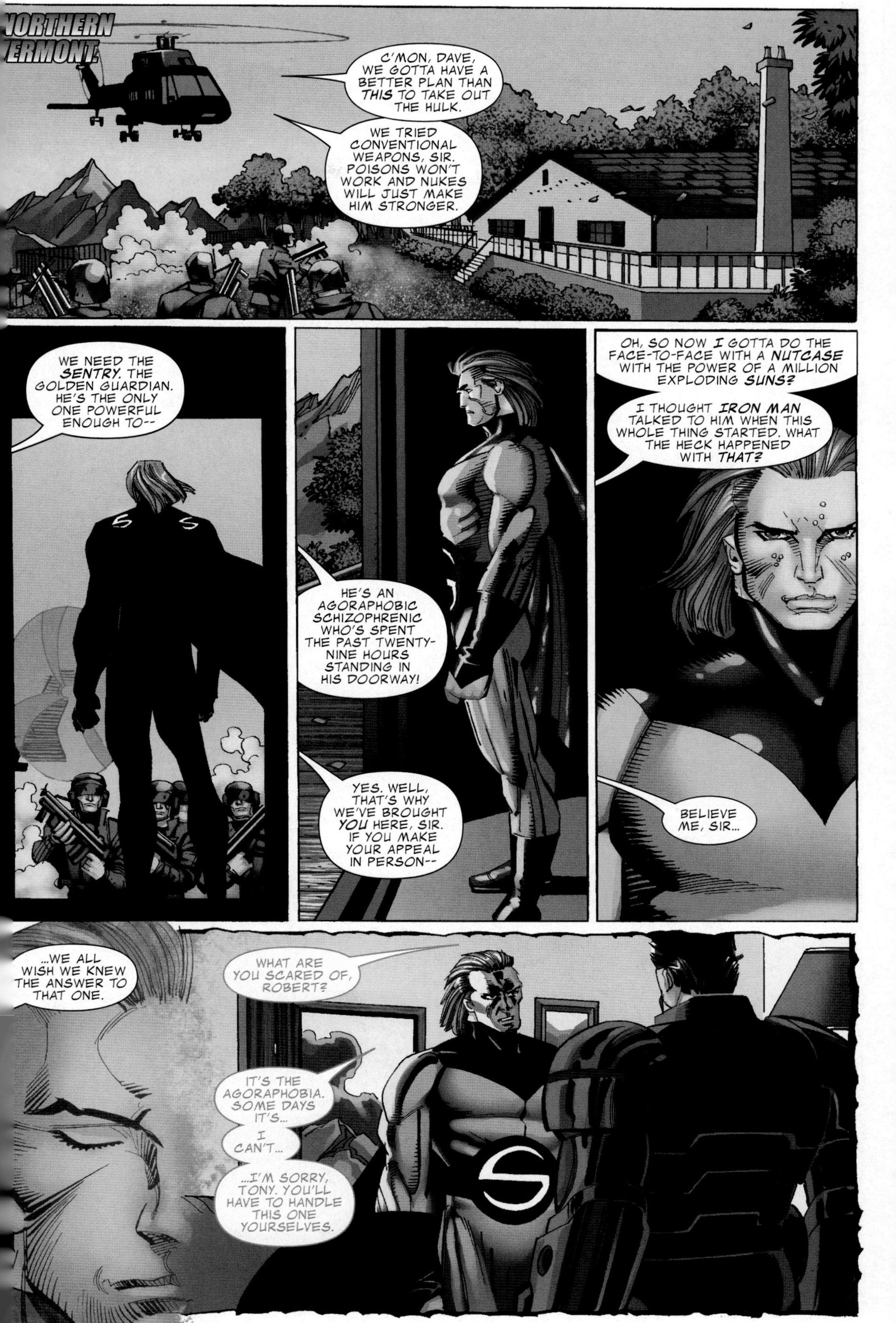
NORTHERN VERMONT.
C'MON, DAVE, WE GOTTA HAVE A BETTER PLAN THAN THIS TO TAKE OUT THE HULK.
WE TRIED CONVENTIONAL WEAPONS, SIR. POISONS WON'T WORK AND NUKES WILL JUST MAKE HIM STRONGER.
WE NEED THE SENTRY. THE GOLDEN GUARDIAN. HE'S THE ONLY ONE POWERFUL ENOUGH TO--
HE'S AN AGORAPHOBIC SCHIZOPHRENIC WHO'S SPENT THE PAST TWENTY-NINE HOURS STANDING IN HIS DOORWAY!
YES. WELL, THAT'S WHY WE'VE BROUGHT YOU HERE, SIR. IF YOU MAKE YOUR APPEAL IN PERSON--
OH, SO NOW I GOTTA DO THE FACE-TO-FACE WITH A NUTCASE WITH THE POWER OF A MILLION EXPLODING SUNS?
I THOUGHT IRON MAN TALKED TO HIM WHEN THIS WHOLE THING STARTED. WHAT THE HECK HAPPENED WITH THAT?
BELIEVE ME, SIR...
...WE ALL WISH WE KNEW THE ANSWER TO THAT ONE.
WHAT ARE YOU SCARED OF, ROBERT?
IT'S THE AGORAPHOBIA. SOME DAYS IT'S...
I CAN'T...
...I'M SORRY, TONY. YOU'LL HAVE TO HANDLE THIS ONE YOURSELVES.

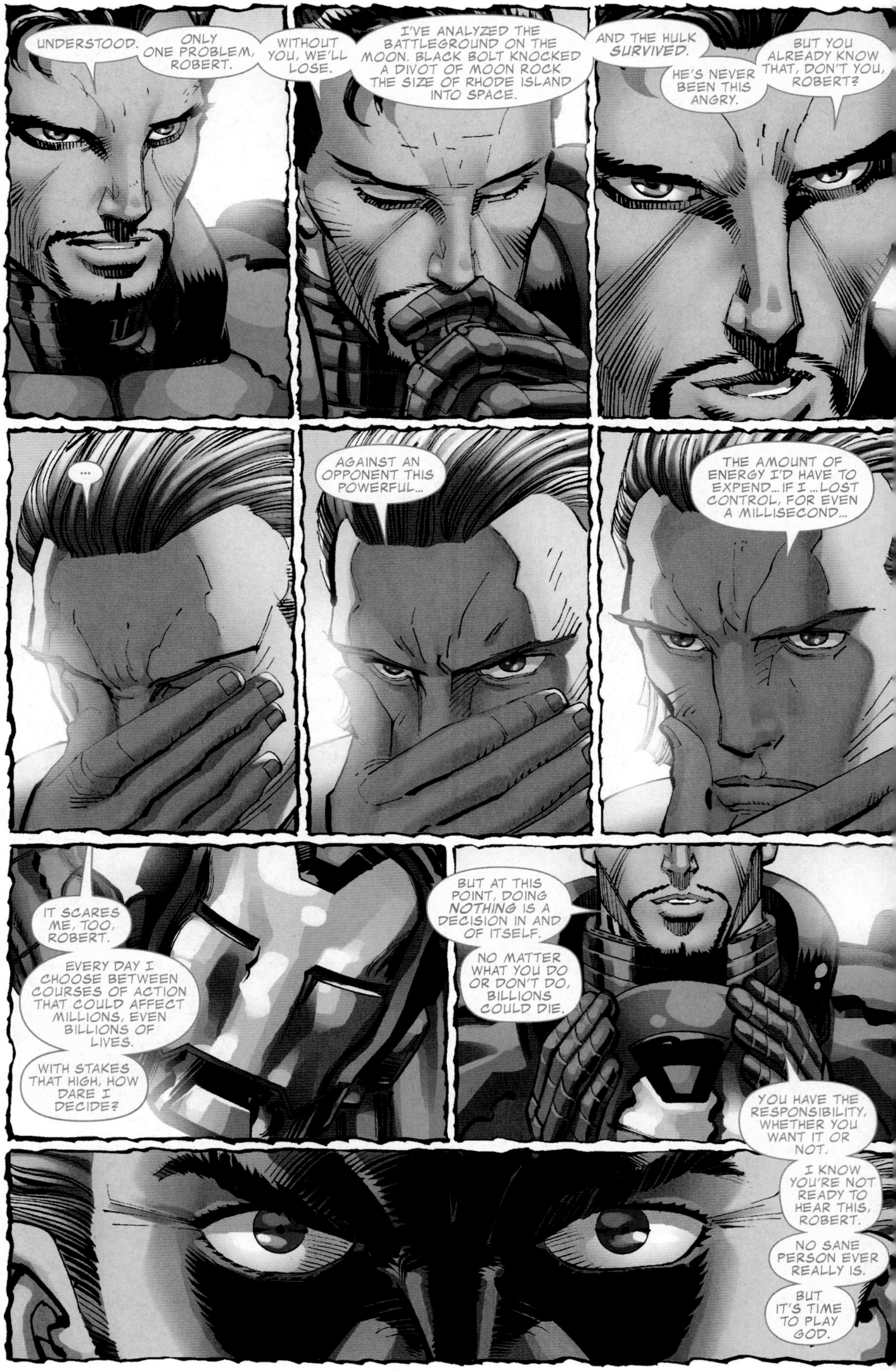
UNDERSTOOD.
ONLY ONE PROBLEM, ROBERT.
WITHOUT YOU, WE'LL LOSE.
I'VE ANALYZED THE BATTLEGROUND ON THE MOON. BLACK BOLT KNOCKED A DIVOT OF MOON ROCK THE SIZE OF RHODE ISLAND INTO SPACE.
AND THE HULK *SURVIVED*.
HE'S NEVER BEEN THIS ANGRY.
BUT YOU ALREADY KNOW THAT, DON'T YOU, ROBERT?
...
AGAINST AN OPPONENT THIS POWERFUL...
THE AMOUNT OF ENERGY I'D HAVE TO EXPEND... IF I ...LOST CONTROL, FOR EVEN A MILLISECOND...
IT SCARES ME, TOO, ROBERT.
EVERY DAY I CHOOSE BETWEEN COURSES OF ACTION THAT COULD AFFECT MILLIONS, EVEN BILLIONS OF LIVES.
WITH STAKES THAT HIGH, HOW DARE I DECIDE?
BUT AT THIS POINT, DOING *NOTHING* IS A DECISION IN AND OF ITSELF.
NO MATTER WHAT YOU DO OR DON'T DO, BILLIONS COULD DIE.
YOU HAVE THE RESPONSIBILITY, WHETHER YOU WANT IT OR NOT.
I KNOW YOU'RE NOT READY TO HEAR THIS, ROBERT.
NO SANE PERSON EVER REALLY IS.
BUT IT'S TIME TO PLAY GOD.

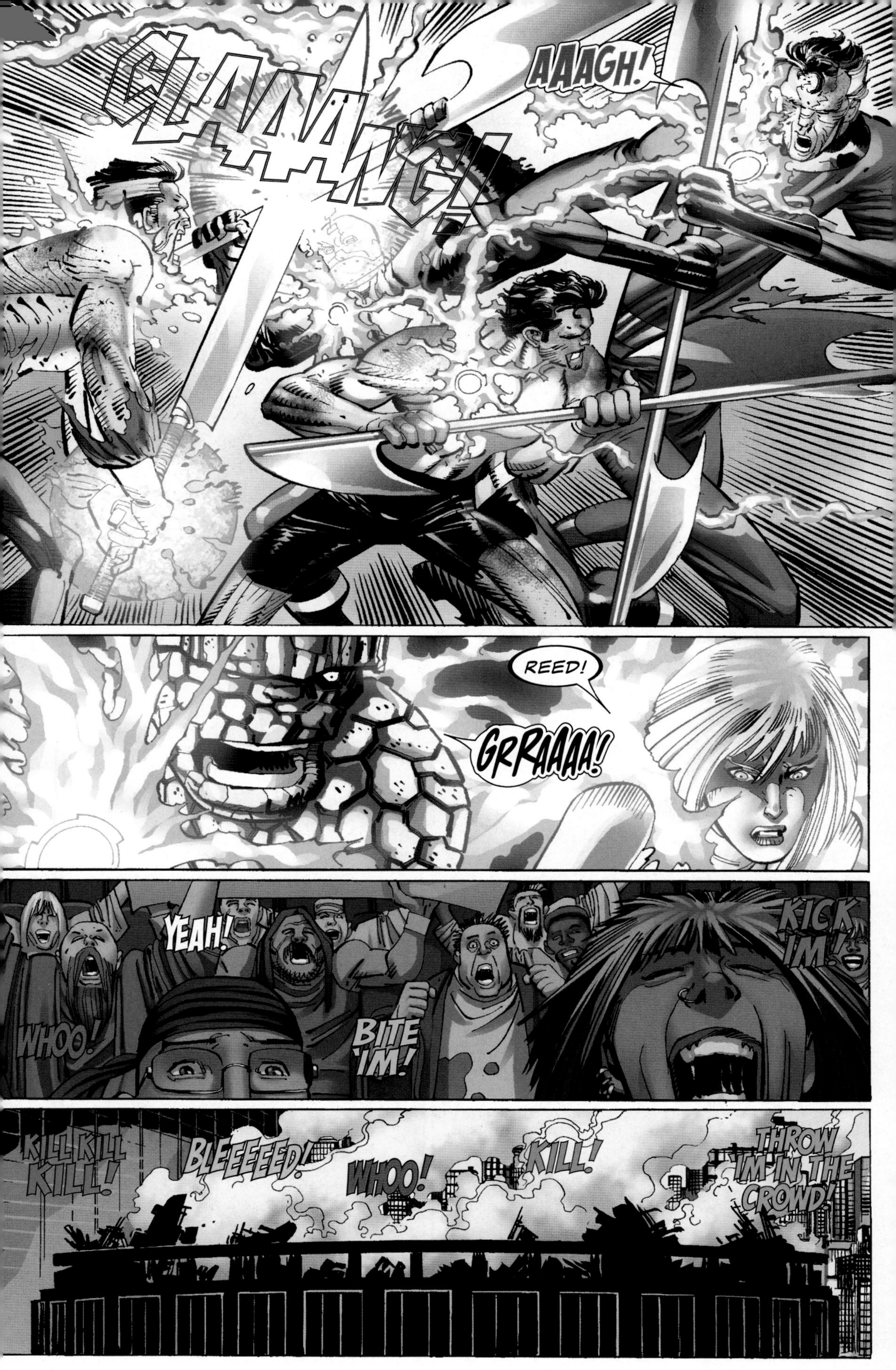
CLAAANG!!
AAAGH!
REED!
GRRAAAA!
YEAH!
KICK 'IM!
WHOO!
BITE 'IM!
KILL KILL KILL!
BLEEEEED!
WHOO!
KILL!
THROW 'IM IN THE CROWD!

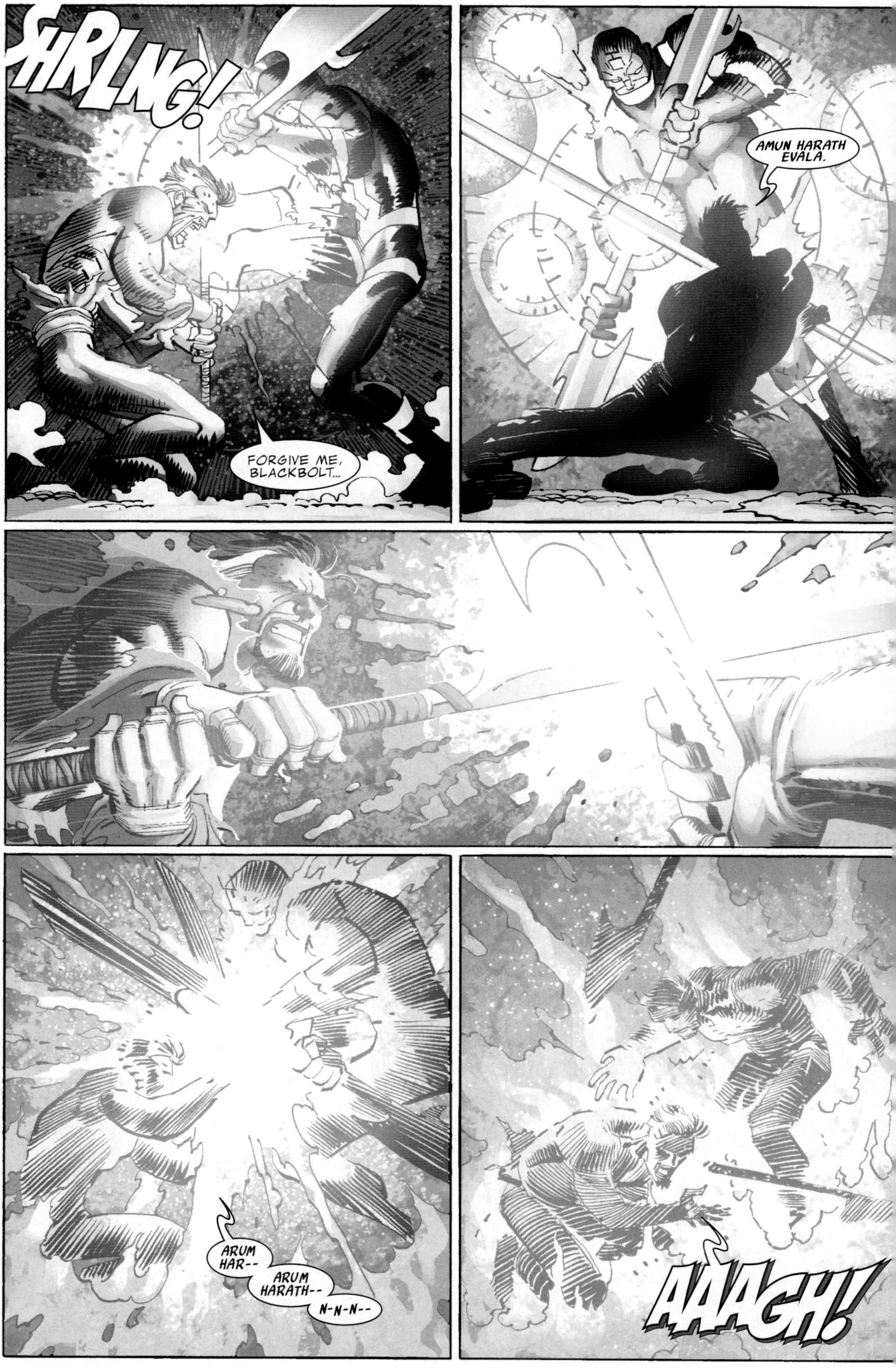
SHRLNG!
FORGIVE ME, BLACKBOLT...
AMUN HARATH EVALA.
ARUM HAR--
ARUM HARATH--
N-N-N--
AAAGH!

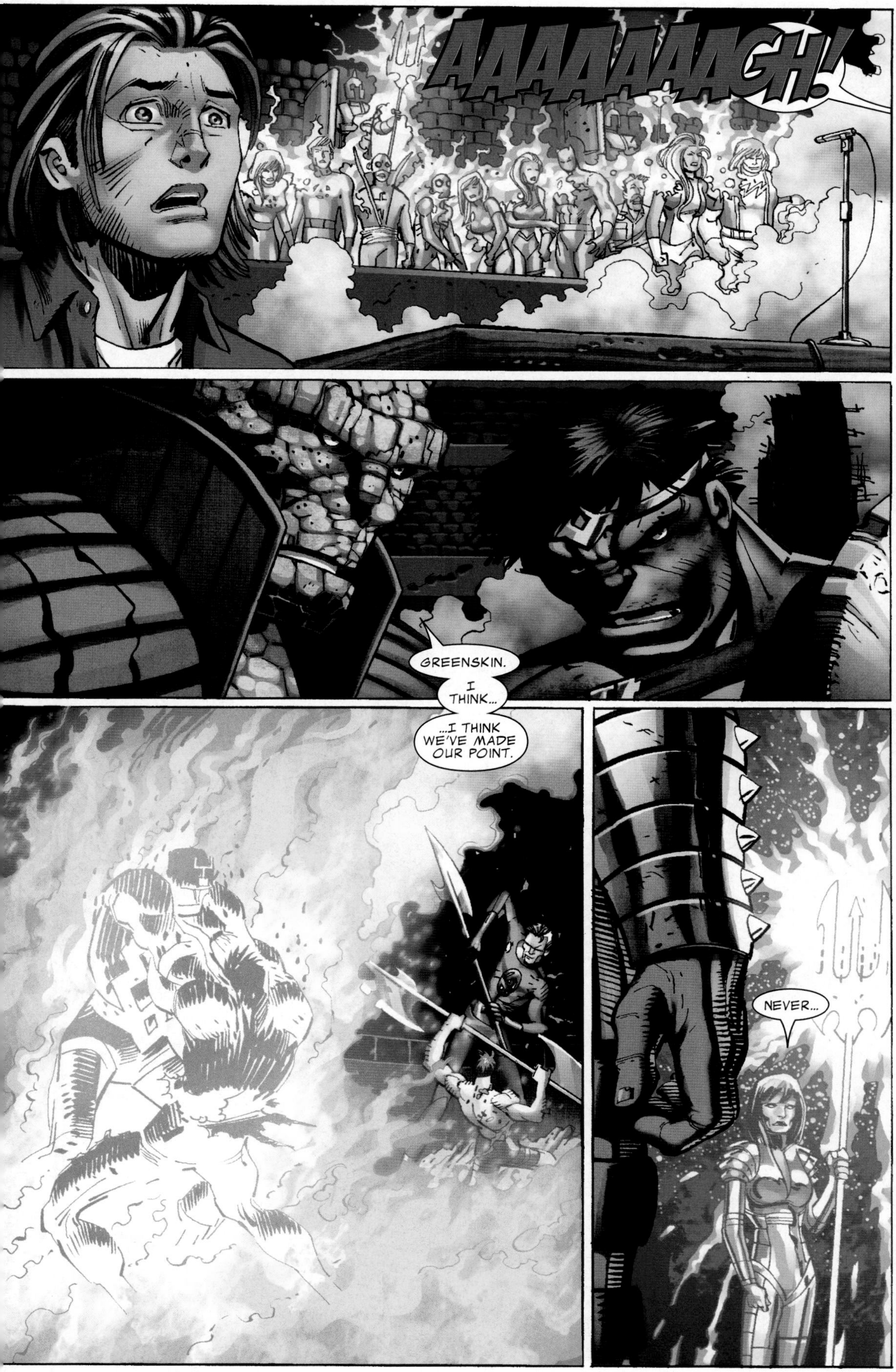
AAAAAAAAGH!
GREENSKIN.
I THINK...
...I THINK WE'VE MADE OUR POINT.
NEVER...

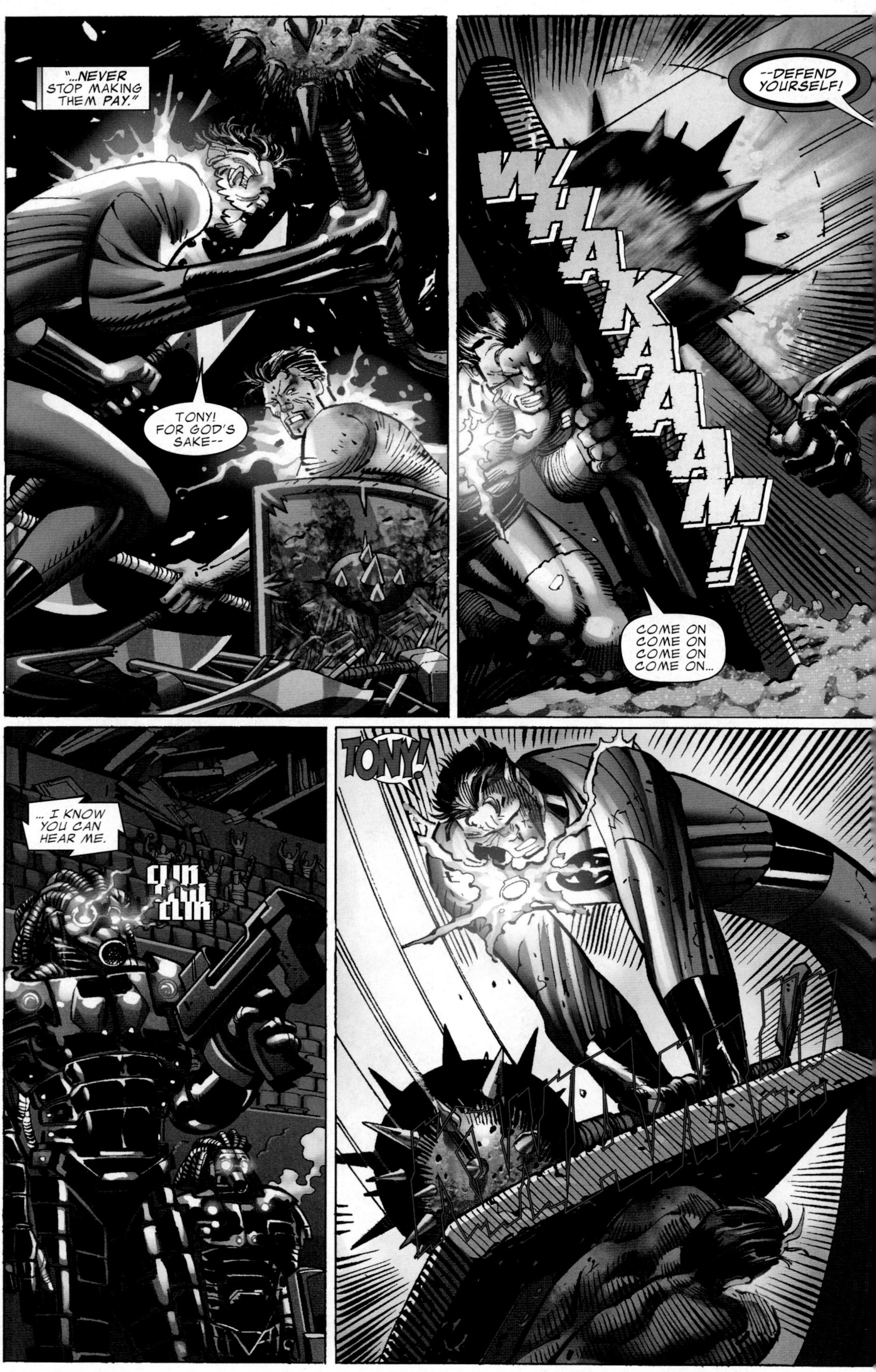
"...NEVER STOP MAKING THEM PAY."
TONY! FOR GOD'S SAKE--
--DEFEND YOURSELF!
WHAKAAAM!
COME ON COME ON COME ON COME ON...
...I KNOW YOU CAN HEAR ME.
CLIK
CLIK
TONY!

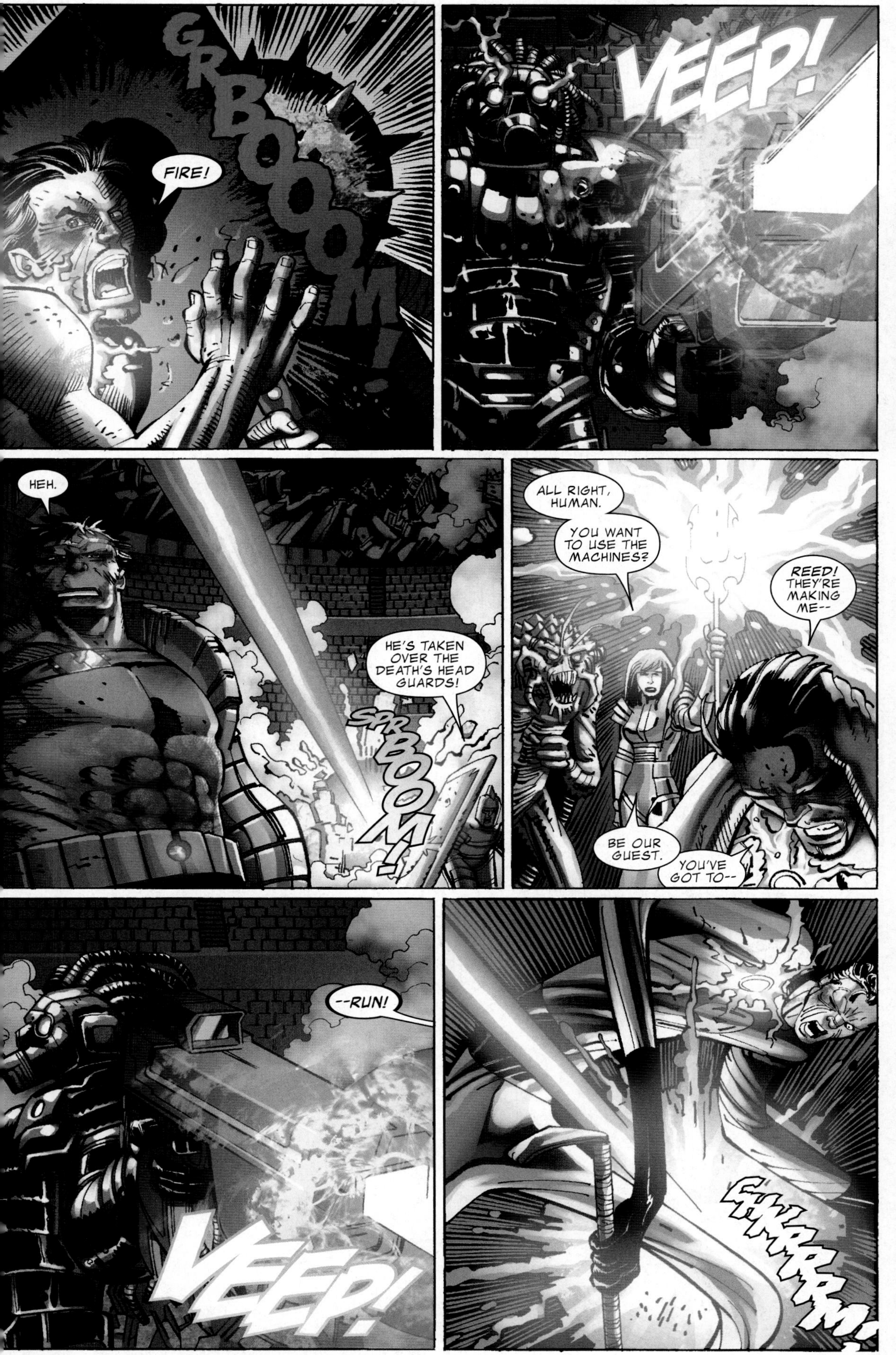
GRBOOOOM
FIRE!
VEEP!
HEH.
HE'S TAKEN OVER THE DEATH'S HEAD GUARDS!
SPRBOOM!
ALL RIGHT, HUMAN.
YOU WANT TO USE THE MACHINES?
REED! THEY'RE MAKING ME--
BE OUR GUEST.
YOU'VE GOT TO--
--RUN!
VEEP!
SKRRRM!

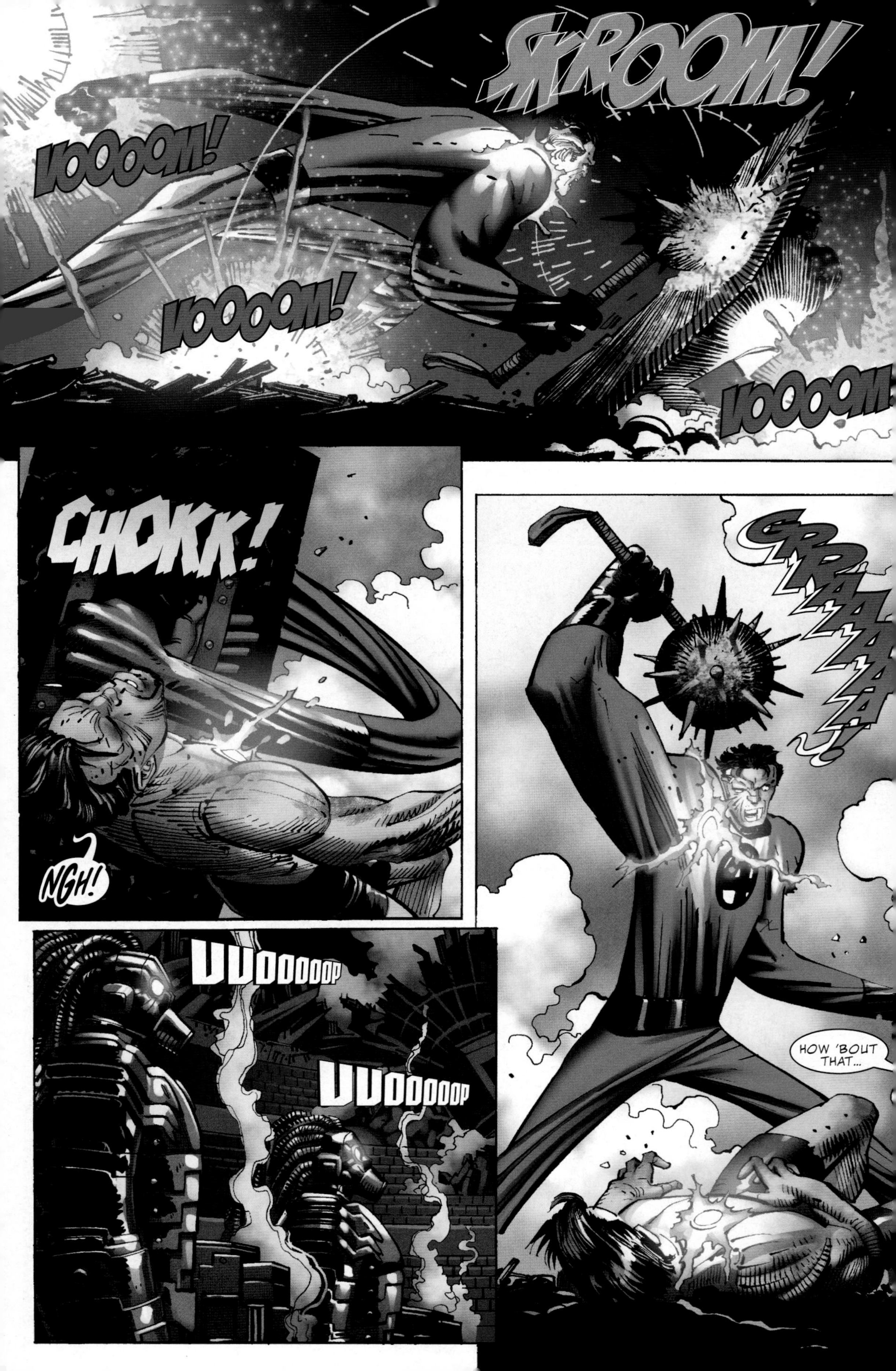
SKROOM!
VOOOOM!
VOOOOM!
VOOOOM
CHOKK!
NGH!
GRRAAAAAA!
UVOOOOOP
UVOOOOOP
HOW 'BOUT THAT...

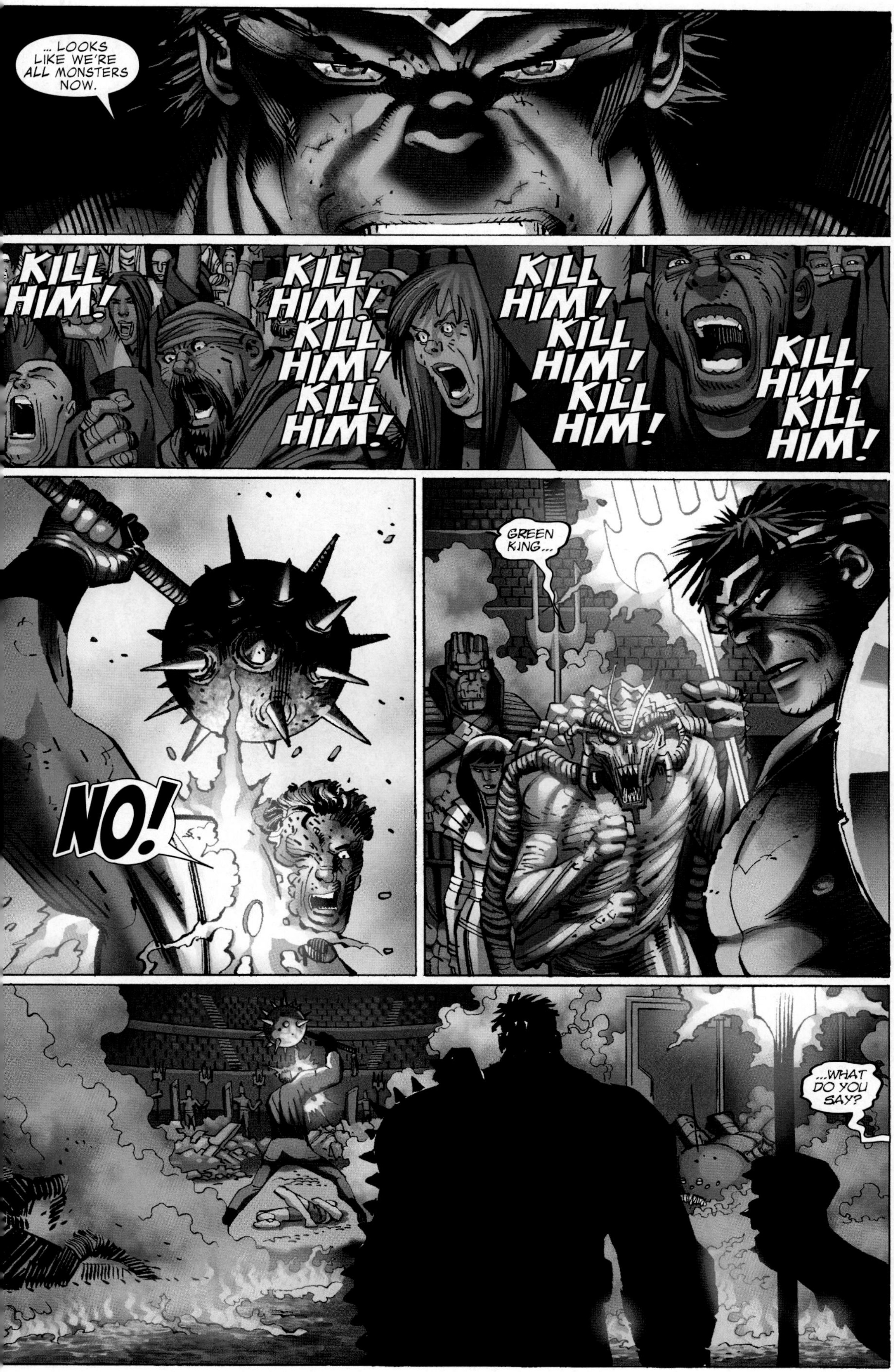
... LOOKS LIKE WE'RE ALL MONSTERS NOW.
KILL HIM!
KILL HIM! KILL HIM! KILL HIM!
KILL HIM! KILL HIM! KILL HIM!
KILL HIM! KILL HIM!
NO!
GREEN KING...
...WHAT DO YOU SAY?

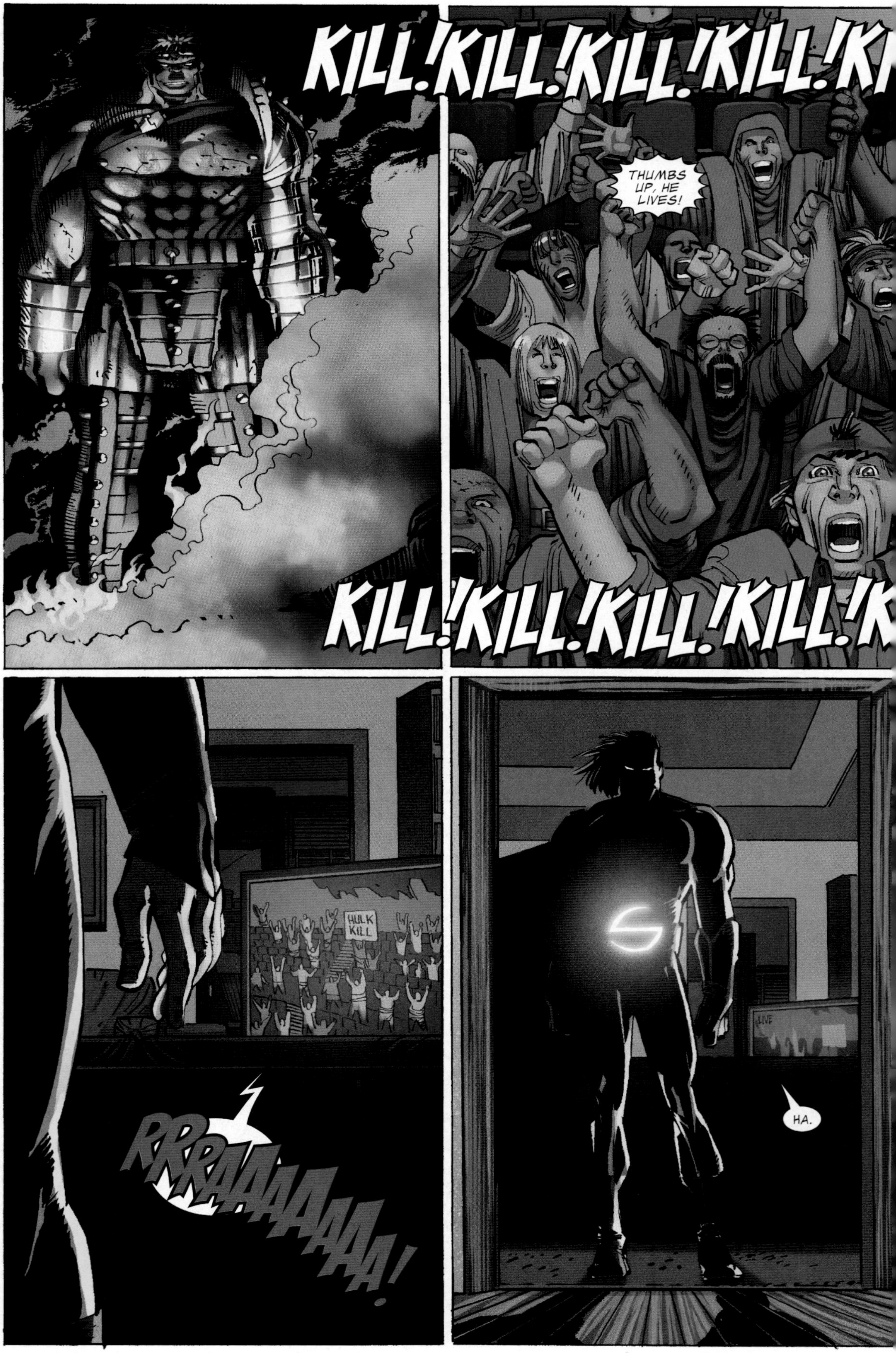

KILL! KILL! KILL! KILL! KI
THUMBS UP, HE LIVES!
KILL! KILL! KILL! KILL! K
HULK KILL
RRRAAAAAAAAA!
HA.

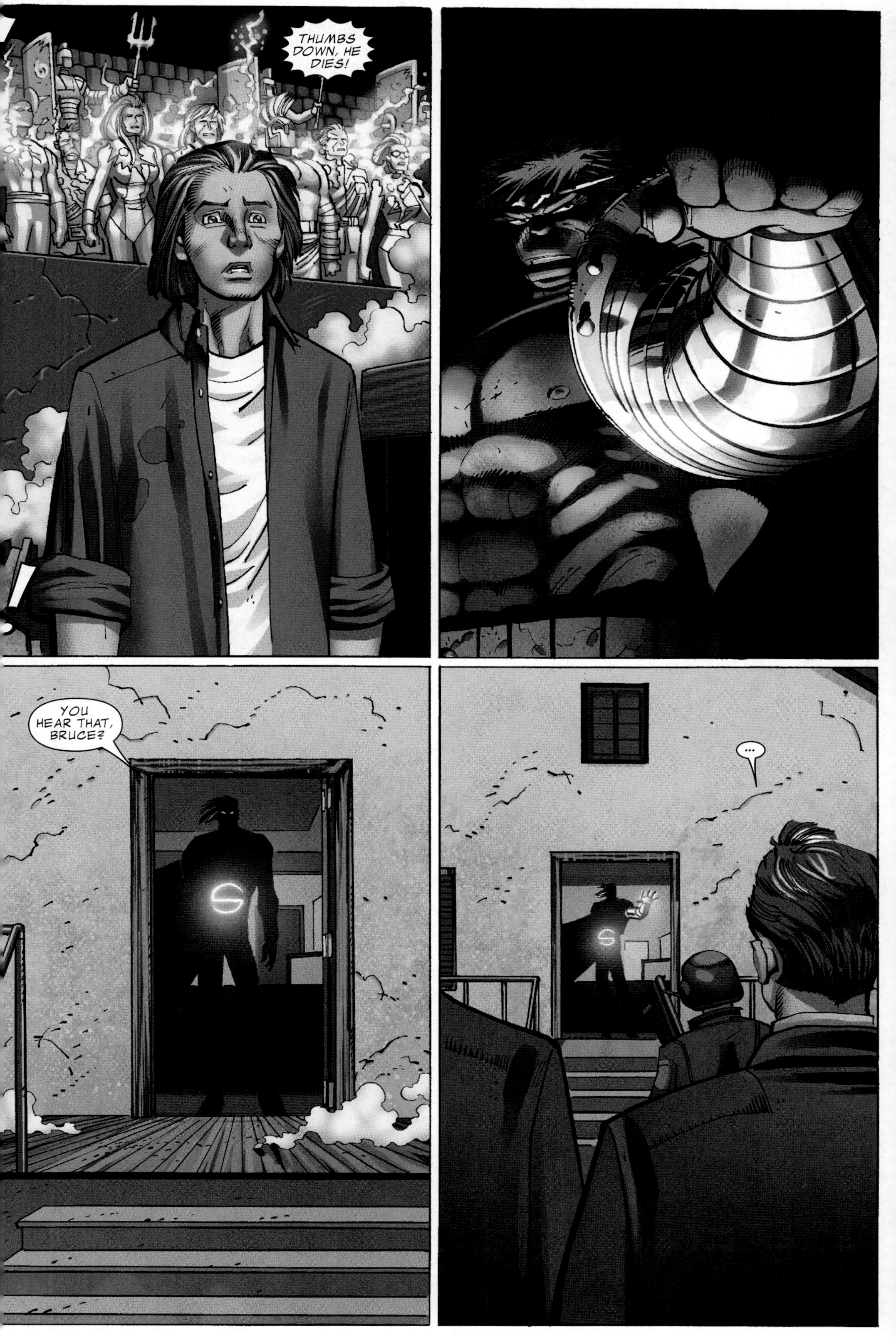
THUMBS DOWN, HE DIES!
YOU HEAR THAT, BRUCE?
...

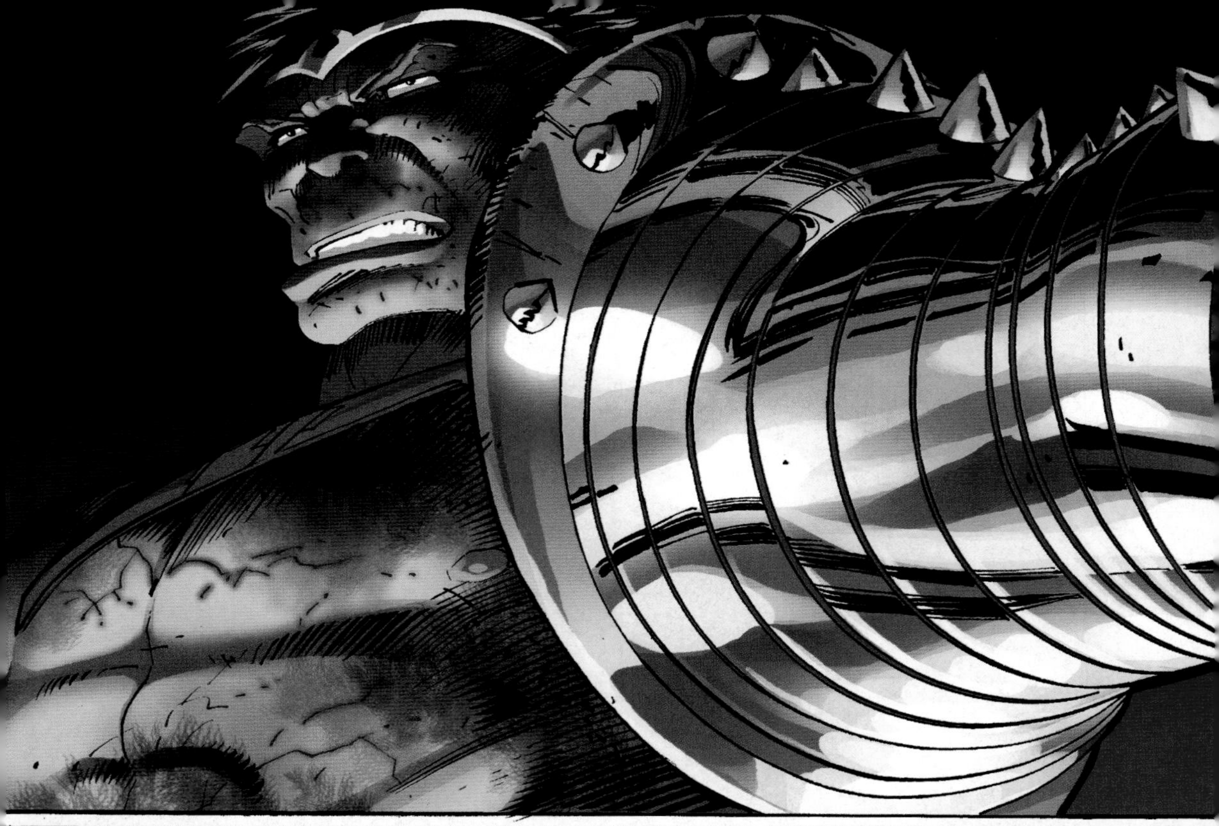

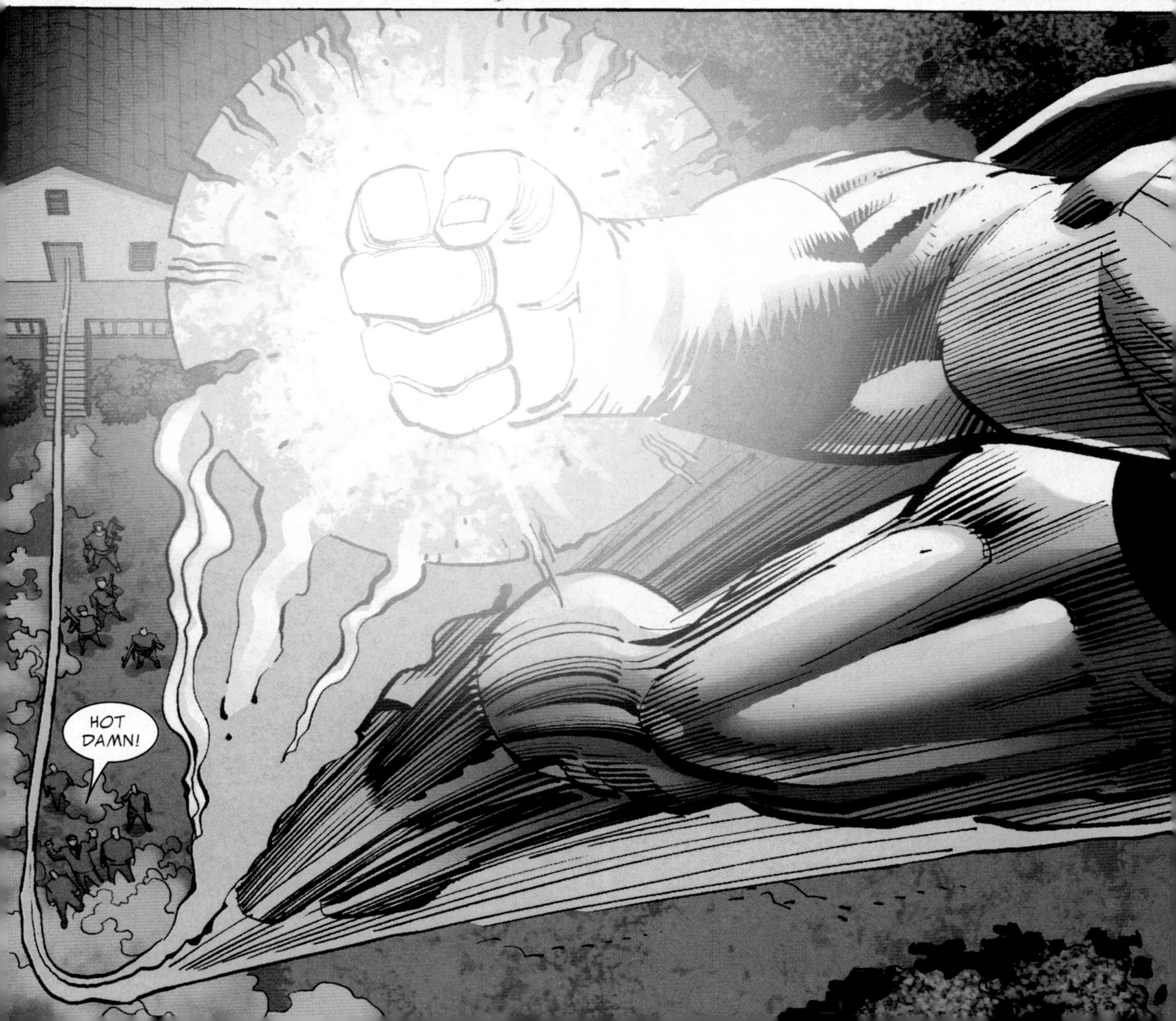
HOT DAMN!

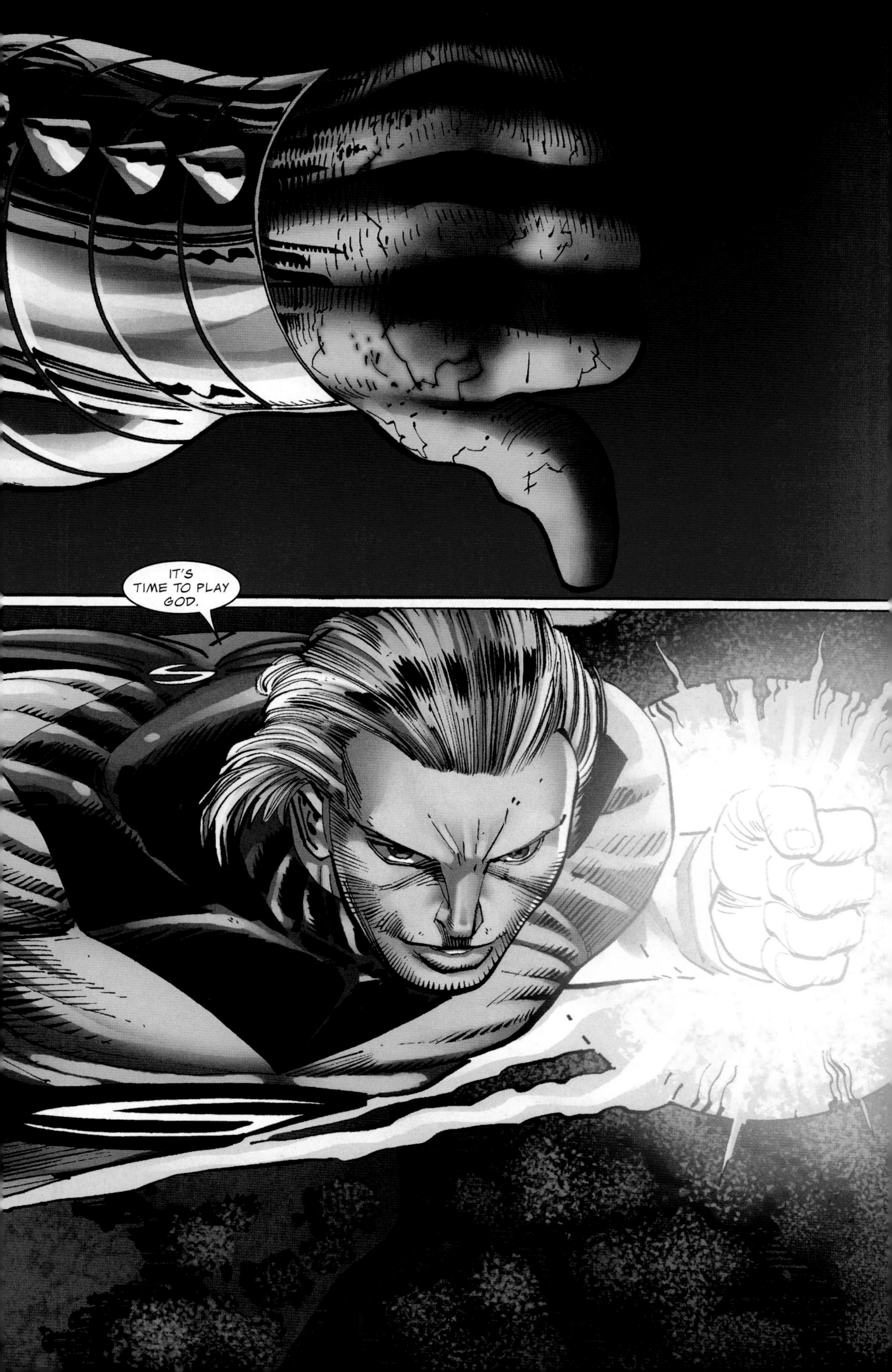
IT'S TIME TO PLAY GOD.

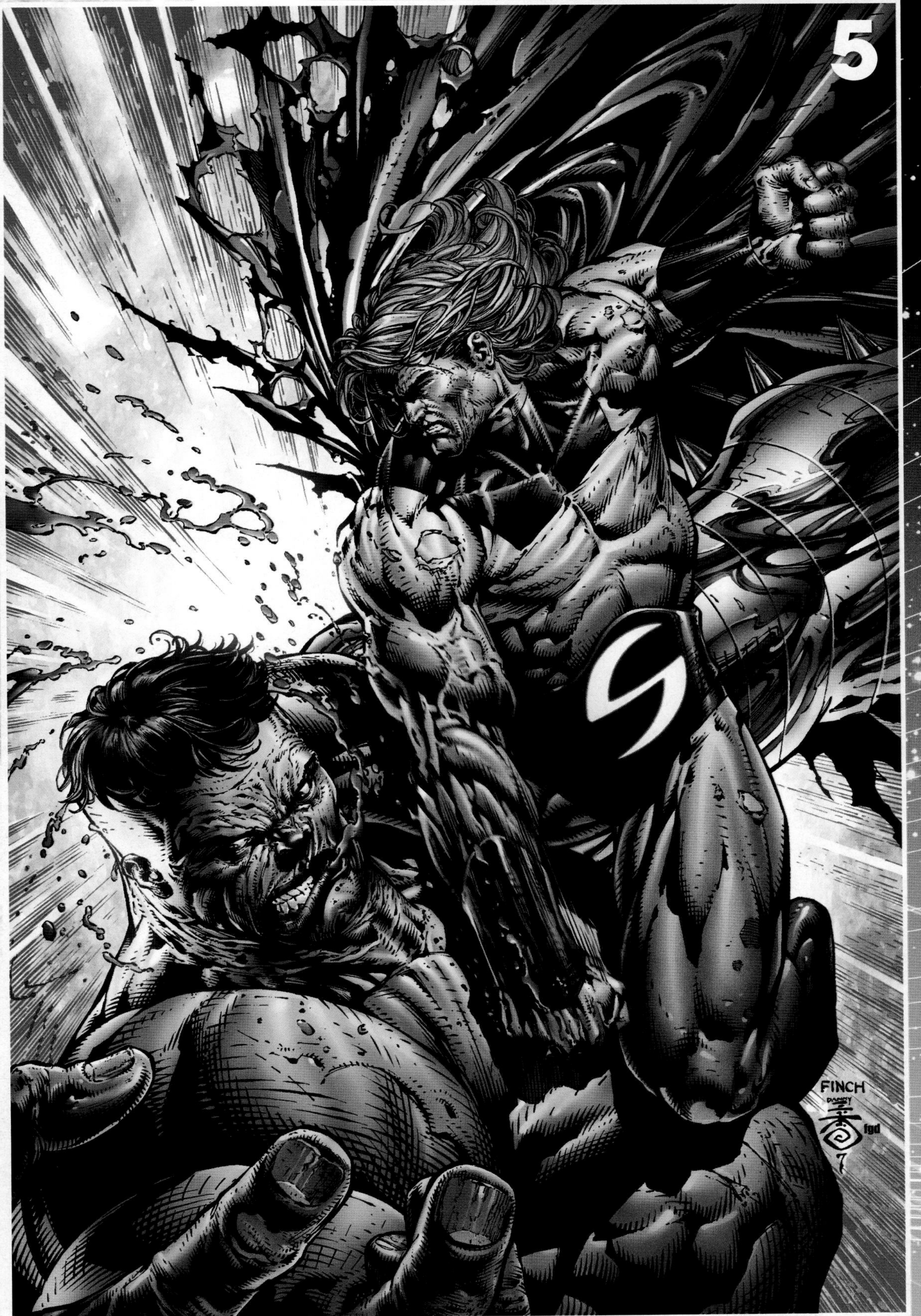
5
FINCH

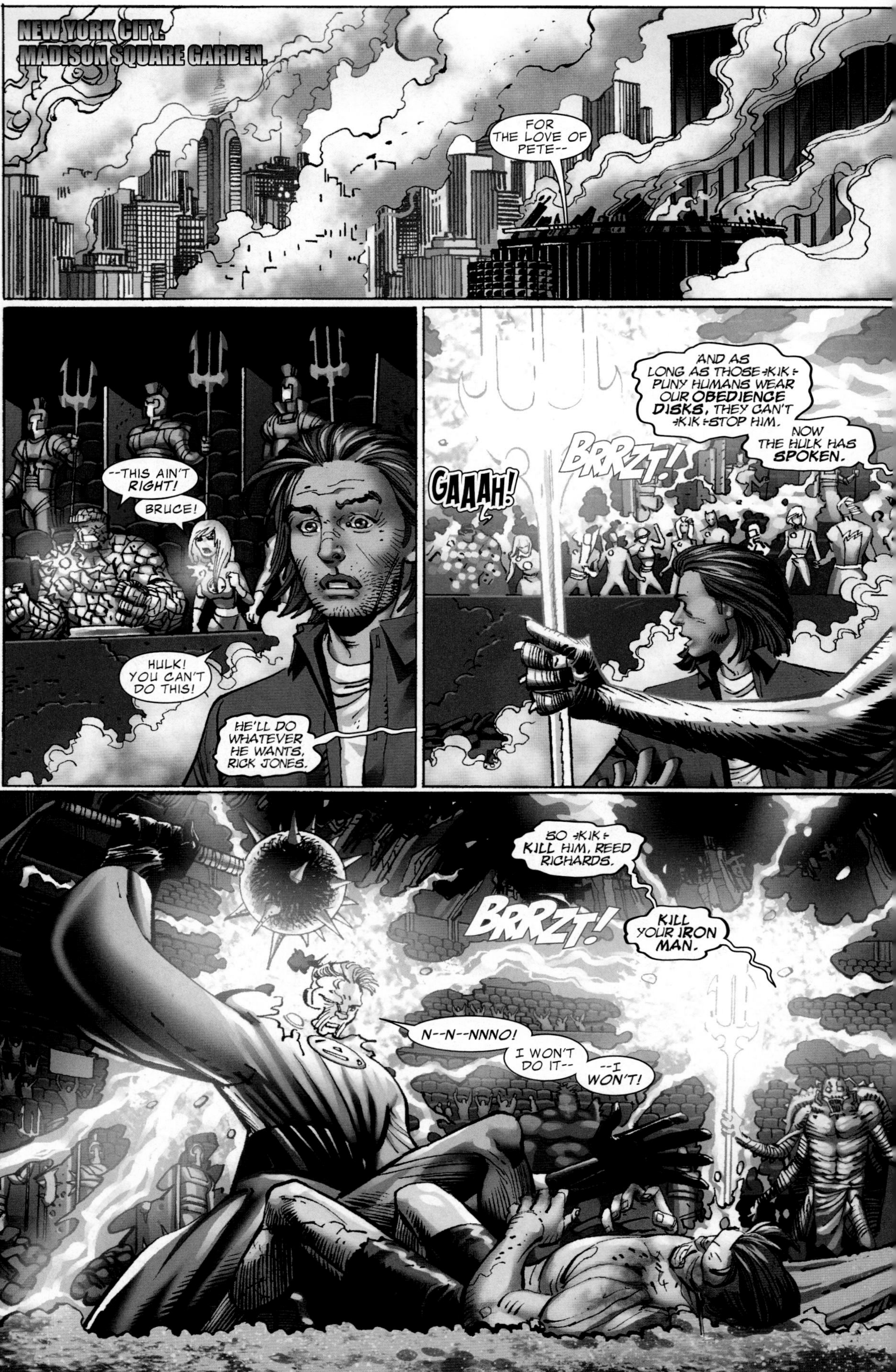
NEW YORK CITY.
MADISON SQUARE GARDEN.
FOR THE LOVE OF PETE--
--THIS AIN'T RIGHT!
BRUCE!
HULK! YOU CAN'T DO THIS!
HE'LL DO WHATEVER HE WANTS, RICK JONES.
AND AS LONG AS THOSE -KIK- PUNY HUMANS WEAR OUR OBEDIENCE DISKS, THEY CAN'T -KIK- STOP HIM.
NOW THE HULK HAS SPOKEN.
BRRZT!
GAAAH!
SO -KIK- KILL HIM, REED RICHARDS.
BRRZT!
KILL YOUR IRON MAN.
N--N--NNNO!
I WON'T DO IT--
--I WON'T!

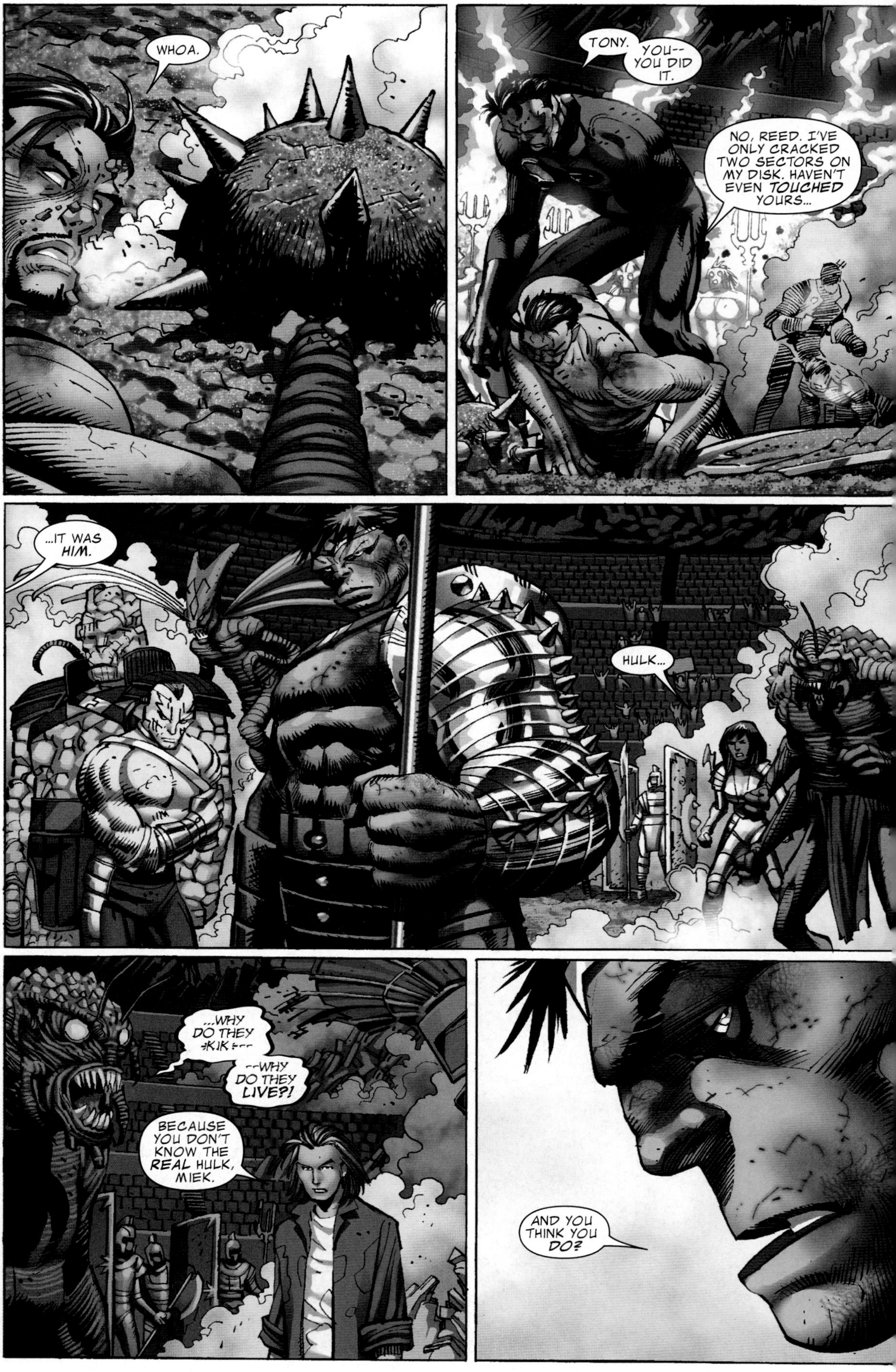
WHOA.
TONY. YOU-- YOU DID IT.
NO, REED. I'VE ONLY CRACKED TWO SECTORS ON MY DISK. HAVEN'T EVEN *TOUCHED* YOURS...
...IT WAS *HIM*.
HULK...
...WHY DO THEY KIK--
--WHY DO THEY *LIVE?!*
BECAUSE YOU DON'T KNOW THE *REAL* HULK, MIEK.
AND YOU THINK YOU *DO?*

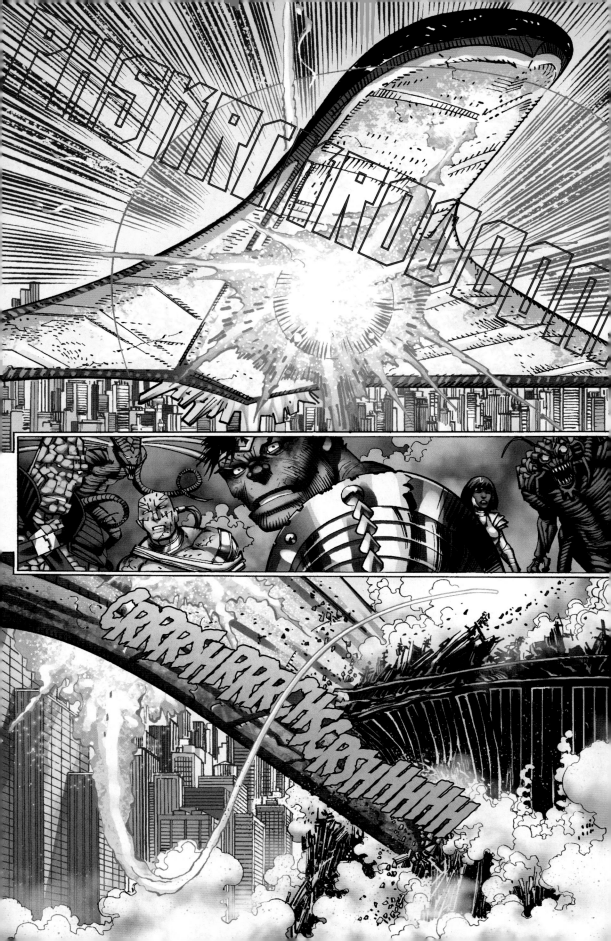

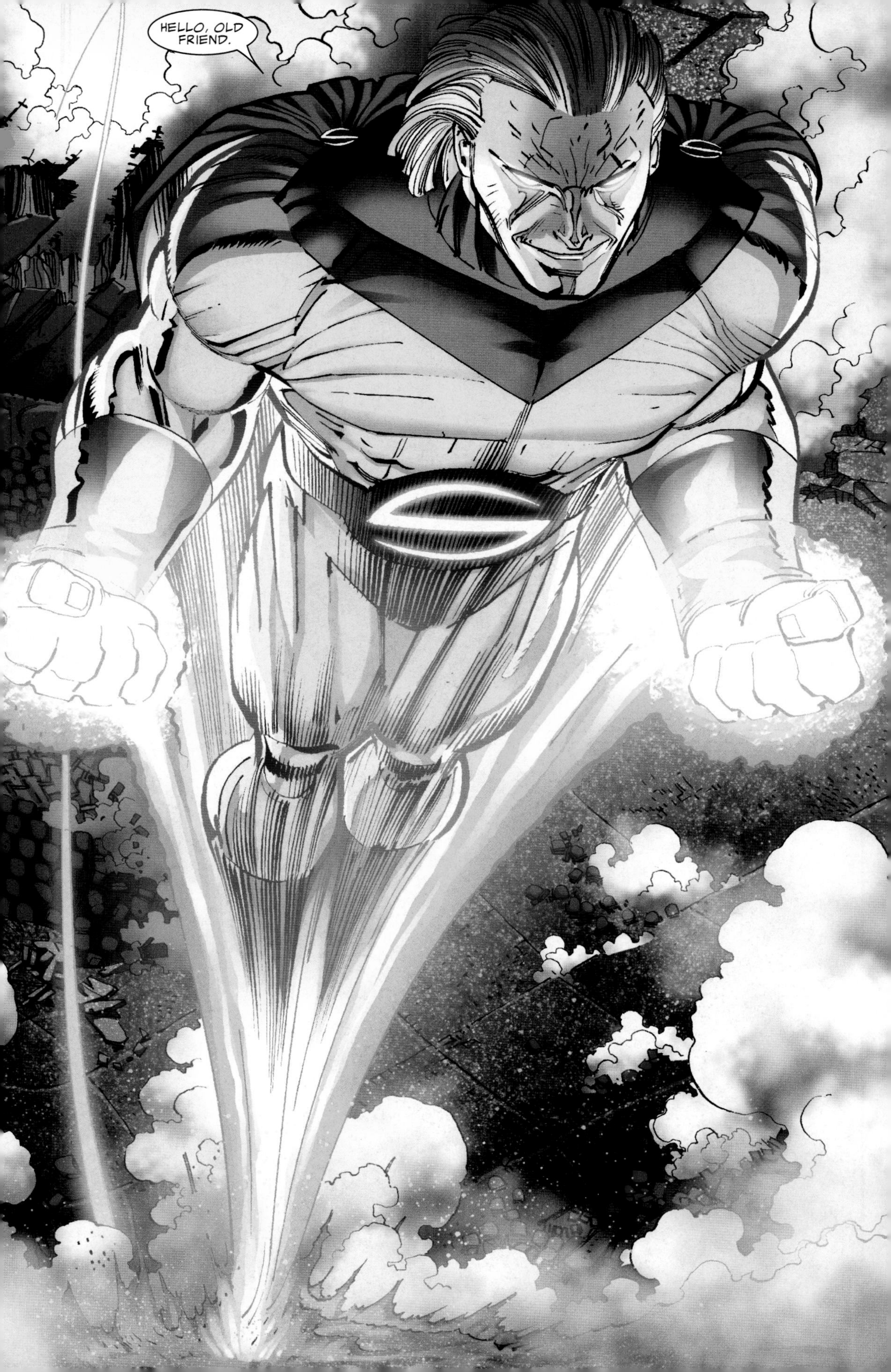
HELLO, OLD FRIEND.

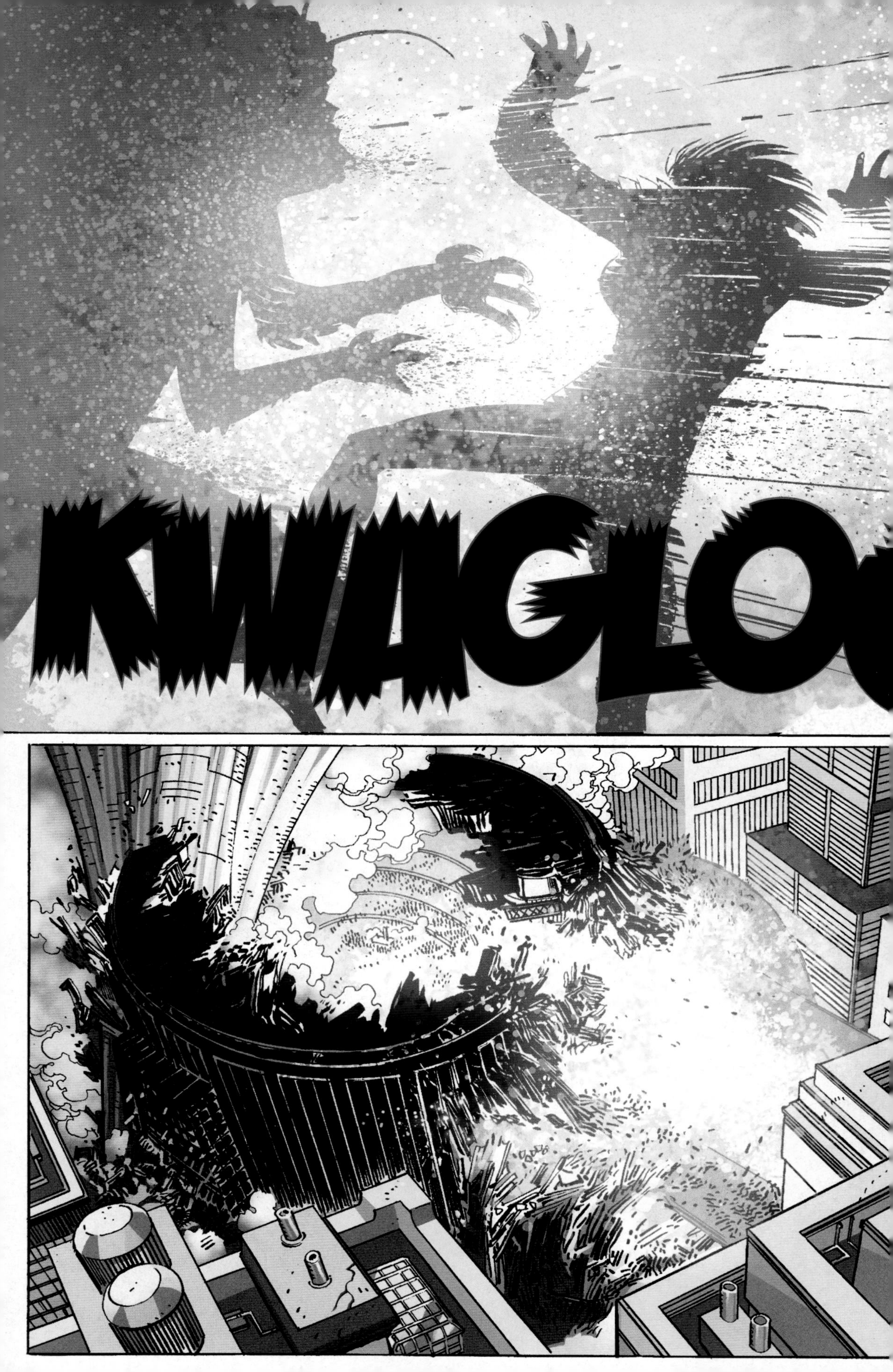
KWAGLO

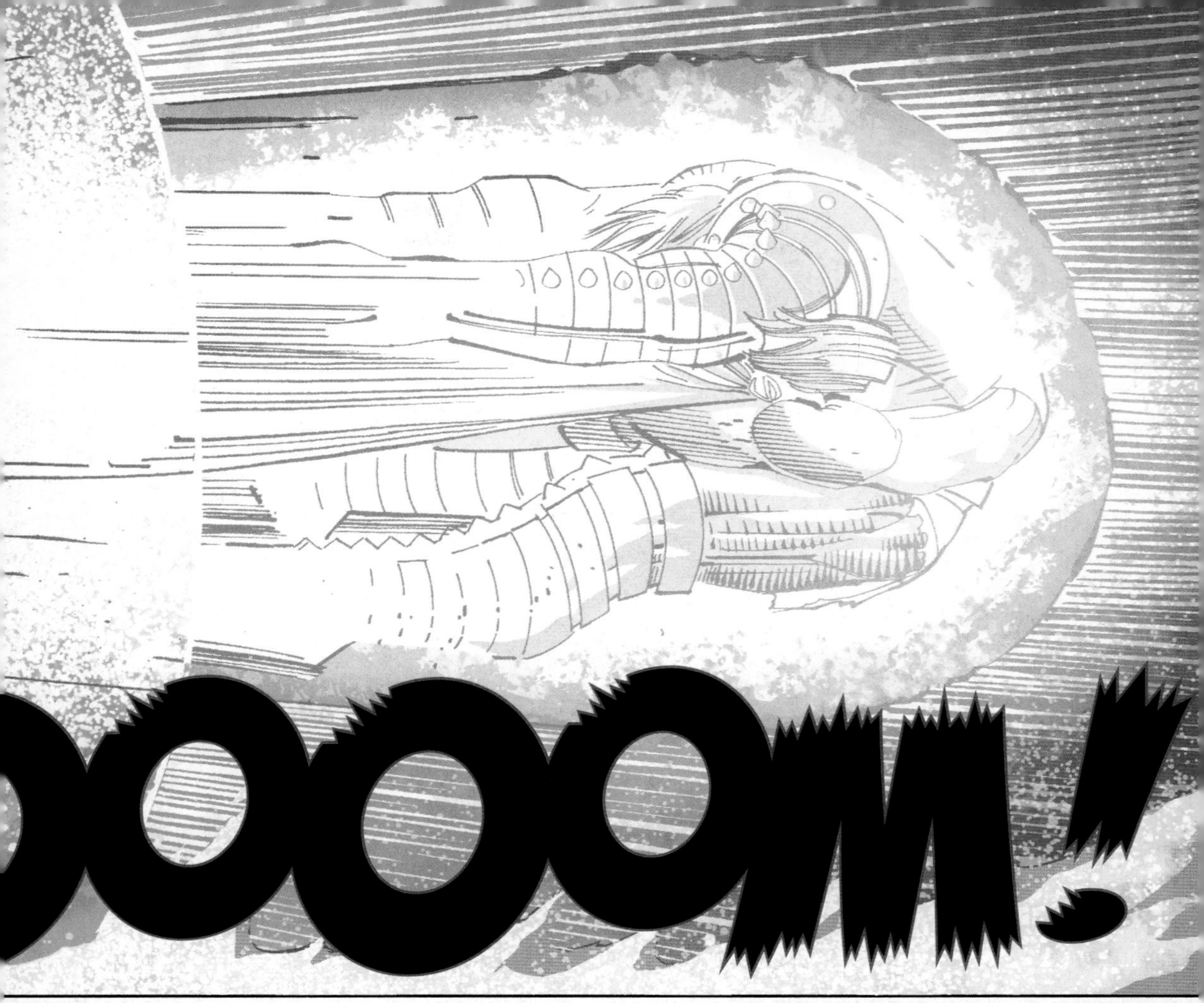
OOOOM!

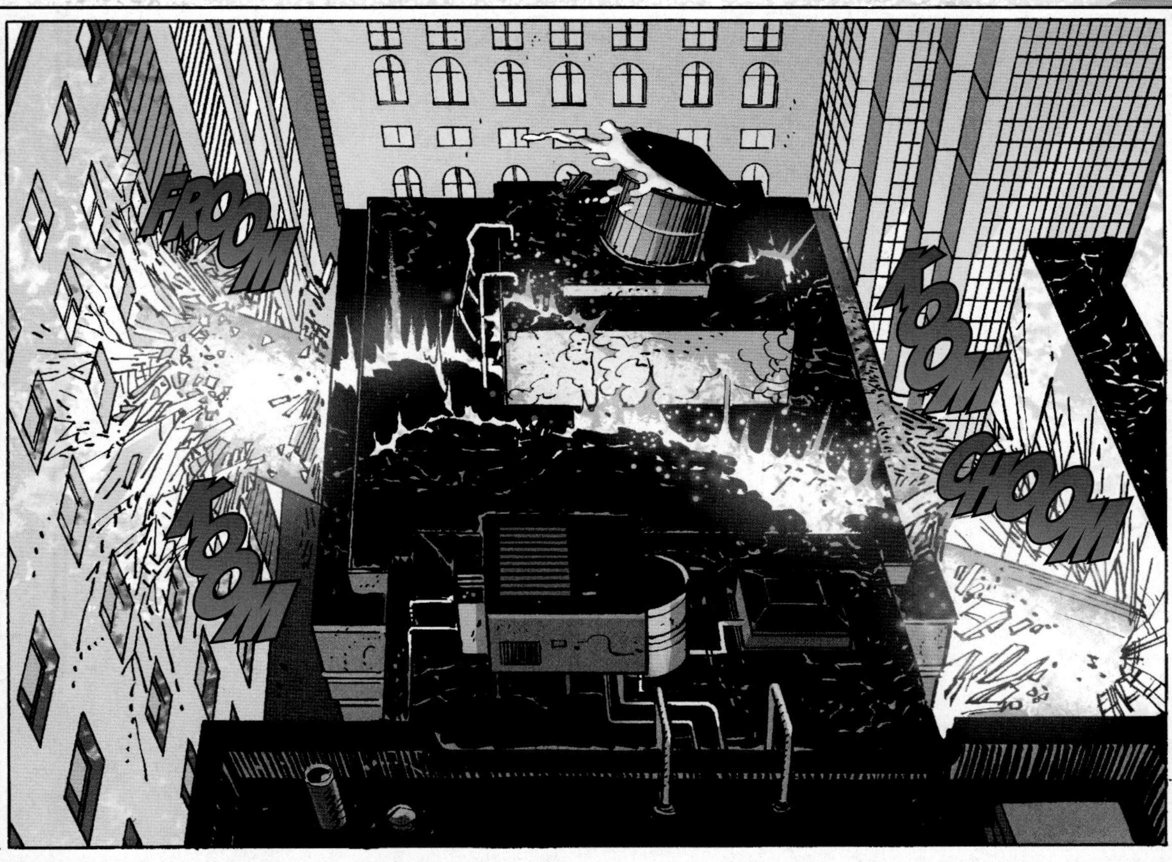
FROOM
KOOM
KOOM
CHOOM

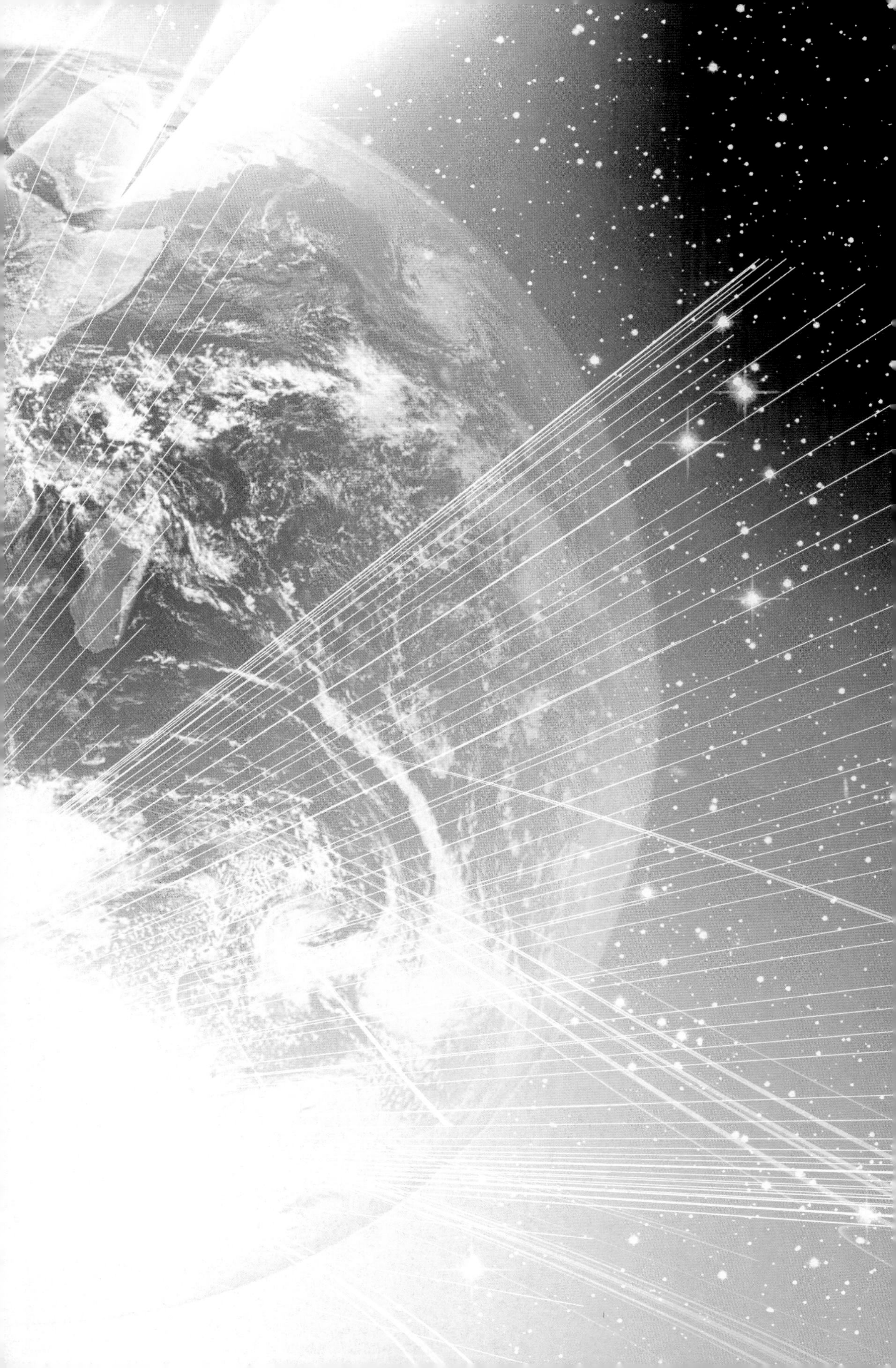

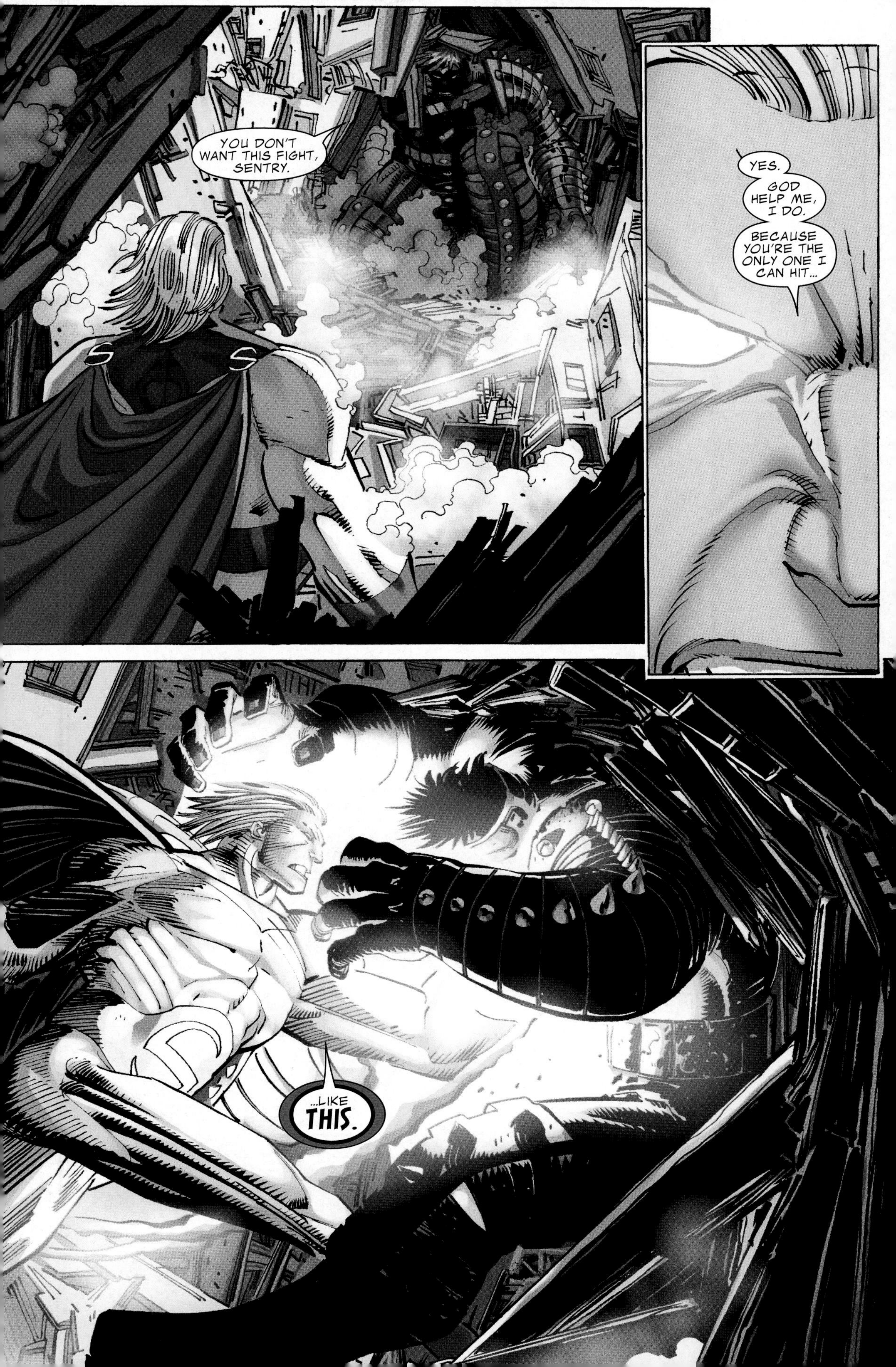
YOU DON'T WANT THIS FIGHT, SENTRY.
YES.
GOD HELP ME, I DO.
BECAUSE YOU'RE THE ONLY ONE I CAN HIT...
...LIKE THIS.

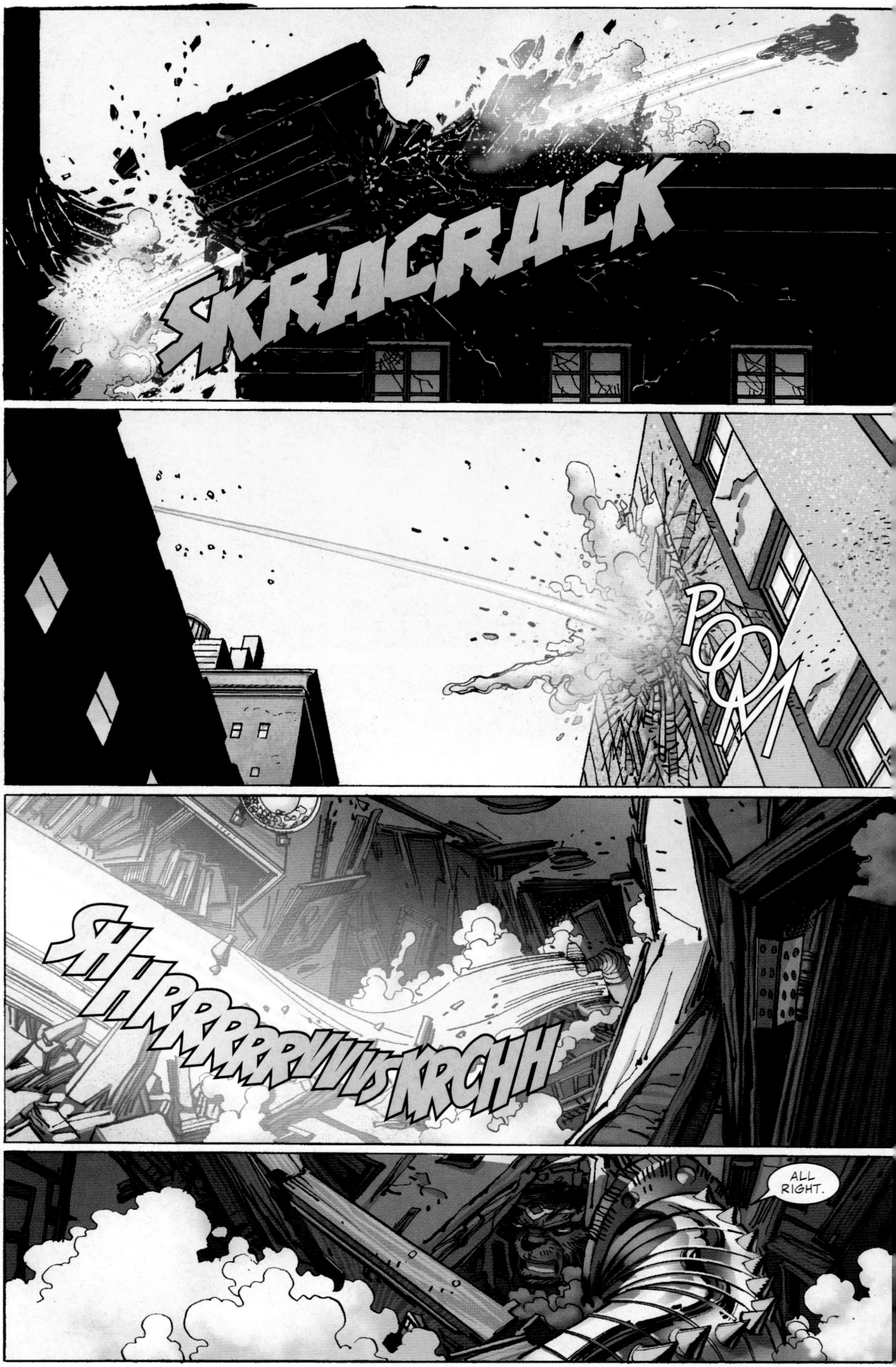
SKRACRACK
POOM
SHHRRRRRRVVVS KRCHH
ALL RIGHT.

STARK!
RICHARDS!

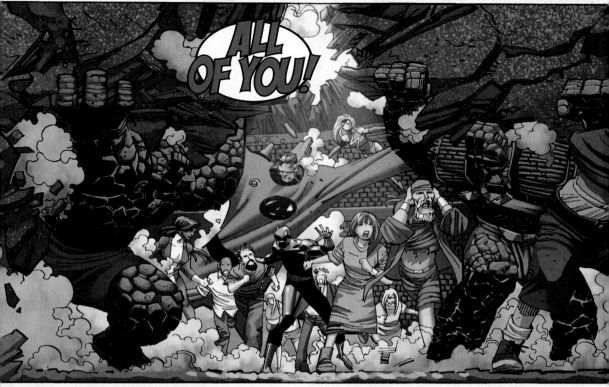

ALL OF YOU!

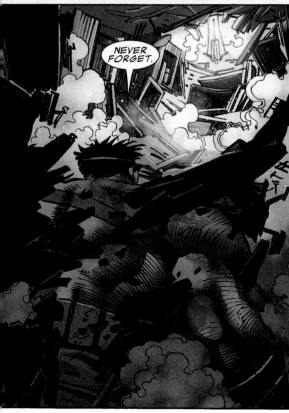

NEVER FORGET.

WHATEVER HAPPENS NEXT...

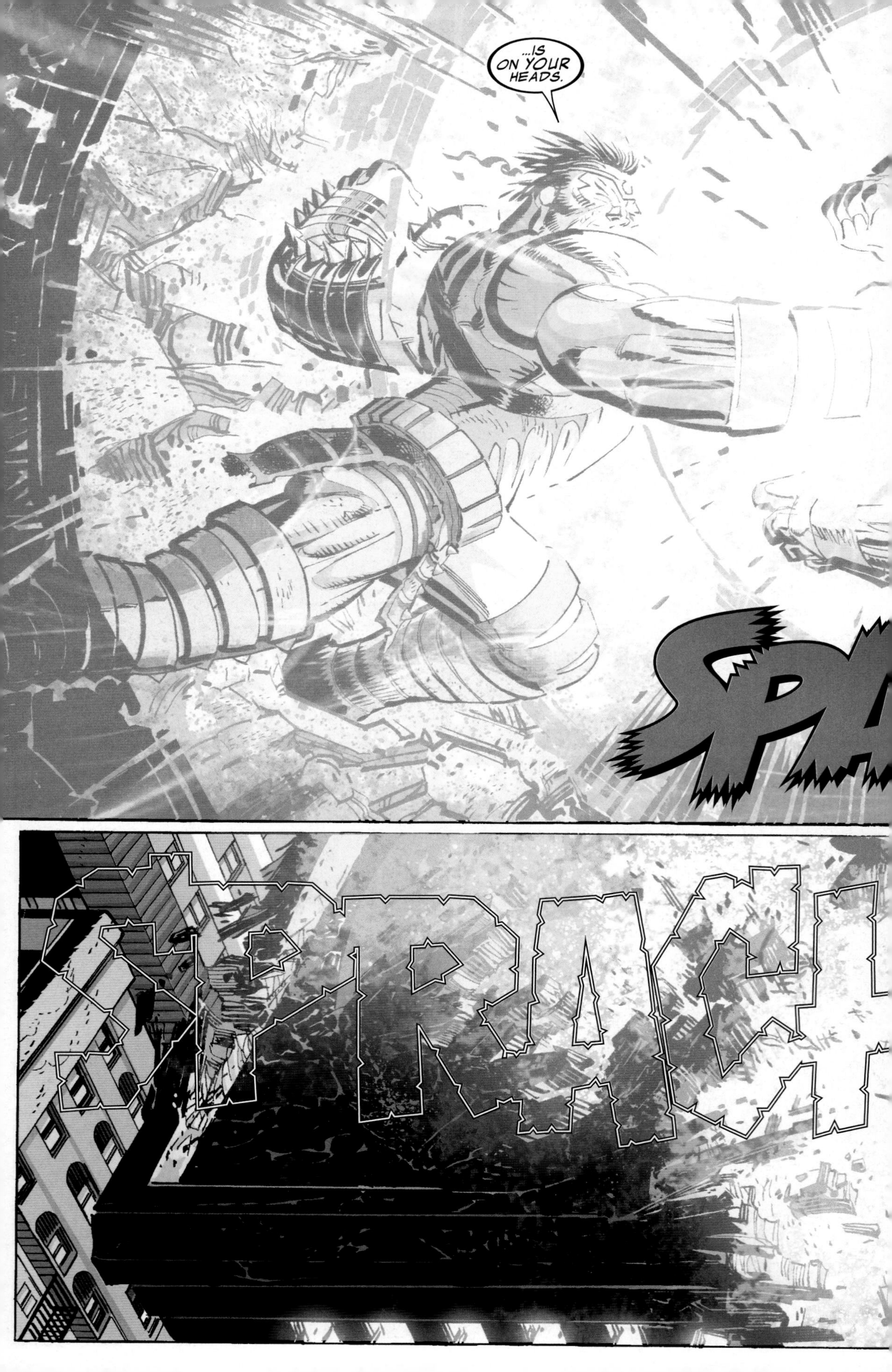
...IS ON YOUR HEADS.

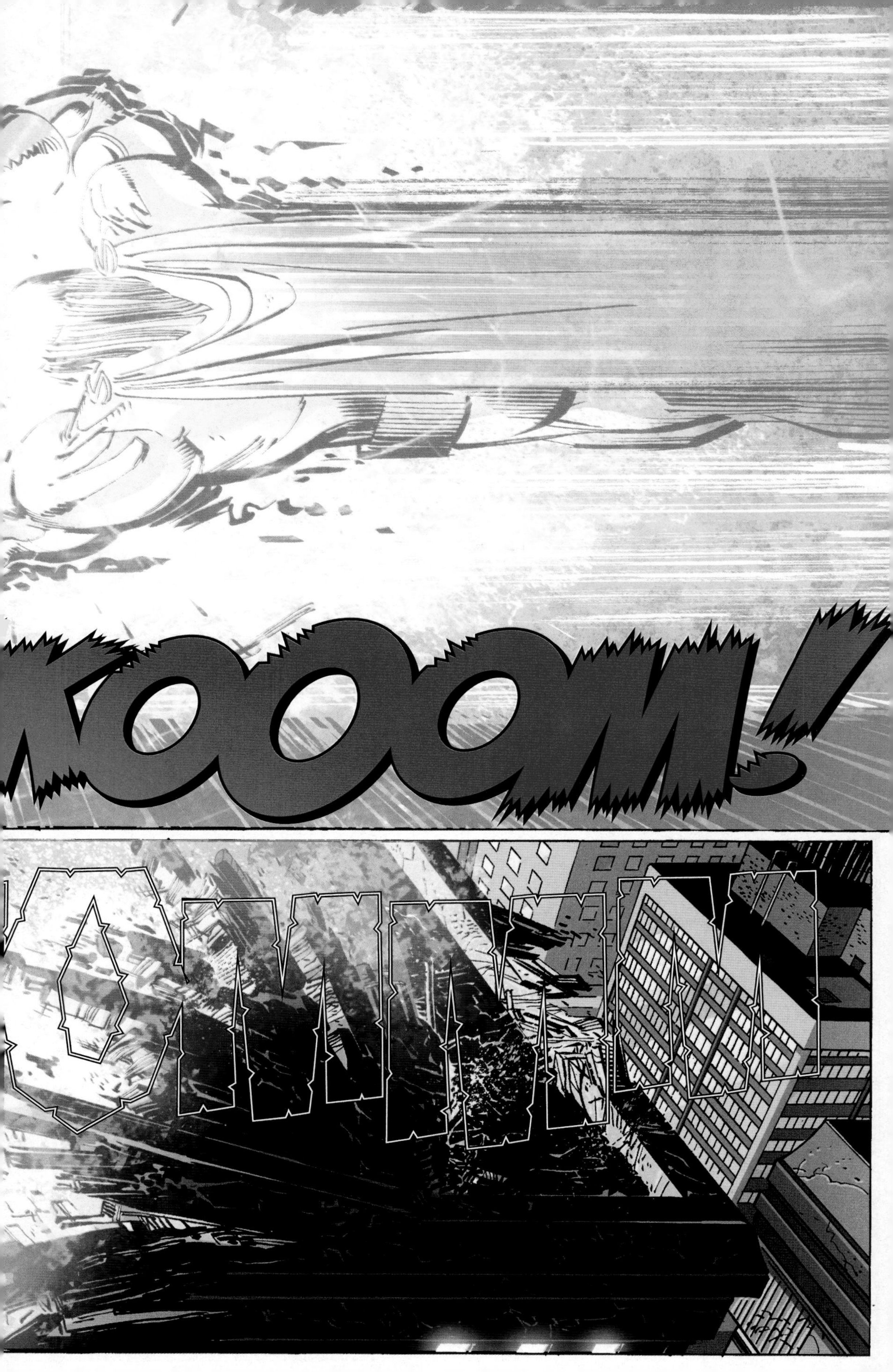
OOOM!

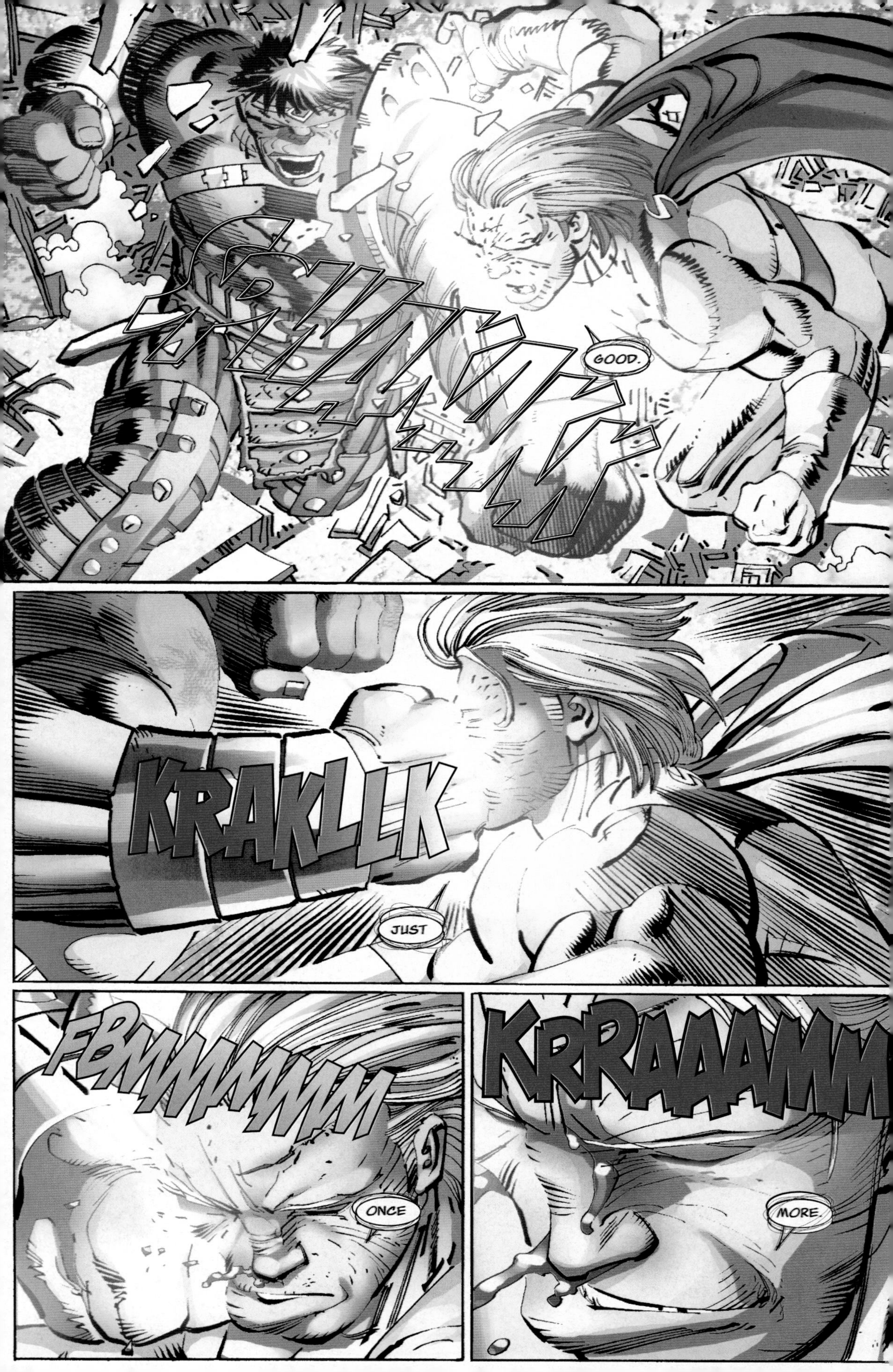
GOOD.
KRAKLLK
JUST
FBMMMMMM
ONCE
KRRAAAMM
MORE.

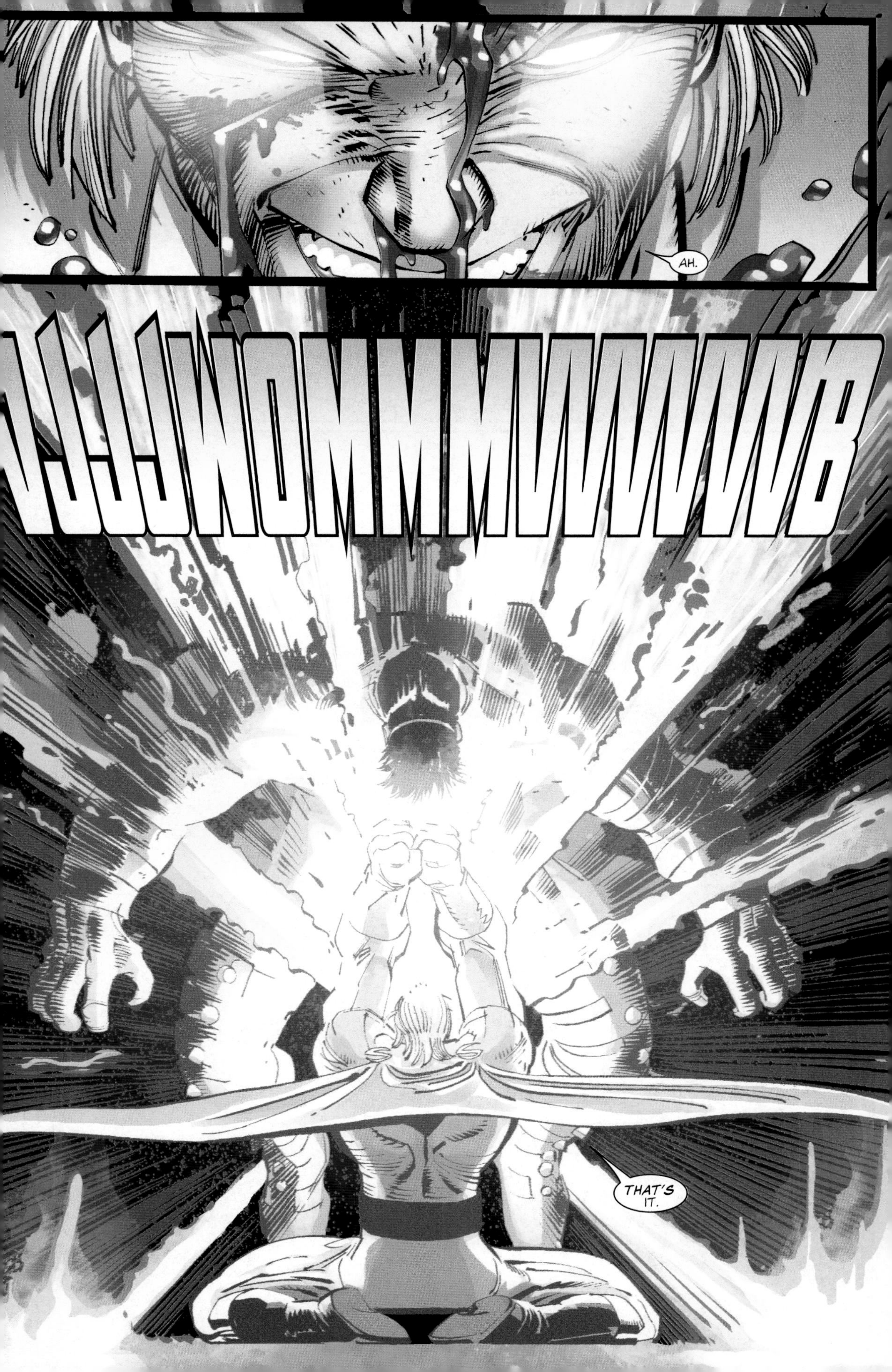

AH.
THAT'S IT.

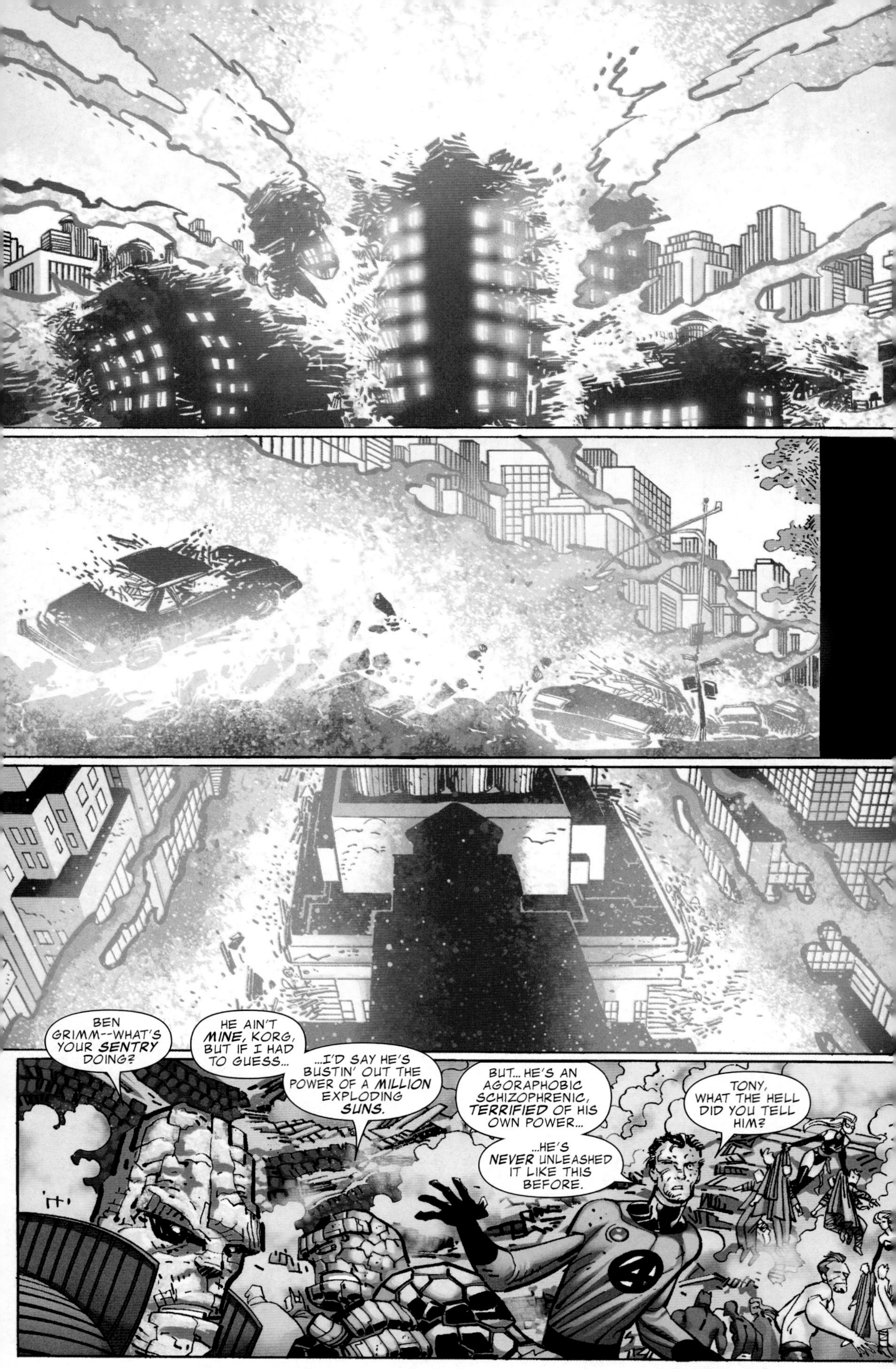

BEN GRIMM--WHAT'S YOUR SENTRY DOING?
HE AIN'T MINE, KORG, BUT IF I HAD TO GUESS...
...I'D SAY HE'S BUSTIN' OUT THE POWER OF A MILLION EXPLODING SUNS.
BUT... HE'S AN AGORAPHOBIC SCHIZOPHRENIC, TERRIFIED OF HIS OWN POWER...
...HE'S NEVER UNLEASHED IT LIKE THIS BEFORE.
TONY, WHAT THE HELL DID YOU TELL HIM?

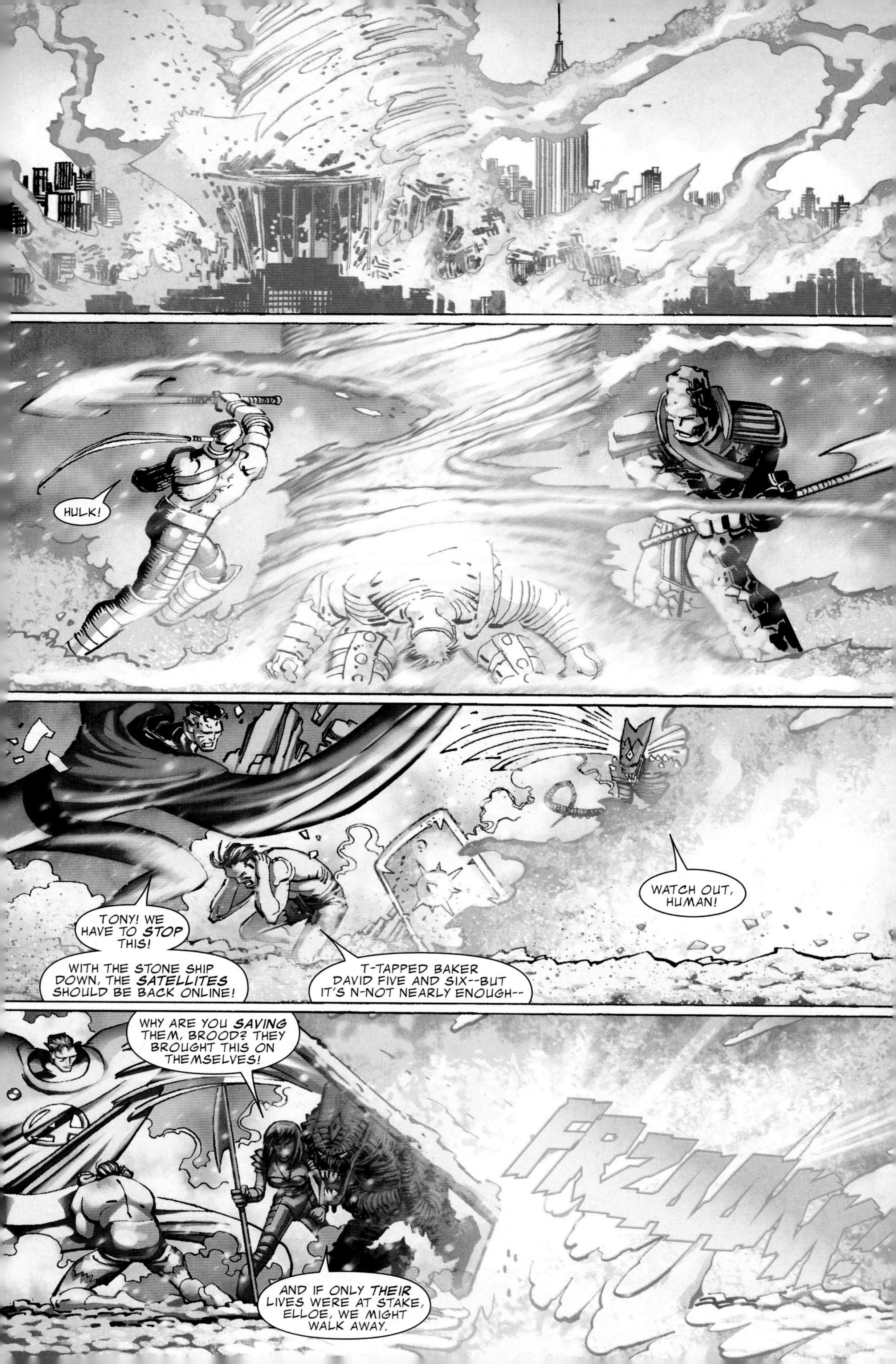
HULK!
TONY! WE HAVE TO STOP THIS!
WITH THE STONE SHIP DOWN, THE SATELLITES SHOULD BE BACK ONLINE!
T-TAPPED BAKER DAVID FIVE AND SIX--BUT IT'S N-NOT NEARLY ENOUGH--
WATCH OUT, HUMAN!
WHY ARE YOU SAVING THEM, BROOD? THEY BROUGHT THIS ON THEMSELVES!
AND IF ONLY THEIR LIVES WERE AT STAKE, ELLOE, WE MIGHT WALK AWAY.
FRZAAKT

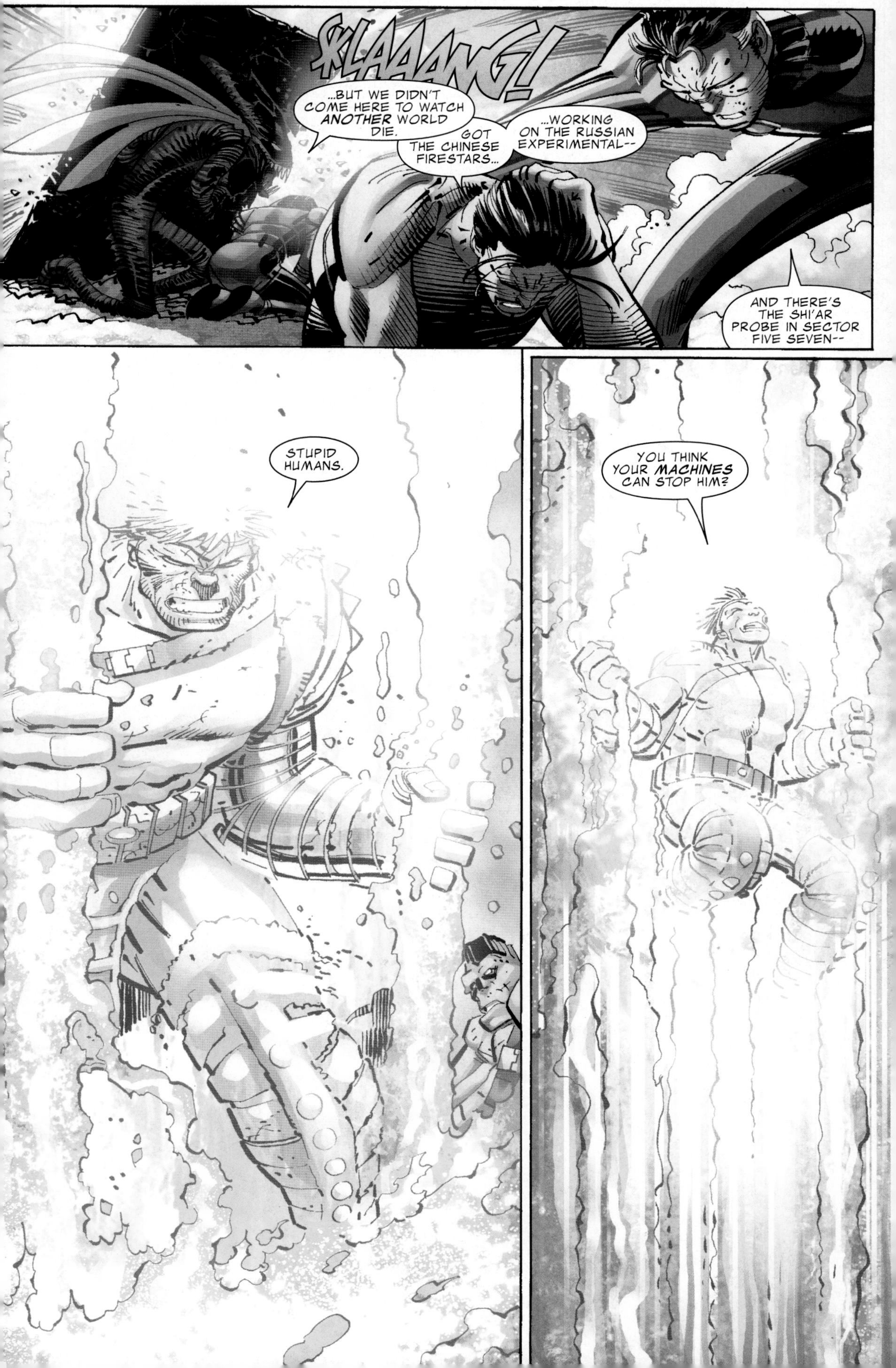
SKLAAANG!
...BUT WE DIDN'T COME HERE TO WATCH ANOTHER WORLD DIE.
GOT THE CHINESE FIRESTARS...
...WORKING ON THE RUSSIAN EXPERIMENTAL--
AND THERE'S THE SHI'AR PROBE IN SECTOR FIVE SEVEN--
STUPID HUMANS.
YOU THINK YOUR MACHINES CAN STOP HIM?

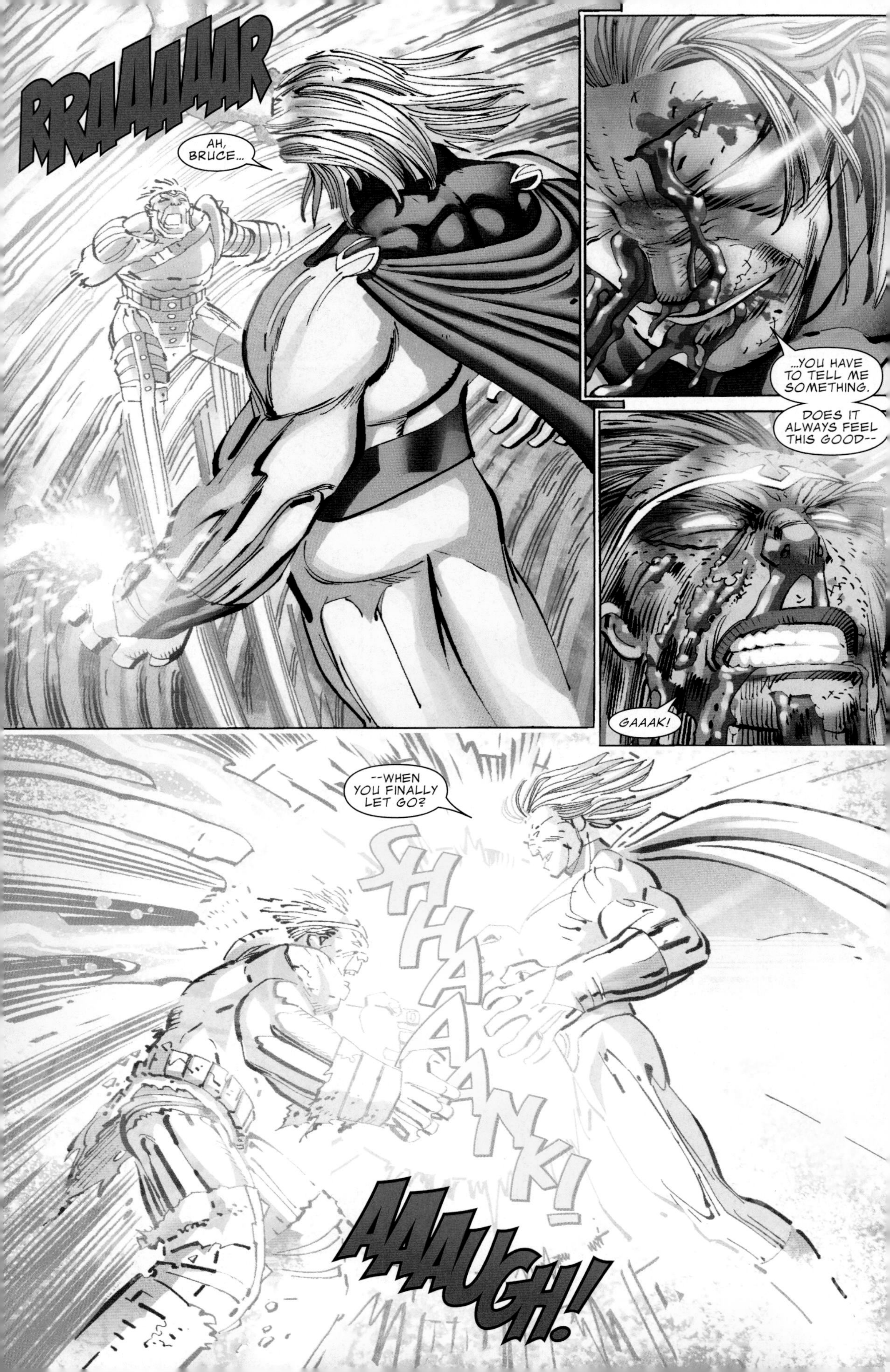
RRAAAAAR
AH, BRUCE...
...YOU HAVE TO TELL ME SOMETHING.
DOES IT ALWAYS FEEL THIS GOOD--
GAAAK!
--WHEN YOU FINALLY LET GO?
SHHAAANK!
AAAAUGH!

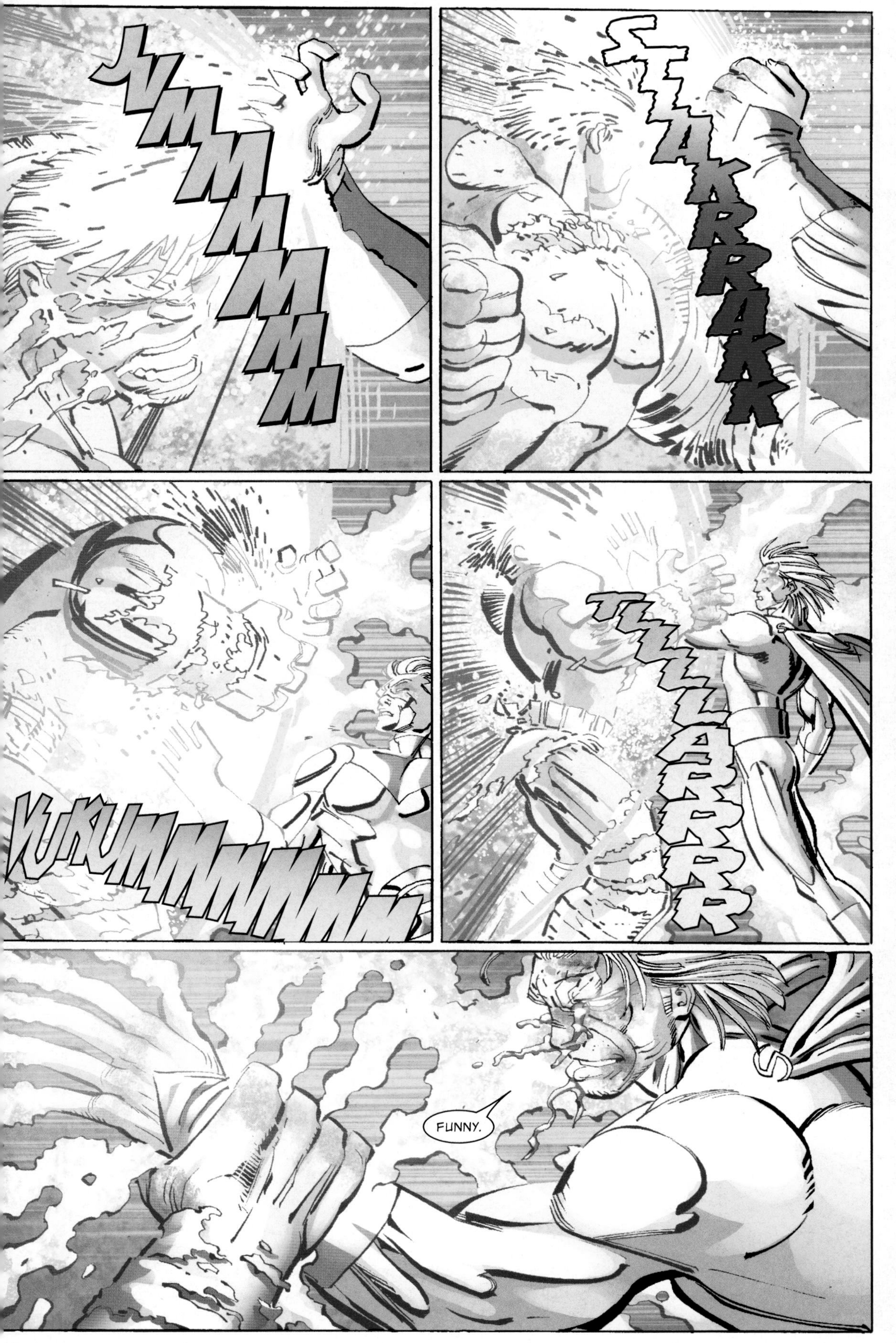

JVMMMMMM
STAKRRAKK
VUKUMMMMMMM
TLLLLARRR
FUNNY.

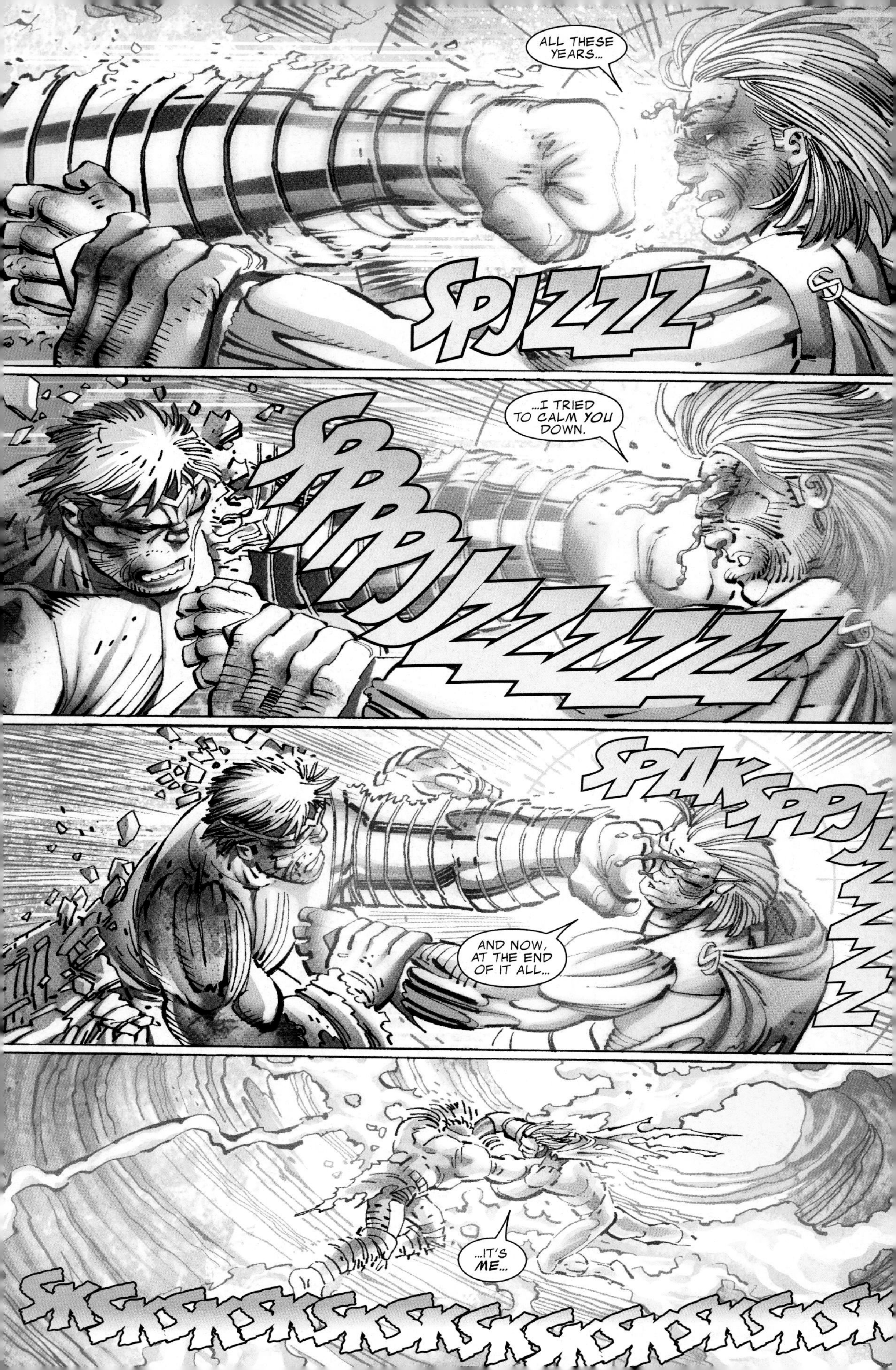
ALL THESE YEARS...
SPJZZZ
...I TRIED TO CALM YOU DOWN.
SPPPJZZZZZ
SPAK
SPPJ
AND NOW, AT THE END OF IT ALL...
...IT'S ME...
SKSKSKSKSKSKSKSKSKSKSKSKSKSKSK

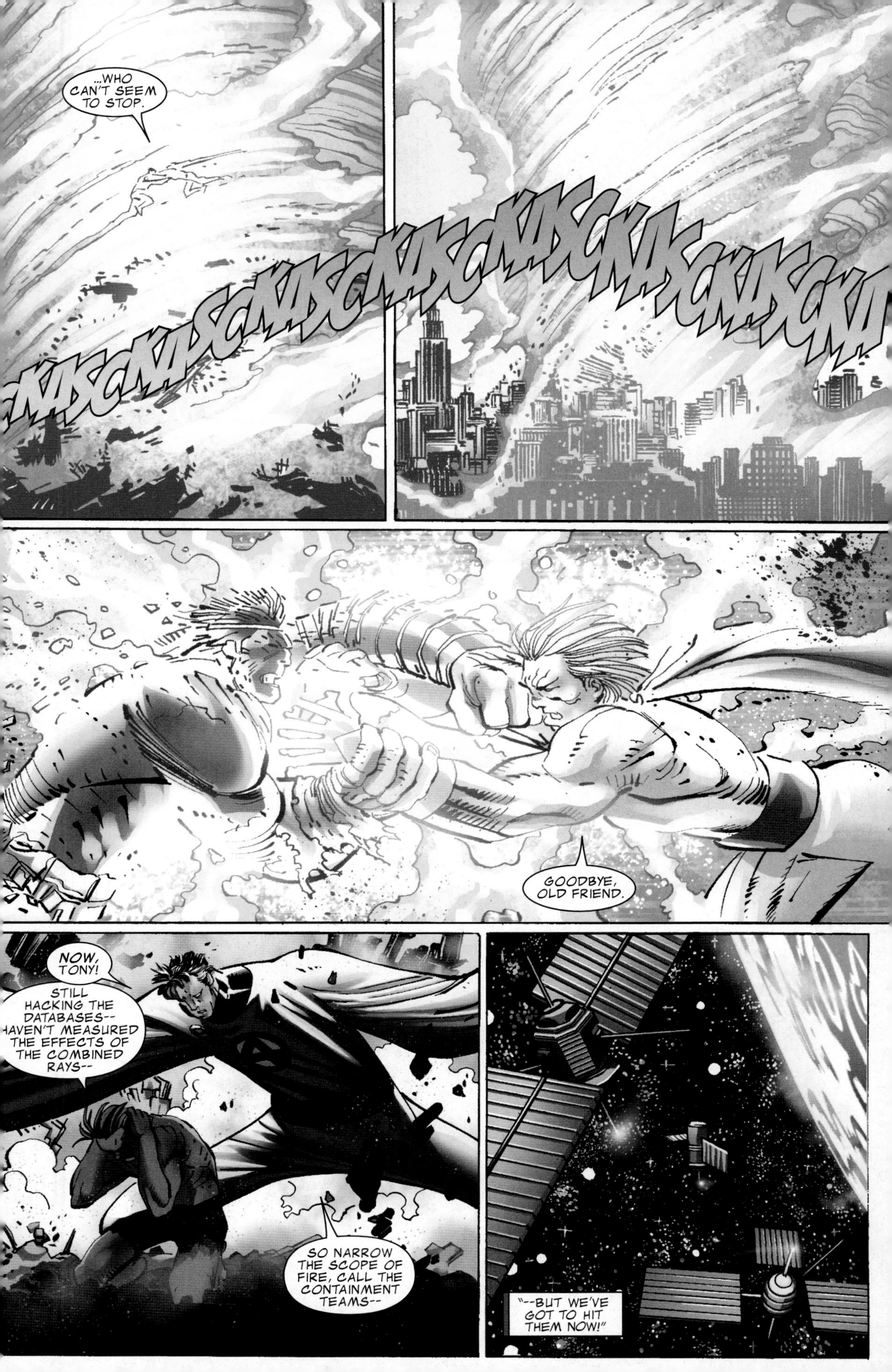
...WHO CAN'T SEEM TO STOP.
GOODBYE, OLD FRIEND.
NOW, TONY!
STILL HACKING THE DATABASES--HAVEN'T MEASURED THE EFFECTS OF THE COMBINED RAYS--
SO NARROW THE SCOPE OF FIRE, CALL THE CONTAINMENT TEAMS--
"--BUT WE'VE GOT TO HIT THEM NOW!"

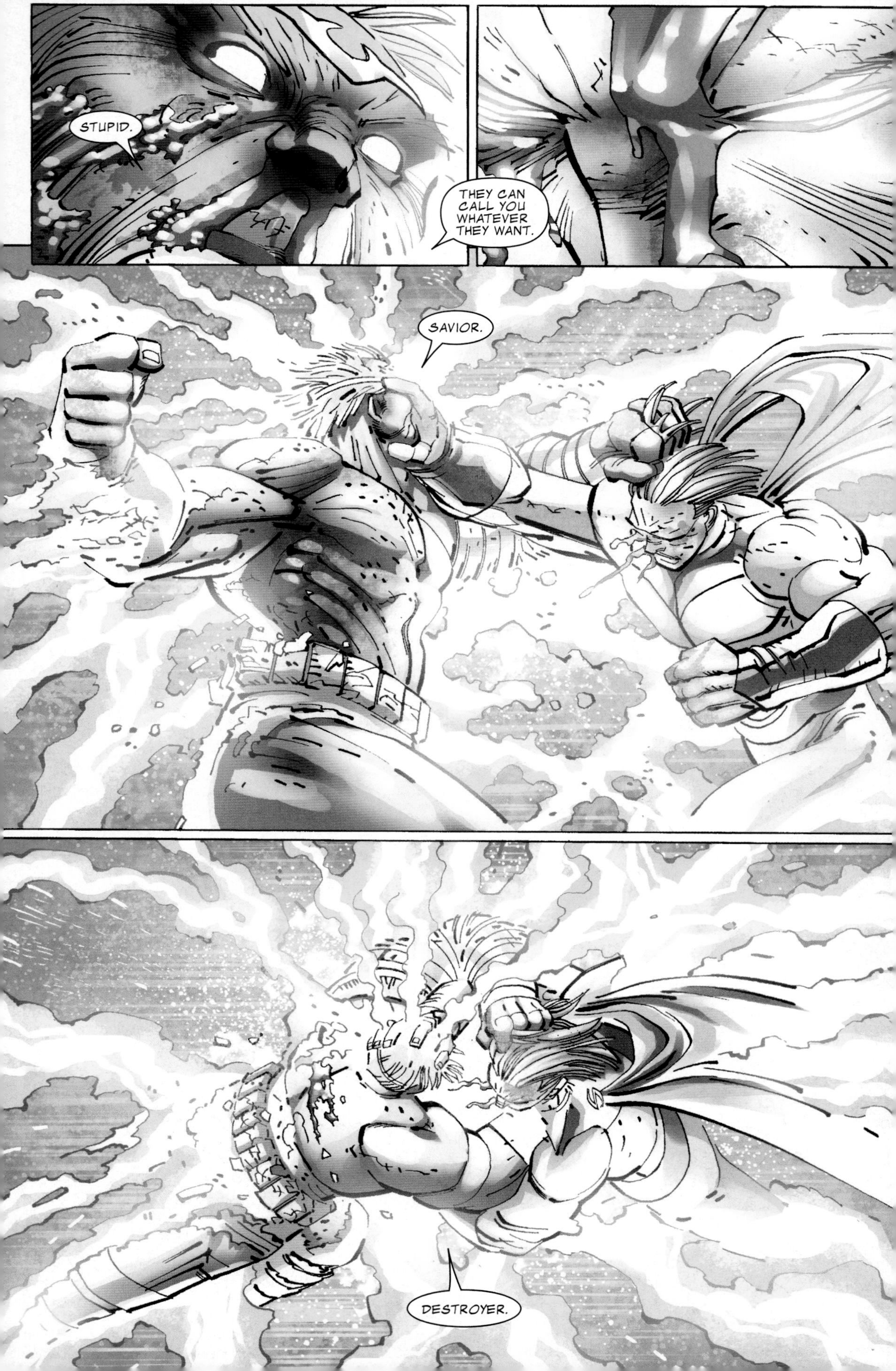
STUPID.
THEY CAN CALL YOU WHATEVER THEY WANT.
SAVIOR.
DESTROYER.

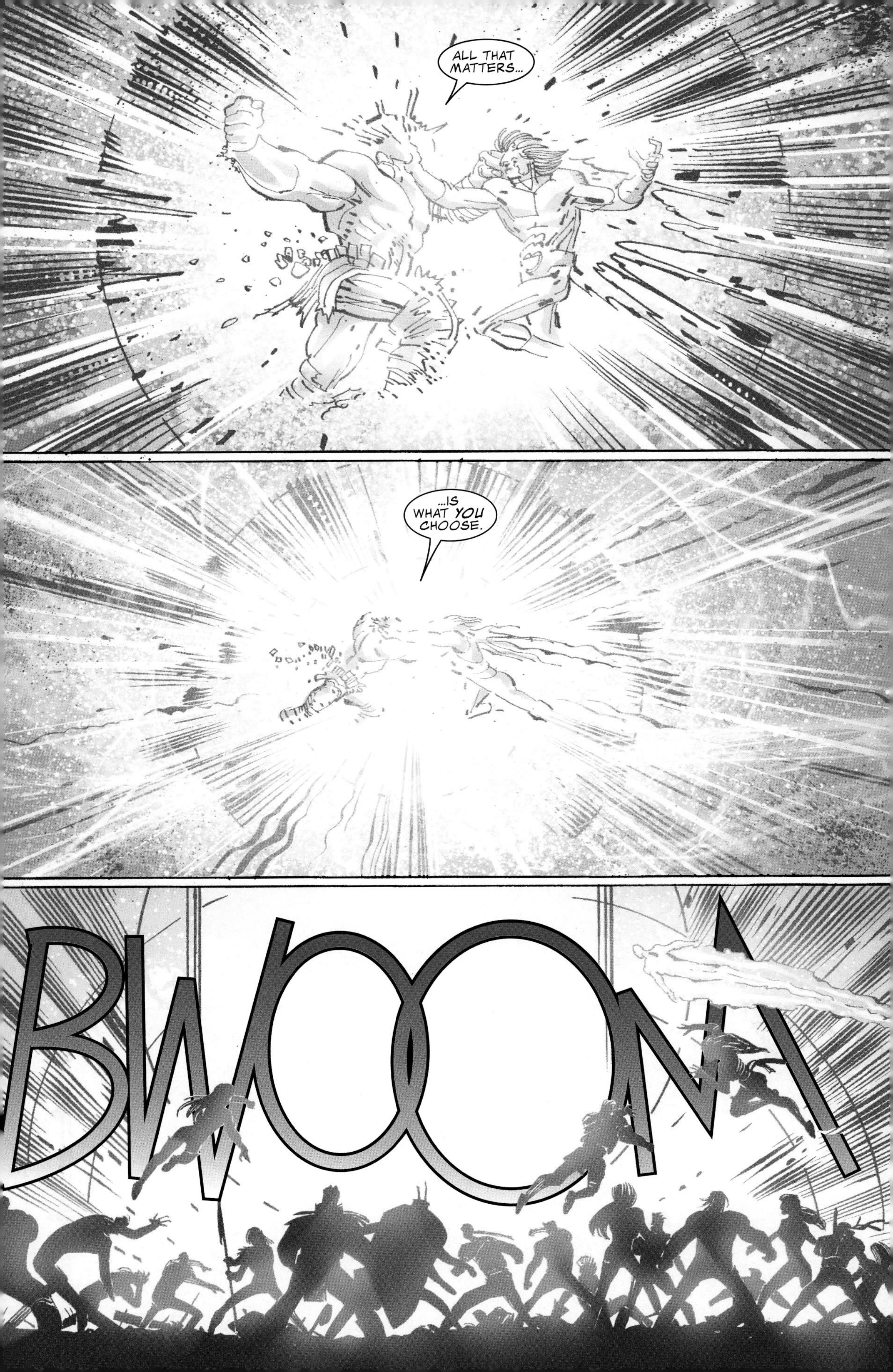
ALL THAT MATTERS...
...IS WHAT YOU CHOOSE.
BWOOM!

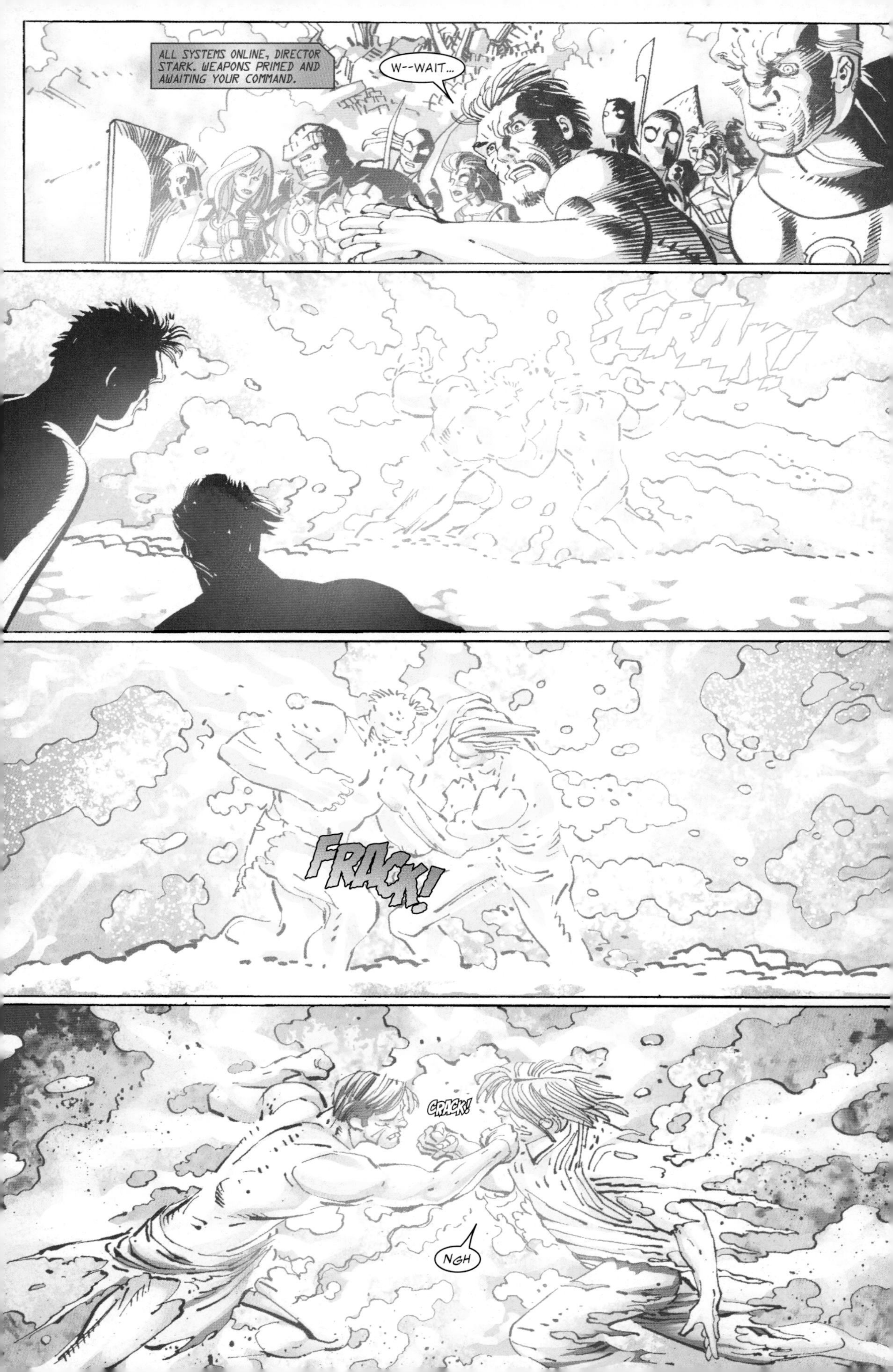
ALL SYSTEMS ONLINE, DIRECTOR STARK. WEAPONS PRIMED AND AWAITING YOUR COMMAND.
W--WAIT...
SCRAK!
FRACK!
CRACK!
NGH

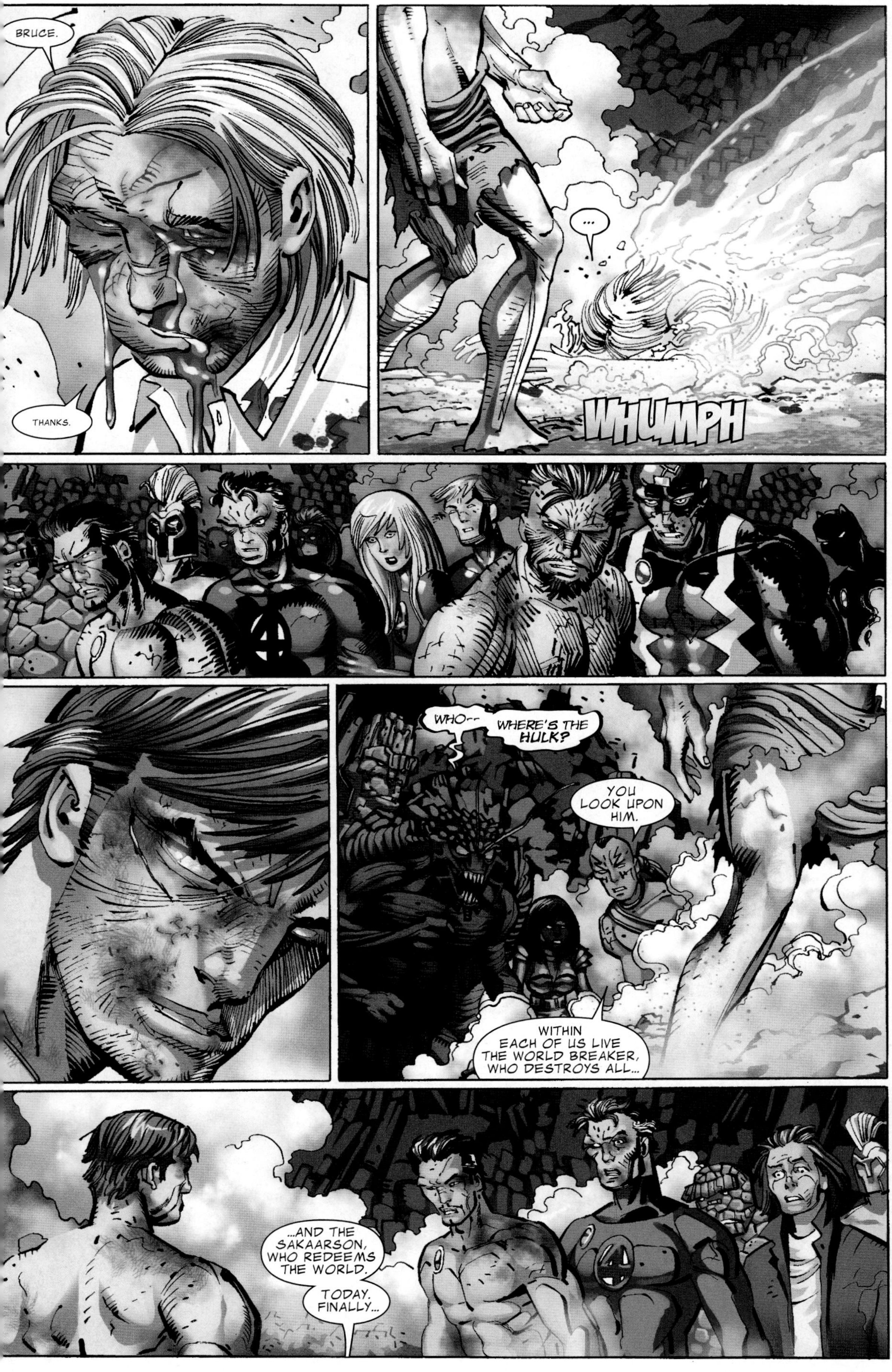
BRUCE.
THANKS.
...
WHUMPH
WHO--
WHERE'S THE HULK?
YOU LOOK UPON HIM.
WITHIN EACH OF US LIVE THE WORLD BREAKER, WHO DESTROYS ALL...
...AND THE SAKAARSON, WHO REDEEMS THE WORLD.
TODAY. FINALLY...

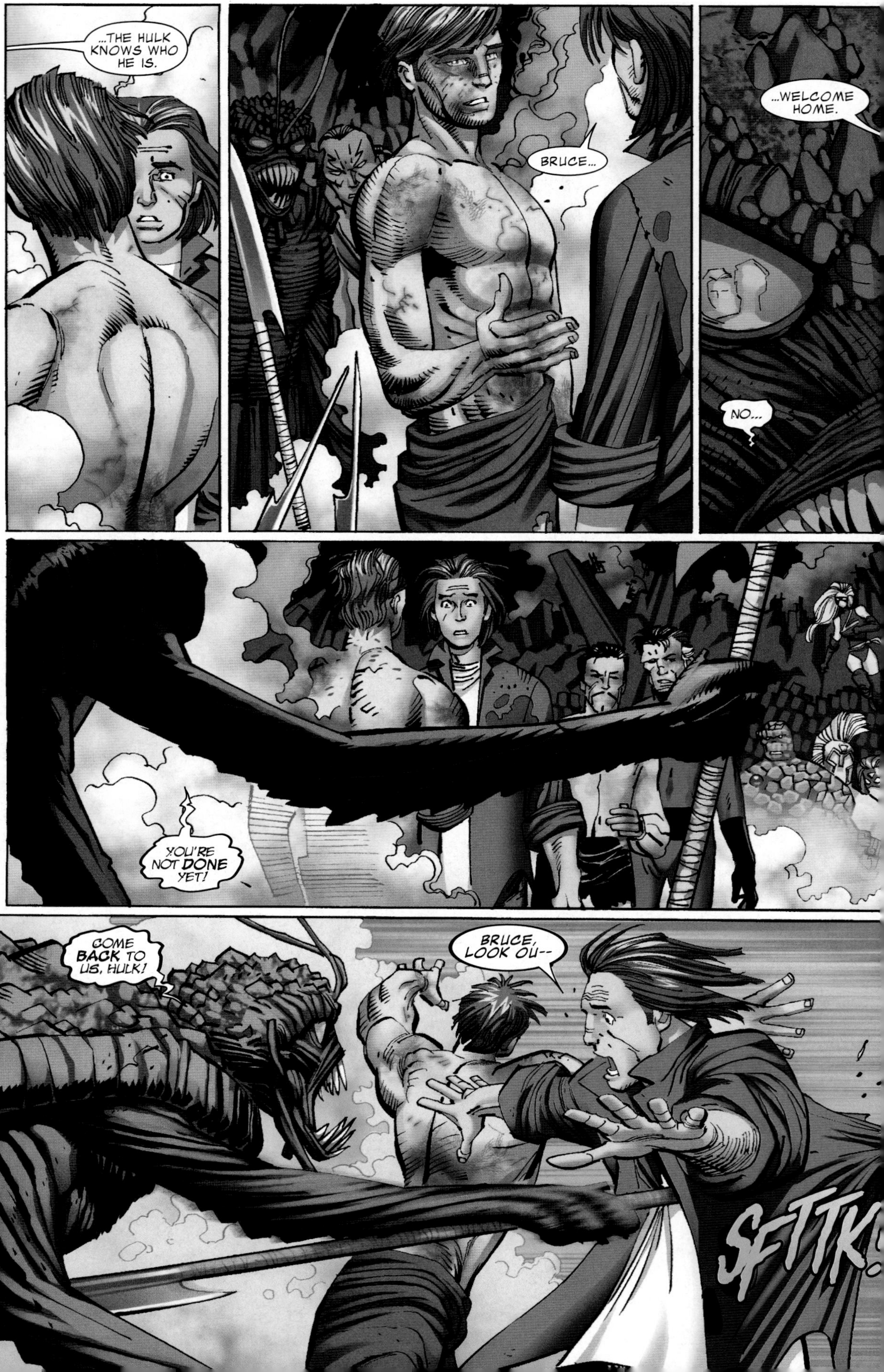
...THE HULK KNOWS WHO HE IS.
BRUCE...
...WELCOME HOME.
NO...
YOU'RE NOT DONE YET!
COME BACK TO US, HULK!
BRUCE, LOOK OU--
SFTTK!

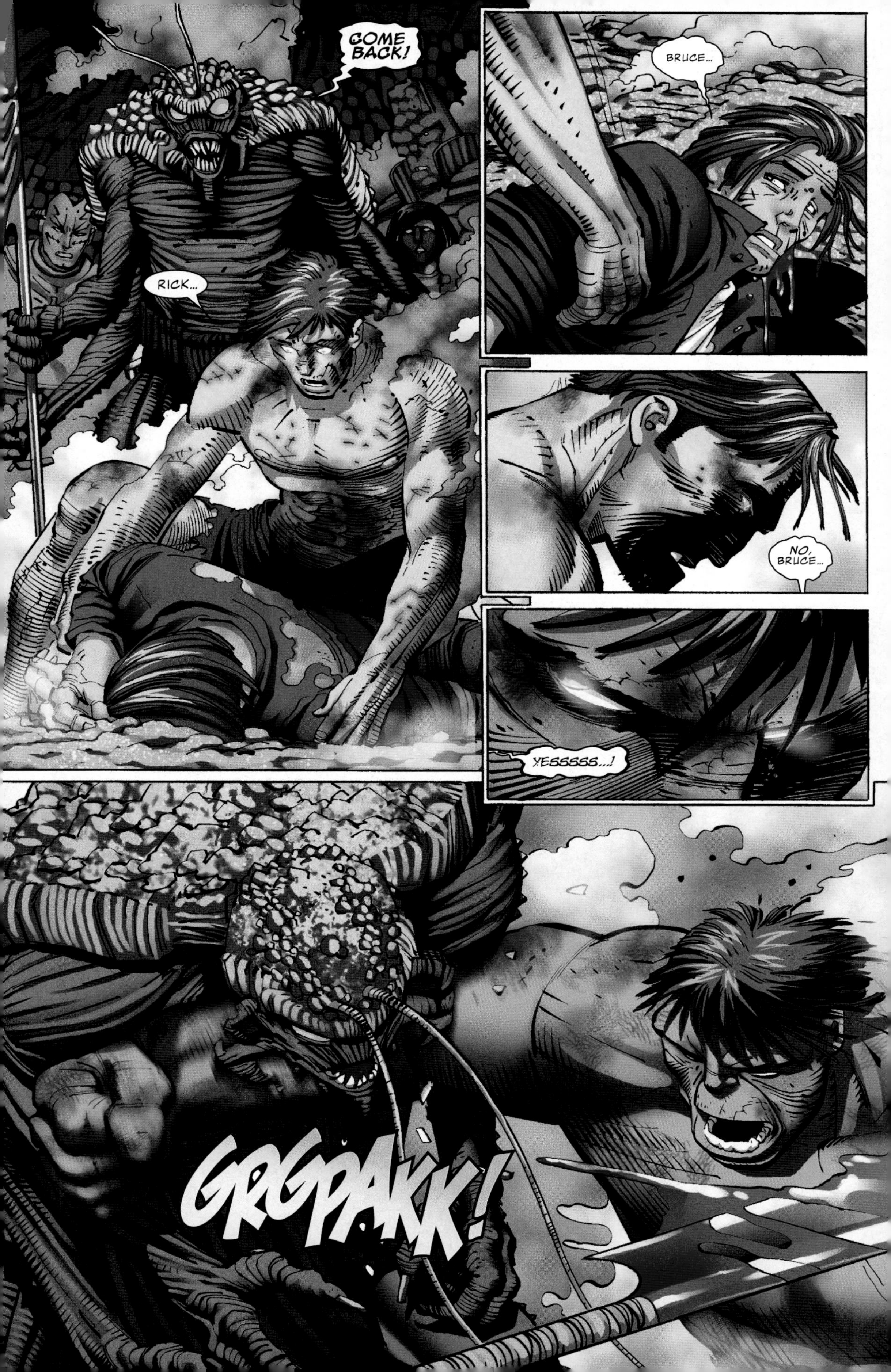
COME BACK!
RICK...
BRUCE...
NO, BRUCE...
YESSSSS...!
GRGPAKK!

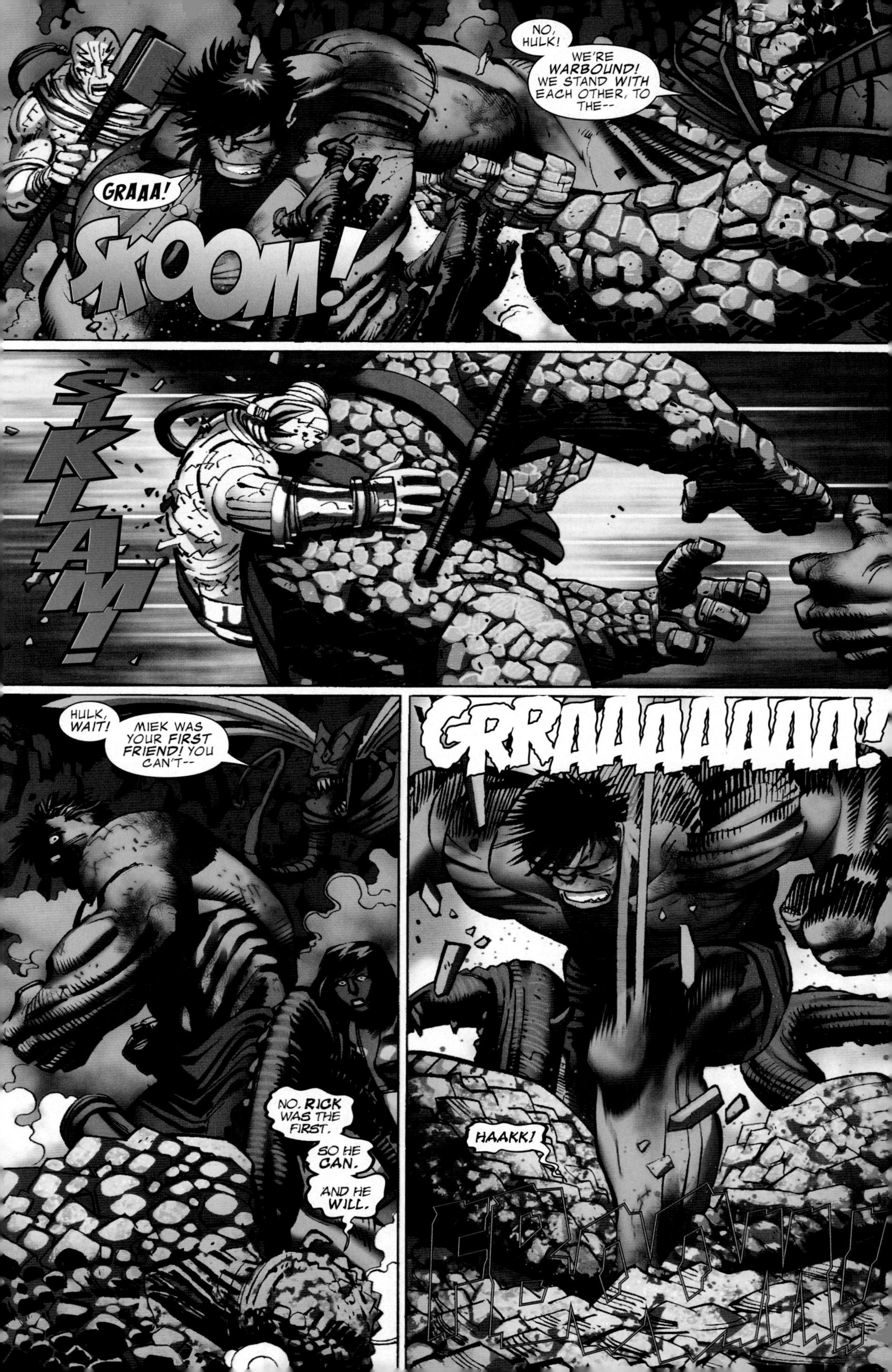
NO, HULK!
WE'RE WARBOUND! WE STAND WITH EACH OTHER, TO THE--
GRAAA!
SKOOM!
SKLAM!
HULK, WAIT!
MIEK WAS YOUR FIRST FRIEND! YOU CAN'T--
NO. RICK WAS THE FIRST.
SO HE CAN.
AND HE WILL.
GRRAAAAAAAA!
HAAKK!

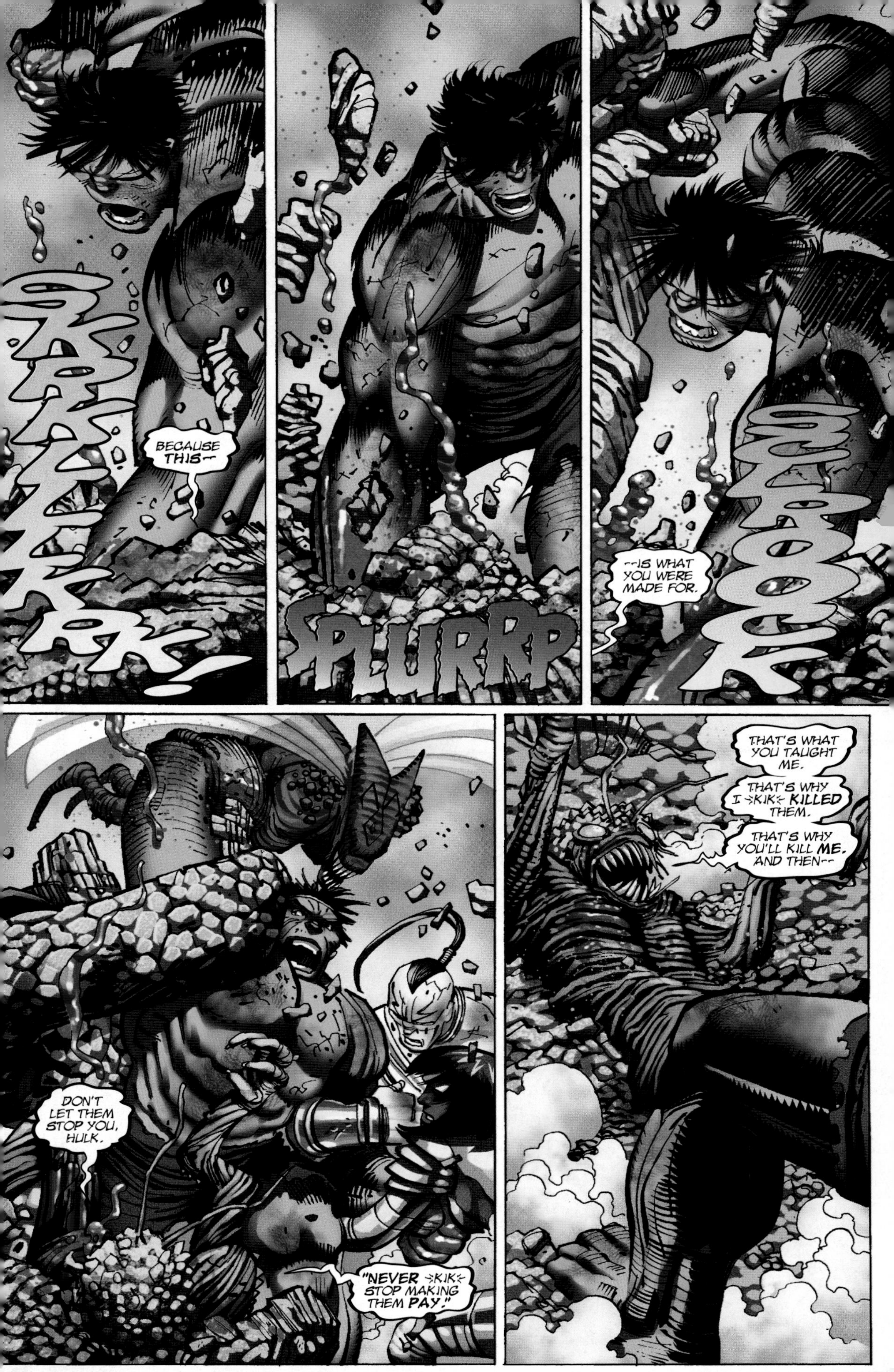
BECAUSE THIS--
SPLURRP
--IS WHAT YOU WERE MADE FOR.
DON'T LET THEM STOP YOU, HULK.
"NEVER -KIK- STOP MAKING THEM PAY."
THAT'S WHAT YOU TAUGHT ME.
THAT'S WHY I -KIK- KILLED THEM.
THAT'S WHY YOU'LL KILL ME. AND THEN--

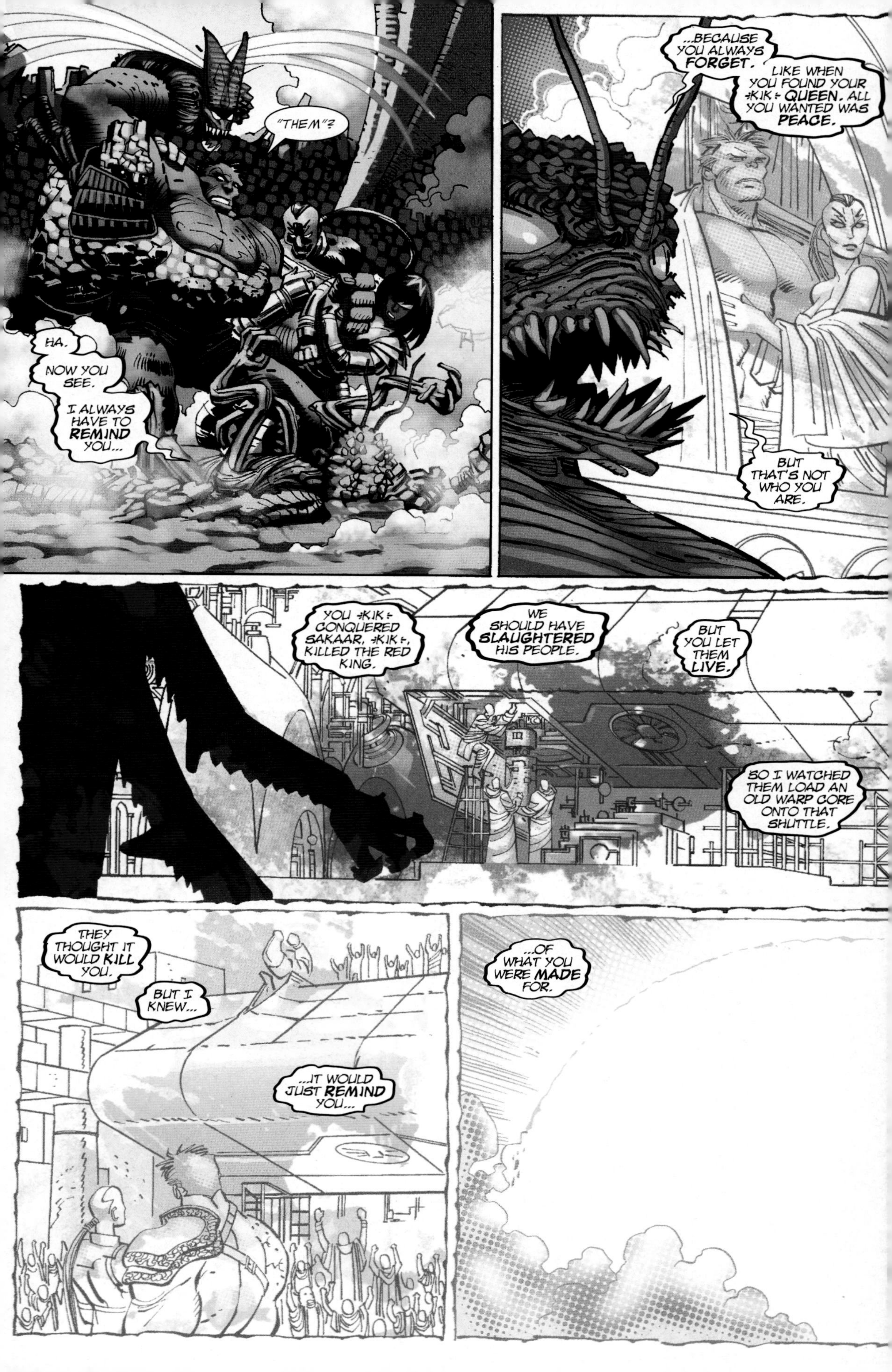
"THEM"?
HA.
NOW YOU SEE.
I ALWAYS HAVE TO REMIND YOU...
...BECAUSE YOU ALWAYS FORGET.
LIKE WHEN YOU FOUND YOUR ≠KIK≠ QUEEN. ALL YOU WANTED WAS PEACE.
BUT THAT'S NOT WHO YOU ARE.
YOU ≠KIK≠ CONQUERED SAKAAR, ≠KIK≠, KILLED THE RED KING.
WE SHOULD HAVE SLAUGHTERED HIS PEOPLE.
BUT YOU LET THEM LIVE.
SO I WATCHED THEM LOAD AN OLD WARP CORE ONTO THAT SHUTTLE.
THEY THOUGHT IT WOULD KILL YOU.
BUT I KNEW...
...IT WOULD JUST REMIND YOU...
...OF WHAT YOU WERE MADE FOR.

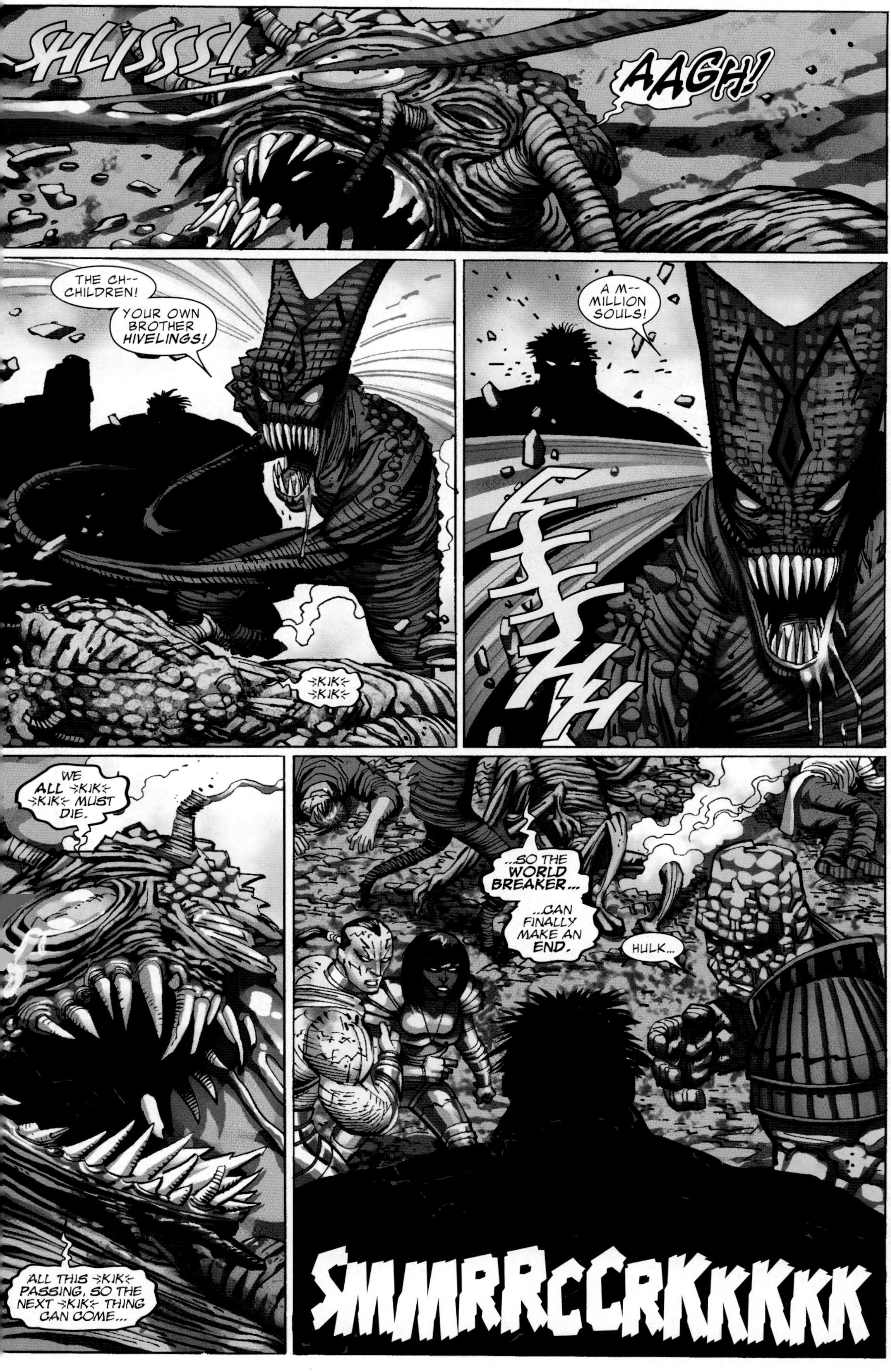
SHLISSS!
AAGH!
THE CH-- CHILDREN!
YOUR OWN BROTHER HIVELINGS!
KIK KIK
A M-- MILLION SOULS!
WE ALL KIK KIK MUST DIE.
ALL THIS KIK PASSING, SO THE NEXT KIK THING CAN COME...
...SO THE WORLD BREAKER...
...CAN FINALLY MAKE AN END.
HULK...
SMMRRCCRKKKKK

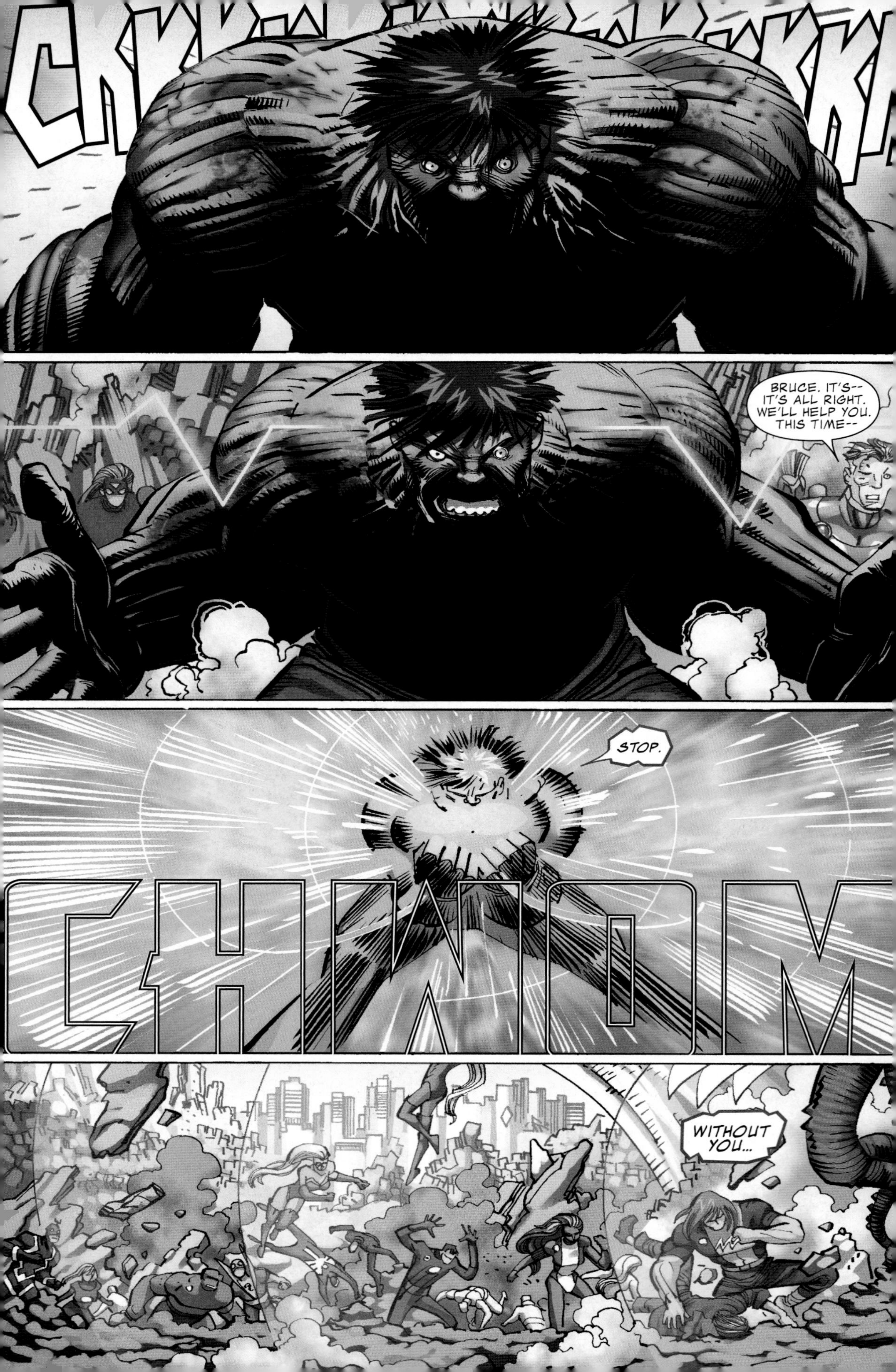
BRUCE. IT'S-- IT'S ALL RIGHT. WE'LL HELP YOU. THIS TIME--
STOP.
WITHOUT YOU...

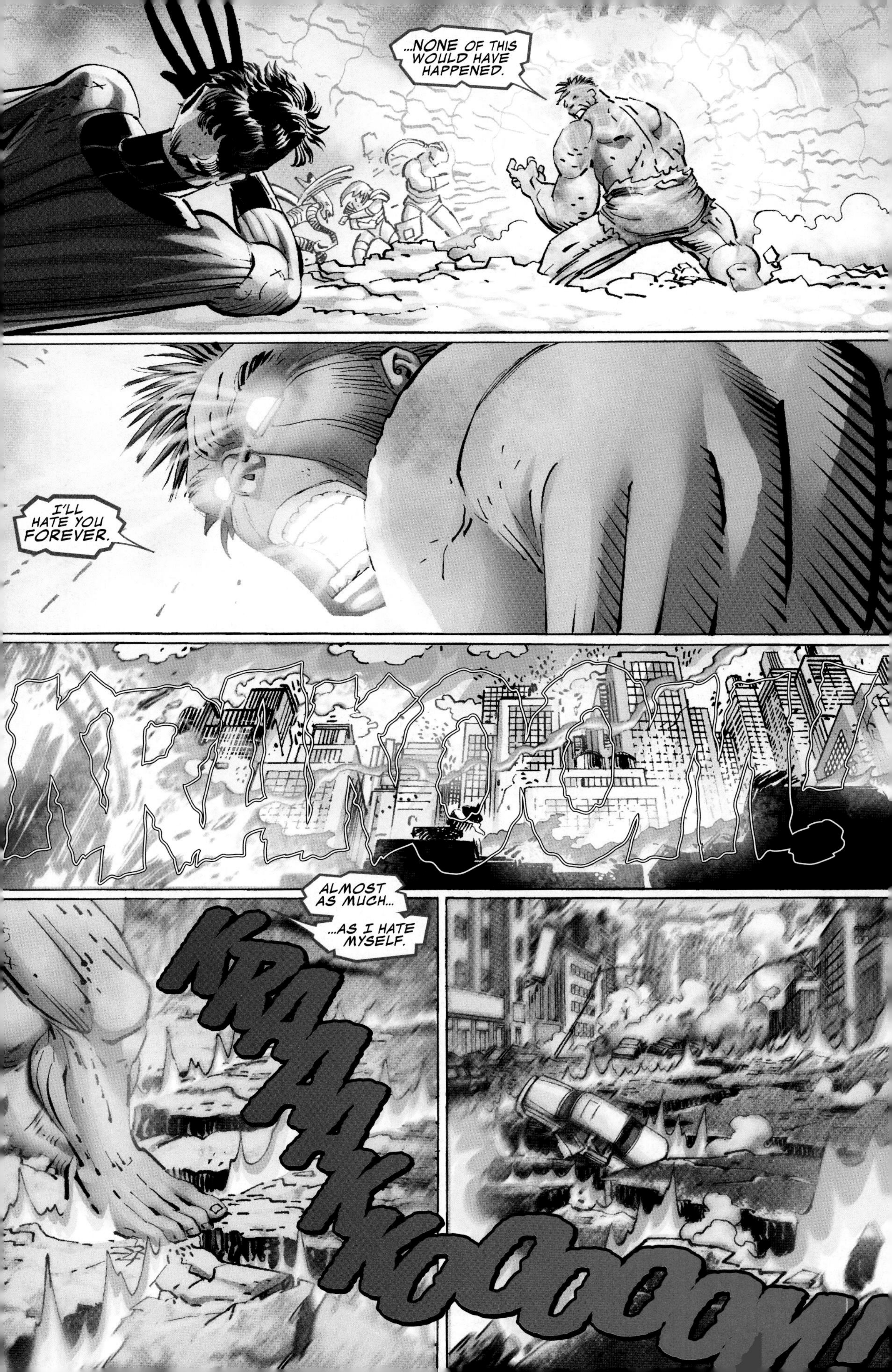
...NONE OF THIS WOULD HAVE HAPPENED.
I'LL HATE YOU FOREVER.
ALMOST AS MUCH...
...AS I HATE MYSELF.

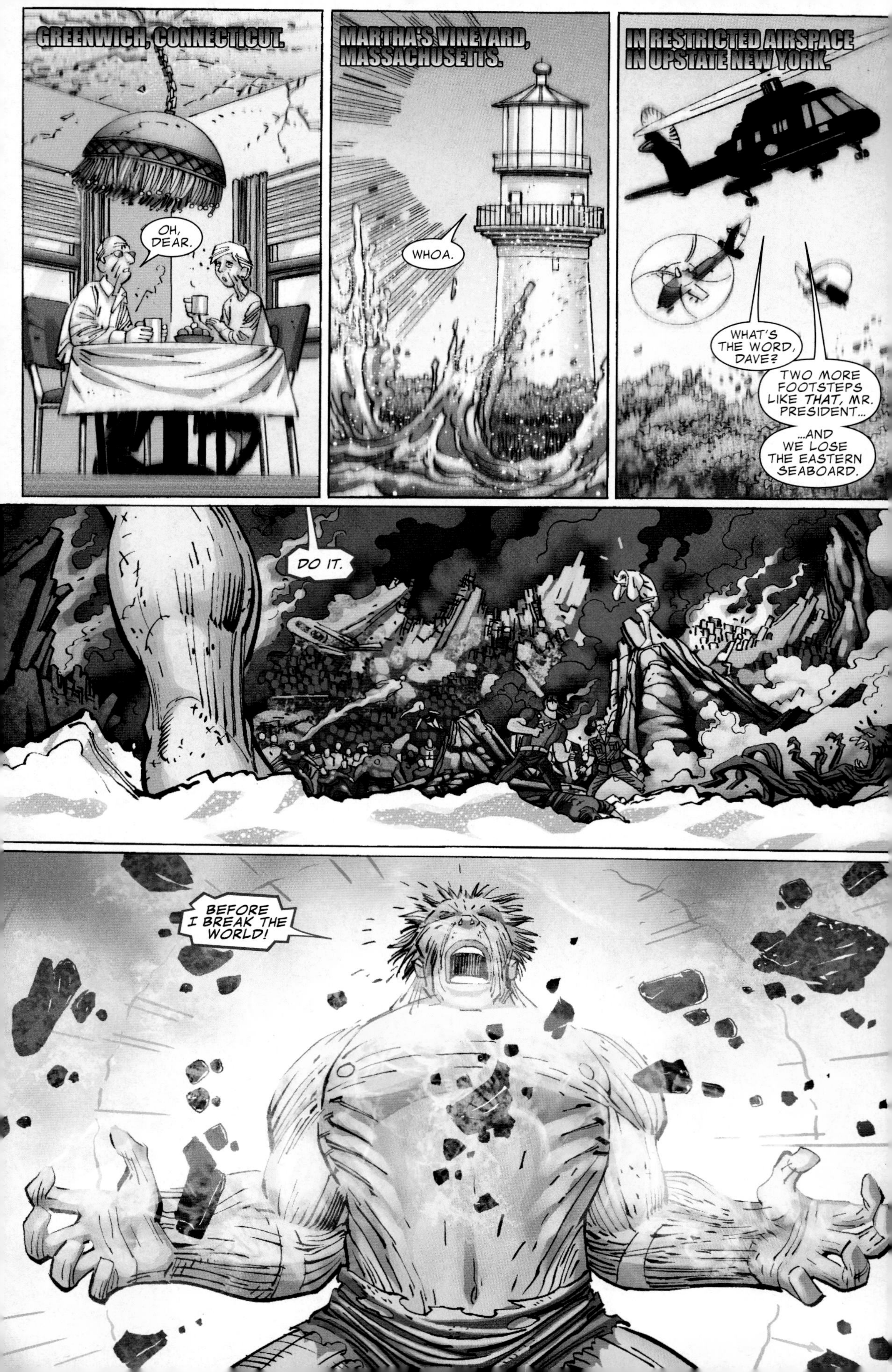
GREENWICH, CONNECTICUT.
OH, DEAR.
MARTHA'S VINEYARD, MASSACHUSETTS.
WHOA.
IN RESTRICTED AIRSPACE IN UPSTATE NEW YORK.
WHAT'S THE WORD, DAVE?
TWO MORE FOOTSTEPS LIKE THAT, MR. PRESIDENT...
...AND WE LOSE THE EASTERN SEABOARD.
DO IT.
BEFORE I BREAK THE WORLD!

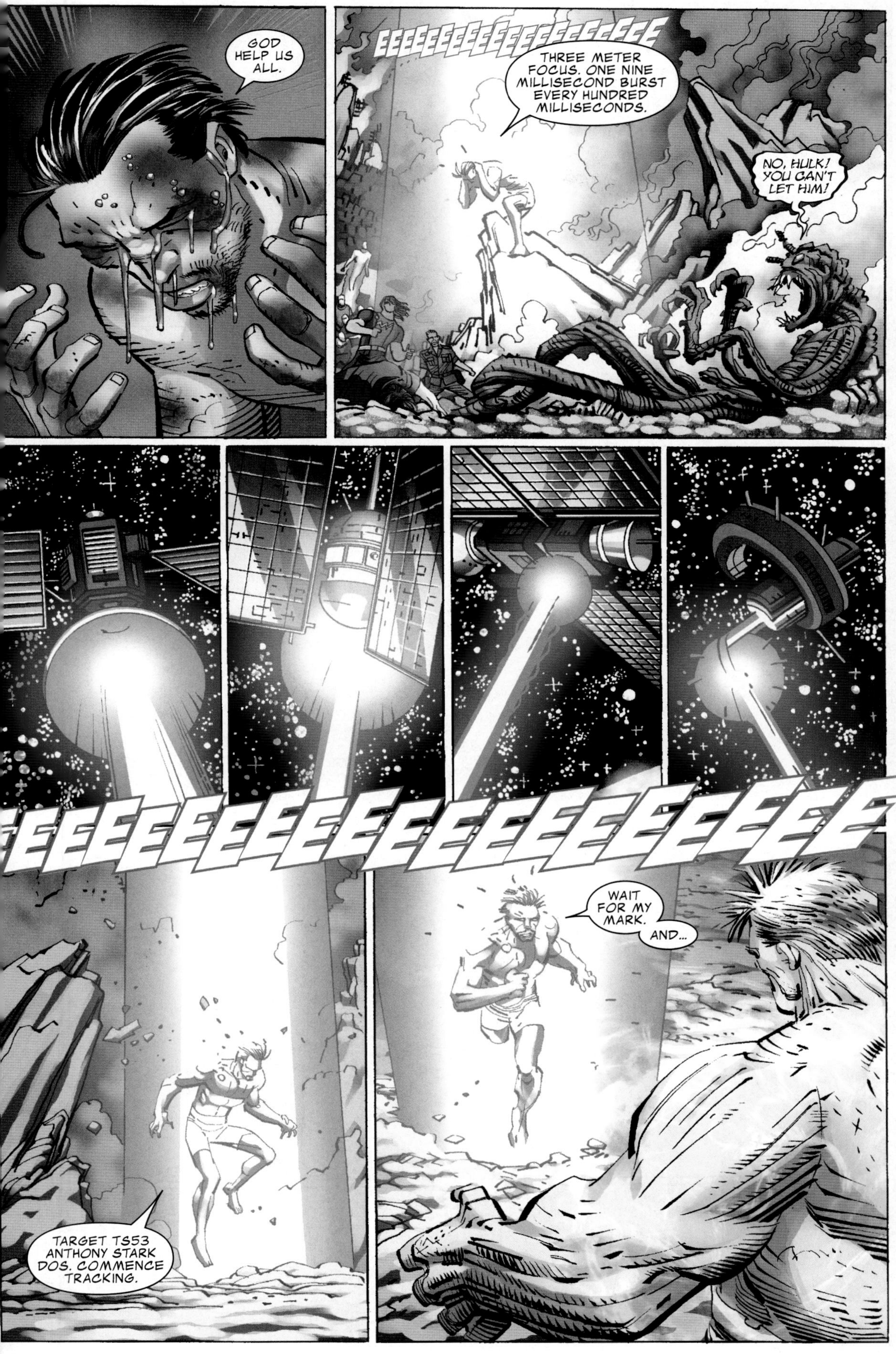
GOD HELP US ALL.
EEEEEEEEEEEEEEEEEE
THREE METER FOCUS. ONE NINE MILLISECOND BURST EVERY HUNDRED MILLISECONDS.
NO, HULK! YOU CAN'T LET HIM!
EEEEEEEEEEEEEEEEEE
TARGET TS53 ANTHONY STARK DOS. COMMENCE TRACKING.
WAIT FOR MY MARK.
AND...

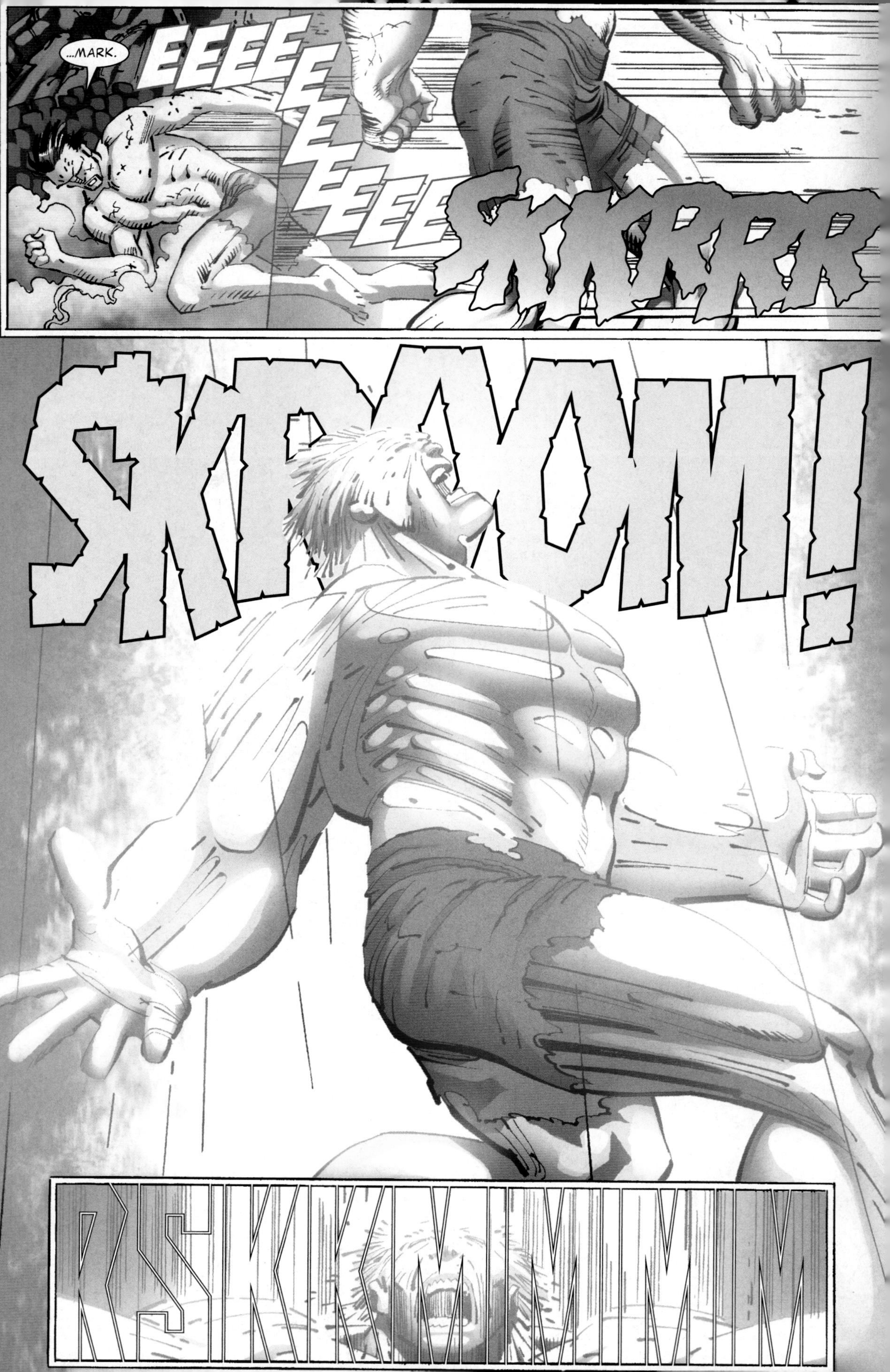
...MARK.

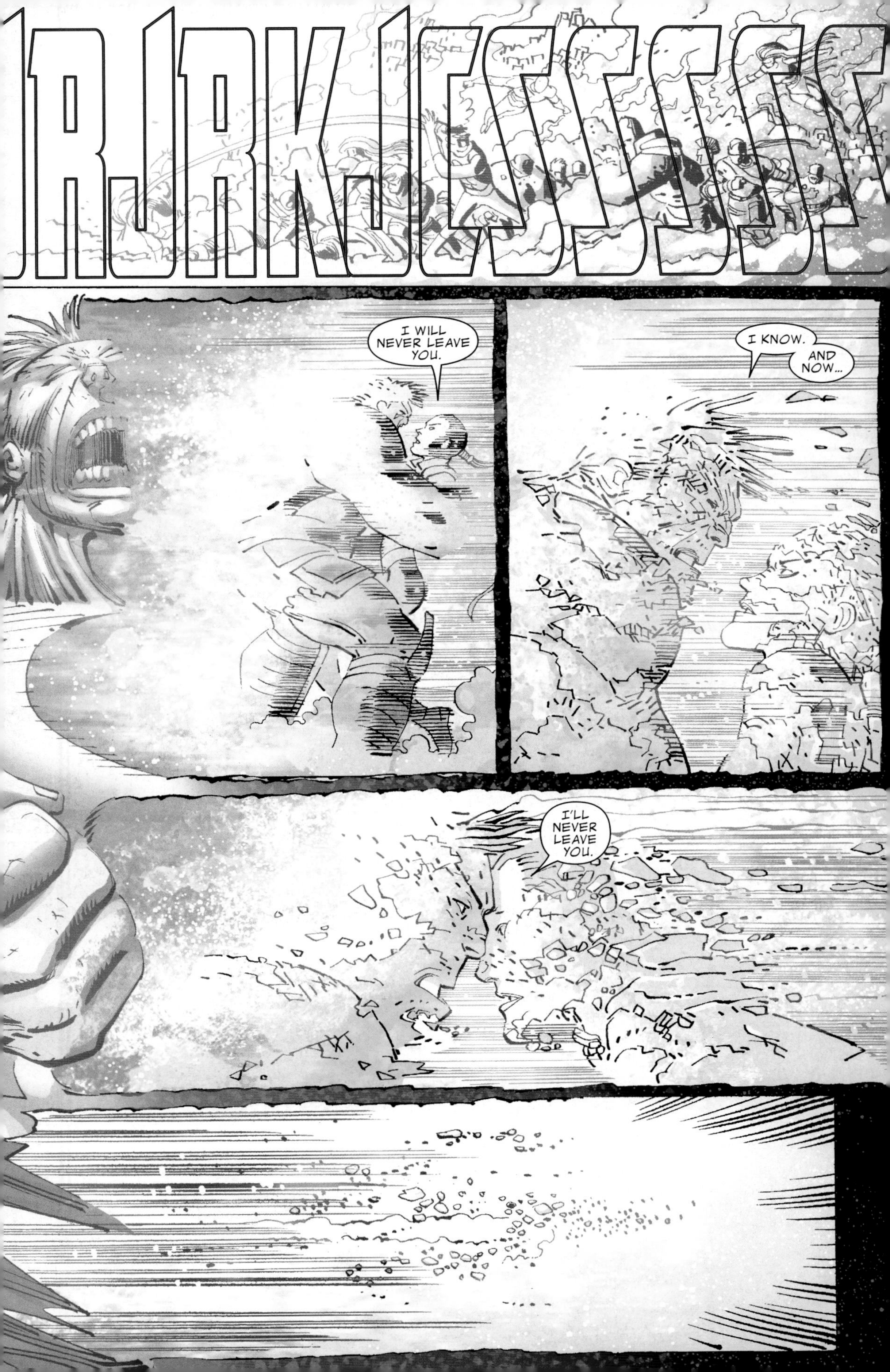
I WILL NEVER LEAVE YOU.
I KNOW.
AND NOW...
I'LL NEVER LEAVE YOU.

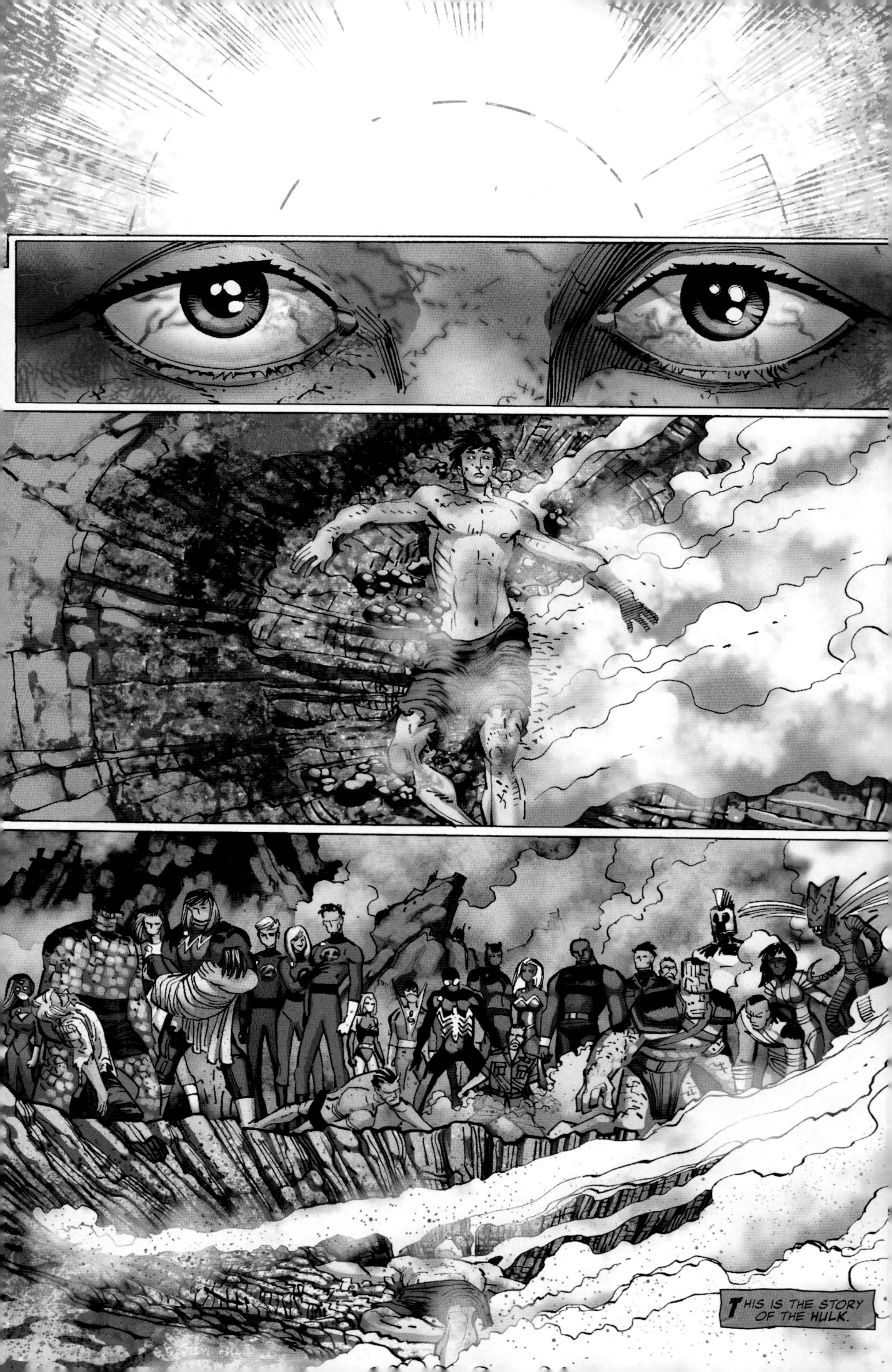
THIS IS THE STORY OF THE HULK.

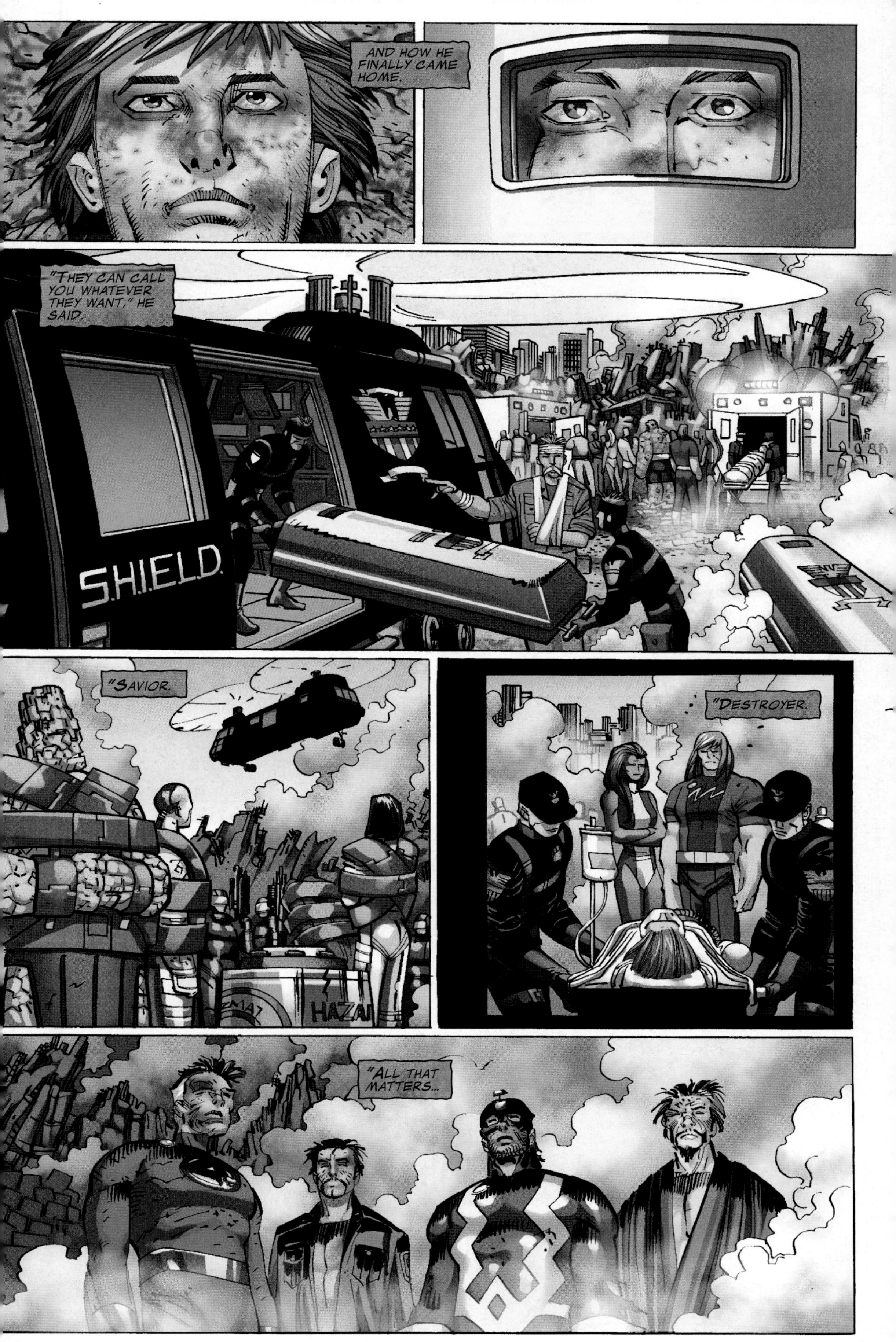
AND HOW HE FINALLY CAME HOME.
"THEY CAN CALL YOU WHATEVER THEY WANT," HE SAID.
S.H.I.E.L.D.
"SAVIOR.
HAZA
"DESTROYER.
"ALL THAT MATTERS...

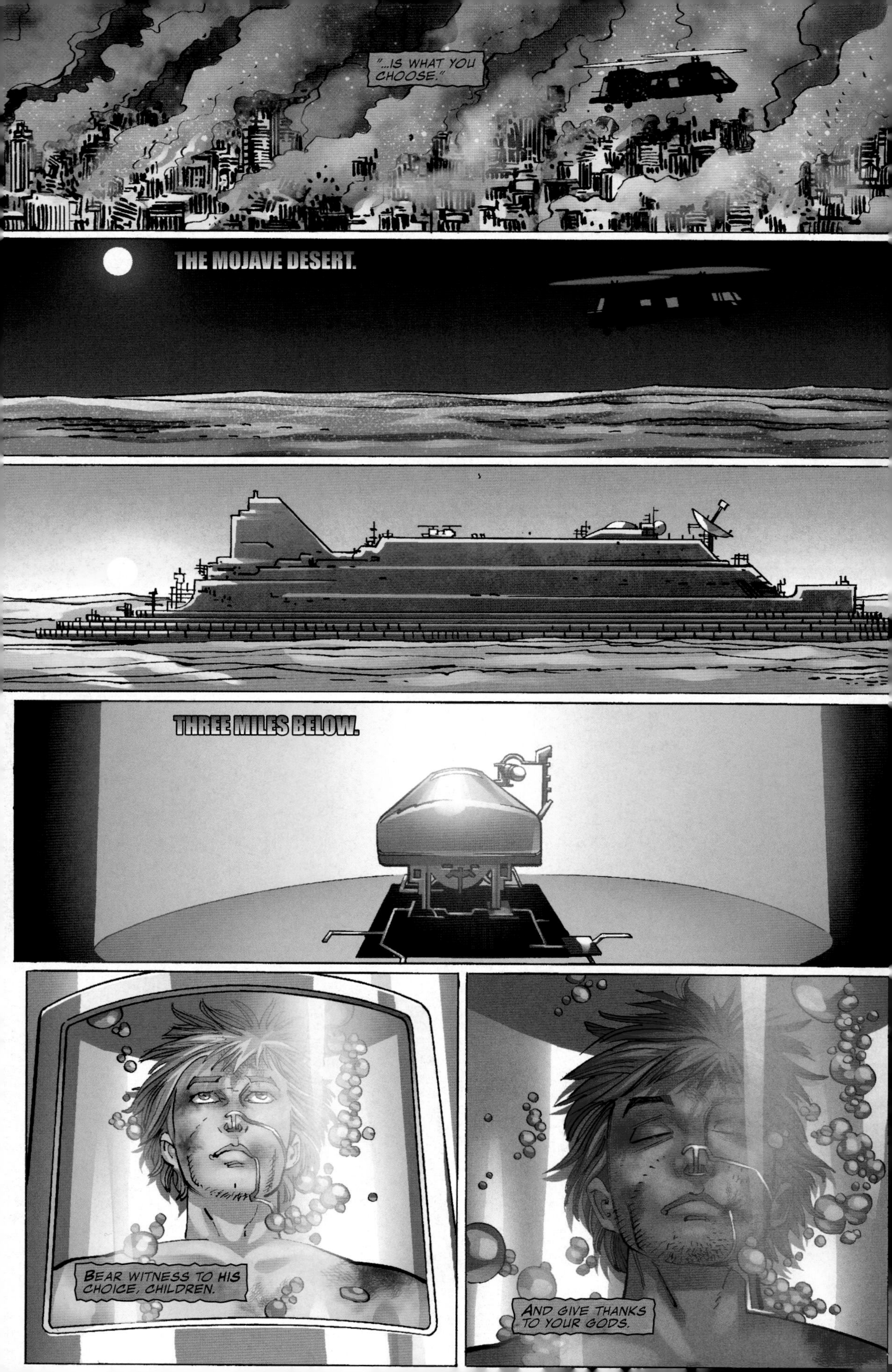
"...IS WHAT YOU CHOOSE."
THE MOJAVE DESERT.
THREE MILES BELOW.
BEAR WITNESS TO HIS CHOICE, CHILDREN.
AND GIVE THANKS TO YOUR GODS.

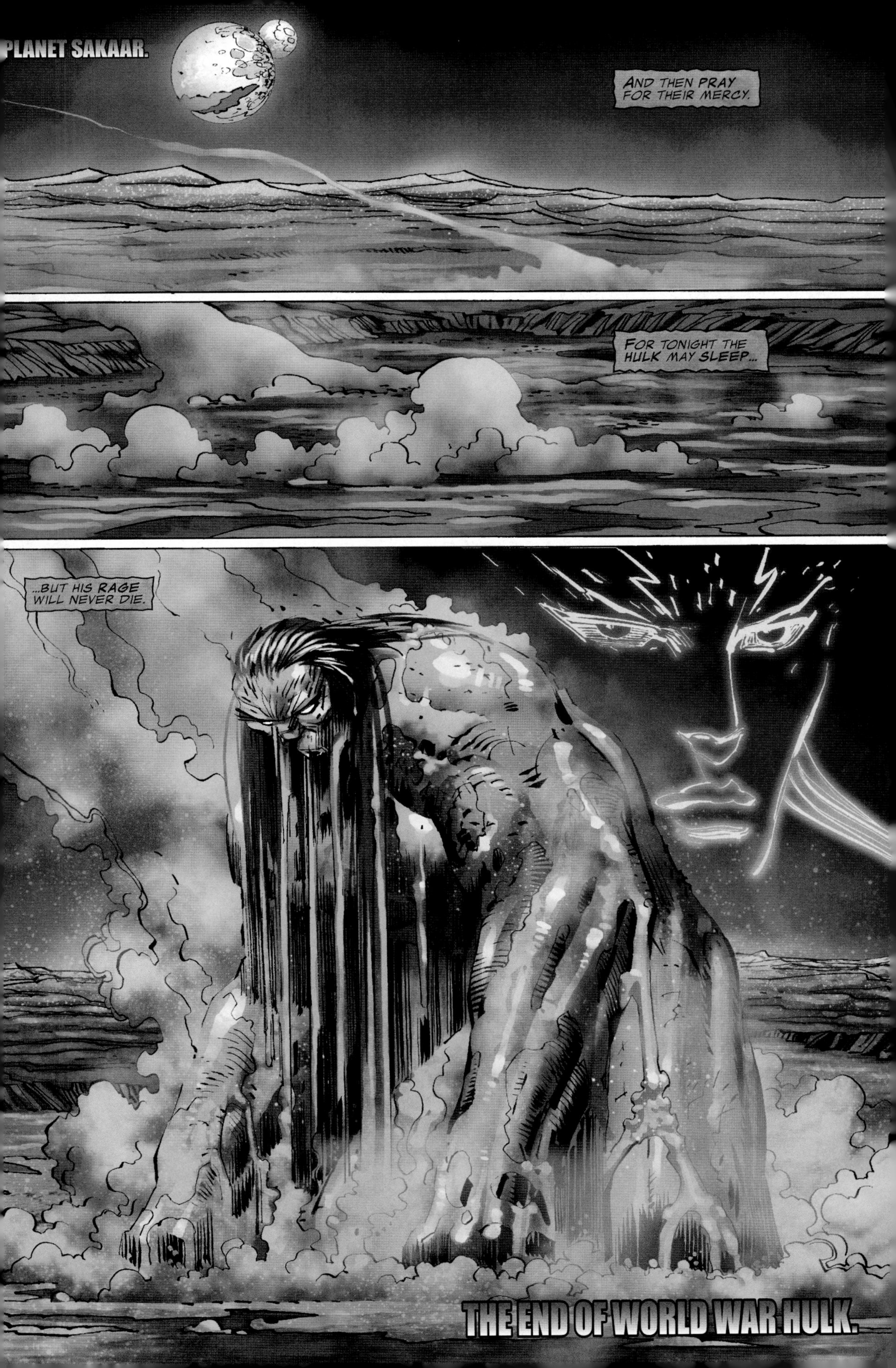
PLANET SAKAAR.
AND THEN PRAY FOR THEIR MERCY.
FOR TONIGHT THE HULK MAY SLEEP...
...BUT HIS RAGE WILL NEVER DIE.
THE END OF WORLD WAR HULK.

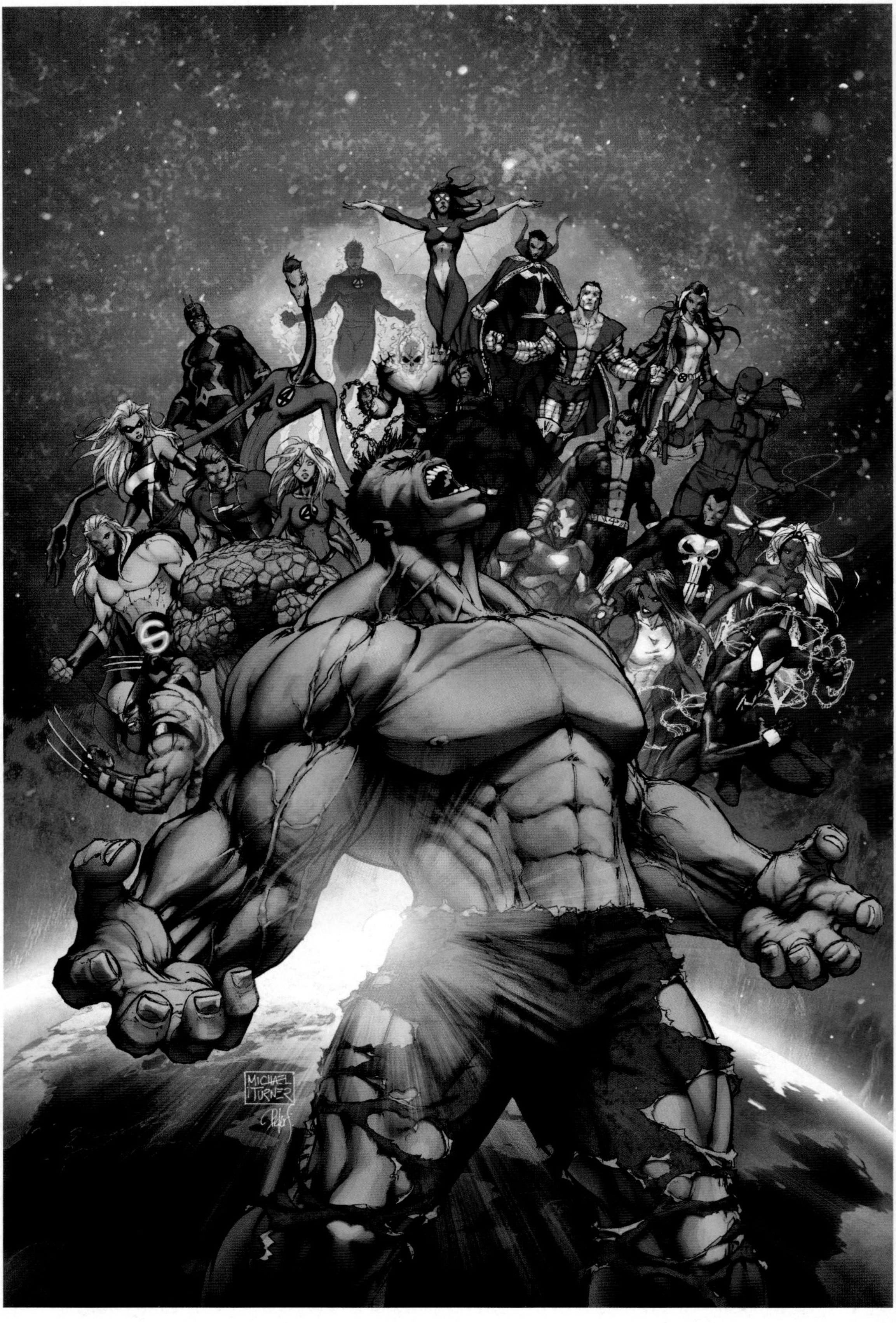
MICHAEL TURNER

WORLD WAR HULK #1 ASPEN COMICS VARIANT by Michael Turner

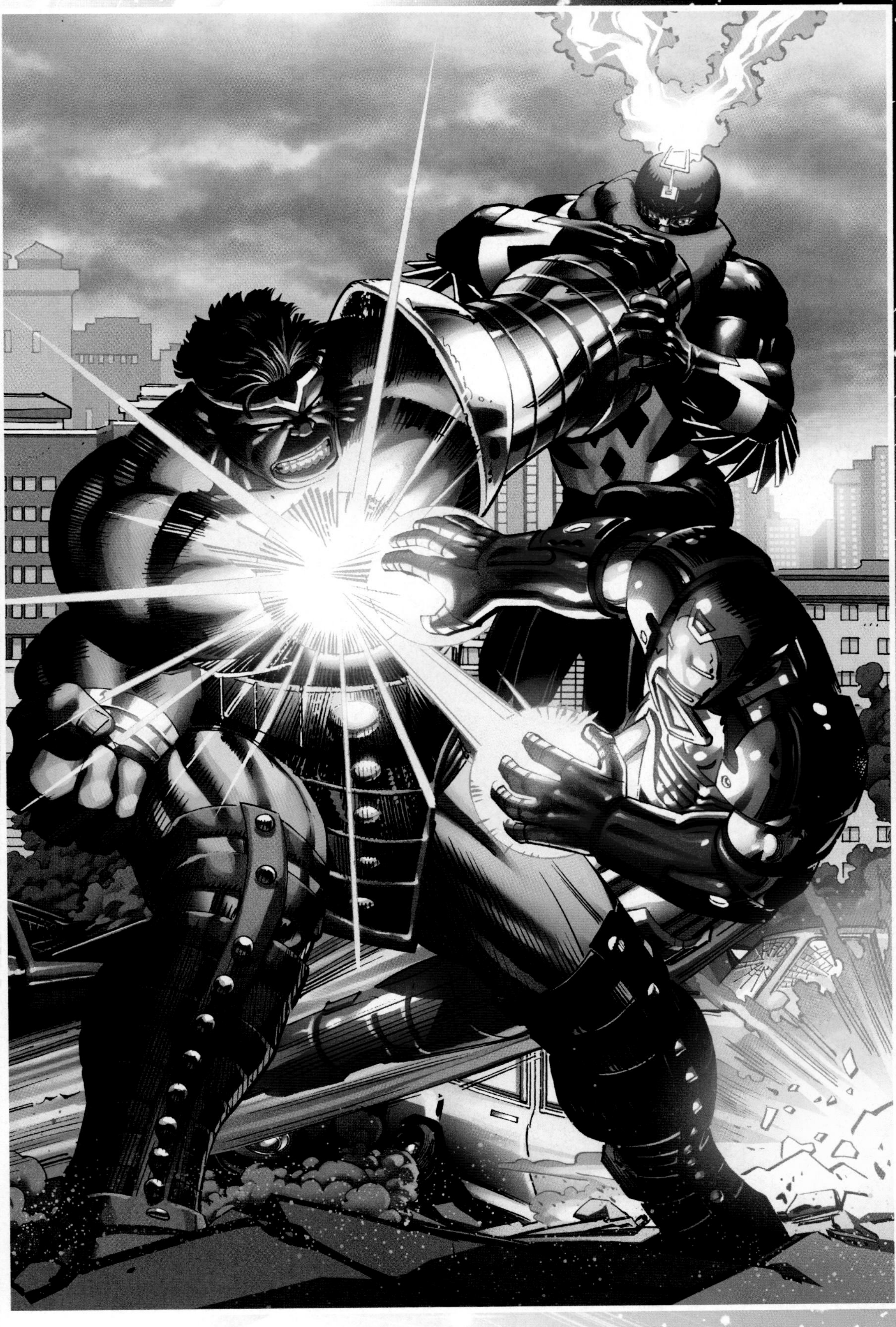

WORLD WAR HULK #1 VARIANT

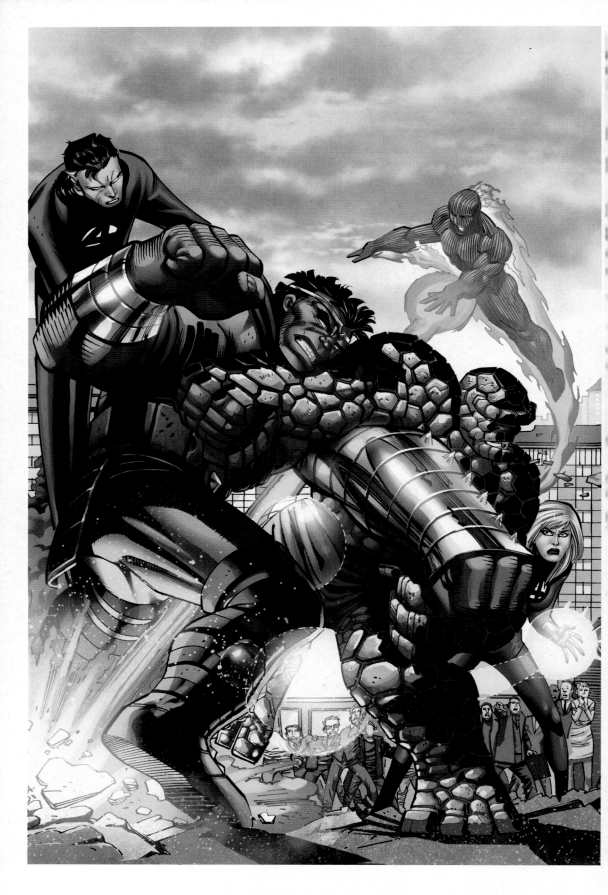

WORLD WAR HULK #2 VARIANT

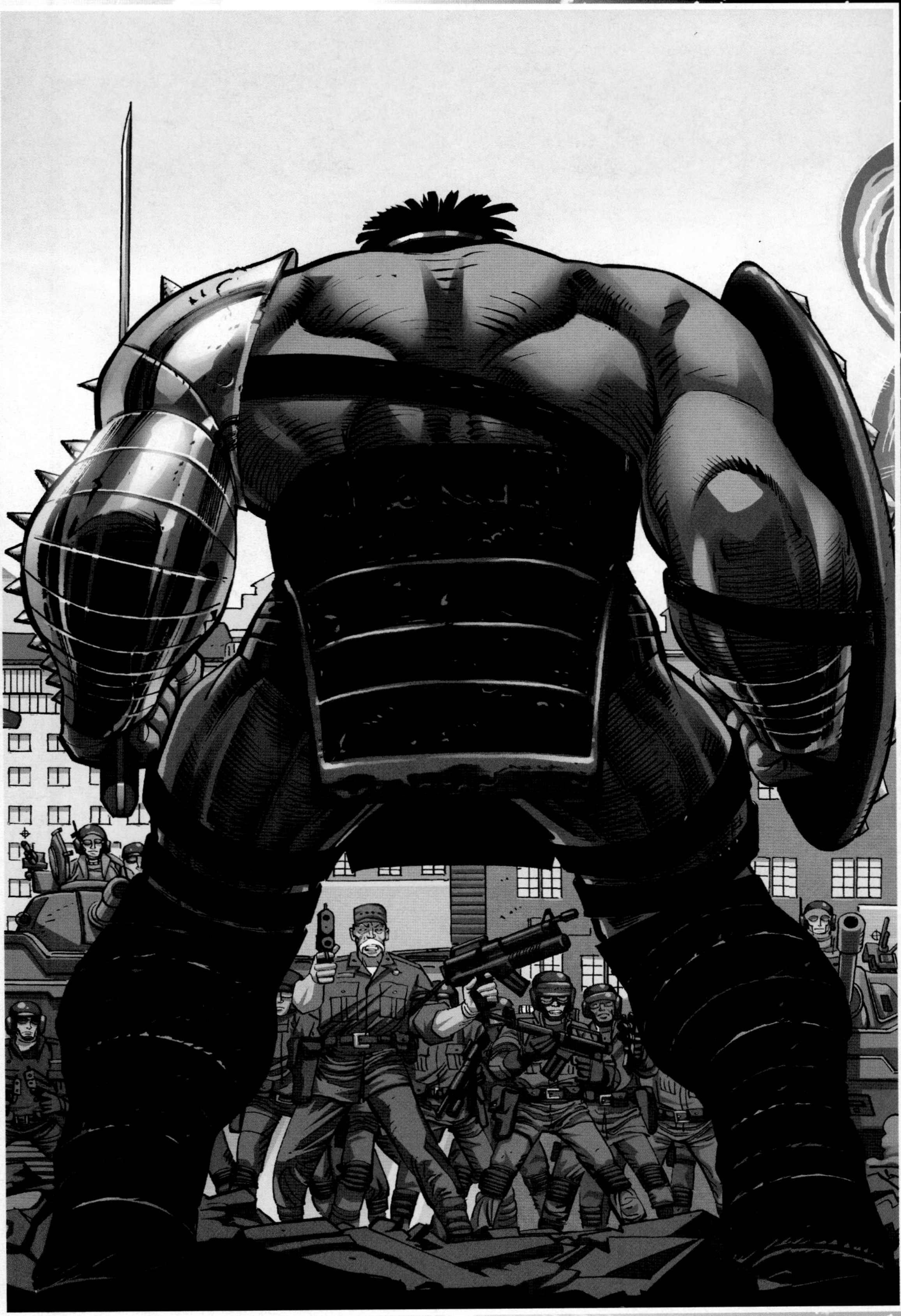

WORLD WAR HULK #3 VARIANT

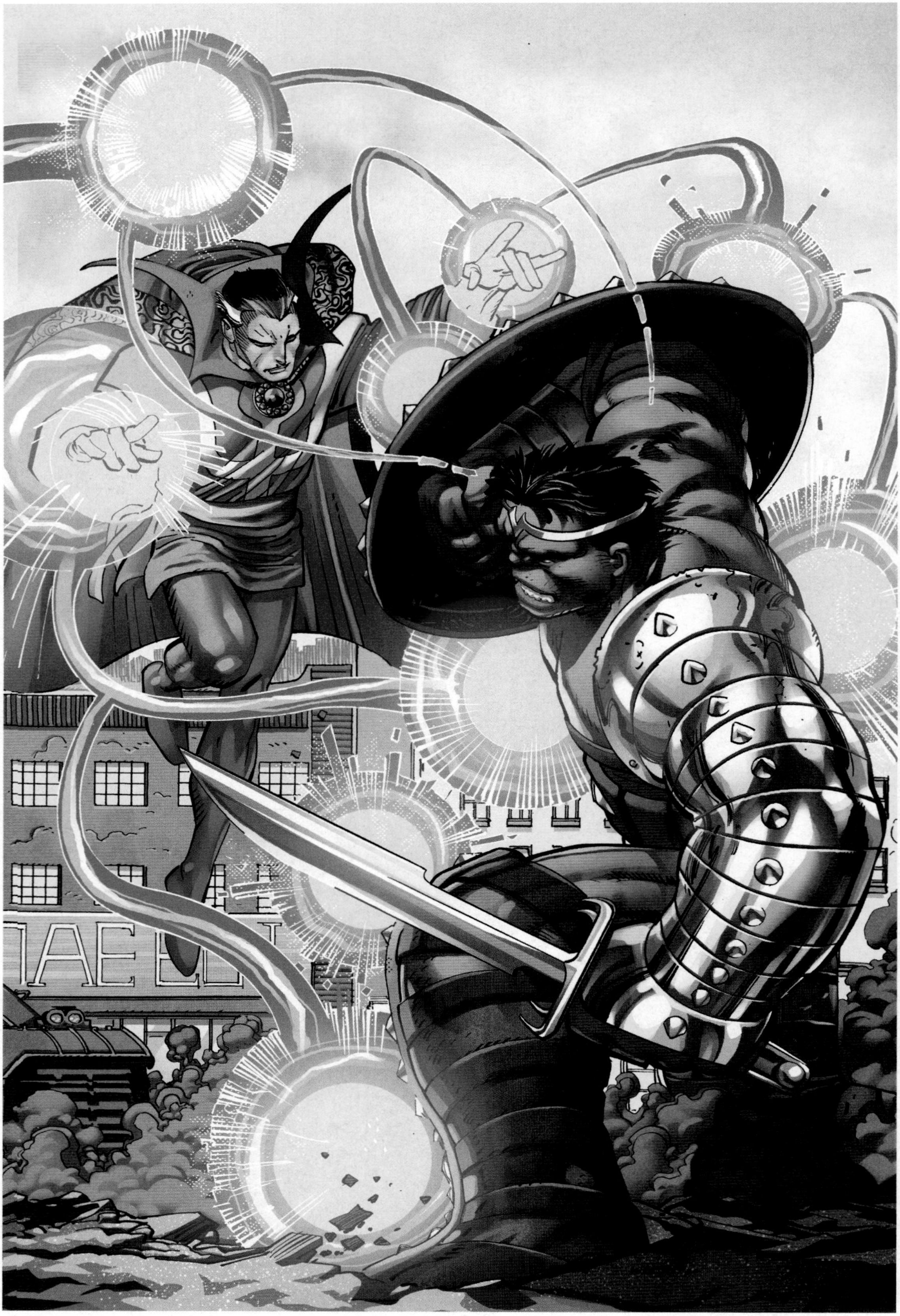

WORLD WAR HULK #4 VARIANT

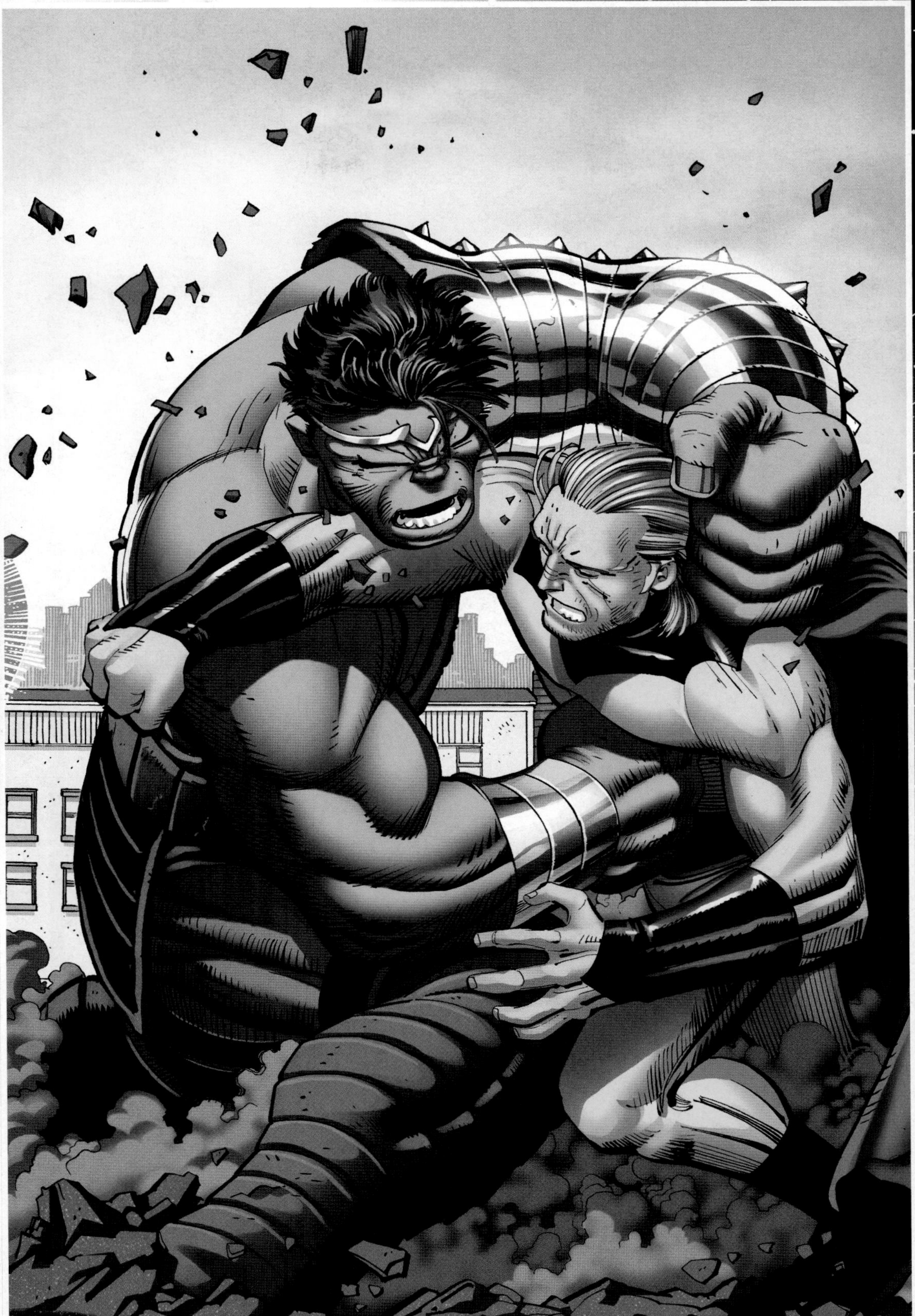

WORLD WAR HULK #5 VARIANT

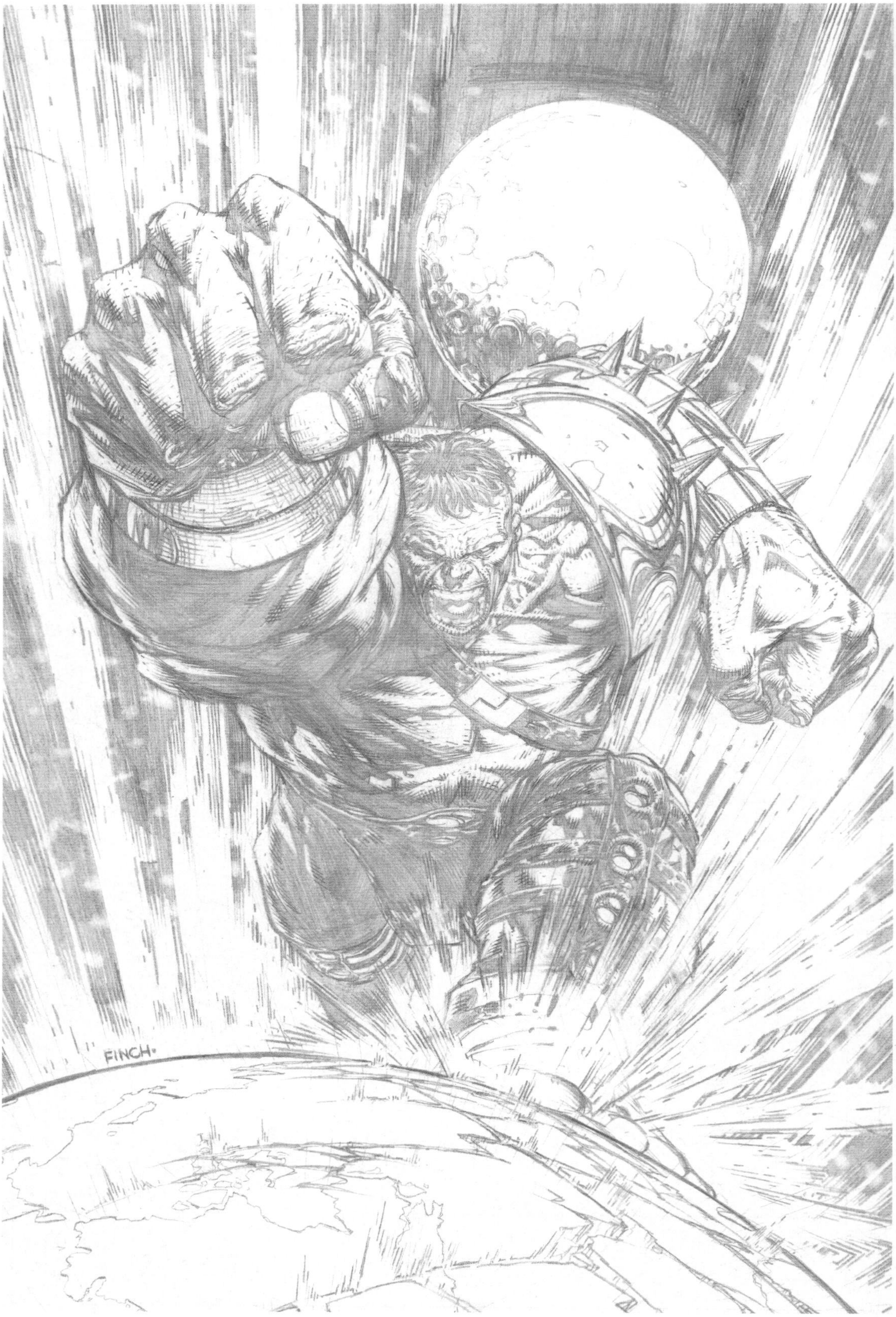
FINCH.

WORLD WAR HULK #1 PENCILS

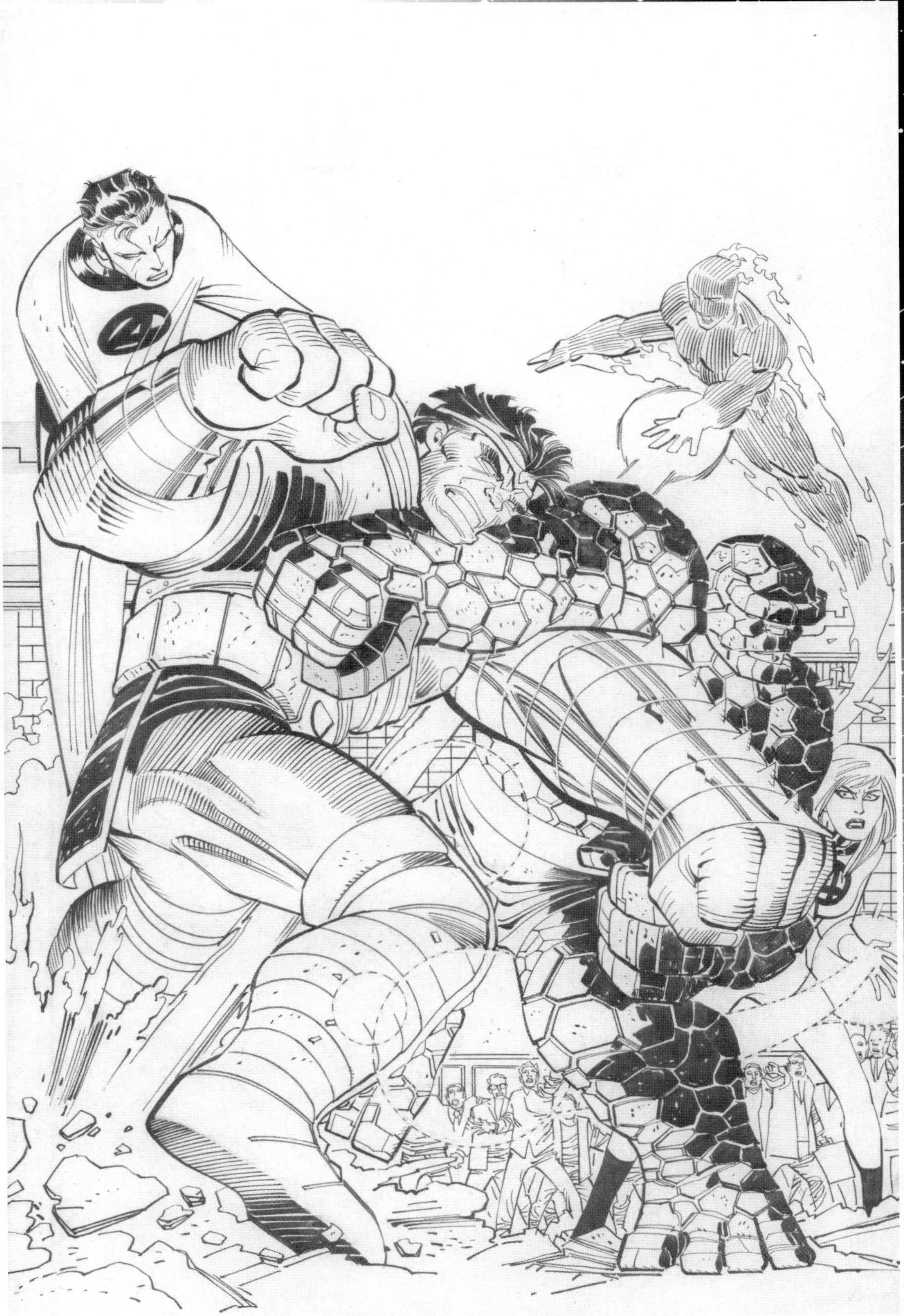

WORLD WAR HULK #2 VARIANT PENCILS

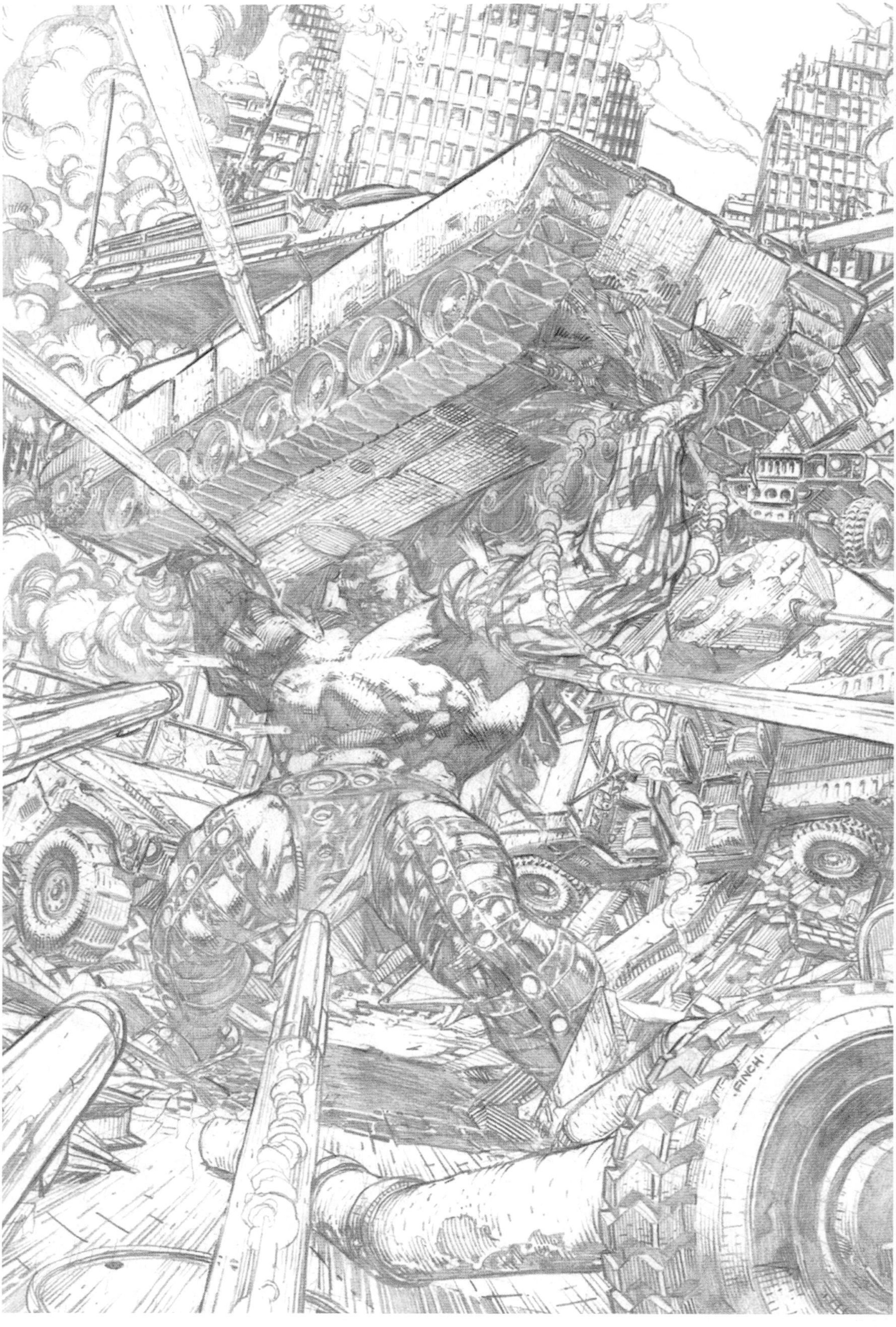
FINCH

WORLD WAR HULK #3 PENCILS

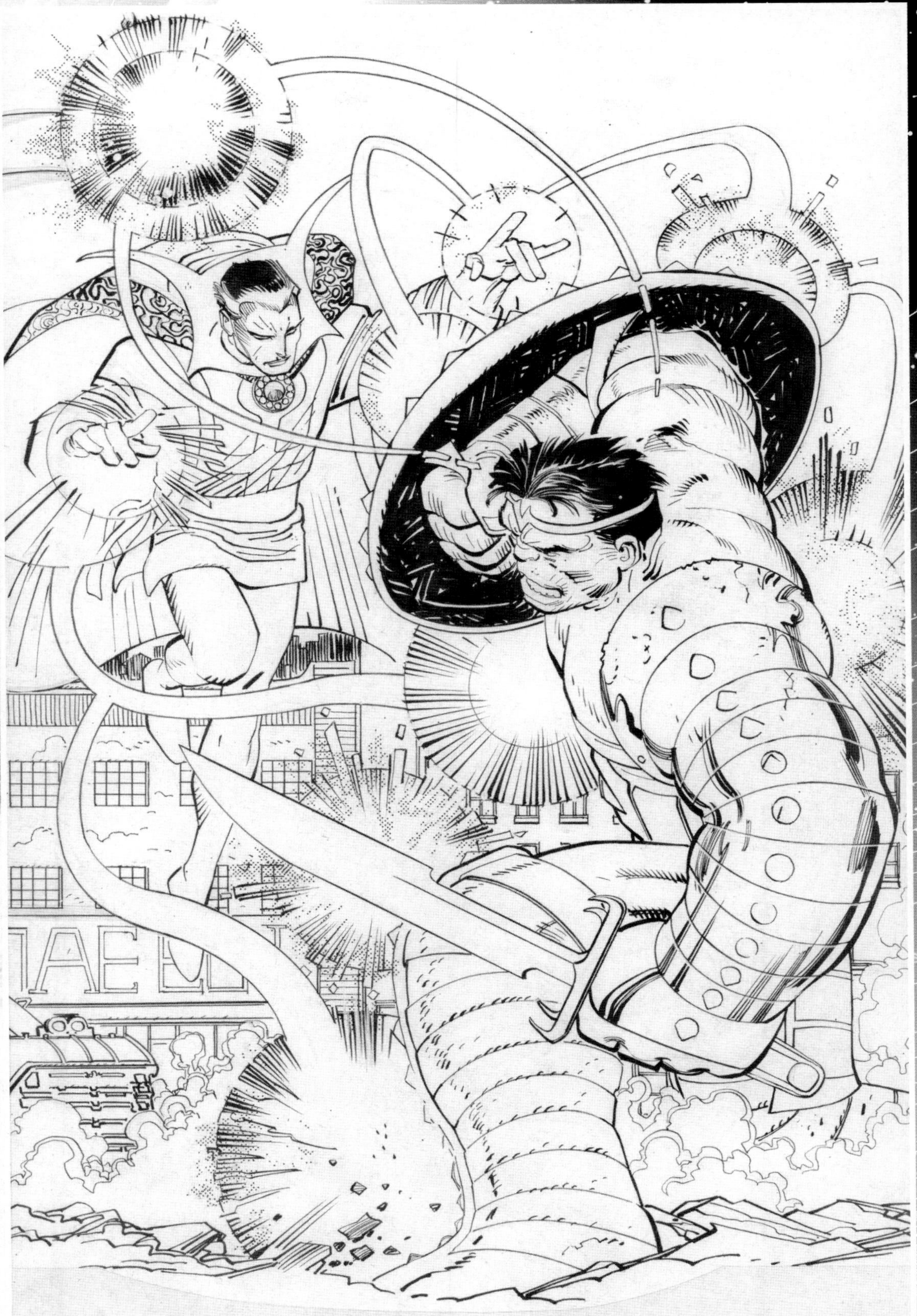

WORLD WAR HULK #4 VARIANT PENCILS

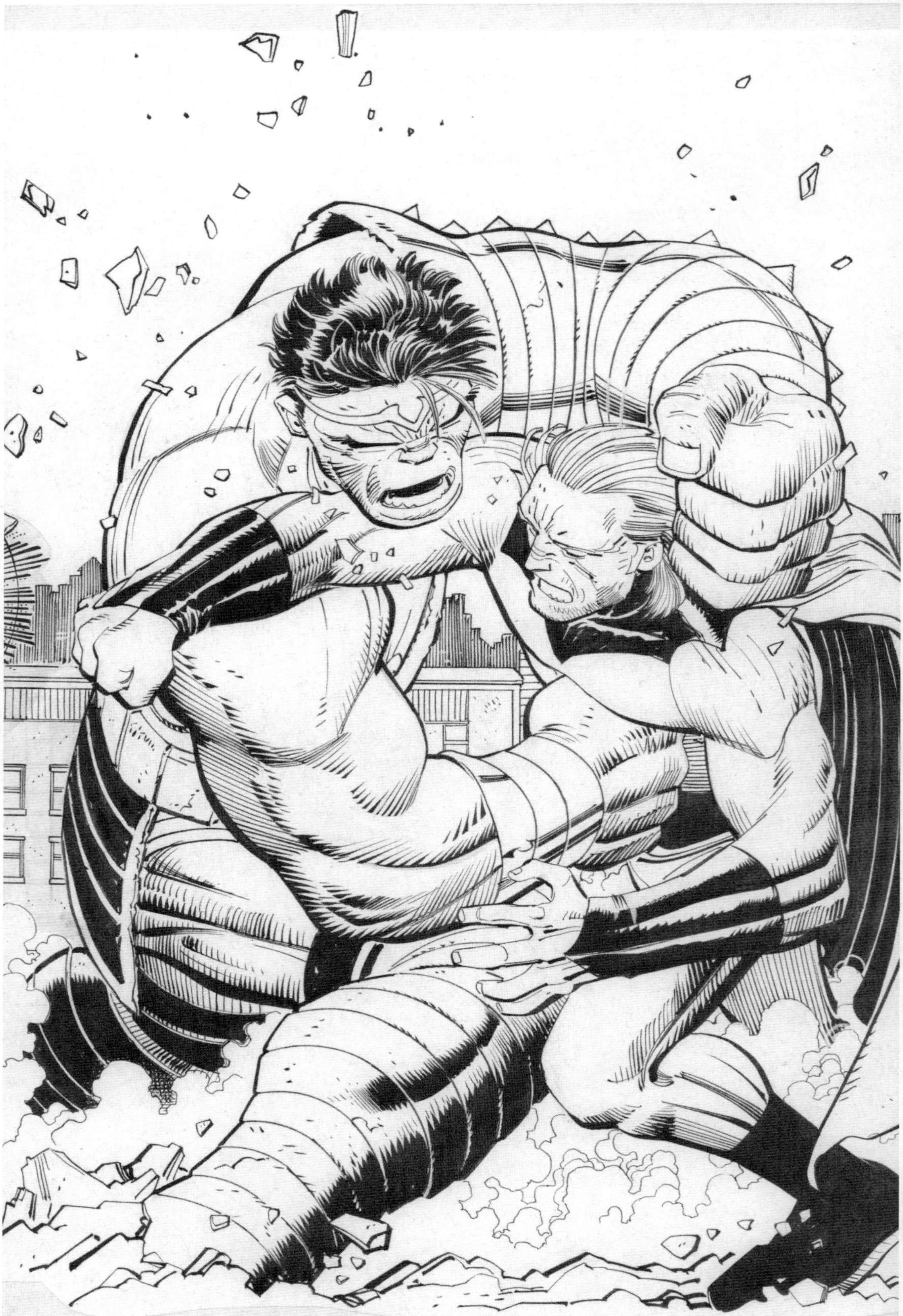

WORLD WAR HULK #5 VARIANT PENCILS